THE WELSH GENTRY
1536–1640

Images of
Status, Honour and Authority

J. Gwynfor Jones

UNIVERSITY OF WALES PRESS
CARDIFF
1998

© J. Gwynfor Jones, 1998

British Library Cataloguing-in-Publication Data.
A catalogue record for this book is available from the British Library.

ISBN   0-7083-1471-6

Typeset at the University of Wales Press
Printed in Great Britain by Dinefwr Press, Llandybïe

Contents

Preface   vii

Abbreviations   ix

Introduction   xi

Part One: CONCEPTS OF HONOUR AND AUTHORITY

Chapter 1   The Gentry Order   1

Chapter 2   Status and Reputation   60

Chapter 3   Honour, Order and Authority   95

Part Two: THE EXERCISE OF AUTHORITY

Chapter 4   The Defence of the Realm   133

Chapter 5   The Protestant Church   164

Chapter 6   Family and Household   203

Conclusion   233

Notes   247

Bibliography   274

Index   288

I'M TEULU AC ER COF AM FY RHIENI

Preface

The 'renaissance' in the publication of Welsh historical studies during the last few decades has led to a significant increase in works relating to early modern themes. The details of the Acts of Union and the main themes in Welsh Tudor and Stuart society are now well known and are contained in several publications, and the impact of constitutional, religious and cultural matters has been admirably covered by Professor Sir Glanmor Williams, Dr Peter R. Roberts, Professor R. Geraint Gruffydd, Dr William P. Griffith and others. They have enlightened their fellow historians by offering new interpretations of major trends and lines of development which have formed the subject-matter of textbooks over the years, and have afforded insights into areas which seriously needed reinterpretation.

In recent years I have directed my research interests to examine another theme, not entirely unrelated to those mentioned above, namely the conceptual role of Welsh Tudor and early Stuart gentry and the manner in which it revealed the survival of old Welsh cultural conventions and the influences of Renaissance ideals. In 1992 I published a volume specifically on the bardic interpretations of the gentry's position in community life, and the present work is designed to take that study further by examining concepts of gentility in a broader context, concentrating on status, honour and authority, the three prime manifestations of their contribution to that life. It is essentially meant to be a study in the history of ideas investigating, using a variety of source material, the manner in which the gentry thought of themselves and how they appeared to others higher and lower than them in the social hierarchy. Concepts of status, honour and authority are examined with a view to exposing some of the salient features of Welsh gentility, traditionally known as *uchelwriaeth*, which made a dominant contribution to all aspects of the history of early modern Wales.

I am greatly indebted to Mr Brian Ll. James and Dr A. M. Johnson for their useful comments on the text and to Mr Peter Keelan, of the Arts and Social Studies Library at the University of Wales, Cardiff, and Mr Bryn Jones of Cardiff City Library, for many kindnesses. The staff of the Department of Manuscripts and Records at the National Library of Wales, Aberystwyth, have provided invaluable assistance and I appreciate their co-operation. I also wish to thank Mr Ned Thomas, Mrs Susan Jenkins and Mrs Ceinwen Jones of the University of Wales Press for their forbearance and efficiency during the period when this volume was in the press, and my wife for her constant support.

Abbreviations

Add. MS.	Additional Manuscript
APC	*Acts of the Privy Council*
BBCS	*Bulletin of the Board of Celtic Studies*
BL	British Library
Ca. MS.	Cardiff Manuscript (Cardiff City Library)
Clenennau Letters and Papers	*Calendar of Clenennau Letters and Papers in the Brogyntyn Collection*
CSPD	*Calendar of State Papers Domestic*
DNB	*Dictionary of National Biography*
DWB	*Dictionary of Welsh Biography*
EHR	*English Historical Review*
FHSJ	*Flintshire Historical Society Journal*
HMC	Historical Manuscripts Commission
JMHRS	*Journal of the Merioneth Historical and Record Society*
L. & P.	Letters and Papers, Foreign and Domestic
NLW	National Library of Wales
NLWJ	*National Library of Wales Journal*
Penbrokshire	*Description of Penbrokshire*
PRO	Public Record Office
Rhagymadroddion	*Rhagymadroddion, 1547–1659*, ed. G. H. Hughes (1951)
Rhagymadroddion a Chyflwyniadau Lladin	*Rhagymadroddion a Chyflwyniadau Lladin*, ed. Ceri Davies (1980)
Statutes of Wales	*The Statutes of Wales*
TAAS	*Transactions of the Anglesey Antiquarian Society*
TCHS	*Transactions of the Caernarfonshire Historical Society*
TCS	*Transactions of the Honourable Society of Cymmrodorion*
TDHS	*Transactions of the Denbighshire Historical Society*
UCNW	University College of North Wales
WHR	*Welsh History Review*

Where edited versions of sources are available, modern spelling and punctuation have been used; otherwise, the original format has been retained.

Introduction

This study is not intended to be a history of the gentry in Wales in the Tudor and early Stuart periods nor is it to be regarded as a detailed examination of the social and economic resources of the privileged orders which governed community life and activity. While it contains specific aspects of the social conditions which reveal the main features of gentility in its Welsh context it is primarily designed to discuss the manner in which the Welsh gentry, in the century following the Tudor settlement in 1536–43, reacted to the functioning of the new administrative framework with which they had been entrusted and within which they were expected to exercise their powers as governors of their localities. It also aims to examine the manner in which privileged members of the community sought to project and preserve the public image which assisted in demonstrating their assertiveness and self-sufficiency in their regions while fulfilling their tasks in community affairs. Chapters in the work are conveniently arranged to examine the theory and practice of gentility (*bonedd*) with a view to investigating the manner in which landowners in Wales defined their positions in society and to assessing the degree to which they regarded themselves as being successful rather than to examining the framework of government institutions which enabled a broad section of the landowners in Wales to grasp the reins of power. In other words, the discussion is chiefly concerned with those families which, in a period of social and economic transformation, were able, in varying degrees, to maintain their hegemony in the localities and to avail themselves of the opportunities to become established as members of a modest landed order, some of whom had strong military, commercial, legal and other professional connections. Moreover, it is geared to view attitudes and opinions expressed by members of the gentry in particular circumstances, and to survey contemporary responses to forces which tended either to enhance or undermine their reputations as local governors while at the same time threatening the realm's independence in periods of social and religious tensions.

The volume, therefore, has three broad aims: to examine how men thrust into positions of power interpreted and handled the status and authority they enjoyed; to survey the influence which the concept of the 'island empire' as it emerged in the Tudor and early Stuart periods had on attitudes in the pursuit of public duties, and thirdly to trace the way in which 'loyalties' to the Crown and native kindred groupings played a significant role in any consideration of the public image projected by the Welsh gentry in politics, administration, religion, domestic life and social status. Despite the dangers and problems which persisted during the century following the Tudor settlement of Wales, new opportunities emerged to stimulate local governors into military or administrative action to protect the sovereign state as defined in contemporary sources. It is considered appropriate that the fears and ambitions of those whose services were essential to the administration of the state as applied to Wales under the new dispensation should be subjected to more critical examination. This study, therefore, includes sections on the degree to which long-term effects of the settlement were reflected in the reactions of those whom the Tudors and Stuarts entrusted with the government of Wales.

Despite the gentry's reputation for being aggressive and assertive, the following chapters discuss the ways and means by which their status and authority were deployed to ensure that the organic unity of the realm was maintained and that their powers functioned specifically to defend the Tudor and early Stuart state. Much emphasis has been placed in the past on the degree to which the gentry served their own interests and how they used governmental institutions for purposes other than those considered fundamental to safeguarding the well-being of the state. Authority was frequently misused but its exercise was also highly esteemed and applied more positively to enable the central government to establish firm links with the regions and impose its power within them.

In the context of Welsh history this interaction between government at the centre and the exercise of authority in the provinces prompts a new line of investigation; the broad details of the careers of gentry families are well known, but the complexities of their interrelations in the manner in which their authority was exercised as well as the way in which they defined that authority forms the subject matter of discussion. More emphasis needs to be placed on the growth of the concept of authority among governing families of varying means and interpretations that were placed upon it by the gentry themselves and by those with whom they associated and collaborated in the task of governing. Such considerations involve conceptual as well as practical issues, such as a study of *virtu* and other attributes which, according to Sir Thomas Elyot, appertained 'to all men worthy to be in authority, honour and noblesse'.[1] These basic features and the manner in which they were manifested in community life are considered essential components in any attempt to portray the Tudor and early Stuart gentry in Wales and England as men of 'wisdom linked with courage, moderation tempered with justice'.

This study also attempts to link these conceptual features, which reveal the essence of Renaissance thought on the role of the 'perfect governor' in its relation to the privileged ranks, with the climate of opinion in Tudor Wales where that is available. Concepts of gentility are interlaced with classical notions of aristocratic status, and prime Aristotelian qualities of justice, prudence, fortitude and temperance are essential to portray the image of the English gentleman. To them are added the Christian virtues of faith, hope, charity and humility. The main aim was to concentrate on attaining perfection in the world emphasizing justice and its allied properties as the norm. Doubtless Aristotelian ideals, which were applied by social commentators in references to prominent secular governors, deeply influenced the portrayal of the 'ideal gentleman' in England and Wales in the early sixteenth century. The English gentleman, in fact, derived his virtues from a number of sources. His basic features and private virtues were essentially classical, his conduct in peace and war stemmed from the chivalric code of conduct, his role within the state emerged from medieval political systems and his religious features were cultivated in the Christian tradition reinforced by the Protestant Reformation. Italian fashions were not as evident, although significant dimensions of the impact of gentility on the continent and virtuous conduct in English literature of the period are observed in contemporary writings. Whereas Castiglione placed greater emphasis on the social graces and philosophical attributes, English writers, like Sir Thomas Elyot and Henry Peacham the younger, considered the practical application of moral conduct to be foremost. In *Il Cortegiano* (1528) the court was defined as an aesthetic centre of perfection but, in Elyot's work, it was the place where the art of good government was mastered. When he wrote of courtesy and majesty he had the practical man of affairs in his mind, applying his skills to his duties and publicly exhibiting his qualities.

> In a governor or man having in the public weal some great authority, the foundation of all excellent manners is majesty . . . Yet is not majesty

always . . . in honourable and sober demeanour . . . with such an excellent temperance, that he . . . by his majesty may be espied for a governor.[2]

The Renaissance spirit had introduced the new ideal of the perfect gentleman as well as concepts of urbane conduct, exemplified primarily in the work of Baldassare Castiglione whose *Il Cortegiano* depicted the court of the Montefeltro family of the city of Urbino, which emerges in the work as the pivot of civilization. The essence of the work can be traced back to Petrarch and other Italian writers, such as Francesco Patrizi, Gioviano Pontano and Matteo Palmieri, who published similar treatises on the role of the courtier. Castiglione relied heavily on the works of classical writers such as Plato, Aristotle, Cicero and Quintilian, and this gave other commentators on conduct a foundation upon which to build. In *Il Cortegiano* Frederick di Montefeltro, duke of Urbino, was regarded as the paragon of excellence known for his 'wisedom, courtesie, justice, liberalitie of his invincible courage and policy of warre' as well as a man of broad cultural and intellectual interests.[3] Like his successors, he was representative of the *vir virtutis* who had employed his innate skills to display his versatility. Much of this description is strikingly similar to the virtues which medieval Welsh professional poets were to attribute to worthy *uchelwyr*, the term used generally for freemen of high status, usually described as the 'nobility' or 'gentry' of Wales. In *Pum Llyfr Cerddwriaeth*, the grammar of the poets, the lord and *uchelwr* were accorded similar attributes, of which 'cymhendawd yn llywyaw gwlad a theyrnas' ('orderliness in governing state and kingdom') and exercising effective rule over 'gwladwriaeth' ('the state/ dominion') were prominent.[4]

In *Il Cortegiano* the ideal person is described as being acute in mind, active in spirit, courageous in military leadership, practical in performing public service and cultivated in social conduct. In any examination of the ideal gentleman in western Europe features of this kind were based not only on personal qualities but also on the authority wielded by those acknowledged as governors of their communities. The fifteenth century saw the rise of laymen to places of power and that led to the desire for professional training and education so that good relations with royal and aristocratic courts and sumptuous houses might be fostered. This concept developed as part of Renaissance culture, and the invention of the printing press contributed immensely in spreading images of grace and courtesy. It became a phenomenon in all

countries in western Europe and, in England, had its chief
exponents in Sir Thomas Elyot and later Henry Peacham. In his
dedication of the translation of *Il Cortegiano* into English in 1561
Sir Thomas Hoby described the courtier as follows:

> . . . a mirrour to decke and trimme themselves with vertuous
> conditions, comely behaviours and honest entertainment toward all
> men; And to the[m] all in generall, a storehouse of most necessarie
> implements for the conversation, use and trayning up of mans life with
> courtly demeanours.[5]

These virtues were also incorporated in the authority accorded to
the public governor, which is evidently revealed in *The Book named
the Governor* (for example, p. 58). What Elyot accomplished was to
adapt the humanistic ideal to the needs of the English gentry, and
this ideal was reflected as well in the works of a handful of Welsh
humanist scholars. English humanists, therefore, created 'a new
social norm which the English [and Welsh] ruling class . . . could
and did adopt as its own'.[6] Castiglione's treatise was more urbane
and refined, and demonstrated the brilliance of Italian civilization of
his generation. In England, Elyot, followed by a variety of conduct
writers such as Lawrence Humphrey, Sir Humphrey Gilbert and
Roger Ascham, declared that inalienable birthright, important
though it was, was second to learning and courtesy among other
more essential personal virtues. The *vita activa*, symbolizing the role
of the virtuous in public life, was indeed to assume a central
position in Elyot's concept of the integrity of the sovereign state. It
is the blend of the *sprezzatura*, *grazia* and *gravitas*, although not as
spectacularly displayed in Elyot as in Castiglione, that gave this élite
its speciality and enhanced the concept of the *vita activa*. It was an
age when a search was made for a new *noblesse oblige*, when
education had been secularized and when laymen were rising to
positions of power in the sovereign states of western Europe.
Following early humanist scholars such as Erasmus, Thomas
Linacre, John Colet and Sir Thomas More, Elyot became involved
in analysing social and political issues, thereby evaluating the place
given to education and evolving newer concepts of society. An
examination of Elyot's governor reveals him more as a lawyer-
gentleman type than the courtier and, in his public utterances,
similar to the Ciceronian orator with more attention given to moral
virtues than to courtly graces. The image was evidently meant to fit
the statesman, diplomat and national or regional governor.

The patterns of behaviour expected of the English and Welsh
gentry, as illustrated in the works of social commentators, serve to

explain much of the transition in thought and deed that was taking place even in some of the less well-endowed regions of the Welsh countryside. The fact that a large proportion of the *uchelwyr* failed to achieve the social status enjoyed by their social counterparts in the more affluent English shires does not diminish to any degree their pride in ancestry and their insistence on acquiring the public office that established the basis of their authority. It was such aggrandizement that enabled them and those who revered them to attain privileged status in rural or urban communities. Thus it can be argued that the manner in which the native *uchelwyr* were portrayed reflected, within the traditionally Welsh context, close associations with their *antecessores*. This entailed maintaining a deep-seated pride in their lifestyle and their concepts of gentility, displaying their authority as preservers of values upheld by their predecessors and especially the new Tudor regime, and safeguarding their authority and status in view of the threatening pressures endured by defenders of older concepts of nobility (*uchelwriaeth*). It was this symbolism which encapsulated the most distinctive features of the medieval species of Welsh nobility.

The work is broadly divided into two parts, each comprising three chapters and structured to discuss various dimensions which relate to concepts of government and authority and the practical role of the 'governor' as conceived in the sixteenth century after the Tudor settlement (1536–43). Part I aims specifically to discuss the fundamental features of Welsh gentility as they recognizably emerge in the sixteenth and early seventeenth centuries and emphasize their impact on what A. H. Dodd once called 'a highly elastic and comprehensive' group of gentry families.[7] Also considered are the roots of their local and regional supremacy, the role of status and, building upon that, the sense of honour and other conceptual attributes, as well as the establishment of order and the exercise of authority, which helped to sustain that status. Within that general structure Chapter 1 examines the social, economic and cultural characteristics of the gentry order as they were established in that period, and proceeds to discuss basic features of the activities of heads of gentry families in public life, which contributed to their rise in status in a broader social, economic and political environment. Chapter 2 assesses the preservation of status in relation to underlying principles of gentility in what has often been regarded as an unstable age of rivalry and contention. Chapter 3 extends the theme further to discuss the more abstract lineaments of the exercise of power, order and authority in view of contemporary thought on the subject. These studies serve as the foundations to Part II which investigates three different aspects of gentility revealing the potency of 'concepts of gentility' in the real world that affected, in varying ways and degrees, the livelihood of the privileged orders. The remaining three chapters of the work examine in close detail some of the chief areas of gentry activity, and illustrate the degree to which local governors succeeded in asserting, maintaining and reinforcing their authority in particular conditions and circumstances. These areas are identifiable as the defence of the locality, regarded as essential to preserve the realm's independence, the contribution of the Elizabethan Church and religious life to the defence of the Protestant establishment and creation of an ordered society, and the role of the *pencenedl* (*paterfamilias*) and moral discipline linked with the household and the familial structure. In all three areas the Welsh gentry assumed a formative role as administrators, businessmen, lawyers, heads of families and householders, and Church leaders. At each stage it will be argued that, despite varying social and economic conditions, the gentry were able to maintain their mastery over their communities and command respect among their dependants. Handicapped though they were by their extremely modest resources and often severely reprimanded for their inefficiency by the agencies of the central government, they continued to dominate public affairs in their localities.

In considering these themes this study examines sources in both English and Welsh languages but not extensively the numerous bardic tributes which eulogized the gentry in their position as cultural patrons. Important though such sources are to measure the degree of prestige the traditional *uchelwyr* enjoyed in their localities and the way in which they succeeded in adopting sophisticated modes of behaviour, the study concentrates almost exclusively on the correspondence of gentry, the records of local government, the responses of Welsh humanist scholars, Catholic and Protestant, to the role of lay governors in society and the manner in which the behavioural pattern of the Welsh gentry reflects the ideals expressed by Renaissance scholars.[8] The latter consideration, in turn, necessarily examines the points of contact between the Welsh gentry and the impressions made upon them in more privileged circles and relates it to the degree of influence that such modes of conduct had on the Welsh countryside, in particular the residence (*plasty* or *tŷ cyfrifol*) of the Welsh *uchelwr*. This was a central and most revered institution of social and cultural breeding and hospitality (see Chapter 6, pp. 214–18).

Moreover, it is argued that authority, as manifested in the public and private activities of Tudor and early Stuart Welsh gentry, more than the respect accorded descent and lineage, was their chief characteristic. Their status was not seriously diminished despite severe periods of economic hardship and serious cultural decline. Status, as defined in positions of authority, was hardly ever destroyed by material circumstances. Although social mobility was a factor that sadly affected the standing of individuals in their communities, gentry roots or, more precisely, their regional identities and awareness, were incorporated within them as being the essence of governorship which, in turn, established a close association between them and their native communities. Not that such an alliance, in any practical sense, was permanently effective; theoretically, however, it illustrated how independent communities of all degrees and stations were in the period from the mid-sixteenth century down to the Civil Wars. The organic wholeness of gentry structure survived despite the variations in economic means, social standing and ambitions of estate proprietors, particularly the varying roles of eldest and younger sons, the differences between senior and cadet families and the diverse economic circumstances to which they were subject. In this context it is argued that historians and litterateurs generally, particularly those of 'nationalist' leanings such as Dr Gwynfor Evans, W. Ambrose Bebb and Saunders Lewis, have over-emphasized the impact of social and cultural estrangement from the native scene, even at times when the sons of gentry were being attracted by London's bright lights and the institutions of higher learning.[9]

It is also a factor that authority was regarded, not merely as a privilege to be exercised indiscriminately but rather as an obligation that helped sustain a sense of unity in the localities that, in turn, contributed to maintaining stability within the realm. In that context authority served to defend status at a time when new social forces were threatening to undermine the divinely ordained hierarchical structure upheld by the traditional gentry order. It was through his position in the public life of his locality that the squire or gentleman was able to represent a corporate unity within the local community structure and perform duties as a revered *paterfamilias* in the context of public service. As a private lord and public servant the Welsh *uchelwr* was expected to maintain the same standards of moral integrity and, regardless of the deep divisions that existed between families and underlying animosities between landowners, the ethos of medieval *uchelwriaeth*, tinted by shades of Renaissance thinking, was preserved down to the mid-seventeenth century. Therefore, despite deficiencies in exercising power, 'good lordship', as applied to the shire or locality, and equitable governorship continued very much to be the order of the day.

Thus this study purports to present a distinct hypothesis. Whereas a social and economic transformation was evident and families, by means of their prosperity, were becoming more ambitious, competitive and combative, displaying distinct ambitions to achieve supremacy and gradually developing new lifestyles, the concepts of authority and the ordered society among such groupings continued largely as they had been but were adapted to new conditions. There were integrating factors that maintained elements of traditional *uchelwriaeth* and infused into it invigorating Renaissance characteristics to project some of its most prominent features, particularly leadership, lineage and moral values, of which probity and justice were the most prominent. To that extent, the Welsh gentry shared the same values as their English peers and their interests were not dissimilar. The difference emerges in their racial and ancestral backgrounds and the manner in which they responded to them. It is in the light of such features that it is necessary to proceed to examine the mood of humanist and antiquarian writers commentating on the aspirations of the privileged orders in Welsh society subsequent to the accession of Henry Tudor to the throne and the administrative and judicial changes that occurred in the 1530s and early 1540s. In view of the political settlement it is essential to assess the bases of the *uchelwyr*'s power in the circumstances that befell Wales at that time and how they affected their standing in relation to their community and institutions of local regional and central government during the century that followed. Obsessed though some of these comment-ators are with the achievements of the Tudor dynasty in Wales it is a fact that what they purported to say did not reflect the true nature of Welsh social development nor did they at all times measure accurately the essential qualities and extent of the authority wielded by the gentry families. It is argued that, in addition to their devotion to status, privilege and the practicalities of power, it was fundament-ally the bond of cultural affinity, usually termed *yr iaith*, which enabled the Welsh gentry to cultivate a varied group of homo-geneous qualities considered essential to the formation and preservation of their social order.

It is doubtless the case that the Acts of Union laid the basis of gentry families as they were interpreted in the Tudor period.

Almost half a century earlier the fervour which attended Henry
Tudor's accession to the throne was amply recorded by
contemporary chroniclers and observers since, in their view, it
established foundations for future advances in the emancipation
of the Welsh people as Henry VIII's 'liberal' policies revealed.
Their testimony is heavily-laden with references to past atrocities
and the expected arrival of the 'son of prophecy' (*mab darogan*):
'. . . king Henrie the seuenth . . . knowing and pitieing their
thraldome and iniuries, tooke order to reforme the same, and
granted unto them a charter of liberties, whereby they were
released of that oppression, wherewith they were afflicted by lawes
. . . more heathenish than Christian'.[10] In these words Dr David
Powel, vicar of Rhiwabon and antiquary, set about praising the
first Tudor monarch for his beneficence towards his Welsh subjects
on his accession to the throne in 1485. Powel was not the only
Tudor commentator in Wales to magnify the glories of Henry and
his successors since antiquaries of his generation, principally Rice
Merrick (Rhys ap Meurig), Rice Lewis (possibly of Rhiw'r perrai,
Llanfedw) and later George Owen and Lord Herbert of Chirbury,
described in glowing terms what they considered to be their
enlightened policies in Wales.[11] Such inspired commentators
wrote principally to applaud the accession of the first Tudor and
the legislation which assimilated Wales with England in the 1530s
and 1540s. Both so-called Acts of Union were regarded as the
twin pillars of what George Owen ecstatically described as 'a
joyful metamorphosis' in the social and political life of Wales.[12]
Historians are accustomed to referring to this legislation as a
significant milestone in the history of Wales at a time when the
developing national sovereign state in England, as G. R. Elton
defined it, was extending its powers into the Principality and the
Marcher lordships of Wales. In many respects the legislation is
important for its administrative structure and the equality of
status that it conferred on the Welsh people. The Acts, however,
are often viewed as means by which the favoured classes in Welsh
society progressed with the greatest of ease, consolidating their
political, administrative and economic powers over their localities
and reinforcing their loyalties to the Tudor state at the same time.
That was certainly the way in which sixteenth-century
commentators viewed the situation since proprietors, like others
of their *milieu*, had progressed immensely by flaunting supposedly
authentic pedigrees and by acquiring land and office which they
considered to be at the root of their standing and authority in
Welsh Tudor society. In that age of aspiring *uchelwyr*, it was said,

new agencies based on a variety of new and old legal institutions and practices were successfully employed, enabling the rising gentry to achieve an undisputed ascendancy in the mid-sixteenth century. Their rank and status, therefore, were central to any attempt on their part to exercise a dominant role in the public life of their regions.[13]

Such factors are well known to historians as representing the watershed in the Welsh social structure. Contemporary writers, however, viewed Tudor policy principally in the context of the old vaticinatory tradition. Radical change, it was considered, stemmed from the importance attached to the accession of Henry Tudor, who was portrayed by Dr David Powel and others, as a messianic leader installed in office to redeem his nation and restore the liberties of those whom they regarded as the worthy but oppressed descendants of the inhabitants of the isle of Britain, sprung from Brutus, supposedly the great-grandson of Aeneas of Troy and leader of the Trojans, who founded Britannia and who, in the second century BC was reputed to have brought bards into Britain as heirs of Greek scholars (see p. 134).[14] That tradition was the basic theme of the vaticinatory literary output which, together with the revival of the Arthurian legend, emerged again as powerful pro-Tudor propaganda on Henry Tudor's accession. Powel, in his comment cited above, aimed to identify the new Tudor sovereign with a distinct policy which had supposedly been devised for Wales and which revealed him as the powerful liberator granting emancipation to his own people. Powel referred specifically to a series of charters of enfranchisement granted by Henry VII to the Principality of North Wales and other communities in the north-eastern Marches between 1505 and 1508. They were interpreted by him chiefly as grants of freedom conferred by the 'son of prophecy', which were intended to restore old cherished rights and privileges, to lift oppression and emancipate whole communities from the 'Saxon yoke'.

It was in this context that George Owen, in his 'Dialogue of the Government of Wales' (1594), explained Henry VIII's policy of allowing the Welsh people to have 'magistrates of their own nation' to govern them when referring to the appointment of sheriffs and justices of the peace in the shires.[15] In his view it was part of a liberating exercise whereby Wales was released from the 'thraldom', to which the Welsh nation had been subjected following the anti-Welsh penal statutes of Henry IV. The picture, however, is far from realistic. Whether Henry VIII's father, Henry Tudor, had the opportunity or inclination to accede to the wishes of prophetic poets or not is hardly the point at issue; of more immediate concern is the fact that, towards the end of his reign, Henry felt himself secure enough to act decisively and to grant progressive and loyal freemen, responsibly representing their native areas, opportunities by which they might serve the state and advance their own private designs at the same time. By means of the charters he granted whole communities equality of status, thus abolishing in those lordships and the Principality of North Wales the coercive penal laws which, in the early fifteenth century, severely restricted the progress of some emergent gentry families, especially in the less well-endowed parts of the country.[16] Medieval though he was in mind and spirit Henry VII, by means of this policy, aimed to maintain and consolidate in Wales what the Wars of the Roses had threatened to divide, namely the unity of this group of virile and gregarious *uchelwyr*, the descendants of high-born freemen of the Middle Ages, upon whom devolved the responsibilities of maintaining law and order in their localities. By granting them those privileges which they desired and which had been denied them, namely freedom from the old Welsh laws of inheritance (since the Edwardian settlement of Wales), and the right to hold office under the Crown and equality of status (since the laws of Henry IV), Henry VII fostered in them a sense of unity and loyalty which strengthened their material powers and reinforced their allegiances to the Crown. Such a close identity of interests a quarter of a century later in 1536–43 served to expedite the Tudor settlement of Wales.

The rise of the gentry revolves chiefly around these factors, and it is clear that the decades before the Acts of Union imposed a more positive attitude towards office-holding among a broader group of lay landowners. The dynastic wars divided England politically but in Wales, despite its fractious condition, the gentry were able to extend their provincial domination, chiefly through nurturing ancestral connections. A cursory examination of official sources for the Principality and the Marches in the latter half of the fifteenth century, together with the eulogies that were accorded to powerful men by bards of the rank of Lewys Glyn Cothi, Guto'r Glyn, Gutun Owain and Tudur Aled, illustrate the prominence that was given to status and public office. In bardic sources office was defined not as an end in itself, but rather as a means of attaining benefits which were shared by the Crown, surviving Marcher lords, gentry office-holders and the local community.

Attention has been drawn to the Tudor settlement as the cornerstone of the social and economic advancement and the political principles of the Welsh gentry. Since an examination of the settlement's details do not form a major theme in this study it is appropriate that its prime features should be given some attention at this point. Historians, such as W. Ogwen Williams and Dr Peter R. Roberts, have discussed at length the policies initiated in 1536 and 1543 to assimilate Wales with England.[17] The Acts are considered to have constituted the watershed between the medieval and modern periods in law and administration and to have signified a marked advance in the public careers of the Welsh gentry. Despite the changes that occurred, the framework of government in the old Principality of Wales survived intact into the post-1530s. So also did the vestiges of authority and the way in which it was exercised. It is in this context that Thomas Cromwell's plans for Wales need to be assessed in relation to the power and influence exerted by a growing band of land-based administrators who considered themselves to be beneficiaries of the old and new methods of government in Wales and who applied their skills in adapting themselves to both.

In this context, therefore, how should the 'Act of Union' – 'the new Acte', as John Leland called it – be evaluated?[18] Moreover, how should the Tudor settlement in its entirety be interpreted and what are its principal features in so far as the exercise of public authority is concerned? Certainly, they did not inaugurate a new era in the lives of Welsh community leaders although their impact was to have significant repercussions on all aspects of Welsh national development. The passage of the legislation was smooth and caused no stir among a conservative people despite the religious changes that might have created opposition to the rejection of papal power and a resentment because of further government changes imposed in law and administration. If Sir Rhys ap Gruffudd of Dinefwr, who was executed as a traitor in 1531, had survived in west Wales it might well have been the case that a strong Catholic resistance would have threatened further the new political framework with serious consequences. That, however, was not to be and during the following five years the government, using various tactics, set about initiating a policy devised to strengthen the Crown's authority in its own territories. The statutes of 1536 and 1543 are considered important, not so much for what they created but for what they preserved; not so much for what they actually accomplished but for what the Crown of England, by their means, hoped to achieve in the period 1537–47, and never succeeded in doing.[19] In other words, the legislation continued what had already been in progress in the careers of forward-looking gentry: it was mainly 'transitional' rather than 'innovatory', as James I stated in 1604 when referring to the union of the Scottish and English Crowns: 'the union must be left to the maturity of time', he declared, 'which must piece and piece take away the distinction of nations, as it hath already done laterly between England and Wales'.[20] In this context three aspects of the legal and administrative changes emerge, adding new dimensions to historical interpretations of the Tudor settlement of Wales.

First, the constitutional framework in 1536 requires some attention. Older generations of historians, such as Sir J. Goronwy Edwards, have emphasized the 'Acts of Union' as measures that had created a new and permanent unity between England and Wales that had not previously been achieved. The content of the Acts relating to the Principality is based largely on the *Statutum Walliae* (1284) and its provisions for the government of royal lands in Wales. As Edwards explained, clauses dealing with the conversion of Marcher territories into shires were based chiefly on the structure of the 'three old shires of north Wales'.[21] The legislation, therefore, served to preserve more than it set out to impose anew, and a progression is discernible from the old Principality of Gwynedd, established in 1267 when Llywelyn ap Gruffudd, Prince of Wales, consolidated the semi-feudal native domain created by him and his predecessors in *Pura Wallia*, the areas governed by native rulers, and other adjacent territories, to the new forces that bound Wales to England in the 1530s.

This constitutional development was recognized in 1284 when Edward I imposed his authority upon the conquered lands of Llywelyn and added them to the realm of England and, in 1301, created his eldest son Prince of Wales. When the legislators in 1536 set about their task of establishing tighter constitutional control over Wales they cited the *Statutum Walliae* as a model for the Act of Union, and a comparison of the contents of the preambles of both reveal a striking similarity.[22] Far from creating unity the Act of 1536 maintained and extended it to cover the whole of Wales: the old Principality was enlarged to include those areas of Wales traditionally regarded as independent Marcher lordships. It was the annexation of those sovereign territories to the existing Principality which achieved positive unity in 1536. In purely territorial terms Wales had been united to an extent never seen previously since the days of Gruffudd ap Llywelyn in the 1050s and early 1060s. Wales, within that new structure, was granted its own independent judicial and administrative organization based exclusively on

English common law. It was governed, therefore, as a separate region of the realm so that the complete assimilation that Thomas Cromwell had in mind was not achieved.[23] Moreover, as Dr Peter R. Roberts has shown, to strengthen the Crown's position, 'enabling' clauses 36 (1536) and 119 (1543) were included in the legislation empowering it to exercise its prerogative power, when it so desired, in its relations with Wales. The new Principality, as devised in 1536–43, enabled the King, when circumstances allowed, to grant his lands in Wales to his son and heir who, as Prince of Wales, would govern it constitutionally as a distinct entity within the realm. That, however, was not to be because Edward was not created Prince, but what might have occurred in the political history of Wales suggested that the Crown had envisaged a new role for a Prince of Wales that was even more positive than the rigid uniformity advocated by Thomas Cromwell.[24] The settlement must not be viewed as a final package sketched out in 1536 and elaborated in 1543; the 'second Act of Union', which granted legal autonomy to Wales by the creation of the courts of Great Sessions and placing the Council in the Marches on a statutory basis, was not necessarily a logical development from the Act of 1536. In the intervening period the Crown had been experimenting in order to secure for itself a closer constitutional relationship with Wales.[25]

The second and third dimensions will become apparent in discussions of gentry power and authority in subsequent sections of this volume, particularly Chapters 1 to 3, but the impact of socio-economic trends and governmental duties undertaken by the Welsh gentry form distinctive features of a settlement which sought to establish unity and uniformity in legal and administrative affairs. The imposition of English common law served to rationalize trends that had been in formation generations earlier, and the co-operation between Crown and *uchelwyr*, that had been a major feature of the later Middle Ages despite the ravages of the Glyndŵr Revolt, reached its period of full fruition by 1485.[26] The formal acceptance of primogeniture became a prime feature of the settlement and signified the acceleration of social tendencies which aided the gentry to consolidate properties and broaden the business initiatives of individual proprietors. Moreover, social mobility led to yeomen rising to higher gentry levels and families, old and new, settling in urban communities, establishing a stake in property and investing in landed estates.[27] The integration of interests was advanced further through the implementation of new Tudur legal and administrative structures based on common law and extended throughout the whole of Wales.

In addition to economic progress opportunities were given to willing gentry to shoulder the burdens of regional government. In this context again the emphasis is placed on continuity and maturity in the use and adaptation of government policies, with specific reference to Wales. The pace of socio-economic change demonstrated how much impact it had on all aspects of public life and private ambition among native families. At the basis of gentry power lay land and property and the governmental framework, and the manner in which they were manipulated by skilful operators reveal their motives, namely to advance private interests and consolidate those through promoting Tudor government and administration. What is remarkable about these social and administrative developments in the sixteenth century is that it was largely men of native stock who were entrusted with the responsibility of governing their regions. The system was rapturously welcomed, not merely because it served formally to establish law and order and bring prosperity to Wales but also, more significantly, because it was flexible and adaptable enough to strengthen the bonds of unity between the Crown and government at source and in the localities. It also applied the innate powers and authority possessed by the landed gentry to fulfil the needs of the Tudor state.[28]

Part One
CONCEPTS OF HONOUR AND AUTHORITY

CHAPTER 1

The Gentry Order

The gentry families of Wales have received much attention during the last two decades and their role in Welsh society in the age of the Tudor settlement has been reassessed. Before considering the theoretical basis of their active involvement in the public life of the nation it is necessary to examine some well-defined aspects of their lifestyle and attitudes which contributed significantly to the reputation they enjoyed as leaders of their communities. An examination of the duties and responsibilities of this 'governing élite' is but one dimension; an analysis of the underlying factors which directed and controlled it, and which often accounted for its neglect of public and private duty, is another. Such a discussion is central to a full understanding of the degree to which those who administered law and order in the localities were aware of their obligations as well as their prerogatives. The rise and structure of Welsh families, their links with land and locality, their economic means and their public and social functions as well as the broader cultural ramifications of these factors, therefore, require attention and form the theme of this chapter. The gentry's legacy to their communities is measured largely by the degree to which their authority was respected and the extent to which they applied themselves to protect the interests of the people with whose welfare they had been entrusted.

Self-esteem, even arrogance, were evident features in the responses of gentry to the assertiveness and hauteur of their peers. In reply to a bold claim made by an unidentified Monmouthshire squire to possess equal status with Sir William Herbert of St Julian's, a scion of one of the most illustrious families in south-east Wales, he reassuringly declared:

> if he be as good as myself, it must either be for virtue, for birth, for ability, or for calling and dignity. For virtue, I think he meant not, for it is a matter that exceeds his judgement . . . I am heir in blood of ten earls

... ([and] bear their several coats); besides he must be of the blood royal, for by my grandmother Devereux I am lineally and legitimately descended out of the body of Edward IV.[1]

Doubtless Herbert felt fully confident that no other squire could match his lineage and that he was a landed proprietor who could proudly boast an impeccable line of descent. Moreover, when Sir John Wynn of Gwydir, another avid claimant to royal ancestry, in his case a native one, declared to Henry, Baron Danvers, that he had received 'the breeding of a gentleman' and was 'free from drunkenness and frenzy' he considered himself to be associated with a 'favoured order' whose attributes revealed that it had received the seal of divine approval.[2] The words emphasize the privilege of being an acknowledged ruler within a hierarchically structured society firmly based on order, unity and uniformity.

In his community the gentleman regarded himself as being part of the organic structure of the state, serving as an intermediary between the monarch and its subjects and asserting his power over dependants and subordinates. Within his region his legal duties involved defending the royal status, protecting his own people in war and invasion, maintaining peace and good government in the locality and dispensing charity within his community. In this respect he was 'for his breeding gentlemanlike clad' in the sense that he was endowed with the principal attributes of gentility. That implied that emphasis was placed more on the practice rather than on the theory of gentility, on the *vita activa* rather than the *vita contemplativa*. The basic features of the code of conduct revealed what the *uchelwr* accomplished for the benefit of others as well as stressing the doctrine of the sovereign state and the governor's place and function within it. Most sources, formal and private, which refer to the nature of gentility in Wales largely concentrate on the privileged individual in his relation to others; in other words, on the *uchelwr* in action. They emphasize not only privilege and authority but also the manner in which those properties were applied so that good citizenship might be fully appraised. The rationale of gentility lay fundamentally in its utility and contribution to the community's prosperity.

The Structure of Welsh Society and the Rise of the Gentry

Such ideas about gentility took time to flourish and were conditioned by factors which lay largely outside the state's control. Indeed, in Wales, they had reached their period of full fruition by the Acts of Union. Long-term social and economic changes signified the demise of the old communal structures and practices of the feudal and kindred systems, and the development of trading and commercial communities achieved significant proportions. The new spirit of individualism and enquiry normally associated with the Renaissance movement was to have permanent effects on England in a cultural and political context. Closer economic ties were also established with the continent and were to initiate new religious reforms that began to flow increasingly into the universities. The ages of Erasmus, Luther and Calvin represented the most dynamic periods in the history of western civilization before the quickening pace of urban, industrial and demographic forces introduced immense changes in society from the seventeenth to the nineteenth centuries. It was an age when new commercial and administrative orders and communities in Europe began to assume a dominant role at the expense of the old feudal aristocracy. Educational opportunities aided a new successful order to achieve prominent positions in government, law, administration and the Church. Families extended their social, economic and cultural interests and, as landed gentry tied to their properties, became the most dominant element in early modern society. Their emergence as a privileged and influential group of landed proprietors coincided with fundamental changes in the social structure of western Europe and, in Wales, which was divided into two broad political, economic and cultural regions, the growth of the gentry was arguably its most remarkable feature in the fifteenth and early decades of the sixteenth centuries.

The gentry have a long history. They emerged rather than developed, showing signs of progress and decline in line with economic circumstances. As the dominant social order they doubtless reached their peak of achievement in the sixteenth century. By then they had recognizably sustaining features drawn from a variety of sources. In this context, the history of the *uchelwyr* in Wales is also diverse and stems largely from indigenous origins, most of them identified with the medieval Welsh landed system based on the *gwely*, the original kindred patrimony which became the permanent settlement for family aggregations in the twelfth and thirteenth centuries. Gradually, individual members of kindreds, in different circumstances and for various reasons, asserted their independence and, in succeeding centuries, became prominent public figures as administrators, lawyers, churchmen, law-enforcement officers and military leaders in their respective communities, thus creating a new and powerful *uchelwr* complex.[3]

Between 1284 and 1536 there were in Wales two broad divisions, the Principality and the Marcher lordships. The Principality, which, in the past, formed the nucleus of *Pura Wallia*, was the area conquered by Edward I after the death of Llywelyn ap Gruffudd, and where a new governmental and legal structure was established. The lordships were the survivals of Norman earldoms and other conquests, most of which, by the early sixteenth century, were in royal hands and extended in a crescent-shape from Pembroke in the south-west to the county palatine of Chester in the north-east. Within the Principality and the broad arc of disparate lordships, containing a diversity of administrative and legal customs, changes occurred that gave individual freemen, most of them loyal servants of the Crown, an opportunity to achieve prominence in public office in royal and Marcher territory.[4] The later Middle Ages represented, in many respects, a dynamic period when the spirit of individualism among free Welsh clansmen led them to assert their independence which, in time, distanced them from those conservative features of landholding that had tied their less well-advanced kinsmen to the customary laws of Wales. In material affairs they used what means they could to adopt English methods of possessing land and property so as to avoid the customary practice of partible inheritance or 'gavelkind' – the subdivision of the patrimony among all sons – which was intended to protect the kindred's unity and coherence. 'He could have been a man of fair lands', John Leland, royal antiquary, remarked of Rowland Morgan, a modestly placed landowner from Machen in Monmouthshire, in his *Itinerary in Wales*, 'if the father had not divided it [i.e. the patrimony] partly to others of his sons'.[5] Sir John Wynn of Gwydir also deplored the effects of this practice: 'into so little parts did the gavelkind by many descents chop our inheritance being at first large'.[6] No one was more bitter in his comments on this matter than he. 'But howsoever it be', he maintained further when referring to the unfortunate effects of the practice on some of his less well-endowed forebears in Eifionydd, 'the gavelkind and custom of the country, not yielding to the elder any prerogative or superiority more than to the younger, it is not a matter to be stood upon.'[7] This serious hindrance to the growth of landed estates was avoided only by the most tenacious of Welsh gentry, most of whose descendants were to benefit immensely from Tudor legislation in 1536–43, especially after the dissolution of the monasteries and the final imposition of English property law on Wales in the second Act of Union of 1543.

The free clan community sprang essentially from a military class whose origins extended back to the early centuries. Native families, having settled on land, established permanent patrimonies that formed the basis of the kindred structure in the late Middle Ages. Leading clansmen lived in free *gwelyau*, the permanent resting places or settlements, and subsequent descendants, claiming direct descent from the founder, considered themselves members of once renowned families possessing indomitable military leaders. Social and economic changes in native and Anglo-Norman society in the fourteenth and fifteenth centuries, including the growth in population, the expansion of the wool trade and the gradual use of the circulation of money, enabled the most prominent members of this warrior class to acquire additional properties and to devise legal means by which they could avoid the consequences of Welsh laws of inheritance. In that way they extended their landed interests in the post-Glyndŵr era and in the early Tudor period, exploiting new social forces and settling as landed gentry who gradually adopted a more sophisticated lifestyle. Among them were the Vaughans of Corsygedol (Merioneth), Llwydiarth (Montgomeryshire) and Tretŵr Court (Brecknockshire), Herberts of Raglan and Montgomery and Pryces of Newtown Hall, whose ancestors had firmly established themselves over centuries in their respective communities and had enjoyed positions of power.

From the declining feudal and kindred backgrounds families confidently emerged to match one another in estate-building. The bonds of fealty had gradually weakened in the Englishries of the Marches, absenteeism among lords and royal control over lordships had increased, and political strife and economic instability had intensified.[8] Consequently forward-looking families seized the main chance, contended for the 'sovereignty of the country' and established themselves as prominent gentry. This was the case, as Sir John Wynn of Gwydir observed, regarding the relations between the Kyffins and Trefors in north-east Wales, who jockeyed for primacy and harboured hardened criminals and fugitives in the lordships of Chirk and Oswestry in the latter half of the fifteenth century.[9]

Added to these families were those native court officials, also descendants of clan founders who were given lands by the native princes as rewards for services rendered and who progressed as an administrative order surviving the economic malaise of the fourteenth century and the Glyndŵr Revolt. Such circumstances led to a marked decline in the bond population in the Principality and the Marches. As the social structure disintegrated more free labour became available on the land market as, for example, at Penrhyn in Caernarfonshire where the founder, Gwilym ap Gruffudd, was known to have employed labourers on his estate early in the fifteenth century.[10] The most striking example of a rising gentleman in the last two decades of that century, however, was Maredudd ab Ieuan, founder of the Gwydir estate, who encroached upon bond lands in the hundred of Nanconwy and established himself first at Dolwyddelan Castle before moving to a more comfortable residence at Penamnen in the same township.[11] Similarly, families such as the Vaughans of Golden Grove, Morgans of Tredegar, Mostyns of Flintshire, Nannau of Merioneth and Pryses of Gogerddan rose to ascendancy through the exploitation of their natural resources. At a time when bond and free townships were becoming vacant, ambitious and enterprising freeholders of Maredudd ab Ieuan's type spared no time or energy in exploiting and subsequently benefiting from all that Crown leases or bond land had to offer in the Principality and the Marches.

Properties were extended, leases of Crown and monastic lands were granted to rising gentry, and they in turn sublet those lands to tenants. In due course these properties became private holdings that formed part of 'capitalist' freehold estates owned by prominent families and based on a money economy. The tenants on these lands were surviving bondmen and descendants of the old military order who had failed to maintain their stake in land, chiefly because, as has been observed above, of the serious effects of partible inheritance and dire economic conditions. Gavelkind, however, was not the only reason for the undoing of some families and their inability to make the grade, and it is evident that more tenacious and far-sighted kinsmen, seizing their opportunities, advanced significantly to establish powerful estates, often at their expense. These showed initiative, a spirit of independence and a determination to succeed, and progressed because of their business acumen, political shrewdness, administrative skill, military prowess, economic foresight and often sheer good fortune.

The larger estates in Wales were built up chiefly through the acquisition of Crown and monastic properties. Purchasing individual holdings, however, was a much slower process because it often involved litigation, contention among kinsmen and freeholders who were well aware of their claims to gentility and who resented attempts by unscrupulous landlords to deprive them of their rights. Legal records reveal many references to the rapacity of individual gentry who were steadily improving themselves, and although many were fabricated to strengthen a plaintiff's case, it appears that ambition did often lead to keen rivalry and even oppressive behaviour. During the century following the Acts of Union the establishment and consolidation of landed estates was a central feature in the lives of proprietors. In varying degrees, this process offered them wealth, power and authority. Lineage alone, as has been shown, was inadequate if a Welshman wished to assert his independence, for it had to be matched by a solid land-base.

Not all such families were to become prominent in public affairs but, in a regional context, they continued to be highly respected as natural leaders of their people. Broadly, they were divided into two sections, the native gentry who rose from the ranks of free kindred stock, and the *advenae*, whose ancestors came over with the Norman invaders or soon after in the late eleventh century. Most of the evidence concerning their development is derived from a variety of sources including subsidy and muster rolls, rentals, surveys, terriers, legal, administrative and probate records as well as private family correspondence. Both groups placed emphasis on lineage, and the professional poets in Wales, throughout the period down to the outbreak of the Civil Wars, kept reminding them of their illustrious past. These poets were the custodians of family pride and status as preserved in genealogies which they fully publicized in their traditional strict-metre poems. Safeguarding ancestry implied maintaining special links with *antecessores* which often strengthened their connections with the regions where they exerted power and leadership. Precedence would not normally be recognized unless the family could provide an illustrious ancestry, and the concern to cultivate reputable pedigree was arguably the most prominent feature among gentlefolk. In some instances it had become an obsession among poets who, by maintaining the conventions of their craft, recorded the lines of descent in remarkably accurate detail.[12]

In *The Description of England*, William Harrison referred in some detail to the universal practice of the Welsh language and drew attention to the quality of its usage, especially in the northern regions: 'so in Wales the greatest number . . . retain still their own ancient language, that of the north part of the said country being less corrupted than the other, and therefore reputed for the better in their own estimation and judgement.'[13] It is a fact, however, that many heads of households in the fifteenth and early sixteenth centuries, especially in the most accessible locations, were bilingual because of the increased intercourse between English and Welsh families and the attraction of official posts. In the more inhospitable areas, however, it appears that several freeholders were still monoglot or at least less familiar with the English language compared with gentry in the low-lying areas of the Principality and in the Marches. Sir John Wynn, in the *History*, testified to that in relation to his ancestor, John ap Maredudd of Eifionydd, a redoubtable clan leader whose followers were described as being of 'goodly stature and personage but wholly destitute of bringing up and nurture' and who, according to the chronicler of the Gwydir family, stood dumb in the presence of Henry V's queen Catherine de Valois![14] Moreover, in the 1570s Christopher Saxton, the famous cartographer and antiquary, employed Welsh- as well as English-speaking horsemen to guide him during his tour of the Welsh shires.[15] In a letter in 1613 to his father-in-law Sir Roger Mostyn strongly advised that his son and heir should return home from his tour of the continent to attend to estate business at Gwydir and Llanfrothen, and declared that 'he hath seen enough and more than ever any of his ancestors in the later ages hath, yet they lived in some esteem in their country without any other language than their own'.[16] It was reported that William Herbert, first earl of Pembroke, spoke better Welsh than English,[17] and Thomas Vaughan of Radnorshire, coroner and justice of the peace, was said to hold office even though he knew no English.[18] Barbara Bret of Somerset, the wife of Sir George Mathew of Radyr, it was said, had learnt Welsh,[19] and Sir John Wynn hoped that his daughter-in-law might be able to converse with the Merioneth tenants in the language.[20] George Owen of Henllys, like most of his contemporaries, confessed to being able to speak the native language fluently but, like his fellow gentry, preferred to write and correspond in English.[21] Where monoglot conditions existed they chiefly affected members of native families that had married within the kin structure and had very limited means of extending their influence outside their *patria*. On the increase, however, were those families which, through inter-marriage and economic growth, became more receptive to foreign influence and whose founders, who wished to get on in the world, were characterized by tenacity and overriding ambition. It is difficult to assess the degree to which *uchelwyr* in the hinterland were proficient in writing their own language but, according to William Camden in *Remaines concerning Britaine* (1623), it appears that most of those whom he met during his travels in Wales were unprepared to admit that they could write in the vernacular.[22] Sir John Price of Brecon, however, believed that many were able to read it,[23] and in 1585 the recusant Robert Gwyn of Penyberth, Llŷn, assuming that the gentry were literate, urged them to read and write their language.[24] The picture, however, is not as clear as it might be and further research needs to be undertaken into the subject of literacy among all ranks in early modern Wales before c.1700.

The most prominent families were established near or within the boroughs and in the more prosperous low-lying areas of Wales. Although their material means varied from one area to another, they continued to exert considerable power and invariably established cadet families that also grew to become centres of local influence. The Vaughans of Trawsgoed in Cardiganshire and of Golden Grove in Carmarthenshire, Morgans of Tredegar in Monmouthshire, Prices of Rhiwlas in Merioneth and Trefors of Trefalun and Plas Teg in east Denbighshire, for example, were families well-connected in their respective regions.[25] Among the incoming English stocks whose ancestors had introduced new cultural features into the Marches from the late eleventh century onwards, there were similar families who had entrenched themselves principally in urban centres, such as the Bulkeleys of Beaumaris, Salusburys of Lleweni and Pulestons of Maelor. The powerful Stradlings of St Donat's and Mansels of Margam, on the other hand, were not urban but settled as lords of manors and maintained the traditions and customs established and practised by their Norman forebears. Sir Rice Mansel of Penrice and Oxwich was an influential figure who raised his house to a prominent position in west Glamorgan by the mid-sixteenth century.[26] He purchased Margam Abbey and moved the family residence to that most salubrious site; similarly, the Catholic Carnes of Ewenni, a native family descended from old Gwent rulers, converted the former Benedictine priory into their principal residence after purchasing it in 1545. Mansel became Chamberlain of South Wales in 1553 and held all the other important offices in his shire. By the mid-sixteenth century the alien families had become fully integrated into the social structure of the communities in which they settled. An increasing number intermarried with Welsh families and some became popular supporters of professional poets, the chief exponents of their gentility. These immigrant families settled, for the most part, in the castellated boroughs and the towns in the Marches, and the power which they accumulated came their way through the acquisition of offices and clan properties which, in due course, formed freeholds on their expanding estates.

The legal forms of landholding and the settlement patterns associated with the growth of estates in native Wales cannot be traced in all parts of the country. There was no uniformity in social organization. Most native families stemmed from forebears who had settled in kindred patrimonies or who had obtained rewards for holding offices under the native princes of Gwynedd and the English Crown from the thirteenth century onwards. The *uchelwyr* (high-born clansmen), known in earlier days as *priodorion* (free clansmen), were the equivalent of the *nobiliatores* and *optimates* arising out of free clan status that had constituted most of the native population in the Middle Ages.[27] Their origins derived from their common obligations and the defined privileges which they enjoyed within the clan structure. They perpetuated a system whereby land was never owned but held by family groups and passed down through the generations. For legal and social reasons it became necessary for each individual to know his pedigree since it helped to establish his claim to *priodoldeb* (free clansmanship) and to maintain the integrated features of the clan structure. In the Englishries of the southern lowlands and coastal areas of Wales a transformation had also occurred in the manorial system from the mid-fourteenth century onwards. Lords had ceased to exploit their demesnes which were leased, and un-inhabited bond townships became liable to engrossment. This engrossing of holdings and leasing of demesnes and enclosure of land laid the basis of a new landed structure in regions outside the Principality. The old subsistence economy had yielded to exploitation, leading to the growth of landed estates and consolidated farms, a trend well-established by the accession of Henry Tudor.

In view of this 'land revolution' and the rapacity of those who benefited by it, it is fitting to examine the principal attributes of the Welsh gentry in the period spanning the Acts of Union and the Civil Wars. There were strong unifying forces that revealed common features. First and foremost, they placed emphasis on lineage and descent, thus identifying their origins and protecting their 'credit' or reputation. Status will be discussed at greater length in Chapter 2, but since it is a central feature of gentility it deserves some attention at this point. In Tudor and early Stuart times it was not self-evident and could not be maintained independently of other attributes: inalienable birthright had to be defended and fortified by the cultivation of virtues that served to enhance the *uchelwr*'s privileged position. According to that eccentric character William Vaughan of Llangyndeyrn, Carmarthenshire, *gravitas*, courtesy and the spirit of adventure were regarded as the 'properties of a gentleman'.[28] Be that as it may, it is certain that the gentry made up in their pride in ancestry what they lacked in material resources. This phenomenon gave them unique qualities that their English counterparts regarded as excessive and derisory, serving only to camouflage what was essentially an impoverished existence. Generally, however, the Welsh gentry securely established links with forebears who were usually heads of kindreds. It was evident that the further back in time they went the better it was for a family's reputation.

Important though the kindred complexes were, the sixteenth century saw the gradual emergence of a new territorial or regional concept, not universally accepted among historians, namely the 'county community' which, in governmental and family affairs, largely loosened the old bonds with the Principality or the individual lordship, especially after the Acts of Union and the extension of the shire system into the Marches of Wales. Many of the gentry within the county structure built up their power primarily in the commote or hundred where they resided and subsequently in the shire itself. The close-knit regional community gradually became a well-established social feature, and the shire-towns, operating as the fulcrum, emerged as centres of social, economic, political and administrative life. Despite the emergence of territorial unity and identity there also existed regional diversity, even within parishes and townships. Wales, like England, was composed of small communal entities. Jealously guarded customs varied in their features as much as did the shires and regions in which they were cherished. Besides these divisions perpetuated in local government, the organic entity of the region based on the shire was maintained and given cohesion through the Quarter Sessions, the County Court and other lower courts, as well as administrative institutions.

Within this structure emphasis was placed on the social role of the *uchelwr* and *bonheddig* class in Tudor and Stuart society. The *uchelwr* might broadly be regarded as the late-medieval equivalent of the *bonheddig*, the privileged men and women of impeccable descent: courteous, refined and typifying the Renaissance prototype. Professional poets were in the vanguard of this process of granting status to the gentry by reminding them of an illustrious past and the social demeanour expected of them. The

Act of Union had imposed English property law, thus reducing the need to flaunt pedigrees for purely legal reasons, particularly with regard to partible inheritance, *galanas* (compensation or blood-fine) and *sarhad* (insult- or honour-price), but they were still often used for litigious purposes in the Courts of Great Sessions, especially when complications arose concerning the old land tenure. Together with official extents and surveys, genealogical sources shed much light on ancient Welsh and Norman land tenures from which families emerged. The sources focus on the composition of the *gafaelion*, parcels of land once the properties of free clans, and other features of landholding that gradually formed an essential part of the new estate structure.

In view of their pedigree, *uchelwyr* in the sixteenth century were still aware of their membership of free clans. They also sought to exploit their privileged positions to protect their interests and confirm their rights as they defined them. To that extent pedigrees were rendered public and were well-distributed among all gentry families in Tudor Wales. Although the Act of Union deprived such compilations of any legal importance with regard to property inheritance they continued to contribute significantly to anti-quarian scholarship and to maintain the social disposition of the gentry and added to their prestige in their localities. Pedigree certainly reminded them of past glories identified with the family and, in the present, encouraged them to cling to standards of behaviour worthy of their ancestors. To deny a man's gentility was a mark of disgrace and, by the mid-Tudor period, that gentility represented a degree of material wealth, well-proven descent, prominence in public service and a cultured upbringing. It is hardly surprising that the poets placed continual emphasis on *ach* ('lineage') and *gwehelyth* ('stock'), and that the correspondence of the gentry referred to the bonds of kinship and the privilege of good ancestry. Doubtless lineage was a paramount feature of English gentry but the Welsh *uchelwr* prototype claimed for it a distinctively unique significance in that it underpinned his claim to superiority.

The Foundations of Landed Power, Wealth and Status

The power which men claiming gentle birth possessed was visibly displayed in the land and properties which they held or owned or coveted. The most ambitious among them increasingly attempted to avoid the consequences of old Welsh property laws and used their initiative to exert influence in regional affairs. They enjoyed a close relationship with their tenants, many of them less fortunate kinsmen with inadequate resources, and obtained from them the loyalty and support that a traditional lord of the manor customarily enjoyed. Professional poets consistently reminded them of the values they were expected to uphold, primarily those attached to reputable *uchelwriaeth*, and the communal leadership which they claimed to possess. They were elevated in their localities, not only as representatives of worthy families but also, on a higher level, as personifications of virtuous qualities in the community. Although political fluctuations in the fifteenth century had deeply affected the fortunes of Welsh *uchelwyr* it is noteworthy that, gradually during that century, there came into existence a cultural stability that characterized a peculiar brand of *uchelwriaeth* that was to achieve greater prominence later.

The economy was principally dependent on land, its use and resources, and this was being exploited and cultivated more intensively. With the growth of new estates arable farming still remained important, especially in the most prosperous low-lying areas of south-east and south-west Wales and the Vale of Glamorgan. Fertilizers, especially lime, were used and the enclosure of strips gradually advanced. On the increase was the rearing of livestock, particularly in the upland regions, although it was also practised extensively in the lowlands, such as Glamorgan and north-east Wales. Cattle-rearing was important in Glamorgan and in the counties of Gwynedd and the western parts of Denbighshire. The wool and cloth trades also flourished, forming a brisk commercial exchange with the borderlands and in the export market in France, Italy, Spain, Ireland and the Low Countries.[29] Many of the gentry prospered as a result; in addition to engrossing lands the liveliest proprietors set about intensifying their farming on existing demesnes, and their accounts and rentals reveal their dependence on stewards and overseers employed to supervise management and husbandry.

More enterprising gentry developed mineral resources on their estates and the extent of their success depended largely on the size and nature of their properties, on the stimulus of industrial agents and on their own adventurous spirit. Profitable exploitation improved the estate's value and, next to rents, became the chief method of increasing its income. In 1526 Sir Mathew Cradock of Swansea leased coalmines in Kilvey and Gower, and the Mostyn family in north-east Wales shipped coal from Mostyn to Beaumaris.[30] The Mathew family of Radyr built an iron furnace at

Pentyrch in 1565, and a wireworks and foundry was established by the Society of the Mineral and Battery Works at Tintern in the 1560s and leased to Richard Hanbury and his partners in 1571.[31] Sir Thomas Middleton set up an ironworks on his estate at Chirk[32] and Huw Nannau Hen leased lands at Ganllwyd in Merioneth to English speculators in 1588 to build an ironworks.[33] Hugh Middleton leased Cardiganshire mines in 1617 at a rent of £400 a year, and Thomas Bushell, a speculator in leadmining who was particularly successful on Middleton lands in Cardiganshire after receiving confirmation of the lease in 1637, opened a mine at Aberystwyth in that year for coining silver.[34] There were other aspects of industrial enterprise, such as maritime activity, marketing agricultural produce and the cloth, cattle and drover trades, which were the mainstays of the Welsh economy.

These families were allowed freedom to develop and expand by the terms of the Acts of Union which formally recognized their contribution to public life in Wales. Not that they had been inactive previously: the social and economic history of the Welsh gentry has shown that they had increasingly become involved in local government affairs well before the Tudors came to the throne. The consequences of the Glyndŵr Revolt served mainly to advance their fortunes, especially those who chose either to support, or at least submit to, the English Crown. In 1536 Cromwell adopted a less coercive policy which enabled the Welsh gentry to become the backbone of administration in the localities. They had built their *plastai* (see pp.24–8) and had enjoyed supremacy at a time when the foundations of Tudor government were being well laid. Some of these were materially better endowed than others but a broad stratum of land proprietors participated actively in government throughout the period down to the Civil Wars. It was an era when the gentry became, by law, masters of their communities and servants of the state, holding public office and other positions of trust. Regardless of the inability of many, as Rowland Lee put it in 1536, to 'dispend £10 land' (£10 less than the property qualification for the justice of the peace in England at the time), and although lawlessness in parts of the country was often deplored, Cromwell went ahead to establish uniformity in administration introducing into Wales the same type of local government organization as had been success-fully employed in England.[35] Soon after their appointment in 1536 magistrates and other public officials became 'cocks of the walk . . . the *de jure* as well as *de facto* rulers' of their communities,[36] or, as was stated in 1542, 'Wales is true to the Crown because it is not under one ruler but several in each shire', a direct reference to the collaborative structure of regional government.[37]

Any examination of the constitutional framework of Tudor policy needs to be placed within the social and economic structure of Tudor Wales. The settlement occurred at a time when far-reaching developments were already taking place in its community life. Indeed, Thomas Cromwell might never have entertained planning any major policy of annexation had there been no strong social and economic basis to support it. If Wales was as lawless as it had been reported then Cromwell most certainly would not have risked initiating such a conciliatory policy; hence the content of the settlement was based on what Cromwell – well advised at Court by leading Welsh gentry – saw as being feasible. Doubtless the 1530s in Wales represented the climax of existing tendencies, not only in law and administration but also in the growth and development of the new gentry in the social order who, despite their disabilities in terms of wealth and influence, were determined to grasp all that was readily available for them in the same spirit which had characterized their predecessors.

Economic trends which gradually changed landholding and created a virile group of proprietors characterized by their tenacity and business acumen indicated the gradual erosion of the medieval structure based on kindred law or, in the Englishries of the Marcher lands, feudal tenure. As noted above, Welsh property laws had declined in the process of estate building, and the Welsh land system suffered badly.[38] Primogeniture was replacing the old system of partible inheritance and forward-looking freeholders took every opportunity to extend their interests by encroaching on bond tenancies and acquiring valuable properties. The final decision in 1543 that English land law only was to be practised in Wales (cl. 91–4) came as no surprise.[39] Welsh law lacked patronage and the newly established estates created a new social unity based on a system of private properties owned by families distinguished by their ties with the soil and bonds of communal relationships. Their prestige, in many cases, was based essentially on their claims to a stake in property and status duly acknowledged by common consent. Material means and social ostentation, important though they were, were subordinate to the bonds of consanguinity. As Subsidy Rolls indicate, income levels were exceedingly modest within each rank of freeholders, suggesting that Rowland Lee's stricture in 1536 on their impoverished state of Wales north of Brecknock was fairly near the mark.[40]

An examination of the social structure of gentry families in all regions in Wales in the middle years of the sixteenth century, for example, reveals that an élite group of relatively wealthy families had emerged, superior in status and means to a much greater number of mere gentry, the vast majority of whom were materially inferior to their English counterparts.[41] Many of them were encumbered by poor physical conditions in the more remote and isolated upland regions, while those in the more anglicized and largely coastal and lowland areas of Wales thrived because they were better positioned. Such divergencies are often revealed in the attitudes of individual members of families, especially in relation to kindred affairs, administrative duties and cultural interests. Fundamentally, however, their views on the values of authority and loyalty to the Crown were similar. They were subject to the same single higher authority in the state, performed the same tasks, administered the same institutions of government, and were expected to protect and control communities harassed by a host of social and economic problems. The distinction between them occurred in the social climate of the communities which they governed and in the means at their command to exert their authority. Having said that, wealth was not everything, for a fair proportion of modest upland gentry asserted considerable power in the least accessible areas in the Welsh shires and enjoyed the same authority as their counterparts elsewhere. It is evident, however, that the more opulent gentry of eastern and southern Monmouthshire, the Vale of Glamorgan, southern Pembrokeshire and north-east Wales, for example, were generally better situated to assert their authority within a wider area and to associate with people of their rank and above it who were themselves more acquainted with the sophisticated surroundings of the royal court and the attractions of London life.

These factors raise an essential point concerning the composition of the gentry order in Wales in this age of trans-formation. There was a substantial growth in population: it is broadly estimated to have risen in Wales from approximately 278,000 in 1536 to 405,000 in 1630.[42] Owing to financial inflation, the changes in agrarian economy and the increasing demand for foodstuffs, severe conditions afflicted all sections of the community. Gradually there emerged a group of property owners, known as the 'middling sort', who, by creeping up the social ladder, established themselves as reasonably prosperous and respected gentry in the towns and their surroundings. In material terms they were appreciably better off than many of the

backwoods or parish gentry, but it appears that the competition
for status was not as evident in the Welsh countryside as it was in
England. Yeomen farmers, claiming worthy lineage, also increased
their hold on property and became men of some substance in
their neighbourhood. They held offices as bailiffs and high
constables and served on jury panels, thus identifying themselves
with the task of maintaining law and order. Below the sheriffs and
justices of the peace, they formed the backbone of community life
and upheld royal authority in hundreds and parishes.[43]
Nevertheless, the struggle to acquire and maintain status, at whatever level, constantly occupied all ranks within the landowning
and landholding orders, chiefly because the traditional families
eagerly protected their 'credit, good name and fame' and the
rising newcomers concentrated on economic advancement.

Impoverished though the economic condition of the country
was, the 'middling gentry' made a mark for themselves and
gradually acquired a social status. Compared to the gentry in
England, the majority of the Welsh landed families were of the
'middling sort', and not all of them were necessarily involved in
developing their modest estates on commercial lines.[44] In that
respect, some were conservative, but those who consolidated their
stake in land by traditional means, namely by claiming inalienable birthright, considered their properties to be the chief
manifestation of their gentility. Since the general level of income
was low compared to that of prosperous English gentry households, many of which kept servants, it appears that the majority of
Welsh landowners struggled to maintain a standard of living
commensurate with their assumed status, and in depressed
economic circumstances many were not far off the poverty line.
Compared to the smaller and substantial professional families
representing commercial, legal and administrative families, and
usually associated with the towns and dependent on official status
and a favourable economic climate, the majority of Welsh gentry
appeared to be rural-based, largely conservative and obtaining
incomes that would often compare with those of well-to-do
yeomen farmers in the more affluent English counties.

The rivalry between the newer urban-orientated families and
the traditional stocks seems not to have been intense. It emerged
normally in the courts of law, as illustrated in the inordinately
large number of lawsuits involving the lesser gentry and
freeholders contending with their superiors, and the disputes
between tenants and landlords, servants and masters, and richer
and poorer relatives within the kin structure. Within the broad

social framework, however, all those who claimed gentility considered that they shared common qualities: 'there are to this day', George Owen remarked, 'many ancient gentlemen which can by good authority derive themselves from divers famous and illustrious families that did possess great patrimonies'. What he said of Pembrokeshire could also be applied to the rest of Wales. 'Gentility', Lord Burghley declared, 'is but ancient riches.'[45] In the Welsh context, however, that wealth needs to be measured chiefly in terms of the ancient attributes of *uchelwriaeth*, and this concept was overtly manifested in the public role of the gentry as maintainers of law, order and government and preservers of kindred affinities that characterized their forebears.

The wider dimensions to the role of families in public affairs varied according to means and power to the extent that their material resources allowed them. Economic circumstances largely governed social mobility and the distribution of wealth. Social commentators began to propagate new doctrines of rank and status that gradually undermined the traditional hierarchical structure cherished by the most conservative native families. What, therefore, did landownership imply in terms of material wealth and how is the prosperity of the Welsh gentry to be measured during this period? Answers to these questions depend largely on studies of individual families, regional divergencies and circumstances that increased or hindered material growth. Families such as the Bulkeleys of Beaumaris and Stradlings of St Donat's dominated their regions because of a variety of factors, not least the entrenched position which they and their fellow incomers had established for themselves in accessible areas where trade and commerce flourished. Doubtless both native and alien families benefited from shared commercial dealings, good marriages and office-holding. During the course of the fifteenth century an increasing number of English gentry married into Welsh families and were 'cymricized', notable examples being the Salusburies of Lleweni and the Mansels of Oxwich and Margam and their satellites which established strong social and cultural connections in north and south Wales respectively.[46] The majority among the rural families. however, stemmed from native stock, such as the Philippses of Picton Castle, Mathews of Radyr and Llandaf, Morgans of Tredegar, Pryses of Gogerddan, Lloyds of Rhiwedog, Trefors of Trefalun and Bryncunallt and Griffiths of Cefnamwlch in Llŷn. Matrimonial alliances strengthened this unified structure but, with social change came another dimension to matrimonial practice, namely the steady increase in marriages between families in distant as well as neighbouring regions, thus broadening their interests and tying together families of repute in Wales in a bond of unity and in the spirit of kinship.

The material wealth of the Welsh gentry drew the attention of social commentators. George Owen of Henllys confidently declared that standards and values among them had increased significantly. Whereas freeholders generally were hardly worth £20 in land in the 1530s, by the 1590s, he declared, they were reasonably well off, an encouraging token which enabled him to applaud Tudor policy which, in his opinion, had benefited the inhabitants of Pembrokeshire:

> Generally, for the inclination of the people . . . they all embrace peace, quietness and neighbourly love, hating contentions, troubles, brawls and factions . . . very obediently to the magistrates of the county, undertaking willingly to their power any burden or charge laid upon them for the prince's service or their country's good . . . [47]

It was this 'joyefull metamorphosis' throughout the whole of Wales, as he described it in the 'Dialogue', that had facilitated the building of substantial residences. Whereas it has been calculated that gentry incomes in the 1530s varied broadly between £5 and £20 (gentlemen) and between £20 and £40 (esquires),[48] by the mid-seventeenth century a number of families with substantial annual incomes had emerged, such as the Bulkeleys of Beaumaris (£4,300), Mansels of Margam (£4,300), Mostyns of Mostyn in Flintshire (£3,000), Wynns of Gwydir (£3,000), and Morgans of Tredegar (£3,000). These were privileged families who formed an élite that prospered in trade and commerce, acquiring monastic and other properties, exploiting mineral resources and arranging substantial marriage alliances. Together with large numbers of backwoods gentry valued at no more than £500 a year by the end of the sixteenth century, they kept a wary eye on their material prospects, particularly the matrimonial market.

Since social status was often expressed in occupational terms it is hardly surprising that a large proportion of the minor gentry worked their own lands as farmers. They had not the means nor the inclination to maintain large-scale households or estates and were not within the range of gentry described in the oft-quoted passage by Sir Thomas Smith in his *De Republica Anglorum* (1586) as those 'who can live idly without manual labour'.[49] According to their social standing they did 'bear the port, charge and countenance of a gentleman', but that, in many cases, was inferior to the standards enjoyed in more prosperous English houses.

Their lineage and status dictated that they should aspire to prominent positions and adopt new codes of conduct. Nonetheless, so long as the status they claimed was acknowledged by their communities there was no inconsistency for, in the last resort, it was the manner in which an individual conducted himself among those of the same social milieu that mattered. By the mid-sixteenth century the most eligible native families began to drop the traditional patronymic style and adopted surnames in line with English practice. This was convenient but also abandoned another significant link with the medieval past. Some major families, like the Griffiths of Penrhyn, Morgans of Tredegar, Herberts of Raglan and Vaughans of Tretŵr, had long since discarded the custom in the mid-fifteenth century but most families did so at least a century later as their prosperity increased. Thomas Mostyn obtained permission from Rowland Lee at Great Sessions in 1539 to adopt the name of his estate as his surname, and at about the same time the Vaughans of Corsygedol, Wynns of Gwydir and Lewises of Y Fan followed suit.[50]

Emphasis was placed increasingly on the need to defend one's 'credit' and reputation against the gibing accusations of inferior gentry. One of the most actively engaged in defending his status was Sir John Wynn who, when asserting his and his followers' rights to lands in the Forest of Snowdon in 1598, expressed his fear that to be deprived of such possessions would, in his case, lead to the loss of regional supremacy despite his father's support for the earl of Leicester in previous years. He desired that his honour might be upheld and that his 'friends be not forced first to yield' for, as he maintained, 'that will turn to my great reproof and shame in the country'.[51] Some overbearing gentry often exceeded themselves by tyrannizing over their dependants in matters relating to land and property rights. Piers Holland of Cinmel, Abergele, for example, was reputed to be a ruthless protector of his interests, a proprietor who, it was said, 'is all in all and ruleth and commandeth all men . . . as him listeth, using his will for law and his affection for reason . . . where he willeth there it goeth, be it right or wrong'.[52] Two of the most aggressive landowners with Catholic sympathies who would stop at nothing to achieve their aims in this respect were Edward Kemeys of Cefnmabli, a corrupt and vindictive Glamorgan landowner, and Anthony Mansel of Llantriddyd who was constantly involved in bitter disputes with his tenants. Mansel was the second son of Sir Rice Mansel and, in the years 1571, 1578 and 1583–4, quarrelled violently with his tenants in Swansea and the Vale of Glamorgan concerning enclosure of land, and on one occasion his hedges were destroyed.[53] Moreover, in Eifionydd, Sir William Maurice of Clenennau, was equally quarrelsome and was described in one Star Chamber suit, in which he appeared as a defendant, as being 'a man of great power and authority . . . a turbulent and contentious man amongst his neighbours and carrying a greedy mind unlawfully to enrich himself by other men's goods and lands'.[54] Such exaggerated descriptions of aspiring and tenacious landowners were not uncommon in those days and characterized many of the most unruly; yet, in the Welsh countryside generally, amicable relationships were fostered between landlords and tenants, even in periods of hardship, and the leadership was hardly ever in doubt.

Cadet families also flourished, which may suggest that the case for a substantial movement of younger sons of gentry from Wales has, to a degree, been exaggerated. For example, three of the five sons of Thomas Salusbury of Denbigh established estates of their own: Henry Salusbury at Llanrhaeadr, Robert Salusbury at Plas Isaf, Llanrwst, and John Salusbury at Bachymbyd. Thomas the eldest became the heir of Lleweni and laid the foundations for a prosperous future for the senior branch.[55] The Wynn family of Gwydir also established a group of junior families which extended and consolidated its power virtually throughout the whole of north Wales. Moreover, in Monmouthshire, three younger brothers of Rowland Morgan of Tredegar, became the ancestors of families at Llanfedw, Basaleg and Penllwyn-sarth (or serth) respectively, and his second son, Henry, established the Llanrhymni branch.[56] Many of these offshoots were formed and progressed as a result of propitious marriages, and the patronage which they gave to professional poets boosted their reputations and accompanied their growth in landed power and public office, particularly in the western and northern areas of Wales. Regardless of the grievances expressed by the itinerant bards that patronage among landed proprietors was on the decline in the latter half of the sixteenth century, it is evident that several of them were still being supported by heads even of cadet families which were predominantly of the middling sort. In Merioneth, for example, intermarriage between families either within the county or in areas just over its borders, was common and this accounted for the persistence of a strong Welsh-language cultural tradition among modest gentry in that region down to the eighteenth century.

In this context, the case of Morus Gruffydd of Plas Newydd (Porth-aml) in Anglesey and later of Llanfair-is-gaer in Caernarfon-

shire, and his family is relevant. He was descended from prime
Welsh stock, his ancestor being Sir William Griffith, Chamberlain
of North Wales.[57] In the late Tudor and early Stuart periods he
was a modestly placed country gentleman holding offices in
Anglesey. He married Jane, daughter of John Wyn ap Huw of
Bodfel in Llŷn, by whom he had fourteen children. He personally
recorded the details of their births and marriages, the majority
marrying into Welsh gentry families, thus emphasizing 'the
remarkable extent to which the principal families were bound
together by a network of marriage alliances'.[58]

In any assessment of the gentry in their communities it is
evident that, in many regions of Wales, cadet families may well
have filled a significant gap in the history of the landed gentry in
this crucial period. Several of the younger sons who established
substantial houses had acquired education: some were professional lawyers, others entered commerce and trade and a number
took holy orders. They also set up households which they were
able to maintain as sources of power and influence in generations
to come. They upheld their status by marrying local heiresses who,
on the poetic evidence, were worthy partners by birth and
reputation. Doubtless it was largely the availability of such
heiresses that drew many of the younger sons back to the Welsh
countryside to set up families. In that context emphasis was
placed on the role of the gentlewoman in polite society, not only as
a benign and pious figure but also as a practical governess of her
household and, in the case of the redoubtable Katherine of
Berain, married four times successively to leading north Wales
gentry, as a shrewd and ruthless manipulator of family politics.

The more opulent county families enjoyed a more comfortable
standard of living but all gentry shared some common interests in
claiming illustrious ancestries which indicated the value they
placed collectively on tradition and antiquity. Matrimonial
alliances strengthened family connections and enriched pedigrees.
Whenever an *uchelwr* was called upon to defend his honour he did
so usually by citing his family's lineage and reputation. Allied to
this feature were the virtues which gave the *uchelwr* his special
position in his community. The deference shown to individual
members of reputable families was largely based on the qualities
they had inherited from their forebears. Such attributes were given
publicity in the strict-metre odes which contain sustained
references to the courage, magnanimity and integrity of the
'perfect' gentleman. He who was skilled in all goodness ('Dawnus
ym mhob daioni') and an example in his time ('Yn siampler i'w

amser oedd') was regarded by maintainers of the Welsh cultural tradition as the ideal for others of lower rank, not necessarily to emulate, but to admire and value.[59] This view, as expressed in the poems, often obscured the actual person it was meant to describe who was actively engaged in organizing his family and estate and running public affairs on behalf of the Crown. Emphasis was placed on hierarchy and patriarchy and on maintaining the link between the country seat, usually regarded as the *plasty* or *tŷ cyfrifol*, and kinship.

Patrilineal features in bardic composition, as well as estate and private correspondence, broadly revealed five fundamental aspects of the concept of gentility within the framework of Welsh *uchelwriaeth*: the country seat, land and property, family archives, an esteemed reputation and, where possible, a direct line of descent or hereditary title. Continuity was considered essential in maintaining stability. The emergence of provincial loyalties gave prominent families a stake in land within a defined geographical area that involved establishing a foothold in adjacent counties. A prime example was Mostyn in Flintshire which, by the mid-seventeenth century, had emerged as a major power in the social and political life of north Wales. It showed considerable pride in its past because the family had established connections throughout the region: the uniting of the five courts of Pengwern (Chirk), Trecastell and Tregarnedd (Anglesey), Mostyn (Tegeingl) and Gloddaith (Creuddyn) under Richard ap Hywel (*c*.1500) laid the basis of the family's power and his reputation as a leading landowner. His grandson, William Mostyn, added to the buildings at Mostyn to raise his standing in the community and exercised supervisory authority over the bardic order in north Wales in the mid-sixteenth century.[60] Sir Edward Stradling compiled 'The Winning of the Lordship of Glamorgan' (*c*.1561–6), a spurious family pedigree which identified the Stradlings with Robert Fitzhamo, earl of Gloucester and the Norman conqueror of Glamorgan.[61] Sir John Wynn's observations on the importance of pedigrees are well known and revealed his detailed knowledge of his own stock allegedly traced back to Gruffudd ap Cynan, the twelfth-century king of Gwynedd, and pride in his gentle status.

It was pedigree and status also that accounted for the rise of the Vaughans of Trawsgoed in Llanafan, Cardiganshire, the family enjoying remarkable success through the accumulation of land and arranging successful marriages into the Stedman and Jones families of Strata Florida and Abermarlais respectively.[62] In Carmarthenshire, the Vaughans of Golden Grove rose to fame through acquiring court offices and administering the attainted lands of Sir Rhys ap Gruffudd of Dinefwr.[63] Likewise, in north-east Wales, the Trefors of Trefalun and their cadets achieved prominence in the time of John Trefor (d. 1589), who built Trefalun (1576) and whose native connections were revealed by the inscription in Welsh on his alabaster tomb in Gresford church.[64] Families of this type, which had grown from modest kindred roots and located in different parts of the country, had become fully recognized as supreme in their localities by establishing fortunes in land and office well before the close of the sixteenth century.

Country Seats and Economic Resources

The social and religious features of gentry households will be examined in Chapter 6, but the material aspects of country houses are given attention in this section. When the economic climate was favourable the mansions of the gentry, varying considerably in size, formed a central feature in the Welsh countryside. The living conditions of gentry improved immensely during this period when country houses were rebuilt, extended or renovated. The delight in introducing newer methods of Renaissance architecture and establishing the country mansion on a more elevated plane as a symbol of the aesthetic tastes of the most opulent was becoming more apparent in different parts of the country. As military functions began to recede the luxury and sophistication of the *plasty* assumed greater prominence. The influence of Renaissance architecture gradually penetrated the most richly endowed areas of Wales, particularly the north and south-eastern parts as well as the lowlands of Glamorgan and south Pembrokeshire. The border regions, open as they were to wider influences, also revealed exciting developments. Between *c*.1550 and 1640 there occurred a significant increase in the building, extending and refurbishing of houses, with the object of increasing comfort and privacy and of asserting status and independence.[65] New architectural styles were introduced and the trends reflected a growing prosperity among all sections of landed and urban communities. Closer commercial and cultural contact was established with border English towns and London, and the routes of the drovers and the brisk coastal trade with Bristol, Chester and London, brought into Wales new architectural techniques and ideas. George Owen was constantly alert to the changes that brought new trends into the material life of Wales. His works manifest the benefits and drawbacks of economic development in a country that had gained from the gradual assimilation with England. He offered perceptive comments on a variety of social and economic trends and his testimony revealed how, by the last decades of the sixteenth century, the landscape of Wales was significantly changing. Some houses, like Stackpole, Carew and Picton in Pembrokeshire, and Raglan in Monmouthshire, were rebuilt castles. Other fortifications, such as Powys Castle, Chirk Castle, Cardiff Castle and St Donat's Castle also became sumptuous gentry residences. In his preface to *Cambrobrytannicae Cymraecaeve Linguae Institutiones* (1592) Dr John Davies of Brecon extolled the virtues of Sir Edward Stradling and his wife Agnes Gage, and referred in its early sections to the magnificence of their residence. He mentioned a poem by a Thomas Leyshon who, in Latin metres, considered the castle as being 'stalwart its defences' and praised the sumptuous buildings which Stradling, the writer explained, 'had raised . . . at the very edge of the coast in a most wondrous manner'.[66]

The mansions at Margam (Mansels), Llantarnam (Morgans) and Brecon Priory (purchased but not inhabited by Sir John Price) arose out of monastic establishments. The Gunters and Joneses of Usk and Williamses of Monmouth used materials from the castle nearby or conventual buildings to build their residences and many more modest houses were either renovated or built anew in the hinterland. For example, Gwerclas in Merioneth, owned by Humphrey Hughes, a justice, lawyer and keen litigant, was rebuilt and he extended his lands at the same time.[67] The poet Huw Machno composed a well-known ode for the enlightened squire, Huw Llwyd of Cynfal Fawr in the same county, who had spent some time warring in France and the Low Countries against Spain.[68] On his return he rebuilt his home and provided it with a water supply. He was a typical Renaissance man interested in medicine and a master of the twenty-four feats, and he owned a splendid library. Prosperous conditions in north-east Wales were largely responsible for traces of conspicuous consumption there and elsewhere in the mid-sixteenth century. Plas Clough was built of brick by the entrepreneur Sir Richard Clough in the 1560s with doric columns adorning the porch. Clough, the second husband of the famous Katherine of Berain, was a typical *nouveau riche* who prospered and became a gentleman of means and local influence, a factor for Sir Thomas Gresham in Antwerp and the builder of a second house, Bachegraig, in Tremeirchion which had a remarkable 'revolutionary pyramidical six-storeyed plan'.[69]

Other houses were built, such as Plas Mawr, Conwy (1576) by Robert Wynn, a scion of Gwydir,[70] and Corsygedol by Gruffudd Vaughan (1592–3), and he also added Corsygedol chapel to Llanddwywe church.[71] Gwydir mansion was extended (c.1555) and a chapel was attached to St Grwst church by Sir Richard Wynn, second baronet, in 1633.[72] Carew Castle was renovated at the beginning of the sixteenth century by Sir Rhys ap Thomas,[73] Oxwich Castle became a magnificent abode erected with four storeys as a 'new-style palatial country mansion' for Sir Rice Mansel and his successors before the family moved to Margam,[74] and Plas-y-ward, rebuilt by Simon Thelwall, symbolized his family's advancement in the Vale of Clwyd.[75] When Sir John Perrot died in 1592 the survey of his estates described the house as one of the most elegant in south-west Wales. These examples reveal that, despite economic hardship, even some of the most modest of landed gentry ventured to improve their personal circumstances. How much of this activity involved the use of borrowed money it is difficult to tell but doubtless economic recession bore hard on them. They would go to any lengths to establish for themselves new standards of living, a degree of independence and a firm claim to regional superiority. Ambition was the impetus to their activities but excess in these matters did entail economic stringency.

Domestic architecture enjoyed a remarkable revival and the social progress of the gentry was reflected sometimes in the most flamboyant manner. Brick was used and later glass, and the old halls were replaced by storeyed residences, floors and stairs, masonry, fireplaces and chimneys. The living space increased and rooms were refurbished with expensive furniture. All this became more apparent in the latter half of the sixteenth century and was more prominent in some areas than others, depending largely on the growth of wealth and the abilities of families to increase their power in their respective localities. Owing chiefly to economic constraints it would be inappropriate to suggest that the majority of the Welsh gentry were reputed for their 'conspicuous consumption'. In Glamorgan, where there was a greater spread of wealth, a spate of house-building occurred between 1560 and 1630 indicating a consolidation of family-ranking in the social hierarchy. The habitations of the gentry usually revealed what social standing and degree of power they enjoyed. In this context the town houses of both *noveaux riches* and traditional rural gentry who settled in second houses, usually in shiretowns, further indicate that reputation was being measured in terms of economic progress and the ability to extend family 'credit and fame' into commercial spheres. Henry Herbert, second earl of Pembroke, kept a sumptuous household at Cardiff Castle which he had repaired. There, on his infrequent visits, he lavishly entertained and, as Rhys ap Meurig observed, he and his wife were

> honourably received into Wales by the most part of the gentlemen of Glamorgan and Monmouth shires, and with like entertainment brought to the Castle of Cardiff [1574?] . . . where, keeping a very honourable and sumptuous house to all comers, they continued . . . riding abroad, and visiting their friends, and viewing the country.[76]

Huw Nannau Hen was certainly a less prominent figure but, in his native Dolgellau, equally esteemed as a gentleman of worth. Despite family disputes he was, by Merioneth standards, sufficiently substantial in his remote locality to be able to build an impressive house c.1615–20.[77] In view of the expensive legal battles which had absorbed the owner's attention the poets were amazed that the house had cost so much to build. In addition to his expansionist policy in property Huw Nannau desired to display his ostentation, though in a largely impoverished part of the country. John Wyn ap Maredudd added new dimensions to the Wynn household at Gwydir as did his grandson at Gwydir Uchaf nearby. Sir Richard Clough enriched the two houses mentioned above to satisfy his own taste in Flemish architecture and they were built possibly for commercial purposes in the parishes of Henllan and Tremeirchion respectively. Both of them were also among the first truly representative of the Renaissance in north-east Wales, and doubtless Clough, during his period as factor in Antwerp, was in touch with Flemish builders and building methods. His own pretensions urged him to expand on these lavish houses, Plas Clough, with its crow-stepped gables, being regarded as the first Renaissance house built in Wales.[78] Oxwich Castle, originally redesigned by the powerful Sir Rice Mansel, was repaired by his equally ambitious son Sir Edward Mansel. At Briton Ferry, Leyshon Price built a 'fair new house' and Sir Edward Carne set up 'a goodly home' at Ewenni. The Lewises used stone from Caerphilly Castle to add substantially to Y Fan, and the celebrated Herbert House at Greyfriars in Cardiff was lavishly embellished and, next to the castle, became the largest building in that town. In the Vale, Beaupré contained Greek architecture, principally ionic, doric and corinthian styles, and further west, the houses of Stackpole, Carew and Picton stood out supremely in the Pembrokeshire landscape.[79]

By establishing themselves in the countryside the majority of gentryfolk maintained a most revered practice associated with the old Welsh nobility, namely householdership (*perchentyaeth*). Fifteenth-century poets, such as Dafydd Nanmor, referred to the increased hospitality offered in the emerging *plastai* where *pencenhedloedd*, the heads of households, or *paterfamiliae*, the magnanimous hosts, shared with their immediate family and guests the virtues of good living and the comforts and delights of the material world.[80] The rare surroundings enabled poetic declaimers to emphasize the moral probity of the hospitable *uchelwr* and often drew attention to his expert husbandry and estate management. 'Householdership' prevailed in the sixteenth and seventeenth centuries as a social phenomenon in many residences. Sir Roger Mostyn opposed his son Thomas's intention to contest the Flintshire county election in 1624 because he would be required to live in London while his wife remained in the country.[81] Moreover, Sir Thomas Salusbury, when explaining his decision not to leave Wales in 1632, declared that 'our country-men . . . are a crafty kind of people and . . . bear an internal hate to such as make themselves strangers unto them'.[82] A varied selection of sources, extending from family correspondence and domestic accounts to bardic tributes, testify to the homekeeping habits of a reasonably large proportion of gentry down to the eve of the Civil Wars.

Luxurious though the lifestyle of the most prosperous among the gentry appeared to be they were also subject to periods of hardship and economic tension. To keep up appearances many of them were obliged to employ usurers and were often at the mercy of unscrupulous lawyers. Arduous economic conditions frequently led to bitter conflicts between contending factions to gain the ascendancy. They enabled the most prominent to increase their authority at the expense of others whose landed resources were not as extensive and robust. Indeed, economic insecurity was the prime factor in any contest of this kind since litigation was often caused by rivalries over lands and property, the loss of which could seriously damage their reputation. The gentry by nature were a contentious lot, and when times were hard with bad harvests, drought and disease, as well as the usual 'dead' times of the year, frustration turned into aggression in their efforts to maintain income. In the years 1549–51, 1594–7, 1623 and 1632, for example, even substantial gentry found it almost impossible to make both ends meet and openly voiced their grievances in their correspondence.[83] The 1590s were regarded as a period of crisis

owing mainly to bad weather conditions, successive harvest
failures which led to serious famine, and inefficient estate
management. In 1591 and 1592 drought affected the economy
and, in 1596–7, the price of wheat soared to 92s. a quarter, four
times the average price. The prices of other commodities also rose
and, in communities where there was much poverty, the bad times
affected all levels of society. 'The unseasonable year', lamented Sir
John Wynn, referring to the drastic fall in rents in 1613,

> which hath burnt up the greater part of our corn and grass and hath
> brought down the sale of any cattle being the only means my tenants
> have to live on and to raise my rents hath made them fail payment to
> me and I to his majesty.[84]

Similar examples could be cited: in stock-rearing regions where so
much depended largely on fixed rents and the drover trade, it was
an up-hill task for any squire to maintain his income, pay his dues
to the Crown, defray his household and other expenses and
maintain his reputation in his community. Economic recessions
hit the lower orders more severely, of course, and Rowland Lee, in
1535, considered that dearth led to an increase in lawbreaking:
'this skarsenes of grayne which riseth dayly causeth small roboryes
in Wales, ffor where want [of] bredd, ther must ffleshe be had, the
belly must be fylled somewhatt'.[85]

Half a century later, John Penry, that ardent Puritan agitator,
drew attention to economic adversity in his first treatise entitled
The Aequity of an Humble Supplication . . . (1587), albeit as a divine
penalty for sin: 'The unseasonable harvest 1585 yielded very little
corn . . . The winter . . . destroyed all their cattle well near, so that
now the very sinew of their maintenance is gone.'[86] William
Vaughan of Llangyndeyrn, in *The Golden-fleece* (1626), also
emphasized the poor economic condition of Wales which,
although his own project had failed, prompted him to advocate
colonization in Newfoundland:

> For what is it, which renders a Nation vnhappy? Next to the want of
> Gods knowledge . . . it is the want of necessaries for the sustentation of
> life . . . And when through a long peace, and their ouerspent fields,
> their Country-men doe increase and multiply, so that the extent of
> their natiue Land is not capable nor sufficient to maintaine them.[87]

These comments reflected the condition of society as a whole and
emphasized the intense suffering among an impoverished
peasantry and modest gentry, especially in winter, striving to
make ends meet under stringent conditions.

It was in periods of economic depression that the professional poets also found it extremely difficult to ply their trade. Although many bardic tributes contain references deploring the conditions that caused economic blight, in more temperate times it appears that a considerable amount of patronage was still being offered, even in the less well-endowed parts of the country. A large proportion of privileged families was probably Welsh-speaking, whether they were prepared to practise or even acknowledge that or not in public among their social equals. They would, however, have had no option but to use the vernacular when dealing with local administrative business and in courts of law. Some, of course, were more prepared to maintain the dying craft. Majestic eulogies, while yearning for better times, did praise individual gentry for maintaining the tradition of worthy *perchentyaeth* in times of high inflation, bad harvests and cultural malaise.[88] Stressful conditions, however, did not deter a large group of patrons, lay and cleric, from serving their communities, and there were several families, from a variety of areas in north and south Wales, who continued to support the poets and Welsh cultural pursuits generally down to the pre-Civil War period and beyond. More research is needed to try to uncover the extent to which Welsh gentry adhered to native literary activity in this period for it may, surprisingly, reveal that the process of cultural alienation was not as rapid or as widespread as once supposed by literary historians.

It is evident that the fulcrum of power was not the shire arsenal or the shire courts but rather the country residences where the *uchelwyr* demonstrated moral leadership, authority, and the worthy attributes of *uchelwriaeth*. Whereas in the courts of law they adopted a code of conduct which applied to that brand of Welsh gentility as public servants to meet the needs of the Tudor state, in the country residences they combined their legal status with their skills in granting hospitality. In both areas of activity they served as guardians of their people.[89] In the *plasty* they safeguarded the interests of the patrimony and, as officers in the courts of law, they contributed to the maintenance of unity and good order in the realm. Local government agents often acted corruptly, exploiting their position and lining their own pockets at the expense of the state or less well-endowed kinsmen, neighbours and tenants. It was the law that invariably suffered in such circumstances. Corrupt juries, in the past, had been the order of the day, especially in the Marcher lordships, and the practice continued well after the Tudor settlement. Unscrupulous defendants and

their kinsmen, for example, tainted court proceedings by bribing
sheriffs to empanel partial juries to their private advantage. Oliver
St John, opposed by the powerful Mansel family of Margam,
turned to Sir Edward Stradling for aid in securing an impartial
jury to hear his suit concerning the title to the parsonage of
Penmark: 'send me the names in writing of xxiiii substantial and
honest men', he said, 'such as you are assured will be indifferent,
that we may trust to, so as then I may peruse them and seek to get
them returned with your good help and others of my friends'.[90]
Old practices died hard as the appeal of the desperate correspondent amply reveals.

Governmental Control and Political Faction

The more conservative families who claimed gentle status were
strongly attached to their localities and possessed authority
derived essentially from the traditional kindred organization. It
was that innate link with their respective regions that created an
organic unity in community life and established economic
patterns which bound together all social degrees and gradations
within regional identities. There existed a strong sense of
community in towns, villages and townships, which was reflected
chiefly in local government administration. Maintaining economic
stability, where that was possible, depended largely on the
preservation of law and order at local or regional level. In this
context again the Welsh gentry assumed prominence before and
after the Tudor settlement. Their power in government was
inherited but, subsequent to the Acts of Union, was enhanced
principally as part of a conscious design on the government's
behalf to allow aspiring freemen to enjoy the privilege of office.
Not that they all managed, in material terms, to hold prestigious
positions but they pursued all avenues possible in law and
administration to try to compensate for their narrow means. Their
public stature in the Principality and the native regions, the
Welshries of the Marches, had been achieved by experience and
shrewdness in maintaining law and order, often in the period of
social and political instability before 1536. The reputation of
landed gentry in public affairs by the latter decades of the
sixteenth century stemmed principally from the progress made by
tenacious predecessors in acquiring administrative offices
generations before the Acts of Union. Traditional leadership was a
key force in assuring the *uchelwyr* their prominence in local

government; a strong attachment to the native soil created firm bonds of affinity between them and members of their household and those whom they governed.[91]

The mechanics of local government in Wales following these acts of assimilation reveal that the system introduced was based on the adaptation and use of English law. The Council in the Marches, a Yorkist creation in 1471 revived by Henry VII, was the administrative arm of the Privy Council which advised the Crown and functioned as the chief executive body in the realm. The Council in the Marches, established at Ludlow, and the Courts of Great Sessions, or assize courts, were set up in 1543; the Council as a permanent statutory body and the assizes as a legal organization divided into four circuits, each consisting of three shires, and held twice a year in each shire. They were entrusted with practising English common law and were cheap compared with the central London courts. Within the old shires of the Principality the existing judicial and administrative offices continued to function, particularly the chief justices of the Anglesey and Carmarthen circuits, and added to them were the Chester and Brecknock circuits. Sheriffs had already been appointed in the Principality shires in 1284. They were installed in the five new shires and served from henceforth on an annual basis as the principal royal representatives responsible for organizing fiscal business, presiding over the county and hundred courts and supervising the Crown's affairs in the shire. The sheriff, although subordinate to the justices of the peace and expected to be 'attendant' upon them 'in all and everything concerning their authorities', shouldered many administrative burdens but his responsibilities in military affairs declined after the appointment of deputy-lieutenants in Welsh shires in 1586, arguably the most prestigious office in regional government in the late Elizabethan period.

Government in the shires was co-ordinated by a hierarchy of courts linked to the Council in the Marches through its administrative and judicial mechanisms. That Council's legal duties were divided into criminal and civil, and its jurisdiction overlapped with that of the King's Courts at Westminster, which led to rivalry between them within a single judicial system. These institutions were divided into equity and prerogative courts of Star Chamber, Chancery and Requests and the common law courts of Exchequer, King's Bench and Common Pleas.[92] The increase in litigation, however, supplied the Council in the Marches with ample business. In 1594 it was said that 2,000 cases still remained to be heard and, in 1606–10, it was reported that it had dealt with almost 3,500 cases. Whether Star Chamber, despite its popularity with the more hard-pressed among the gentry, was altogether successful in suppressing overmighty officials is questionable. In many cases the court's verdict is not recorded, but it did threaten the most truculent among the gentry by reminding them that means were at hand to curb their turbulent behaviour.

It was the appointment of justices of the peace, however, that formed one of the most imaginative innovatory features of the settlement of 1536–43 (St 27 Hen.VIII c. 5).[93] Eight magistrates chosen from among the gentry in each shire were granted commissions to preserve law and order. With no property qualification to hinder their appointment they were to meet quarterly in sessions of the peace where they dealt with a diversity of judicial and administrative tasks, especially those concerning breaches of the peace and other matters such as defence, repairs of highways and bridges, weights and measures, the regulation of alehouses and the administration of the Poor Law. Resident justices in the hundreds held petty sessions and supervised the high constables in each of these divisions and the petty constables in each township. The parishes were the smallest units of administration, and at the annual vestry meeting, local surveyors and overseers were respectively appointed to administer roads and bridges and the Poor Law rates.

Doubtless the most highly regarded officials in shire administration were these justices of the peace, who had well established their reputation in England for almost two centuries. The office was the pivot around which local government functioned, an office of which George Owen thought highly despite his reservations concerning the material qualities of its holders. In his opinion, they were the 'chiefest gentlemen in every shire' and their residences frequently sited in inhabited areas. [94] At the head of the commission of the peace was the *custos rotulorum*, 'a man', according to William Lambarde, 'especially picked out either for wisdom, countenance or credit'.[95] He held a prominent position in view of the authority granted to him to collect and preserve sessions' files, build up a corpus of legal convention and establish precedent in the exercise of the law. The *custos rotulorum*, introduced into Wales in 1543, was usually a senior magistrate who, in view of his prominence in county affairs, was expected to keep a vigilant eye on the records and arrange for their safe custody.[96]

According to the statute introducing justices of the peace in 1536 the aim of installing them in Wales was to ensure 'that one order of ministering of his [i.e. the King's] laws should be had, observed and used in the same as in other places of this realm of England'.[97] Consequently, justices of the peace, in conjunction with sheriffs, were engaged by the Tudors as the chief officers of regional government in the sixteenth century. The efficiency of the office was referred to by Sir Thomas Smith as 'a more certain way to rule the people whereby they are kept always, as it were, in a bridle of good order'.[98] That 'good order' was taken by Tudor commentators to be the bedrock of stability in Welsh society in days of administrative reorganization, political faction, economic unease and religious change.

In the context of gentility, privilege at all times entailed obligation, which was principally manifested in the institutions of law in the regions. In the Principality the offices of sheriff, coroner and escheator had been well-established since 1284–5, and from 1536 the justice of the peace.[99] They were all responsible for the smooth running of affairs and the routine of county government. As time went on more duties and responsibilities were heaped upon the justice of the peace whose official status, despite the honour accorded to the county sheriff, was higher than any other in regional government except the justices of assize in the courts of Great Sessions. By the early seventeenth century the office had become so popular among the gentry that the number who served on the bench in all Welsh counties far exceeded that stipulated by law, and unsuccessful attempts were made to weed them, retaining the services of the most efficient. George Owen rejoiced that Henry VIII had installed Welsh governors in official positions: 'for passing by dyuers gentlemens howses', he declared (in Barthol's words), 'it was towld me that a Justice of peace dwelt theare', prompting a further statement that they were, if not the most distinguished members of the county community, at least the best known.[100] Although some were more prominent than others, a broad-based group of gentry served, many as justices of the quorum with a degree of legal knowledge, on the bench of magistrates. Since these two offices were key positions in the counties it is hardly surprising that the bards, in defining the public role of their patrons, constantly drew attention to the dignity that the most favoured of those patrons enjoyed. It was indirectly a means by which the poets gave their consent to the Tudor settlement and, surprisingly though it may seem, heightened a sense of national consciousness among those ranks in society that were in danger of abandoning their native cultural traditions. Such references boosted their morale in three directions: as administrators with special responsibility for their localities, as maintainers of order and discipline among their subordinates and as cultural leaders in those communities. Whatever offices were entrusted to the gentry they added significantly to the prestige of some families and to the responsibilities of magistrates in safeguarding legal precedent and the defence of the realm.[101]

All in all, sources reveal that the local government system in Wales was reasonably efficient during the remainder of the Tudor age after 1541. Not that lawlessness ceased thereafter: it prevailed, particularly in the old Marcher areas where the new system took a long time to settle, and it may have been the case that if the stringent policy adopted by Rowland Lee in the 1530s had been allowed to continue, it might well have achieved some success in solving the problems of law and order in the Principality and, to a lesser extent, outside it. However, it was the system of regional government, initiated by the Tudor settlement, that provided the decisive answer to the chronic disorder in the old Marcher districts and gradually eliminated the more serious legal abuses in the Marches. When it is considered that the malpractices forbidden in a series of statutes in 1534–5 persisted long after the Acts of Union it is hardly surprising that Lee expressed his anxieties at the time when the appointment of justices of the peace was being contemplated. The abused customs of *arddel* (the employment of criminals and outlaws in private armies) and *cymortha* (a communal aid illegally exploited to impose forced exactions on tenants) continued although they had been abolished in 1534,[102] and attention was drawn to their survival by Sir Thomas Holte,[103] Richard Price of Brecon,[104] Henry Herbert, second earl of Pembroke and President of the Council in the Marches,[105] and Dr David Lewis, a native of Abergavenny, a leading government legal adviser and a prominent Admiralty Judge.[106] Lewis commented harshly on conditions in the south-east marchlands of Wales and blamed the Council in the Marches and shire officials for the lack of order. 'Contempts and disorders must be severely punished', he declared in 1576, 'and the better the man offender the greater the offence, and the punishment ought to be the more, which must be rather in body by imprisonment than in purse'. Lewis's rivalry with Sir Henry Sidney, then President of the Council in the Marches, largely accounted for such a bitter condemnation but his criticism probably echoed the views of other worthy lawyers. In addition to his comments on the increasing criminal business involving Welsh clients and defendants in the Court of Star Chamber and on the civil suits in the Chancery and Exchequer courts (which respectively dealt with equity law and with debts or recovery of lands, goods and profits owing to the Crown), what he had to say about the abuse of law was generally a serious cause of concern. George Owen likewise was compelled to draw attention to the abusive character of many of his fellow-gentry, particularly in Glamorgan where, he maintained, 'great troupes of retayners followe every gentleman'.[107]

Surviving Quarter Sessions records for Caernarfonshire clearly show that the court was operational in that shire from 1541 onwards and that its organization and archival material were seemingly in good order during the remainder of the century.[108] Many of the Great Sessions records for Wales have survived from 1541, especially those for the Chester circuit, when the courts began to function, and evidence does strongly suggest that those courts were also regularly held and in reasonably satisfactory order for the remainder of the sixteenth and early decades of the seventeenth centuries. In fact, Sir William Gerard, Sir Henry Sidney and Nicholas Robinson, bishop of Bangor, complimented the standard of government maintained in Wales in the 1560s and 1570s (thus counterbalancing Dr David Lewis's strictures to the contrary) and, despite his constructive review of a variety of procedural matters, George Owen's verdict in the 1590s was that the structure of government was reasonably healthy.[109] The country would soon have noticed the difference, he continued, if the Council in the Marches were to be abolished: 'if o'r ffathers weare nowe lyuinge', he declared, 'they wowld thinke it som straunge Contry inhabited with a forran Nation so altered is the cuntry and cuntrymen, the people chaunged in heartt within . . . from euill to good, and from badd to better'.[110] A glowing testimony indeed but, in view of Owen's devotion to the Tudor settlement, definitely biased and misleading. So also was Robinson's testimony to Sir Francis Walsingham in 1567; although he was aware that the 'dregs of superstition' hindered the spiritual progress in his diocese, he added that 'the people liue in much obedience, fredome and quiet, so yt toward their prince they are like to continew faithfull subiectes, and among themselves peaceable neghboures'.[111]

A similar opinion was expressed in 1603 when the Council's jurisdiction over the border shires was subject to severe attack.[112] If it were dissolved it would 'prove but a deseigne for the Welshmen to free themselves also from the same government', and destroy the spirit of the Tudor settlement.[113] The Council was considered necessary to control Wales and to maintain the unity that had already been achieved. To dissolve it would 'cast a general skorne and contempt upon the remainder of authoritie left in that Court for hereafter and make the Welshmen despised by the English who are now by their common government holden in termes of love'.[114] The Council was still considered to be the linchpin of good government in Wales and the borders. It was the chief means to vindicate the political harmony already established. To tamper with its authority would, it was maintained, destroy 'all traffique and commerce betweene the English and Welsh . . . and so both [countries] must retorne to that povertie, rudnes and disorder which was amongst them before this Coort made them quiet and rich'.

The structure of government manifestly revealed, therefore, how the Tudor gentry and their successors adapted themselves with comparative ease to its workings, and although they were often hampered by the interference of Crown agents pressing them to perform their duties more efficiently, they were doubtless masters of their communities and adept at manipulating offices in royal institutions. Devoted servants of the state they might well have been, but their authority, and the manner in which it was exercised by them, bore clear signs of their independence and, in some instances, of their incontestable supremacy in regional affairs.

Landed wealth and the exercise of public control created leadership and the authority associated with it; both were exercised within the household, over tenants and kinsmen and generally within a locality. The prerogatives were also asserted quite often in courts of law. The ideal gentleman was not merely a person demonstrating the social graces for he was also regarded as a governor of his patrimony or region of jurisdiction. It is not known how many gentry in Wales knew of or had read Sir Thomas Elyot's *The Book named the Governor*, but the type of authority which they wielded, especially after the 1530s, compared well with his description of the governor or administrator as a man of influence, responsibility and integrity.[115] It was expected that the educated gentleman would engage himself in public affairs. The emergence of the new sovereign state led to the demand for the services of a loyal administrative class chosen from among the gentry to organize and administer local government and maintain law and order.

The protective qualities of the gentry and their obligations to their immediate communities were extended to include the supervision of regional defence. Catholic threats made the Welsh coasts vulnerable to attack from the continent and from Ireland.

The coastal areas of Anglesey, Caernarfonshire and Pembroke-shire, in particular, were exposed to constant danger in times of war or when hostilities were imminent (see Chapter 4). In the summer of 1545 Sir Richard Bulkeley I of Beaumaris informed John Wyn ap Maredudd of Gwydir, sheriff of Caernarfonshire, of the need for constant vigilance in defence matters at a time when a third war had broken out between England and France.[116] It was an urgent appeal for concerted action to defend the two counties. 'I hertily pray you and all others . . .', he declared,

> to shew yoresellves at this tyme according to the trust and expectacon whiche I have had always in you . . . ffor now a frynd and ev' a frynd, and what so ev' he be that is faynte and slak at this tyme lett hym nev' loke for no favor nor good turne at my handes.

Roman Catholic threats and the seditious activities of Jesuit priests were also causes of concern. In 1587 the Privy Council commanded that the activities of recusants were to 'be looked unto and restrained as they shall neither be able to give assistance to the enemy nor that the enemy shall have any hope of relief or succour by them'.[117] Moreover, Sir John Perrot of Haroldston was concerned in the 1580s about the danger to Milford Haven and the coasts of Pembrokeshire and in September 1590, for example, there was a general call to musters because it was reported that Spain was making further preparations to invade England and Wales from northern Spain and the Indies. In 1593 it was directed that enquiries should be made into the activities of the children of gentry who were educated abroad and whose homes were to be searched for Jesuit priests, books, letters and other treasonable material.[118] In 1611–12 and 1627 Perrot and his co-adminis-trators also expressed concern about the increase in recusant families in south-east Wales and feared the consequences of overland immigration into Pembrokeshire and adjacent areas from the eastern borders of Wales (for further discussion of this theme see Chapter 4).[119]

In perilous times emphasis was placed on co-ordinating resources in all counties and on organizing an efficient deputy-lieutenancy. Assuming authority in local regional government entailed preserving the state's unity and welfare. In his frequent addresses to the juries of Kent Quarter Sessions William Lambarde consistently reminded them of the need to defend the best interests of the realm, and his observations on the nature of equitable government could easily be applied to the Welsh context. 'The very end of law', he declared, 'is obedience, and the end of obedience is the life and safety of the Commonwealth.'[120] That statement is fundamental in any assessment of the responses of local governors to their duties. The communications of the Privy Council to the Council in the Marches also demanded that local officials be more diligent in attending to their public duties.

In the broader context of gentry activity it is noteworthy that, in some respects, concepts of *uchelwriaeth* in the Welsh countryside and in the formal surroundings of the courts and other institutions, were 'at variance and in conflict with the English and Renaissance idea of a gentleman'.[121] This was revealed in the emphasis placed on kindred relations and on an undeviating attachment to pedigree, hierarchy, native culture and close-knit racial affinities based on a common language. Nevertheless, there were strong points of resemblance as well for, in the period between the Acts of Union and the Civil Wars, they adopted common criteria in their approach to communal obligation based on the establishment of order and just leadership. That communal obligation was not seriously impaired for, in most cases, relations between squire and tenant were amicable because they were largely interdependent. Moreover, the many cases of umpiring whereby an impartial arbitrator functioned as a daysman settling disputes, usually concerning lands, between parties indicate how law-giving often became an extra-curial practice in civil matters. Arbitration assisted in easing dealings over properties, partly in unburdening the court of its business, avoiding expensive and tedious litigation and clarifying surviving examples of Welsh law concerning land. The system was meant also to promote peace and good government and identified local communities with the expectations of the state of affairs in community life that drew all ranks in society together in obeying a common order. Moreover, attempts were made, in appointments of stewards to supervise landed properties, to seek skilled administrators and to ensure a strict adherence to good order. This was the case when Sir Edward Stradling was appointed by Sir Oliver St John in 1575 as chief steward of his Glamorgan properties. He was not only St John's kinsman but also a man 'of so good government', suitably equipped as an official to maintain order and obedience.[122] Given stable conditions, kinship and the close identity of interests that it fostered were among the foremost factors that kept together the gentry as a cohesive force and created the circumstances that might, if the central government was sufficiently vigilant, induce them to protect the state.

Regardless of the tensions that periodically occurred between local gentry and the agencies of the central government relationships were never, at any time, at breaking point. The basis of their power and allegiance was the Tudor settlement itself; the Crown's authority was acknowledged by the majority and thus common interests were served. Evidence shows that the acquisition of offices locally or elsewhere, aided in strengthening their loyalties to both dynasties and, in James I's reign, an increase occurred in the number of knighthoods conferred upon Welsh gentry and officials at Ludlow and at Court. Although loyalty to the person of the monarch was a marked feature in the sixteenth century, the accumulation of interests in institutions, particularly in Elizabeth's reign, was equally powerful in the making of the landed gentry. Tudor loyalties survived into the seventeenth century and, as A. H. Dodd has shown, Welsh parliamentary representatives gradually began to participate in the Commons more on political principle than on personal adherence to a dynasty.[123] Their apprenticeship in office, especially after the 1570s, enabled them to familiarize themselves with parliamentary procedure and to boost their confidence in dealing with parliamentary business. That business was rapidly increasing as the state expanded, and some Welsh members contributed to debates on such matters as finance, foreign policy, the burning issue of monopolies and economic affairs generally, parliamentary privilege and defence organization. In the early seventeenth century Sir William Maurice of Clenennau and Sir James Perrot became ardent spokesmen for issues that increasingly occupied the House of Commons and had special relevance to Wales. Maurice, in particular, keenly supported the union of Crowns in 1603 and the 'Cambro-British' tradition associated with the Welsh ruling class which he considered worth reviving so as to promote the unity of the realm on the accession of James I.[124] The sturdy puritan Perrot, on the other hand, became a more conspicuous figure through his ardent speeches in the House on more thorny political and economic matters which constantly occupied it in the 1620s and 1630s.

Increased experience in parliamentary business led a proportion of members to participate more actively in committees and as spokesmen on religious and political issues. The taciturn behaviour of the majority during the first half-century of Welsh representation stood in marked contrast to the remarkable buoyancy demonstrated by a few towards the end of the sixteenth century. It became more apparent as governmental business increased and coincided with contested elections in the shires when rival factions arose. Regional supremacy was again at stake among families that had become politically conscious but, basically, it involved the interplay of kin relations and influence as well as disputes over properties. They were largely responsible for the feud in 1571 between the Owens of Llwyn and Salusburies of Rug in Merioneth over the occupation of the township of Dolgellau.[125] Again, in 1597, the Vaughans of Clyro and Prices of Mynachdy contested the Radnorshire seat which uncovered corrupt practices on the sheriff's part.[126] In the 1570s and 1580s doubtless the most powerful figure in north Wales was Robert Dudley, earl of Leicester, who became lord of Denbigh (1564) and Ranger of the Forest of Snowdon (1575). He was expected to recover for the Crown the titles of concealed land encroached upon in north Wales, thus creating bitter resentment among freeholders led, in part, by Sir Richard Bulkeley of Beaumaris and, in part, by conservative Llŷn and Eifionydd freeholders.[127] Leicester also had supporters among influential gentry and his relations with Sir Henry Sidney, Lord President of the Council in the Marches, his kinsman by marriage, and Henry Herbert, Sidney's son-in-law and successor as Lord President, enabled him to build up a strong pro-Leicester alliance among north Wales gentry.

The Montgomeryshire and Denbighshire elections of 1588 and the Denbighshire election of 1601 also exacerbated existing controversies in those regions.[128] The 1601 election was deeply embroiled in local faction. Sir John Salusbury of Lleweni, in the west, opposing Sir Richard Trefor of Trefalun (near Gresford), Sir John Lloyd of Bodidris (near Llandegla) and the Salusburys of Rug (near Corwen) in the east. They had been followers of Robert Devereux, earl of Essex, who was executed for rebellion in that year. Essex was a strong rival of the Cecils and Henry Herbert, earl of Pembroke: he was powerful in south-west Wales and Radnorshire and extended his influence into Denbighshire, many local offices being filled by his nominees. Disputes concerning Cardiff bridge in 1581 led to the earl of Pembroke's involvement in a bitter controversy with the gentry of Glamorgan.[129] Their failure to enlist the support at court of Herbert's relations, Sir Henry Sidney and Robert Dudley, revealed the interrelations between rival gentry families in the locality, particularly the conflict between the Mathew and Mansel families, and the links with factious groups at court. Faction served to control as well as strengthen gentry power and revealed how prominent squires eagerly sought the aid of the aristocracy to achieve political ascendancy. To that extent it is difficult to define Welsh politics *per se* in the late Tudor period and its very existence is questionable.

When all factors are considered, the core of real power in the provinces needs to be identified. Did it lie in the officialdom set up by the central government, the institutions of local administration, the houses of the gentry or in the dominance that often non-resident nobles exerted to aggrandize their political hold over the regions, particularly in urban centres? Record evidence shows that a combination of these forces contributed to create the conditions whereby faction and politics caused disorder and, conversely, to keep some semblance of political order among the unruly.[130] As the constitutional conflict became more acute in the late 1620s and 1630s, criticism of royal ministers at the centre became sharper, revealing that, although the institution of monarchy was almost unanimously supported by the Welsh gentry, its servants were subject to censure. That does not imply that gentry in all parts of Wales were politically active, and in south-west Wales, excepting Perrot, it is considered that 'political awareness was a rare quality' among members of parliament.[131] It was largely the pursuit of family aggrandizement that led the Wynns of Gwydir to contest the Caernarfonshire seat in the 1620 county election. Their opponents were the Griffiths of Cefnamwlch in Llŷn who secured for themselves solid support from neighbouring houses and among their tenantry, even to the point that new freeholders were created to strengthen their campaign. Various clandestine methods were used on both sides in the county and at court to seek assistance, and although the Wynns seemed to have secured the most prosperous northern and eastern parts they eventually lost the election, a bitter blow that signalled, in part, their political demise. The election success of the Llŷn faction on that occasion symbolized the rise of a group of lesser families to destroy the powerful position which the Wynns had enjoyed in county politics for at least half a century.[132]

In an age when movement eastwards over Offa's Dyke was becoming an attractive proposition for an increasing number of gentry, the position held by those gentry who remained at home to maintain the Quarter Sessions courts and attend to routine matters of local administration made them aware of the increasingly strained political climate. How alert they were to the impact of foreign affairs and the welfare of local communities and how knowledgeable in the issues governing the tense constitutional conflict between king and parliament it is difficult to say, other than that they had become increasingly more aware of the intensity of the crisis as it affected their pockets. What is clear, however, is that the continual demands made by the Stuarts for financial aid, culminating in the opposition to the Ship Money tax in the 1630s, showed how actively engaged local governors were despite economic difficulties and their grievances. They responded accordingly to the Privy Council, declaring how difficult it was for communities, hindered by a backward economy, to yield the required levies, particularly the deeply resented Ship Money. Officials referred to their 'poor country' and, in dead times of the year, how impossible it was to levy, collect and safely convey the moneys to London. These officers, for the most part, were the successors of landed gentry who had served under the Tudors. Their support for the Crown was indisputable and based on their interpretation of the monarchy as the fount of law and order. Indeed, they interpreted royal power against the background of their own circumstances and considered that abolishing monarchy would lead to anarchy. For them that struggle revolved around legal rather than political principle for it was considered that a divinely constituted monarchy preserved the fabric of the social order. Since they regarded the Crown as the basis of law, to defend it was the only means of maintaining stability in the realm. Moreover, when war broke out those who participated, and even those who remained on the touchlines, revealed a deep-seated loyalty to the Crown, however cautious and inactive that often was.

It is hardly surprising, therefore, that Wales was called the 'nursery of the King's infantry' and a 'royal fortress' during the Civil Wars. Firm support there certainly was for the monarchy but the most politically active gentry had weighed up the situation carefully. If their resources allowed, and if they were so inclined, they joined the King's armies. Others shied away, not merely because of inadequate means but also because the devastations of war and rebellion were not to their liking and the threat of sequestration and consequent loss of status a daunting prospect. The Crown was aware of the loyalties of the majority of Welsh gentry, a large proportion of whom were its most active supporters. With their expertise, experience and commitment to the military cause they readily supplied resources in men and money to advance the war effort.

Educational, Cultural and Linguistic Aspects

Any examination of the resources used to extend gentry control over their communities must take into account the contribution of education to the formation of the Tudor and Stuart governing élite. Privileged life was clearly associated with the educating process which formed an essential part of the *noblesse oblige*, the promotion and maintenance of status among the gentry. In that respect, education had a functional as well as a moral or ethical role. Their cultural patterns were interwoven within two well-defined traditions that were both fused and at odds with each other in the sixteenth century. The medieval bardic system continued to function at a time when the principles of the New Learning were being disseminated in old and recently founded educational institutions. The traditional and the new cultures blended well until humanist scholars realized what the long-term implications of social development and academic instruction were to be for cultural life. Ideas concerning the type of education that the governing classes required had flowed into England from the continent and had been adapted to the needs of English gentle-folk. At an increasing rate the sons of Welsh gentry were sent to grammar and public schools, universities (particularly Oxford) and the Inns of Court, and a select few, such as Sir Thomas Stradling and his son Sir Edward Stradling, Sir John Stradling, Thomas Mansel, John Trefor III of Trefalun and Sir John Wynn, junior, of Gwydir, broadened their cultural horizons by going on the Grand Tour.[133] In the *Commentarioli Descriptionis Britannicae Fragmentum* (translated by Thomas Twyne as *The Breuiary of Britayne* in 1573) Humphrey Llwyd drew attention to the popularity of higher education among even the most modest gentry in the Welsh hinterland: 'there is no man so poore but for some space he setteth forth his children to Schole, and such as profitte in studie: sendeth them unto the Universities where, for the most part, they enforce them to studie the Ciuile law'.[134]

Between 1570 and 1642 some 2,000 students from Wales were educated at these universities where 'the matrix of gentility and of culture values would be secured through shared companionship'. A sizeable proportion achieved high academic status in these institutions and entered the legal profession, the world of commerce and trade, and the Church. Many others, however, did not stay the full course at university or at the Inns of Court, but obtained there a smattering of legal knowledge and sufficient training in the art of good conduct. They familiarized themselves with the civility and courtesy that characterized privileged circles in London and the border towns. The best example of the scrupulous father anxious to see that his son settled well at Oxford, 'a famous University, the fountain and well-head of all learning', was William Wynn of Glyn Cywarch in the less hospitable part of Merioneth. He urged Cadwaladr to attach himself to all that was considered praiseworthy in the appearance and code of conduct of the gentleman. He was to keep company with 'honest' students, to attend declamations, disputes and other exercises regularly and conduct himself in an exemplary manner.[135] Consequently, he would be suitably prepared to serve the state, although the prime motive was usually social rather than academic. It was a useful, indeed necessary, form of 'conspicuous consumption' and, in that respect, the young Merioneth student prepared himself more adequately to become eventually a governor of his community. It was the continual use of Welsh, even in the border town of Abergavenny, that made a prominent resident send his son to London to improve his English and speak it 'without any corruption from his mother tongue which doth commonly infect men of our country by their vitious pronounciation or idiotisms'.[136] This point, about the Welsh language being inadequate as a vehicle of polite society, had been made by the humanist scholar William Salesbury and professional poet Gruffudd Hiraethog, but from a different angle and with a different motive.

What knowledge and experience of the law young gentry did obtain at the Inns of Court enabled them to administer their estates with a degree of competence, pursue their legal interests, settle tenants' disputes and govern their regions on the bench of magistrates. Society was changing rapidly in the legal world: it was ruthless and competitive, and ambitious proprietors primed themselves in all matters that satisfied their litigious instincts. In an age of high inflation the practice of short leases instead of leases for life and fixed rents was becoming more common and efforts were made to secure title-deeds to land, usually monastic or ancient clan properties. Purchasers in the heartland kept a wary eye on their meagre incomes so as to provide for their heirs. It is fair to conclude that landed proprietors in Wales learnt more about legal procedures and how to handle disputes by being resident on their estates or actively engaged in regional administration than they did at any educational institution. The records of the Exchequer, Chancery and Star Chamber courts, for example, contain a vast corpus of suits relating to Welsh gentry and modestly placed freeholders. So active were they in conducting their private affairs and so aggressively determined to retain what they had and to acquire more, that they willingly overburdened themselves with debts to pay their legal fees and even went further to enhance family status. In part, this entailed borrowing money to purchase land, let alone litigate concerning it. Ellis Wynn, a lawyer and younger brother of Sir John Wynn of Gwydir, severely reprimanded him in 1604 for 'his insatiable passion for purchasing lands with borrowed money'. 'When a man', he observed, 'shall purchase money to purchase land withall it is little for his credit and less for his profit.'[137] In a hand-to-mouth economy the urge to acquire, even among the most eligible of gentle families, often exceeded their purchasing power.

Some individual gentry rose to fame and prominence and made the law their career. George Owen referred to those who 'have proved excellent in ye civil laws',[138] and Humphrey Llwyd added that 'the greater sort of those which profess the Civil or Common Laws of this realm are Welshmen'.[139] During the course of the sixteenth century lawyers began to excel themselves in the Court of Requests, Court of Chancery, the ecclesiastical courts and the Admiralty Court. Among the most eminent lawyers in this period was Simon Thelwall of Plas-y-ward, Denbighshire, who, as deputy judge of the Council in the Marches in 1584, sentenced to death the recusant schoolmaster Richard Gwyn (or White) of Llanidloes at Wrexham.[140] He was a legal writer, served as a baron and justice of the Seven Shires (Chester and the counties of north Wales), and came from a long-serving family of lawyers and administrators. Thelwall was also interested in Welsh cultural affairs and was himself a practising poet. Others who achieved prominence were William Owen of Henllys (George Owen's father), who published a summary of the statutes of the realm; William Aubrey, 'the great civilian' as he was called, of Brecknockshire, an eminent lawyer in secular and ecclesiastical courts, who was among those who condemned John Penry, his distant relative, to death in 1593; Sir Edward Carne, reputed to be one of the most distinguished civil lawyers;[141] Dr David Lewis, Judge of the Court of Admiralty; David Williams of Ystradfellte and Gwernyfed; John Williams, Lord Keeper of the Great Seal, a scion of Cochwillan, Caernarfonshire, and Sir William Jones of Castellmarch in Llŷn, who became judge and lord chief justice of the King's Bench in Ireland and participated in the 'Five Knights' and Ship Money cases.[142] Thomas Trefor of Trefalun, Denbighshire, was another Ship Money judge and a descendant of William Trefor, the famous

Admiralty lawyer. They were all eminent men who, although they were successful in their professions, mostly outside Wales, and exploited their opportunities well enough to achieve powerful positions in the legal world, also maintained close and at times meaningful relations with their native regions.

The law was regarded as the gentry's main profession. Aspiring men did not hesitate to extol the virtues of a successful legal career and considered the educational preparation for it to be worth the financial outlay.[143] Hugh Owen of Gwenynog in Anglesey was regarded as a leading lawyer, albeit self-taught,[144] and Sir Richard Bulkeley III, it was said, was so skilled in legal matters, that 'if any Bill was exhibited ag't him att Ludlow or elsewhere, hee would answer it with his owne hand & subscribe his name to every page'.[145] He was doubtless a remarkable squire, but keenness to prosecute law was a vital factor in the careers of all gentry. Wiliam Cynwal regarded one of his patrons as a wise practitioner of law, a person fully equipped to maintain order in his community:

> Doethder yw d'arfer yn d'oes . . .
> Y gyfraith, ŵr dewr gwiwfryd,
> Yn ddifost gwyddost i gyd.[146]

[You have practised wisdom in your time . . . Bold genuine man, you unboastingly profess your accomplishment in all legal matters]

Despite the corruption that often impaired the practice of law, these statements amply testify to the reputation that lawyers enjoyed as the most accomplished and prosperous professional men of their age. To acquire qualifications in law was the ambition of many a younger son who considered wealth and prestige to be the most valuable attributes of any self-respecting gentleman. Pursuing the law, asserted Robert Wynn of Gwydir and St John's College, Cambridge, younger son of Sir John Wynn, was the only way to 'seek after worldly honours', although he himself was aware that if he intended to enter the Church then 'he must refrain from the world looking only to those heavenly joys prepared for them who do God's will'.[147] This scion of Gwydir did not live to achieve his ambition but he had realized that pursuing the law was a source of wealth and influence.

While some individuals did well out of the legal system with regard to office and privilege, paradoxically the majority of Welsh gentry were not only defenders of peace and good government but often transgressors of law and order. The reaction of the gentry to their privileged positions in public life and private enterprise was at one and the same time both beneficial and a threat to the peace, order and security of the Tudor and early Stuart local administrative machinery. The advantages were revealed principally in the close ties established between a thriving group of landowners and commercial dealers with a monarchy that promoted their prosperity. The threat came as a result of the mishandling of office, corruption and inefficiency that was a constant feature of governmental and legal procedures among officials who took advantage of their positions. To quote examples would be superfluous and it might be more appropriate to note the concern shown by agents of the central government because of such recalcitrant conduct. The Privy Council and the Council in the Marches often reprimanded local governors for their mismanagement and delay in attending to urgent administrative business, particularly with regard to defence matters. The concern centred upon the fear that the unity and safety of the realm might be jeopardized. Henry Herbert, second earl of Pembroke, in his capacity as Lord President of the Council in the Marches, severely reproved the Caernarfonshire deputy-lieutenants in 1591 for neglecting their military duties, and deplored the conflicts between gentry in that county. 'For how can your minds be united in public defence', he maintained, 'when they are divided by private quarrels'.[148] He proceeded by urging them not to perpetuate animosities but rather, in the interest of the state, to establish 'Christian love and neighbourly friendship' so that the business of the realm might be conducted with ease, the lord lieutenant himself satisfied that his supervision was effective and that the offending officers might safeguard their own credit.[149] It is a powerful and revealing letter which reflects on the disreputable practices of the Welsh gentry.

The reasons for inefficiency and negligence in office and a scant regard for the due processes of law are not easily explained unless they can be attributed to personal ambition. After all, the gentry had the means at their disposal to act lawfully and to plan their advancement by maintaining good order rather than perpetuating disruption and contention. On the other hand they were aware of their freedom of action and had the opportunities to 'bend' the rules to their own advantage in the knowledge that laws, in certain circumstances, were meant to be broken. In that context, physical violence – a common feature at that time – arising out of family disputes inevitably concerning land, property and matrimony, tells only part of the story. There would often be political, religious and personal reasons for this instability, but the prime reason was economic depression which caused financial hardship.

The social structure of Wales during the century between the Acts of Union and the Civil Wars reveals that the allegiances of the gentry were normally identified with the Crown, the local community and the native culture. In some respects all three features were integrated but, with the gradual impact of new modes of living on an increasing number of Welsh gentry in all parts of Wales, it became apparent that the third allegiance was losing its appeal. This feature became more prominent by the latter part of Elizabeth's reign when the impact of the Tudor settlement was becoming a favourite topic for Welsh social and administrative commentators. George Owen, constantly on the look out for signs of progress in Tudor Wales, commented on the growing prosperity of Wales by the end of the sixteenth century and described a country that had benefited immensely from Tudor rule. He referred, rather exaggeratedly, to a remarkable transformation and to a desire among the people of Wales, led by shire officials, to be loyal and obedient to a dynasty considered to have sprung from amongst themselves.[150] The complacency revealed by that remark suggested that some families had outpaced others in material prosperity and had established a more powerful foothold for themselves in the Welsh heartland.

Doubtless the century before the Civil Wars saw a marked increase in the use of the English language and social practices among all ranks of the gentry. In 1536 it was declared that English was to be the official language of Wales in law and administration. It had, of course, been used by the gentry previously and Thomas Cromwell would never have risked inserting such a clause in the Act of Union had he thought that leading Welsh freeholders were not in a position to assume public office for any linguistic disability. His decision, however, was reached in discussions held between him and prominent Welshmen at court such as Sir Richard Bulkeley I, Sir Richard Herbert of Montgomery and Sir John Price who keenly advocated uniformity in law and government. Rowland Lee was more concerned about the material circumstances and judgement ('discretion' as he called it) of Welsh gentry rather than any linguistic deficiencies when he criticized the Act creating magistrates in 1536.[151] Welsh and English families had intermarried and Welshmen in the Principality and the Marches, despite the penal legislation of Henry IV, had continued to hold office. These two factors had helped the so-called 'anglicizing' process well before Cromwell's rise to power. This is not to say that modest backwoods gentry and freeholders were necessarily fluent or even literate in English because, as mentioned above (see pp. 7–10), several were monoglot as late as the early sixteenth century. The evidence for the use of English among remoter families varied with the opportunities granted by their heads to advance their prospects. Nevertheless, degrees of fluency in the language were achieved through establishing connections with families in England, educational facilities, the commercial and the droving community, and governmental agencies. The imposition of English as the language of law and administration was, from the government's viewpoint, considered essential since, to establish uniformity, the proper use of English common law in the Principality and the new shires created from the Marches demanded strict supervision of all aspects of legal procedure.

There were so many irregularities following the abolition of partible inheritance in 1543, as well as other 'sinister' practices that had survived, that royal officers had to be constantly on their guard to ensure that legal practices were not transgressed but rather uniformly and equitably adhered to. That could only be done if all proceedings recorded in the courts of law were intelligible to Crown officials. Imposing a uniform body of law demanded that legal precedent be dutifully recorded on court rolls. Procedures, therefore, had to be distinctly defined in line with those practised in other legal institutions. Evidence suggests that Welsh was used in local courts in several areas, which was unavoidable in view of the large monoglot population in Wales.[152] In 1576, when drastic reforms were proposed for the Council in the Marches and other courts, an additional Judge of Great Sessions was appointed for each circuit and it was suggested by Sir William Gerard, vice-president of the Council in the Marches, that one of them should be Welsh-speaking to help George Fetiplace in the Carmarthen circuit because, it was observed, 'many times the evidence is told according to the mind of the interpreter whereby the evidence is expounded contrary to that which is said by the examinate, so the judge giveth a wrong charge'.[153] In this context Sir John Wynn expressed his concern about his own circumstances in 1615 when monoglot witnesses were expected to give testimony against him at Ludlow. They were 'illiterat simple people, not knowing the English tounge', he declared, so that the court 'was fayne to use an interpreter, and whether the same did interprett right is to be doubted'.[154] Gerard's request, however, was not granted and it does not appear that a Welsh-speaking justice of assize served in Wales until the

seventeenth century with the appointment of John Jeffreys of
Acton, Denbighshire, for the Anglesey circuit 1617, David Jenkins
of Hensol (Carmarthen circuit 1642), Richard Prydderch of
Anglesey (second Justice of Chester 1636) and Sir Marmaduke
Lloyd of Maesyfelin, Cardiganshire (Brecknock circuit 1636).[155]

How literate, therefore, were the Welsh gentry who exercised
their authority on the bench of magistrates and elsewhere? The
majority in many areas, in the period down to the Civil Wars, were
thoroughly bilingual. A sizeable proportion also knew some Latin
which they had learnt at school and university and which they
conveniently deployed in legal matters. Since they were heads of
well-established families or educated younger sons who had
established cadet branches and extended patronage to practi-
tioners of the bardic craft, it is evident that routine business would
often be conducted in Welsh in their houses and verbal testimony
expressed in that language in their presence in the Quarter and
Petty Sessions, County and Hundred Courts. Depositions in the
Caernarfonshire Quarter Sessions files in the early seventeenth
century, for example, reveal that Welsh was used in court,
especially in matters involving the lower orders, but that the clerk
of the peace, in accordance with legal requirements, would record
the business in English or Latin or both. When officials of
hundreds and parishes attempted to avoid appointment as
constables they did so usually on grounds of ill-health, material
insufficiency or inability to speak English.[156]

Intellectual activity was stimulated among an increasing
number of the gentry. This followed their contact with centres of
learning: indeed, the Renaissance in Wales owed much to the
support and aid of a small band of heads of gentry families who
were prepared to finance and publish Welsh literature. In all parts
of Wales groups of gentry of varying material means continued to
involve themselves in cultural matters extending from the modest
Merioneth and Cardiganshire squires steeped in native tradition
to William Herbert, first earl of Pembroke, Sir Edward Stradling,
Sir Thomas Mostyn, Sir John Wynn and others, all of whom
showed a lively interest in Welsh antiquities and history and the
wider fields of literary activities. Herbert was more proficient in
Welsh than in English,[157] and Stradling set out to learn the native
language.[158] The heir to the Kemeys estate was given a Welsh
instructor,[159] and the Lewis family of Y Fan employed a tutor to
teach Latin, French and Welsh.[160] For practical purposes William
Herbert of Cogan Pill was advised by William Gamage to learn
Welsh: 'You are a gent borne to good meanes in ye native soyle',

he declared, 'and therefore not to deale in y'r affaires by interpreters, w'ch oft are deceitful but rather . . . to answere all in theire own language.'[161] Be that as it may, it is in this context that the 'cultural attachments' of the gentry and the degree of stability attained in Wales, factors that are closely associated with socio-cultural features and burning issues among historians, need further consideration.[162]

Conclusion

In view of the breadth of their activities, the distinctive cultural characteristics and attitudes of the Welsh gentry need to be placed in perspective before we can proceed to discuss further their authority in public life. Concerning the interrelationships between Welsh gentry, their cultural milieu, their aspirations in the context of their national awareness, their allegiance to law and their role as protectors of their dependants, four features emerge. Interpretations of these trends have occupied several literary historians and need to be elucidated within the context of existing trends in the sixteenth and early seventeenth centuries. The gentry and their class, it is declared, 'moved with the times' and forged new relationships, new identities and new attitudes. While such interpretations are considered valid it is necessary, before examining the bases of gentry power in the localities, to pause and, in the broadest cultural context, to reflect on certain features which are valuable pointers towards understanding and appraising Welsh gentry culture in the early modern age.

1. It can be argued that far too much emphasis has been placed on the 'anglicization' of the Welsh gentry. It is a nebulous term that is used rather arbitrarily to describe a social development that itself eludes strict definition. Usually, it is taken to mean the movement away from native customs and culture, increased absenteeism and a marked lack of commitment to the traditional arts. It cannot be denied that gentry, especially younger sons, were, by the very nature of their circumstances, expected to seek employment elsewhere and were therefore less likely to be familiar with the bardic tradition and the native cultural genre. Many of them prospered as servants in noble households, professional soldiers, churchmen, entrepreneurs, administrators, lawyers and such like. Two factors, however, need to be borne in mind. First, this feature was not unique to Wales since complaints were voiced that country gentry in the remoter parts of England (and not all necessarily

younger sons) were making their way to London to taste the
rarified atmosphere of the royal court and to seek employment.
Secondly, it is equally important to consider how many younger
sons, in fact, stayed at home or returned to Wales, married locally,
set up what became well-established cadet families in the
countryside, and continued the tradition of granting patronage to
the bards. That process did not lead such heads of households to
abandon their contacts or interests elsewhere over Offa's Dyke.
Some stayed at home and others, who had moved to England,
maintained close ties with their native regions, returned and
married locally, having acquired some social graces.

   Several cadet families continued to keep up appearances in their
respective regions by patronizing the traditional bards. Of course,
there were also families which discouraged the use of the Welsh
language among their sons. The example of the Abergavenny
squire (noted in the last section) is significant, as is the firm advice
given by William Wynn of Glyn Cywarch, Merioneth, to his son
not to speak Welsh at Oxford to any who could speak English, not
even to those nearest to him, so that he might 'attain . . . and freely
speak the English tongue perfectly'.[163] In this particular case it
may well be that the father, himself a staunch patron of itinerant
poets, was more concerned about the standard of his younger
son's conduct and bearing in English circles since he had been
reared in a thoroughly Welsh environment. In fact, he was typical
of the country squires of his day in Wales, supportive of traditional
culture and well-respected in local society but, at the same time,
eager to grasp all the vestiges of status available in his county and
urging his offspring to 'get on' in the world, even though it meant
depriving native culture of the sustenance it so badly needed.

   It is evident that a more thorough examination is required of the
socio-cultural structure during the early modern period to
discover how alienated from the countryside the gentry had in fact
become by the eve of the Civil Wars. Evidence shows that some
employed Welsh tutors for their children (see above pp. 50–1). Sir
John Wynn hoped that his daughter-in-law might learn Welsh
among her husband's tenants in Llanfrothen,[164] and Sir Edward
Stradling, as Dr John Davies of Brecon declared, learnt the
language to edify himself and be more able to appreciate the
literary works of contemporary Renaissance scholars. There were
exceptions and deep-seated problems, of course, and poets
complained that the standards and incidence of patronage were
declining. Expressing grievance had almost become a convention
by the early seventeenth century. Nevertheless, by blaming the

gentry as apathetic for the lack of patronage and laxity among an increasing number of former patrons, the poets were largely ignoring the fundamental reasons for their own lack of vitality. Inflation severely hit the real incomes of would-be patrons who found that they could no longer extend hospitality, especially to bards, to the extent that they might have wished in an age of rising prices and poor agricultural conditions.

The poets also found it very difficult to adapt themselves to inflationary processes (*drudaniaeth*), and they doubtless found the nine-year apprenticeship increasingly burdensome. Well might Edmwnd Prys, Edwart ap Raff and Siôn Phylip reprimand the gentry for their wayward conduct and for forsaking their native way of life; however, unless their arguments showed some awareness of the real problems that beset the patrons the situation might well become distorted.[165] Of the poets only Siôn Tudur, in his bitter diatribe against those of his fraternity who betrayed their craft, turned the tables, emphasizing how corrupt their system had become because they accorded false pedigrees to the *nouveaux riches* and elevated them to positions in Welsh society which they hardly deserved.[166] Did that occur because of the relative prosperity of urban-based individuals, usually of English stock, upon whose resources they could rely for sustenance, or did that take place because the poets had ceased to appeal to native patrons? Their strictures on the 'estranged' clientele of patrons touched on a rather sensitive matter, and indicated that they were departing from their original purpose of offering paeans of praise to the ideal *uchelwr*. That convention did not allow them to deplore a patron's actions, however dubious, but rather to counsel and admire him: their function had been purely social but, by the close of the Tudor gentry, it had developed a sharper edge. The eulogy had lost much of its traditional appeal and the poets themselves had become somewhat disillusioned.

2. The concept of 'national consciousness' when applied to the Welsh gentry is at best elusive in early modern Wales. Normally, historians associate an awareness of nationality in this period with the aspirations of the poets, humanist scholars and antiquarians, guardians both of Renaissance standards and of the antiquity of the language and its literature. In view of the nature and interpretation of Tudor legislation in the 1530s and 1540s an examination of this issue needs to be taken further. This legislation had, according to some, accelerated the swift 'anglicization' of the governing classes; to others it had transformed and consolidated what had already been in progress over previous generations. In

that respect it acted as a catalyst drawing together factors and changing them so as to create a new legal and administrative entity within the national sovereign state. On the one hand nationalist historians believe that the legislation, in due course, weakened any sense of national awareness that the Welsh gentry had in the past and almost destroyed it and, on the other, strengthened and fostered a new English mentality. The functions of royal institutions, it is said, brought them into closer association with the English realm and tied them inextricably to an English mode of life. To be 'made English', in other words, implied adapting social, cultural and political values to the needs of the times. The concept of 'national consciousness' can be applied specifically to define the manner in which the Welsh poets interpreted their affinities with the gentry class in relation to the Tudor settlement.

Not unexpectedly, no direct bardic response to the Acts of Union has survived since it was not considered appropriate for poets to observe or comment on public legislation, even in relation to Wales. Nevertheless, the nature and content of the eulogistic compositions reveal that they favoured the opportunities granted to their patrons to participate in government, on condition that they did so as resident officials serving in a dual capacity in their native communities. By magnifying their pedigrees and virtues and admiring their official status, particularly as sheriffs and justices of the peace, they underlined the benefits of the Tudor system for Wales. The references associate these and other offices narrowly with the native environment. The *uchelwyr* assumed governorship as natural leaders, originally of the clan patrimony, and later, in the sixteenth century, of the broader administrative region; the offices which they enjoyed were identified essentially with the finer traits of Welsh *uchelwriaeth*.[167] The lord's obligation to protect his community or patrimony was transformed after the Acts of Union into the responsibilities exercised by the Tudor governor appointed to preserve the stability of his region, an essential component in the nation-state. The sheriff and justices of the peace, for example, were respected in bardic tributes primarily because they had inherited their rightful places as governors in their own localities or, as George Owen put it, as 'magistrates of their own nation'.[168] To that extent the poets urged their patrons to adopt a distinct feeling of national consciousness and succeeded in doing so, judging by the large corpus of bardic material that has survived in manuscript.

Regardless of the long-term effects of Tudor legislation, the almost obsolete medieval bardic system continued to survive. It had redirected a sense of regional awareness among the gentry and, in that context, had projected a more sympathetic view of the Tudor settlement in relation to cultural matters. Indeed, the concept of patrimony persisted well into the seventeenth century when gentry in public life regarded themselves as true Ancient Britons and Cambrians, attitudes that deeply affected their political opinions in the early decades of that century in parliament. The liaison between the poets and their patrons was disrupted when office-holding became a means of acquiring positions and of enrichment which divorced those patrons from their obligations. This occurred most seriously in the more anglicized areas of Wales close to the border and in south Pembrokeshire where they hoped to feather their own nests. Most of them, however, regardless of their material advancement, seemed not in this period to have lost their identity. A proportion of the most assertive considered their status to be compatible with that of their forebears and even went some way to sustain the main features of the ancient culture. That was Sir Edward Stradling's intention, influenced by his protégé Dr John Davies.[169] 'Therefore, you may see that antiquity had some reason to honour the bards', it was declared, 'were it but to preserve memory to their future ages, a matter in other nations and in other times much esteemed of.'[170] The dual nature of country gentry remained a distinct feature despite the pressures which they endured, and these natural leaders in the countryside considered that poetic eulogy still had some relevance in their generation if only to boost their reputations. In the early decades of the seventeenth century the politics of the gentry were primarily tied to the Welsh countryside and commercial centres and their attitudes reflected a deep-seated concern for the welfare of the regional community. Despite changing social perspectives in English circles they were still recognizably Welsh.

3. Although the Renaissance is considered to have been an 'unfulfilled dream' for both Catholic and Protestant humanist scholars in late Tudor and early Stuart Wales, there were some encouraging signs that a proportion of Welsh gentry, despite their advancement within their social order as individuals of modest economic means, were aware of the cultural crisis in Wales and had endeavoured to maintain the tradition. This culture, it is said, survived largely because of the impact of religious forces in England.[171] In time, the statute for the translation of the scriptures into Welsh laid the basis of Welsh Protestant literature and heightened a sense of national awareness for the future, even

among modestly placed gentry, and Church leaders were prepared to acknowledge the Queen's magnanimity in granting them to the nation in the vernacular. The humanists established an indigenous Protestant tradition, based on the spurious history of the twelfth-century writings of Geoffrey of Monmouth and other sources, that combined and identified early British antiquity and religion with the Protestant tradition, asserting that it was the pristine apostolic faith, introduced by St Joseph of Arimathea, that laid the foundations of the Elizabethan Church. It is hardly surprising, therefore, that the small but significant corpus of literature that appeared drew support from among a small band of ardent Protestant gentry (see Chapter 5).[172]

In that context it is relevant to assess how critical humanist scholars could be of those leaders in lay society. A general grievance was voiced against those who might have given their people a better example by purchasing and reading Welsh books. Some of these scholars were Catholics and it is doubtful whether their works circulated among most of the gentry. William Salesbury blamed the gentry for their lack of initiative and, in his preface to the New Testament, Richard Davies hit back at the harsh dealings of men in authority with their subordinates.[173] Robert Gwyn, the recusant priest and reputed author of *Y Drych Cristianogawl* (*c*.1585), got to the heart of the matter by accusing gentry of not being able to read or write their own language, thus discouraging their dependants from doing so.[174] In similar vein Henri Perri, chaplain to Sir Richard Bulkeley, in his preamble to *Egluryn Phraethineb* (1595) urged the gentry to write to each other in Welsh,[175] and 'Sir' Thomas Wiliems of Trefriw deplored their churlishness in neglecting their language.[176]

It is doubtless the case that certain sections of the privileged class ignored their culture but it is difficult to gauge the extent of the 'alienation'. From available sources it appears that it was from among the lower gentry that staunch devotees of the language, collectors of manuscripts and patrons of poets emerged. By the eve of the Civil Wars the social and economic structure of Wales had developed considerably.[177] Over the previous century large estates had been established and certain families had become relatively prosperous. Landownership had made them pragmatic and ruthless, grasping at all opportunities to advance their own interests. Even the more modest among them developed to the full what resources they had so that they might establish reasonably substantial senior and junior houses. In the political context the transference of loyalties to the Stuarts paved the way for the support granted to Charles I in 1642. On completing a period of parliamentary apprenticeship the Welsh gentry gained a degree of maturity in dealing with public affairs.[178] While they maintained traditional allegiances they developed political principles based largely on their own concerns. Coupled with their supremacy in local administration it is certain that the foundations of gentry power were established in a century which saw the rise and fall of a monarchy that still commanded their support.

4. It is against the broader background of conservatism blended into innovatory features that the fundamental question, of the extent to which law, order and government were maintained, must be examined. Rather than the quality of government in Wales on the eve of the Civil Wars and the gentry's contribution to public affairs, the aim is to evaluate the manner in which authority was defined and applied by them. Doubtless the administrative and legal structures established by the Tudors had provided the means by which that efficiency might be measured. The machinery of government, as established in 1536–43, was only partly innovative but it gave members of the new freeholder class the opportunity to demonstrate their experience and, depending on circumstances, to defend the state. Such an issue raises the question whether or not the Welsh gentry, in view of their social and economic status and broadening links with their more auspicious counterparts elsewhere, were concerned chiefly about establishing their own supremacy or serving the government. Both aspects of their conduct are vital to an understanding of the nature of Tudor rule in Wales but attaining pre-eminence would not have been possible without an ordered governmental structure. Order was gradually restored in the old Marcher lordships chiefly because they had been incorporated within a new administrative framework governed under the same jurisdictional system as were other Welsh shires. The Edwardian settlement, despite its shortcomings, was strong enough to ensure the continuation of government whatever the imperfections of the gentry.

Parallels can be drawn with other parts of Britain at this juncture. Unlike Ireland, which was not entirely subdued after the spate of rebellions, Wales had been conquered two and a half centuries before the Acts of Union and, excepting the Glyndŵr period, had never seriously threatened existing government. Rather, a gradual process of interaction and peaceful assimilation by legislation had taken place. The Tudor settlement was essentially different from the circumstances that made the union with Scotland (1707) and Ireland (1800) possible. The gentry, therefore, adapted themselves to a situation that the government considered best suited to them and the central administration. Contemporary opinions were divided on the degree to which order and good government were achieved. The most scathing commentators were Dr David Lewis of Abergavenny and Richard Price of Brecon, but even the milder toned George Owen, despite his fulsome praise of Tudor rule, drew attention to several grievances and loopholes in the law that continued to cause concern in the latter years of the century.

Ambitious and aggressive Tudor and early Stuart gentry might have been, but it is necessary to observe that, in the first instance, private interest was not necessarily destructive; it did not damage the machinery of local government to the extent that it ceased to function at any time. Secondly, despite the constant appeals to improve the quality of local government, its well-established system guaranteed its survival even beyond the period of civil war. Thirdly, the way that system worked was based essentially on the interests, reactions, attitudes and co-operative spirit of the governing classes at the time. The struggle to establish economic supremacy or, in the case of the majority, merely to enjoy a reputable status, not only entailed unprincipled dealings, conflicts and the exploitation of office and position but also a calculated determination to maintain a successful working partnership with governmental agencies at local and regional levels. It is not the boisterous show of arms, the legal chicanery or the delayed and often reluctant responses to the demands for active and purpose-ful public service that should be considered as the main features of gentry life in Wales but rather the subtle underlying processes that transformed the pre-Tudor gentry into an essential, if not at all times efficient, ingredient in the making of the Tudor and early Stuart state. Indeed, down to the eve of the Civil Wars, they continued to maintain the organic unity of regional communities under increasing political, religious and economic pressures. Regardless of future developments that changed further the nature and role of the Welsh gentry in the eighteenth century, the foundations had been laid in the century following the Acts of Union for an enterprising and integrated system of government operated by a social order of privileged families who governed as much by common consent as by their own initiative. Further consideration needs to be given to the background to the emerging privileged order, the theme of Chapter 2, which will examine the conceptual roots of their power-base within the context of the Welsh medieval social structure.

Status and Reputation

This chapter examines further the role of status and social standing in the careers of the gentry as royal administrators. It aims to assess status or degree as an inbuilt attribute of power, in the assumption and exercise of public obligation, and thus contributes an essential theme in any discussion of public service. The century following the Tudor settlement highlighted the chief characteristics of rank and position, and revealed how privileged families succeeded in maintaining their supremacy in shire, hundred or parish and in making status the prime feature of their distinctiveness. It is considered here that the governor's awareness of status, together with honour, is a central feature in any assessment of his duties as a regional administrator, and private and legal sources provide ample evidence of the sensitive nature of the circumstances in which individuals set about defending or claiming supremacy. To deny a man's status or to cast aspersions on it publicly was considered a cardinal sin, for any suspicions might also question his integrity, honour and authority. In the Welsh context the position assumed by status in the exercise of power is fundamental to an understanding of the character of the *uchelwr* in his relations with others in his community.

Justice, Status and Authority

The essence of true nobility or *uchelwriaeth* was 'goodness' as identified in classical literature, a virtue to which all social commentators and philosophers gave priority in the Tudor and early Stuart periods. The spirit was Aristotelian and 'goodness' was achieved in the exercise of justice interpreted fundamentally in a Christian context. Despite social inequalities and the economic challenges of the age the privileged assumed leadership which placed emphasis on the blend of the older pagan virtues of prudence, fortitude and moderation based on justice. The more subjective qualities, revealing the character of the true gentleman, were considered necessary to display good conduct in public life. Justice was inextricably identified with authority. Both were regarded as essential in the life of any self-respecting *uchelwr*.

Justice was the basis of Elyot's *The Book named the Governor*, the most elaborate treatise on the chief characteristics of the 'perfect gentleman' in English prose, and was considered to be the most conspicuous quality possessed by the regional leader:

> I have enterprised to describe . . . the form of a just public weal . . . to the intent that men which will be studious about the weal public may find the thing thereto expedient compendiously written . . . the present book treateth of the education of them that hereafter maybe deemed worthy to be governors of the public weal . . .[1]

While this declaration had a practical aim to it, the concept of gentility, in the context of the Italian Renaissance, is more flamboyant, involving *galanterie*. Although the character of the gentleman did contain some well-defined features of Castiglione's *Il Cortegiano* in Wales and England, it was more narrowly defined to fit the needs of the state and to serve the Prince. The cultivation of social graces was considered essential but the emphasis was primarily on prestige and obligation rooted in wisdom and integrity acquired by means of education and good breeding. Society was based on the rule of law dispensed by those chosen through divine grace to fulfil the needs of the community. 'Take away Kings, Princes, rulers, magistrates, judges and such estates of God's order', it was maintained in *The Homily of Obedience* (1547), '. . . there must needs follow all mischief and utter destruction both of souls, bodies, goods and commonwealths.'[2] The rule of law was uppermost and held to be the paramount feature of any well-governed state.

The attempts made to fortify and advance gentility, in this context, entailed strengthening relations with the institutions of English government and the royal court. That court was a magnet attracting all ambitious young gentry; it served as a prism focusing on a wide variety of cultural dimensions. The court was, in many respects, what can be described as the smallest shire, reflecting political attitudes far and wide. It was an institution which projected the aims of the most aspiring among the privileged, and the pageantry displayed by the most auspicious Welsh gentry at home reflected what they had themselves experienced in London. Much of what they absorbed in the social circles of the metropolis was adapted, on a more modest scale, in the country mansion. George Owen's testimony to such gentry in the 'Dialogue of the Government of Wales' is perhaps overindulgent but is corroborated by other sources such as the following:

We heare in Anglesey good commendation of the gentleman you live with and by followinge and observinge of him you may gaine learning, knowledge and experience, for in England curtisie, humanitie and civillite doth abound with generositie as far as uncivilitie doth exceed in Wales.[3]

In the same county Sir Richard Bulkeley III (d. 1621) was described as a typical *paterfamilias*, conservative in some ways but always out for the main chance and constantly aware of events outside his native Beaumaris. He was a country gentleman but it was said that 'Hee had powerful frinds att court & had the gentrie & Com'onaltie of the Countery att his service . . . In his latter dayes hee built the House of Baron Hill . . . for the Entertaynment of Henry Prince of Wales in his way to Ireland . . .'[4] Bulkeley was doubtless foremost among the most eligible gentry of his age in north Wales, having used all his resources to build a fine house and an extensive estate on both sides of the Menai Straits and in Cheshire.

The authority granted to the *uchelwr* was conditional in that he was expected to exercise it in maintaining law and order. The law which had entrusted him with the power to serve the 'commonwealth' had to be fully imposed so that subjects of the realm might, through good example, be induced to honour it. The need to maintain the realm's welfare through the practice of law, William Lambarde declared following the triumph over the Spanish Armada, was based on loyalty and obedience to the state as an institution.[5] Divinely ordained power, it was said, implied that the 'insistence on obedience to authority [was] the linch-pin of the whole order of society'.[6] Why was it, as George Owen observed, that justices of the peace were not able to exert the authority expected of them as efficiently as they might in the 1590s? The reason, in his view, was that inferior status debarred them from doing so. He deplored the inadequacies of magistrates of the third and fourth generations and placed the blame squarely on the incompetence of government officials who had failed to read the signs of the times.[7] In other words, they had not the legitimate authority granted to them by status and reputation. It was to this deficiency that Rowland Lee, Lord President of the Council in the Marches, referred in 1536 when he deplored the Welsh gentry's lack of discretion, regarding that as being partly responsible for the inadequacies of local governors. A man's reputation was made known in his active role as leader and benefactor in his community and the state as well as his line of descent, a point on which Henry Peacham clearly focused in *The Complete Gentleman*.[8] That action was often military, a trait which survived almost down to the Civil Wars, but it also implied action in government, again with an emphasis on educational training. The long peace established in Elizabeth's reign and highly praised by contemporary commentators was a benefit of which local governors were expected to take advantage by ensuring that their authority was justly proven through their adherence to basic moral values. Despite the emphasis on lineage and time-honoured kin associations, the role of virtue, as Richard Pace maintained in 1517, was more significant: 'Et illa demum vera est nobilitas, quam virtus facit, magis quam clara longaque generis series' ('And true nobility is that made by virtue rather than by a famous and long pedigree').[9] In the Welsh context, the place given to ancestry was pivotal in any consideration of status and authority (see Chap. 1, pp. 1–7). Although few Welsh families were ennobled in the sixteenth century the pedigree of ostentation took the place of economic pedigrees upon which privilege, land claims, protection and suchlike tied to the bonds of consanguinity were dependent. The establishment of ancestral families, fraudulent though some may well have been, grew to be a major industry among bards and genealogists. It was a significant legacy of the Middle Ages when emphasis was placed on the *bonheddig* (men of pedigree), all branches, senior, intermediate and junior, of the lineage, unlike the practice in England, being given due consideration.[10] More attention was given to the bonds of blood rather than to political and economic wealth, which created a remarkable feeling of independence among Welshmen of all ranks. 'The Welsh', Gerald of Wales (Giraldus Cambrensis) maintained, 'value distinguished birth and, noble descent more than anything else in the world. They would rather marry into a noble family than into a rich one.'[11] Gerald's observation was not totally accurate when placed in a broader chronological context, especially in relation to the late Middle Ages. During the two centuries before the Acts of Union family relations had changed and some of the well-positioned among them managed to acquire power through intermarriage and by deploying their material resources. The professional bards ecstatically applauded the qualities and ancestral connections, both Welsh and English, of their patrons, the main motive being to exalt status and maintain familial pride and unity.

Despite the change in nomenclature in the sixteenth century the ties of kindred remained strong, withstanding all attempts to undermine them by the state, and bardic testimony and deputy-heralds ensured that the medieval practices survived. Whereas in the past respect for pedigrees was related to the customs of land tenure, political structures and customary law, pedigrees, as shown by M. P. Siddons in his study of heraldry in Wales, became more clearly focused on attaining social grandeur.[12] 'The passport to Welsh citizenship', Francis Jones observed when summarizing the role of lineage in Welsh family life, 'was the pedigree.'[13] With the greater influence exerted by the College of Arms, especially through the appointment of Lewys Dwnn in 1586 as deputy-herald in Wales, notable forebears were being increasingly regarded as magnanimous, heraldic and associated with national as well as regional history.[14]

In the century following the Acts of Union effective government in Wales depended largely on the degree to which the gentry's reputation was safeguarded, and that reputation relied largely on their claim to legitimate pedigree. Local officials were constantly occupied in the latter half of the sixteenth century with maintaining order and government in an atmosphere of growing international tension. Whatever their deficiencies they managed to display a deep-felt pride, even arrogance, in lineage. The juxtaposition of political, economic and religious factors caused anxieties in the localities. In religious affairs the Protestant settlement in 1559 formed the basis of the loyalty nurtured by the gentry to the Tudor monarchy at a time when they were assiduously establishing their power in the localities. Legitimate authority in the state was based essentially on the opportunities given to groups of gentry to exercise their power as servants of the central government. As duties in local government increased so also did the awareness among the *uchelwyr* that they had an obligation to protect communities within their jurisdiction. Maintaining a good reputation was considered a foremost duty and localities were pressed to protect the 'good name and fame' of those selected to govern them and to maintain their integrity. Source material on this theme is easily come by and amply illustrates the constant involvement of gentry of all ranks in the defence of status and the preservation of the family tradition of service and leadership (see Chapter 3, p. 108 *et seq.*). Much of the concern expressed by the landowning and commercial families in such sensitive matters sprang from their collective responsibilities. They were continually involved in co-ordinating matters which ensured their self-preservation in their respective counties.

Status and the Social Order

After the Reformation, in an age when social and political instability was a major problem in Europe, the threats to the 'old order' became more discernible.[15] The traditional hierarchical structure and patriarchalism were gradually being eroded and the accepted patterns of deference were in danger of being undermined. The symbolic divinely ordained order was manifest at its most explicit in James I's *Trew Law of Free Monarchies* (1598) and *Basilikon Doron* (1598); his ideas were underpinned by Edward Forset, who emphasized the rule of nature, and Sir Robert Filmer, whose chief guide on the matter was the law.[16] Filmer believed James to be divinely appointed to head a national patriarchal structure. 'As the father over one family', he asserted, 'so the king, as father over many families, extends his care to preserve, feed, clothe, instruct and defend the whole commonwealth.'[17] Others, such as John Donne, reacted against Galilean and Copernican thought which destroyed the hierarchical concept of the universe and the earth's central position within it.[18] Much of the literary output of the mid-seventeenth century was devoted to defending the accepted view of patriarchy and sought to oppose contrary theories. New features accounted largely for this crisis in interpreting the social order, including the increase in literacy, education, social mobility, the abandoning of a communal for a money economy, the growth in population and a new urban society, together with the emergence of egalitarian tendencies set to challenge conservatism and continuity. Moreover, scientific literature, empiricism and the cultural impact of the Grand Tour were also important factors in forming radical intellectual changes in an increasingly literate society. Sir John Hayward, for example, in his reply to the Jesuit Robert Parson's attack on James I in 1603, stood for the 'old order' and argued firmly for monarchy:[19]

> The whole world is nothing but a great state . . . a state is no other than a great family, and a family is not other than a great body. As one God ruleth the world, one master the family, as all members of one body receiveth both sense and motion from one head . . . so it seemeth no less natural, that one state should be governed by one commander.

This concept of order was identified in a number of practical ways, such as the seating arrangements in parish churches which was a hierarchy in itself – for any upheaval that mis-seating might cause was viewed as a threat to established order. The Llandygái church dispute in 1576, concerning Sir Rhys Griffith of Penrhyn's pew, was made an issue in the Council in the Marches.[20] Rowland Meredith of Bodowyr, Anglesey, and Morus Kyffin of Maenan were entrusted with the task of examining witnesses, and it was finally decided that 'the said plaintief [Griffith] is of great worshipp & calling, and the Deffs [defendants] troblesome poore men & not meete to be Puefellowes in one Pue or seate w[i]th the said plaintief his wief, children or fameluye'. Garden and park arrangements, the *plasty*, architectural features, sculpture, portrait painting and suchlike displays of grandeur represented a 'symmetry of authority'. In that context the defence of personal and family status was tied to the visual as well as the theoretical image of order.[21]

The prime factor in any examination of status in public life was the central position in the hierarchy assumed by the monarchy, commanding the loyalties of gentry within their communities. It was regarded as the fount of law which was the cornerstone of their power. Without respect for law it would be impossible to perform administrative functions. Deference to common law was considered essential for the well-being of the state: it was uniform, equitable and designed to reinforce the authority of the state.

In this context, when applied to regional circumstances, the family entity in communal life was fundamental to any under-standing of how status was projected (see Chapter 6). The institution which co-ordinated the exercise of authority among the gentry enabling them to maintain their regional precedence was the family, and its sound reputation based largely on continuity and solidarity. By its very nature it also reflected the exercise of political and administrative power inside and outside the kindred structure. It is remarkable how often prominent gentry were required to justify their positions by drawing attention to their personal prestige in public matters. Whereas power was often demonstrated in a purely political or administrative context, it was established on the claims to pre-eminence made by the individual or on his behalf.

One factor that emerged clearly in inter-family relations was the awareness of authority as it was overtly revealed in the display of status. Private correspondence often relates the eagerness of families to underline the validity of their pedigree, which implied far more than mere 'pride in ancestry'. It enabled the most assertive among them to demonstrate the essential characteristics of gentility in the most practical manner. Although they varied in temperament and in the degree of jurisdiction they exercised, their basic attitudes to power and precedence were unmistakably similar. They emerged distinctly as governing agencies, including their authority in their *plastai* and the courts of law.

Despite the emphasis on status gentry families did not at all times abide by law. The persistence of old feuds led to open conflicts which were resolved increasingly in the Court of Star Chamber and the Council in the Marches. Violence was endemic in English and Welsh Tudor society and concern was constantly expressed in government circles, particularly in times of religious, political and economic instability. The Tudor state, without a standing army, relied on the services of the aristocracy and gentry to combat rebellion and subversive activity. The concept of power was highly valued, principally because it was instrumental in asserting personal ascendancy. Honourable presence often disclosed warlike qualities but, in peacetime, it was manifested by self-assertiveness, kinship and courtesy, all of which were implicit in the code of conduct of the Tudor gentleman. It also entailed a degree of competitiveness as well as magnanimity. Emphasis was placed in the sixteenth and early seventeenth centuries on a society composed of an organically structured and divinely approved hierarchy.

Although universally recognized, such a rigid hierarchical concept did make individuals and families sensitively aware of their code of honour and of the need to contest for primacy, hence the private disputes which arose more often than not from the conflict to achieve supremacy. It was his concern for the well-being of the community that led Henry Herbert, second earl of Pembroke, to express his anxiety in 1591.

> And what hope of succour in the field may any man have from him who is his professed enemie at home. Or how shall her Majesty's service . . . in this tyme of danger go forwards yf one of yo'w crosse the same because the dealinge therein is comytted to another.[22]

His queries echo misgivings expressed by his contemporaries, especially those holding prestigious regional offices. Herbert considered it essential that he should protect his reputation and, as the government's chief agent in Wales, denounce strife and dissension among ambitious gentry. Failure to attend to his duty would reflect adversely on his ability to use his resources effectively and to reinforce his authority. All this amounted to a recognition that reputation, legitimacy and an equitable social order was the accepted norm. George Owen's treatise on government in post-Union Wales was devoted almost entirely to exposing the features that strengthened the defensive mechanism of the Protestant realm. In his view law, where appropriately applied, offered protection as well as punitive solutions to social problems. This is again revealed in Owen's interpretation of early Tudor government in Wales: when, as he put it, Henry VIII 'made such beneficial laws for the good government of the country' these laws were made, not only to maintain peace but, in his view, to protect the interests of a newly emerging society nurtured by an enlightened monarchy. [23]

Emphasis was again placed on preserving the social and political order. Contemporary commentators favoured traditional views on the special structure, hence the emphasis on obedience, order and stability. At the head of the governmental structure responsible for the security of the realm was the Privy Council, and links were established between the central government and the localities principally through the agency of the Council in the Marches. Of vital importance was the relationship between county administrators and those whom they governed and, despite their shortcomings, it was doubtless their links with their communities that maintained the integrity of county government in Wales and which enhanced their standing. Status depended not only on the individual's ability to demonstrate his skills in government but also, in conjunction with others of his rank, to apply those skills to ensure stability. Thus he was expected to give priority to the welfare of the 'commonweal'.

In the sixteenth century the defence of status in civil life assumed greater importance than establishing a reputation solely on a military basis. That did not imply that home defence was abandoned, for that became a crucial issue when Counter-Reformation forces at home and abroad were at work seeking to undermine the Protestant state. The growth in landed power, as a result of the redistribution of properties, enabled the most auspicious families to prosper. It was an age when the country house, the fulcrum of regional power, dominated the landscape. It would not be inappropriate to suggest that the appearance and function of privileged residences symbolized law and order. These residences were centres of administration, estate management and territorial power for those in authority and those without it; in other words, they were the bedrock of power. At times they reflected power at the centre and, for those who exerted less influence in public affairs, were often the embodiment of established reputation. They were clearly the main attribute of the *uchelwr*'s claim to deference, and centres for exercising paternalistic authority in the Welsh countryside. Sir Gelly Meyricke, one of

the most powerful and wily men in Wales in his capacity as the earl
of Essex's agent in the 1590s, was not favourably regarded by the
earl of Pembroke when selecting the deputy-lieutenant for
Radnorshire in 1598. That was not because he lacked status but
because his power lay outside the county, and on that point
Pembroke was adamant:

> I know that Sir Gilly [sic] Meyricke is a knight; I hear that he is rich; I
> mislike not his credit, and envy not his wealth; but I know that he is the
> Earl of Essex's household servant, not resident in Radnorshire and
> born and bred elsewhere, nor of kin to any there, only brought thither
> by marriage with his wife, and she no inheritrix neither.[24]

Meyricke, despite his pretensions, was a man of power much in
the same way as was his contemporary, the celebrated Dr Ellis
Price of Plas Iolyn, a time-server and the earl of Leicester's long-
serving 'creature' and henchman, who served in a public capacity
in most north Wales shires.[25] George Owen was intent on
revealing that the medieval castles in Wales were not protective but
rather oppressive and that the mansions of the gentry had
replaced them as centres designed to advance the welfare of a
people ruled by a benevolent monarchy.[26] Similarly, William
Lambarde, from a slightly different viewpoint, emphasized the
obligations of local governors in their capacity as protectors of
their communities.[27] The cleric Robert Holland, rector of
Prendergast in Pembrokeshire, encouraged by Sir James Perrot,
Sir John Philipps of Picton Castle and George Owen, set about
translating part of James I's *Basilikon Doron*, principally because
he considered it necessary that Henry, Prince of Wales, by the very
nature of his position and disposition should, in relation to the
Principality, become truly representative of Wales. That would
enable him to defend his dominion and command his subjects'
allegiance by communicating with them in their own language,
thereby fostering a common aspiration:

> ... now thorough the goodness of our euer-merciful God adorned with
> that precious iewell which theirs and our hearts much desired to see, a
> sweet & gracious Prince, whose presence amongst vs would
> wonderfully reioyce all your Highnesse Subiects heere, whose Weale it
> would procure with much contentment to their hearts: and a taste of
> the tongue (which he now might easely attaine vnto) would verily
> hereafter please and satisfie him, as being thereby made able both to
> speake vnto his people, and also to vnderstand them speaking vnto
> him, without interpretors . . . A matter of very great moment and
> desired to bee in princes: for, Officers many times in the ecclesiasticall

and ciuill state, the Church and common weale, grow rich, & the
people poore, where the chiefest Gouernours know not their
complaints.[28]

The emphasis in this section is principally on the authority
embodied in the Prince – the first since the death of Arthur, eldest
son of Henry VII, in 1502 – as a protector of his people's well-
being and, as a ruler, wholly identified with the concept of Welsh
nationality.

How did this sense of control and ruling authority actually
relate to the defence of status and practical use of power exercised
by individual gentry? Patterns of authority can be divided into
several categories. In the first instance there was the regional or
territorial authority which manifestly revealed the governing
potential and control exercised by men of status within a
community or an estate. One example was Edward Morgan of
Llantarnam who maintained a strong Catholic presence among
his tenants:

> by reason of his greate living, power and allegiance . . . [he was]
> accounted the chief pillar and only mainteyner of the parish . . . thereby
> . . . masse is more usually said in the house of the said Edward Morgan
> and the parishe of Llantarnam . . . Llandenny . . . and other places . . .
> then divine service in the said parishe churches.[29]

Morgan appeared to exert feudal control over his people,
combining loyalty to the lord with an allegiance to religious
conviction. There was also the more arbitrary and autocratic type
of conduct which, according to legal records, characterized a large
number of landed proprietors, such as Sir John Wynn, Sir John
Salusbury II of Lleweni and the Mansels of Margam and their
peers. One of Wynn's servants complained in an Exchequer suit
brought against him that he was utterly powerless to curb his
oppressive behaviour. In this instance, the tenant's response
revealed how serious the effects of abused authority could be:

> Whereupon the servant said; look upon these stones (beinge a walle or
> hedge of stones), my Master . . . ys able to make theese stones to be
> greene cheese if he list . . . [he] was able and could prove any thinge
> against him, though the same was never so untrue . . .[30]

Another form of authority was more personal, normally
employed in a public capacity and using local resources to
advance private ambition. This type of conduct emerged, for
example, in the letter by Robert Devereux, second earl of Essex, to

Lord Keeper John Puckering in 1595, requesting that his relatives retain their position on the local bench of magistrates:

> Although I am verie loth to leave the name of master to so manie honest gentlemen in Wales, as out of there love desire to serve and followe me . . . praying your l'p that they may not by the late order be subject to the losse of their places for this cause . . .[31]

In fact, it was a blunt reminder to Puckering that Essex's authority was not to be undermined. Men strongly allied to him were required in office, and he was not prepared to accept any other arrangement although, a few months earlier, Sir William Cecil had disallowed private retainers from becoming magistrates.[32] Closely connected with Essex's response, but with a more political motive in mind, was the authority exercised by Brian Crowther, a long-serving Radnorshire magistrate, in the County Court in 1611 where he publicly denounced the Crown's financial exactions. 'He did animate and encourage the countrey', it was stated in the indictment, 'not to yield in the payment of tallage or mizes deliveringe openly in his words and speeches, due or payable unto your Highness.'[33] As a justice of the quorum his voice was highest among his fellow magistrates and his opposition to royal policy was based on principle: 'if your Ma'tie would looke to have customes performed to you', he remarked, 'you should likewise performe for your part what belonged'. His power was essentially territorial in that his viewpoint was respected and shared by other men of influence in his neighbourhood and beyond.[34]

Social commentators often associated the benign type of authority with the man of integrity, but it also possessed its own inherent qualities. These revealed paternal instincts that formed an extension to the domestic role of the *uchelwr*. It was such qualities that were highlighted in the preface to Richard Davies's *Funerall Sermon* on the death of the first earl of Essex in 1577: 'True religion and wisedome doe proceede from God by grace . . . but the other vertues as Fortitude, temperaunce, courtesie, affabilitie, liberalitie and constancie, be peculiar to your house, discending by nature, and graffted . . . in your principles.'[35] These qualities were basic in any evaluation of the Renaissance gentleman and were frequently cited in commentaries on courtly etiquette. In the Welsh context the *gŵr bonheddig* was distinguished by what he and his community considered his positive attributes to be. The *nobiles* regarded themselves as being essentially different from the unworthy who aspired to their ranks. They were characterized by their historical ties to the soil and their inherent attachment to kindred. In the seventeenth century such was the definition advanced by the assiduous copyist John Jones of Gellilyfdy:

> There is no man admitted by the law to be called *Gwr Bonheddic*, but he that paternally descendeth from the kings and princes of this land of Britain, for *bonheddic* is as much as *nobilis* in Latin . . . Common persons of late years have taken upon them the title of *bonhedd* or generosity, but they are not really *bonheddic*, but are so called or termed for fashion's sake by reason of their wealth, offices or behaviour which are but transitory things and *bonhedd* consisteth in no transitory thing but in a permanent.[36]

Welsh nobility, therefore, according to this extract, was deemed to have stemmed from regal status and was distinguishable from that which characterized the *nouveaux riches*, allegedly self-promoted upstarts, aspiring to privileged ranks by virtue of economic advantage. While it is true that most of the new families gradually merged through marriage into ancient Welsh stocks, the more conservative heads of families based their authority on what they considered to be more enduring features. To them, authority was historical; it not only maintained links with the past but also used that past to reinforce their pre-eminence in the present and to provide for its continuation. In this context history had a civilizing role. It had a moral as well as a practical duty to perform and, as Philip Styles states: 'in the broadest sense . . . [it] is part of the very nature of the Renaissance state. It provides the statesman with rules of policy and the individual citizen with inspiring examples of moral excellence.'[37] The heraldic and sepulchral decorations that have survived are a distinctive aspect of historical ethics. Peacham was keenly aware of the importance of heraldry:

> How should we give Nobility her true value, respect, and title, without notice of her Merit? and how may we guesse her merit, without these outward ensignes and badges of Vertue, which anciently have beene accounted sacred and precious . . . for a Gentleman Honourably descended to bee utterly ignorant herein, argueth in him either a disregard of his owne worth . . . [38]

In *Tri Chof Ynys Brydain* bards were expected to extol the virtues associated with 'pedigrees, or descents of the nobility, their division of lands, and blazoning of arms'.[39] In the generation before the famous Robert Vaughan of Hengwrt, antiquaries and historians such as Rice Merrick, George Owen, George Owen

Harry, Thomas Jones of Fountain Gate and Anthony Powell of Llwydarth were actively engaged in discovering and preserving genealogical and other material.[40] In the latter half of the sixteenth century notable poets such as Wiliam Llŷn, Wiliam Cynwal, Simwnt Fychan and Siôn Tudur, all disciples of the renowned herald-poet and bardic teacher Gruffudd Hiraethog, were also recording pedigrees and describing heraldic achievements in their poetry.[41] In 1647 Wiliam Bodwrda, the cleric-genealogist of Llŷn, in a letter to Siôn Cain of Mechain Iscoed, the last of the herald poets, lamented the low ebb of the bardic and genealogical craft.[42] In an undated letter by Robert Vaughan to a distant kinsman he reveals the serious impact of the movement away from the native environment on the gentry:

> I thought it my duty . . . to present you with a view of ye eminent &
> worthy descents of your fathers ancestors (happily unknowne unto you
> by reason of your birth & breeding in England) whereby you & your
> posteritie may not onely receive some solace and content in the
> reading, but also repell and disesteeme that might iniuriously be
> opposed therunto.[43]

Some weight was given to 'credit' as having derived from consanguineous relationships with native or foreign stocks, and the most prestigious among the incoming English families, such as the Mansels and Stradlings, were acknowledged as respected *uchelwyr*. Sir Edward Stradling, for example, was complimented for the 'seale you beare to the publique commodity of your country before yor owne p'vate wealth'. He was also applauded for maintaining his reputation above all else: 'yow p'ferr yo'r credite before any worldly comoditie', it was remarked, 'and the peace of a religioues conscience before the p'vse pelf [wealth regarded with contempt] of this transitory worlde'.[44] The grace with which he conducted his affairs was a matter of comment as was the picture of the upright magistrate or governor set in the image of Elyot's statesman. That is how authority is portrayed by Henry Salusbury in his address to Henry Herbert, second earl of Pembroke:

> . . . seren ddisglair a llachar y genedl Frytanaidd . . . o dan ein hareulaf
> frenhines Elisabeth . . . yn eich llongyfarch am y modd yr ydych wedi
> gwarchod ein buddiannau cyhoeddus a chyffredin, trwy weithredu
> cyfiawnder a thrugaredd . . . pwy a ddylai dderbyn materion perthynol i
> Gymru yn fwy i'w ddiogelwch a'i nodded na Llywydd Cymru, dyn y mae'n
> arfer ganddo ffrwyno a disbyddu holl drais a llid pob gwrthwynebydd,
> a sydd hefyd yn ddigon cryf i'w gorfodi oll i fod yn dawel.[45]

[. . . the shining and resplendent star of the Brythonic nation . . . under our most exalted queen Elizabeth . . . greeting you for the manner in which you have guarded our public and common interests, through exercising justice and mercy . . . who should receive matters relating to Wales so that he may protect and patronize than the President of Wales, a man who is accustomed to curb and exhaust all oppression and the rancour of every opponent, and who also is strong enough to appease them with force.]

This is the epitome of good governorship but hardly a reflection of the reality that characterized the con... ... f the r. of power when private interests were at stak

Status in Regional Government and Relations

The theme of status, as applied to responsibilities in law and administration, needs to be taken further since it assumes significance in relations between persons in power and all other ranks in community life. They were sworn in office so that they, on behalf of the Crown, might protect the subject's interests within the law. In the domestic scene, they and others of their milieu were drawn together to pursue common interests. Circumstances, however, often revealed differences of opinion and perpetuated old animosities. Private feuds did intensify family relations and occasionally marred the government's efficiency but, in view of the involved and inbred nature of such rivalries, their impact on law and order should not be overstated.

One of the most arbitrary and powerful landowners was Sir John Perrot of Haroldston who, as mayor of Haverfordwest in 1570, when required to impress men for the musters, conscripted the servants of his enemies who were 'acting to the revenge of his own private malice and displeasure'.[46] Star Chamber records abound in suits designed to curb corrupt gentry practices in local government, especially regarding the finances of the defence system. So much independence was enjoyed by persons of rank that fiscal maladministration was not uncommon. In 1599 David Lloyd of Aber-mad complained of the use made by Richard Pryse of Gogerddan and Morgan Lloyd of Llan-ddew of their positions as deputy-lieutenants of Cardiganshire to enrich themselves for, in addition to several other misdemeanours, they were accused of keeping the artillery and munition, valued at £1,000, for themselves, converting the armour 'to their own private wealth'.[47] It was this illicit activity that gave their rivals the opportunity needed to expose and exploit their malpractices. Although guidelines were issued and a degree of strict control exercised, agencies of the central government were entirely dependent on the goodwill and integrity of local officials, and they allowed them to attend to their duties as best they might. A number of Merioneth gentry, including Huw and Gruffudd Nannau, together with Edmwnd Prys, archdeacon of Merioneth, were accused in Star Chamber of 'being men of great Power and long service in the commission of the peace' who had 'confederated only to make themselves great men in the county'.[48] Their status had already entitled them to 'greatness' but the complainant in this case had specific grievances demonstrating that they had assumed for themselves more power through oppression than their position in society warranted. Such a phrase is regularly used in Star Chamber and other records of the central courts, implying that men who monopolized local government offices earned for themselves a reputation for high-handedness over and above what the community itself was prepared to allow. Power was legitimate so long as the status of the individual was sufficient to sustain it.

The Games family of Aberbrân and Newton and elsewhere in Brecknockshire were equally notorious for misusing local offices, suborning juries and similar offences. Three of them were reported in 1579 to have attended the Quarter Sessions with 'many others armed with swords and bucklers, and other weapons . . . some stepping up on the bench, some upon the forms near the bench, some on the lower form where the clerk of the peace did sit with their weapons ready'.[49] In his position as sheriff of his county John Games was described in 1601 as a 'gentleman of great countenance . . . well kinned and allied . . . although disposed to quarrel and brawl and presuming in respect of his greatness that none . . . durst offer to punish correct or imprison any of his followers'.[50] Countless other examples could be cited which reveal that misused authority, exercised chiefly as a symbol of status by the most powerful, was common. It was not so much what John Games desired that was important but the fact that he was himself representative of an order which placed status before obligation and a person who manipulated his position to assert his pride.[51]

Doubtless corruption was found among all ranks of military officials but the prestigious deputy-lieutenancy, introduced into Wales in 1586, served to supplement the duties shouldered by the lord president. The office was a prime mark of status. The numbers of such officials were increased in due course owing to continued threats from abroad. In Glamorgan numbers were increased to four in 1590, and the office was shared between the Herberts of

Swansea, the Lewises of Y Fan, the Stradlings of St Donat's, the Mansels of Margam and the Bassets of Beaupré.[52] When serving officials were replaced the numbers of new deputies were usually increased. In Caernarfonshire, Sir John Wynn and Sir William Maurice, much of whose correspondence regarding defence matters has survived, were assisted in 1615 by Sir William Thomas of Coed Alun and John Griffith of Cefnamwlch, each representing powerful families in the northern ('lower') and western ('upper') parts of the county respectively.[53] These additions implied not only that security matters meant that authority had to be supplemented, but that officials had opportunities to demonstrate their leadership in a responsible manner and to consolidate families considered eligible to serve at the highest level in local government affairs. What did this power mean to the upper gentry and what did they gain by their participation in these activities? Officials of this kind enhanced their social stature. The poets regularly injected into their verse references to their duties because they were considered vital to maintaining the community, a crucial factor in any examination of provincial life. A number of features made up the role of the local governor among his people.[54]

Military service, usually conducted abroad, gave younger members of gentry families the opportunity to display their prowess on fields of battle, particularly in Ireland and on the continent, thus adding substantially to their prestige as individuals and to the status of their families (see Chapter 4). At home as well, the threat of war and involvement in the defence mechanism enhanced the reputations of heads of the most powerful families, even in the less accessible parts of the county community. In attending to military affairs they revealed one of the most remarkable features of their order, namely the privilege of being men of private means entrusted with performing public duties. Central to their power was their knowledge of, and respect for, the law, which enabled them to assert their own authority and, within limits, ensure that the commands of the central government were obeyed in the localities. Their contribution to local government served as a defence of all that was considered worthy in public life. More deference was accorded to the 'rule of law' and, despite lapses in service, it was the gentry's adherence to this principle that largely saved the realm from internal turmoil before the 1640s. This is shown in Sir John Wynn's response to the criticism aimed at him and his colleague Maurice c.1600 when he declared that he had not been ashamed of his 'doyngs' and would be prepared to 'cleer my credyt' at all costs.[55] It was in order to protect his own good name that Sir Richard Bulkeley II of Beaumaris in 1545 appealed to Caernarfonshire administrators for assistance to defend Anglesey against a French and Scottish invasion: 'And therfor eftsones', he maintained, 'I hertily pray you and all other my lovyng fryndes to show yor selfes at this tyme according to the trust and expectacon whiche I have hade alwayes in you.'[56] It was his responsibility to defend his county and to denounce lack of military support from neighbouring counties since Caernarfonshire and Merioneth were spared foreign service in order that they might defend the island when the need arose.

Status also, of course, related to the lower orders and was exhibited chiefly in the response of those considered 'non-gentle' to their superiors who exercised authority over them. An investigation of the term 'lower orders' raises many difficulties. Normally, it is taken to mean those ranks in society inferior to acknowledged 'gentlemen', namely tenant-farmers, husbandmen, artisans and the landless. William Harrison was quite clear in his mind regarding the status of the landless: 'This fourth and last sort of people . . .', he maintained, 'have neither voice nor authority in the Commonwealth but are to be ruled and not to rule other.'[57] Social inferiors, however, did readily object to the use and abuse of authority among their superiors. Tenants did take their masters to court with a view to exposing and checking oppression. A good example is the Nanconwy yeoman threatened with the loss of his tenancy because of the power which his master, Sir John Wynn of Gwydir, it was alleged, unfairly exercised over him.[58] In equally belligerent mood the squire of Gwydir vindictively denigrated the status of William Morgan, reputedly the most erudite churchman of his generation in Wales, to undermine his lineage and assert his own superiority over those whose ancestors had held land of the Wynns, worthy though their claims to gentility might have been.[59] Morgan's assertive defence of his position indicated that he was not, on grounds of conscience or status, prepared to yield to the demands of this recalcitrant landowner:

> It seemeth that Mr Wynn thinketh that I do but pretend conscience, but I assure you *in verbo sacerdotis* that I think in my heart that I were better rob by the highway side than do that which he requesteth [i.e. grant him the benefice of Llanrwst] . . . If my father and mother were living and made the request that Mr Wynn maketh I hope that I should have the grace to say them nay.[60]

Morgan's response was based on a number of factors, his status and authority as a bishop, his honest opinion of Wynn's motives and his own conscience. That authority, when generally applied in less hostile circumstances, was often interpreted as being benign and beneficial rather than injurious to the tenant. Many of the 'followers' who, according to judicial records, assisted a belligerent landlord to gain superiority over his rivals, were his tenants. The bond of loyalty was a force not easily broken and, despite the increasing attempts of tenants, some of whom were women, to seek justice when threatened by a refractory landlord, the rank and file were prepared to submit to his imperious behaviour. Wynn's servant, in the above-mentioned example (p.70), was playing on the tenant's susceptibilities, intending to display how powerful the authority of the landowner really was. George Owen admitted that the material means of justices of the peace in Wales generally had, before his generation, been well below the standard required; moreover, in his own time towards the end of the Elizabethan era, since there was no property qualification and the quality of the magistracy was still poor, the rank and file of the population would not acknowledge their authority: 'dyuers men of mean lyuing', he observed, 'are clymbd vpp to the bench by whom . . . the people will not be ruled'.[61] He proceeded to explain that the situation had changed by his time since there were men perfectly eligible to hold the office 'and the cause of yt inconueny-ence being taken away I wowld wish the inconuenyence it selfe weare allso remoued'.[62] Doubtless there was a feeling that inferiority of status impaired the administration of justice, a view which Dr David Lewis had shared some years earlier when, in a letter to Sir Francis Walsingham, he deplored the inadequacies and abuses of county government officials in south-east Wales and suggested improvements:

> Men of no substance nor of credyte made Sheriffes and Justicers of the peace w'ch moste lyve be [sic] pollinge & pyllynge. The auctoritie of the counsaile [in the Marches] there is not regarded as it hathe ben for [the] sheriffe, and [the] Justice of the peace . . . will playe bo pype, seest me, & seest me not, and this haue growen by impunitye whereof Do proceade all manner of Disorders.[63]

Abused authority exacerbated conditions of instability which, in periods of economic upheaval, had direct consequences on all ranks. It was in such times that status was endangered and liable to be tarnished by the failure to maintain the family's prestige. In such circumstances men in authority imposed their will under pretence of the statutory powers granted to them. In most cases the relationship between master and tenant or labourer was amicable;

the landowner who proclaimed that none of his tenants would accept a lease in writing from him because they trusted him may well have been more eager to defend himself rather than praise his dependants' goodwill but he did, in severe economic times, reveal concern when they suffered privations and bore 'the impression of hunger in their faces'.[64] Economic stringency was a matter of grave concern since landed proprietors suffered as well as their tenants. As magistrates, they were also expected to operate the Poor Laws and, in an age when Tudor paternalism urged them to attend to the urgent needs of the poor, when their right to impose the rule of law by virtue of their status was asserted, priority was given to good order and discipline and the exercise of mercy and leniency. Scores of regulations were imposed on magistrates in the expectation that they would try to alleviate chronic hardship. Landed families were aware that their involvement in politics and economics was essentially to establish order. Despite their private interests they wished to maintain economic equilibrium and the chief advocate of stability was George Owen who, when praising the Council in the Marches to the German lawyer Barthol, noted that it had succeeded in establishing 'civility and quietness . . . from that wild and outrageous state that you shall here of'.[65]

Status employed as an adjunct to authority, however, was subject on occasions to control by government agencies. In 1573, for example, when the Council set about asserting its power more effectively and controlling alehouses, criticism was levelled against local magistrates who indifferently administered their obligations, and it was declared: 'that they should attend more diligently to their duties so that they may have regard to their credit' and 'bend their whole study' to that end 'by what means good order may be continued'.[66] A series of legislative measures was heaped upon them from the mid-sixteenth century onwards, many of them supplementary to normal responsibilities and geared to relieving the poverty and social dislocation in urban and rural areas. Increasing concern was shown to improve economic conditions so that 'the riche shall not oppresse the poor, and that the poore iniurey not the wealthy'. Sir Edward Stradling was acknowledged by 'sondrye credible gentlemen . . . of the great care [he] . . . had to equitie and justice'.[67] Doubtless his status had guaranteed his standing among his people.

The routine duties of local governors increased as economic circumstances became more severe; regulating corn prices, attending to the needs of the poor, restricting the movement of unemployed vagrants and setting men to work. An example of the

way in which the Council in the Marches, in its last years of
decline in 1637–8, sought to exert its authority appears in the
orders given to the Anglesey magistrates in March 1637
commanding them to examine the condition of impotent poor,
provide a competent stock of material for those able to work, raise
money weekly or monthly to relieve the needy, discover which
able-bodied poor people refused to work, organize apprenticeships
and make their presentments at Great Sessions.[68] These
requirements, chiefly contained in the Books of Orders (1630–1),
were issued at a time when attempts were made to improve
efficiency in local government. The hard-pressed Privy Council,
however, only acted arbitrarily, usually in periods of crisis, and the
desired impact was often lost. In the 1630s steps were taken to
tighten control over economic affairs in the localities; it was a
period when increasing corn prices and unemployment
endangered law and order. The Books of Orders were intended to
instruct magistrates on how to deal with such matters. They
differed from other books issued in the 1570s and 1580s in that
strict procedure was laid down. Authority was vested in local
governors supervised by the conciliar system and that authority,
once the critical period was over, became again the sole monopoly
of the country gentry, whose numbers by then had become
inflated. The Books of Orders displayed more often than not the
government's intention rather than its accomplishment in social
and economic policy. The gentry were firmly lodged in their
position in county government; their authority, although
sometimes feared, continued supreme and neither Crown nor
parliament was able to depose them.[69] Status once again protected
their interests and made most of them immune to the more
arduous consequences of economic stringency.

It was when private disagreements between officials, particularly magistrates, became serious that the lord president became
concerned because such animosities undermined the *uchelwr*'s
role in defence and impaired his personal status (see Chapter 4,
pp.140–6). Henry Herbert unsuccessfully attempted to solve such
problems; his sharp letter to the Caernarfonshire deputies was
sufficient proof of that. The cause of the friction was the supply of
troops and raising voluntary contributions for their maintenance
to serve in Ireland under the earl of Essex. Delay in the matter
prompted a reprimand from Ludlow:

Therefore if thes noble men [i.e military generals] doe thinke it their
duties to spende their goodes and hazard their owne persones in so

honourable and behoofull an action, I thinke it should prejudice your credyttes accordinge to your abilities you should shewe yourselves worse affected.[70]

It was a stern riposte cautioning that rival *uchelwyr* entrusted with responsible office should care for their own good reputations. That reprimand was carried further by his successor, Lord Zouche, who also expressed his concern for the protection of the local community, and he administered a timely reminder that the government's standing in the country rested largely on the integrity of those appointed to govern. He expressed his sorrow that men's affections hindered the maintenance of good order for, 'when blood called for vengence', he observed, 'the commonwealth will suffer'.[71]

Henry Herbert was a powerful figure in Glamorgan, and jealously guarded his interests in the county, particularly in Cardiff. He was continually concerned about preserving his own status as well as controlling local gentry with a view to rescuing their good reputations. In 1586 he rather petulantly remarked about the attempts made by Sir Edward Stradling and William Mathew of Radyr to investigate piratical activities:

Are you alone carefully mynded to respect the good of yo'r countrey or alone authorized to chasten such faultes, or continually accustomed to use such integritie in yo'r offices that neither you may be thought for favour to wyncke at, or for malyce to prye into offences?

The squires had reported their findings to the Privy Council and not to him, thus diminishing his public stature in the country: 'for that it concerneth my self in regarde of my vizadmirallty and p'cidencye, some like mynded to yo'r selves may interprett the same to be more for maynten'nce of myne aucthority then for just blame of yo'r dealinges.'[72] Regardless of the effrontery which Pembroke observed in the actions of these two officials, he focused on three factors in any consideration of the role of status in the course of public functions, namely collective responsibilities, the authority which all gentry relished and the integrity upon which all claims to power were founded.

Zouche, like other lord presidents, was handicapped by his inability to attend personally to the defence needs of maritime counties when it was most urgently needed, and his reliance on deputy-lieutenants was clearly revealed in his declarations to ensure the preservation of law and order. That was his plea in April 1603 when he desired to 'see by all meanes the peace kept and the disturbers thereof punished even if necessitye required by the raysinge of common forces' in the counties.[73] It was a plea to protect his own honour as much as to defend the coasts. Lord presidents, more than any other officials in the administration of Wales, were sensitive to their vulnerable position if the defence mechanism proved to be ineffective. The collective directives issued from the Council from the mid-sixteenth century reveal both the strengths and weaknesses of the Council at Ludlow in this context and go far to explain why successive lord presidents were eager to defend what they considered to be worthy governorship, as practised by themselves, in Wales and the Marches.

Any examination of the status and role of lord lieutenant or his deputies does reveal the emphasis on administrative as well as military skill. Both aspects of the service entailed protecting the best interests of the realm and maintaining civil order. In that respect these officials performed tasks similar to those assigned to sheriffs and justices of the peace. Whatever the drawbacks that prevented the Welsh gentry from claiming equal material status with their counterparts in England it is clear that, in terms of real power in the localities, their position was supreme. To be deprived of such an office for malpractice brought disgrace, as happened to Sir Richard Trefor of Trefalun in 1601 who suffered a temporary setback after his failure to capture the county's parliamentary seat.[74] In 1598 Cadwaladr Price of Rhiwlas and John Lewis Owen of Llwyn, Dolgellau, were dismissed from their positions in county administration. Both deputies were found guilty of embezzling armour valued at £1,000 and other misdemeanours in office and were arraigned before Star Chamber.[75] Likewise, Richard Pryse of Gogerddan and Morgan Lloyd, who held the office in Cardiganshire, were accused and found guilty of similar offences (see p. 74).[76]

After the Union settlement local administrators had gained in confidence, and second- and third-generation squires increasingly strengthened their hold over the institutions of local government. In their relationships with others, they had also demonstrated what had emerged as being a distinctly updated brand of *uchelwriaeth* highly regarded for the protective values which it shared with its English counterpart. Their independence had been well established by the 1580s and 1590s. Despite the vigilant eye kept on these custodians of law and order the state allowed them to organize their own patterns of activity in public affairs, to express their opinions, to decide on what they considered to be the most pressing matters to which attention should be given and, when they considered it to be opportune, to shy away from performing some of the duties expected of them by the central government.

Attention has already been drawn to the close links between status and the powers exercised by the gentry in a protective capacity. Equally important was the association between leadership and historic patrimony which was another feature of status, an aspect which focuses again on the origin of the gentry order (see Chapter 1, pp. 2–12). The individual *priodawr* was intent on establishing his own estate on the patrimony by declaring his independence. Privilege (*braint*), as applied to the native *uchelwyr*, contained primitive elements of *jura regalia*; it also shared concepts of emancipation and freedom to pursue one's own initiative and establish one's own good fortune. The common ancestor created the native lineage group (*cenedl*). This entailed establishing a title and claims to land and matters regarding kin relations were placed on that kindred. A complicated network of relations to the agnatic second cousins male became a significant factor in the build-up of native medieval Welsh society. Ancestry became a central feature in any attempt to establish a reputable lineage. The rights of the free clansman were maintained and protected by the kindred: by law it defended his interests and, in a social context, he assumed responsibility, especially in matters regarding the inheritance and transference of land. The emphasis on kinship and lineage played a vital role in the development of the family group and, despite the limitations which legal custom imposed on the individual clansman, he emerged as the independent owner of a landed estate in the late Middle Ages in a period when the older forms of social life and practice were in a state of disintegration. Despite the continued importance of kindred in the development of new gentry families their power and influence were based largely on their own initiative and broadening social contacts. Although the old bonds of clientage and patronage were gradually loosening, the new wealthy gentry, dependent on a moneyed economy, clung to the basic elements of status, kin allegiance and territorial identity as they consolidated their power in the sixteenth century.[77]

It is in this context that landed proprietors and public administrators in Wales assumed a territorial role. The old 'royal' authority once claimed but later abandoned did survive, however, in the rise to power of *uchelwyr*; it emerged in the way in which individual gentry viewed their territorial rights, not least within commotes (or hundreds after 1536–43) and other administrative 'limits'. In the 1570s and 1580s the Council in the Marches zealously supervised the partition of duties in each shire and hundred when issuing its commands.[78] In the *Description of Penbrokshire* George Owen asserted that 'there is to this day many ancient gentlemen which can by good authority drive themselves from diverse famous and illustrious families that did possess great patrimonies in this country'.[79] A reference to these 'patrimonies' amounted to direct observations on their free status, and to the independence that gave the *uchelwyr* that confidence equipping them to perform their public duties. Relations were not at all times amicable between county administrators with regard to the 'limits' allocated to the most prominent among them to deal with military and related administrative affairs. In 1615, for example, Sir Roger Mostyn of Gloddaith sharply resisted attempts by his fellow magistrates to trespass in his 'limit', namely the commote of Creuddyn in Caernarfonshire where he regarded himself as enjoying full jurisdiction.[80] He who was acknowledged as the *rhuwliwr* ('ruler') and who served as governor of his region ('a dynn y wlad dan ei law') was essentially the independent *priodawr*, originally the free clansman but now the landed proprietor who was endowed with all the qualities of the sophisticated Renaissance gentleman.[81] He possessed an independence of spirit adapted to the needs of the new Tudor sovereign state.

Those who became magistrates enjoyed a status which had been enjoyed by their counterparts in the English shires for almost two centuries. Before taking office they 'took out their *Dedimus Potestatem*', the prescribed oath granting them the authority to serve in a judicial capacity, usually in the presence of a justice of assize or the President of the Council at Ludlow or, on occasions, in the Quarter Sessions where the oaths were administered by the clerk of the peace or *custos rotulorum*.[82]

These central features for the status-conscious *uchelwr* revealed one other notable link between defensive skills and the practicalities of local government, namely military leadership and organization. The office of deputy-lieutenant was complementary to the territorial role of the traditional gentleman as protector of his patrimony whose particular feature was leadership in war and peace. The contribution of free Welshmen to the campaigns of English kings in the later Middle Ages at home and abroad revealed how crucial that really was to their success. Leadership was offered by the new generation of *uchelwyr*, and honour, in this context, was based chiefly on personal achievement on the battle-field. In this connection importance was attached to *plaid* or retinue. The bardic grammar and the *Graduelys*, the sixteenth-century treatise on the 'Great Chain of Being', describes the qualities possessed by the lord and nobleman considered worthy of praise, and attention is given to their strength, courage, magnanimity, 'nobleness in action' and militarism as well as their ability to control men, horses and arms, their wealth, expenditure, wisdom and proficiency in governing land and kingdom ('o'i gadernyd, a'i ddewredd, a'i vilwriaeth, a'i allv ar wyr a meirch ac arfav, a chyfoeth, a thravl a'i ddoethineb, a'i gymhendawd yn llywyaw gwlad a theyrnas').[83] Less is said of the *uchelwr*, in this context, but his militarism is emphasized. The *Graduelys* gives a detailed breakdown of the social strata extending from the 'emperor' down to the bondman. Of importance, and next in line to the seven orders of knighthood, are the three grades of esquire and *uchelwyr*. Emphasis is placed on order and the versatile regional governor. There were ample opportunities, even in the sixteenth century, for individual *uchelwyr* to apply themselves to the martial arts.

The Defence and Preservation of Status and Stability

It is evident that status had to be defended, an undertaking which often occupied gentry of all ranks. All proceedings in the lawcourts, regardless of the accusations laid, reveal the intention to save one's face, to defend status, to demonstrate how malicious social attitudes could be towards a reputedly unworthy person. Siôn Tudur, in his *cywydd* to John Salusbury of Lleweni, counselled him to maintain the integrity of his family by appeasing and befriending his jealous kindred for the good of his house:

> A gado'i dŷ fry, a'i fraint,
> A gâr yn fawr ei geraint.[84]

[He who enjoys an exalted house and his privilege has deep affection for his kinsmen.]

The couplet hints at deep-seated animosities in the Welsh rural society, principally the destabilizing forces which weakened what was considered most worthy in gentle society. Although the repercussions of such disruptions were often exaggerated they were apt to cause animosities within the family circle and it is evident that social commentators were concerned that stability be established in the country. Maintaining the principles of human conduct, John Lyly remarked in 1581, entailed knowing what should be cultivated and be avoided: 'Howe wee shoulde worshippe God, be duetifull to our Fathers, stand in awe of our superiours, obey lawes, give place to Officers, howe we may . . . nurture our children and that which is most noble'.[85] These words concentrated on what was required of the man of gentle birth, extending from the praise accorded to God down to the preservation of what was considered 'most noble' in his life. In other words, it was a concentration on what was regarded as his *braint*, namely prerogative or credit. It is an appeal to the practical as well as the moral qualities of the individual, to his sense of honour, and to the skills cultivated to defend and protect himself within the hierarchical structure to which Elizabethan society adhered despite newer less rigorous concepts of the social order that threatened to disrupt it. Shakespeare, in an age of new social trends, continued to emphasize 'degree, priority and place' and to warn that, if 'degree' were undermined, nothing but 'discord' would follow.[86] Much of what he has to say is echoed in Elyot and, in a Welsh setting, the bardic compositions. Elyot was emphatically conservative in his views:

> . . . where there is any lack of order needs must be perpetual conflict . . . so that in everything is order, and without order may be nothing stable or permanent; and it may not be called order, except it do contain in it degrees, high and base, according to the merit or estimation of the thing that is ordered.[87]

Such qualities covered the whole spectrum of civilized society and symbolized the power which status or *braint* offered to the most eligible sections of the community.

Within the structure of local government the gentry who defended their status also exercised supervisory powers over subordinate officials. The ideal was expounded again by Elyot: 'it is expedient and also needful that under the capital governor be sundry mean authorities as it were aiding him in the distribution of justice in sundry parts of a high multitude'.[88] Governing status was linked with the second major factor that contributed to the defence mechanism, namely the emphasis on supporting the individual's independence in performing public duty. Elyot proceeded to describe and explain the importance of instruction for the privileged; it was to be provided 'in such manner and way may be found worthy, and also able to be governors of a public weal'.[89] Since Elyot is concerned with nurturing the governors actively from birth so the bards, who were in closer personal contact, honoured the *uchelwyr* by virtue of their ancestry. As previously explained, their brand of authority was built upon the kindred structure based on the *gwely* or patrimony. The *priodawr*, or free clansman, based his power on military leadership and his skills in defending the patrimony and his co-parceners. The survival of kindred entities represented territorial domination and the honour which individual members derived from exercising their defensive skills. Hence the association of the *uchelwyr* with the administrative system in the Tudor age was identified with inborn qualities of leadership, and gentry attitudes when that power was threatened indicate how jealously they guarded their interests. The purport of bardic tributes was to give publicity to qualities of custodianship, the preservation of estates, family prestige, public service and a prescribed code of conduct through exercising effective leadership which, in turn, was dependent on the preservation of social values and an established order. By the age of Elizabeth humanism in England had reached full fruition, building upon previous developments, especially in the field of education and the qualities of virtue, creating a theory of the *uchelwr*'s character and contribution to the governmental mechanism.

In a purely domestic context defensive skills are manifested in the manner in which an *uchelwr*, even in an age when greater emphasis was placed on rebuilding homes, defended his *llys* or hall (see Chapter 1, pp. 24–8). The concept of householdership played an important role in placing and defining the function of the *uchelwr* in his native environment, which is amply shown in the quality of domestic life in gentry houses as observed by professional poets and often reflected upon in personal memoranda and correspondence.[90] The *plasty* possessed particular features. It was there that both material artefacts and conceptual values were treasured, symbolizing the essence of *uchelwriaeth*. The householder was a custodian, an anchor and the defender of an organized and sophisticated life. It was there that *uchelwriaeth* was exhibited at its most honourable. It not only contributed to the growth of economic strength but to consolidating the 'good name and fame' of the family which it represented. It was the focal point of gentility 'in action' and highlighted the patrilineal structure and other elements of continuity, such as the family heirlooms, the land (which normally provided the means for its upkeep), the family name and, where possible, the hereditary title, all of which, in a Welsh context, were equivalent to English squirearchical features. Thus in 1594 Sir William Maurice was acknowledged by a kinsman as 'a man of . . . callinge and credit' who had graciously treated 'a poor gentleman born to nothing head and honour of so ancient a house . . .' in dealing with a marriage proposal.[91] The cringing tone of the letter revealed a central feature of the upper gentry, namely that Maurice, who had by then married his second wife Ellen, widow of John Lewis of Chwaen Wen, Anglesey, was regarded as the representative of the senior branch of a worthy family. He was a comfortably placed squire safeguarding his interests with the utmost integrity. The methods adopted by him to conduct his property affairs are beside the point: in accordance with contemporary practice he used his country seat as a means of enhancing his power in Eifionydd and adjacent territories. Correspondence relating to Sir Edward Stradling likewise reflects the importance attached to the country seat for it was regarded as central to regional power, emphasizing qualities derived from honourable foundations, and that honour gave the head of the household a sense of his own worth and a standard by which others could judge him. In cultural affairs Stradling was warmly regarded as the 'chief succourer of our Welsh language in south Wales' and of men of 'virtue and valour' as well as a paragon of excellence in the public life of Glamorgan.[92] Again, in this connection, he maintained his superiority among others of his milieu.

Prose works also give the same impression of grandeur as, for example, in the opening section of Dr David Powel's address to Sir Henry Sidney, prefacing Ponticus's *Britannicae Historiae Libri Sex:*

> Y mae dau beth sy'n rhoi'r urddas pennaf ar wladwriaeth a hefyd, fel arfer, yn gosod dynion yn y safle fwyaf anrhydeddus ac uchelradd: y naill wedi'i seilio ar ddefnydd o wyddor milwriaeth, ond y llall ar ymroddiad i lên ac ar wladweinyddiaeth.[93]

> [There are two things which accord the highest prestige to a state and also, usually, place men in the most honourable and elevated position, the one established on the use of the martial arts but the other on a devotedness to literature and statesmanship.]

The author then stated that, by broadening his intellectual horizons, his skills became more apparent to his fellow men:

> Yn union yr un modd ag y mae'r dyn hwnnw sydd â dewrder gwych yn amddiffyn ei gyd-ddinasyddion rhag niwed gelynion a rhag grym arfau, yn ceisio gogoniant tragwyddol i'w wrolder ei hun, felly hefyd y mae'n gwbl iawn . . . fod y dyn sydd wedi'i gynysgaeddu â gwybodaeth amrywddull mewn llên, sy'n gyfarwydd â delio'n barhaus â gorchwylion sifil, ac sydd wedi ennill iddo'i hun glod am ei ddysg a'i ddoethineb, yn derbyn yr un gogoniant trwy gyfrwng y teitlau a'r anrhydeddau uchaf.[94]

[Exactly in the same way as that splendidly courageous man who
defends his fellow citizens from the harm done by enemies and from
the force of arms, attempts to obtain eternal glory to his own valour so
also it is very proper . . . that the man who is endowed with a diversity
of knowledge in literature, who is familiar with dealing continually with
civil duties, and who has gained glory for himself for his learning and
wisdom, receives the same glory by means of the highest titles and
honours.]

In his comment Powel combines two virtues, namely the skill to
defend peace and good order by show of arms and to preserve a
civilized mode of life by moral excellence. Similarly, Henry
Salusbury, the grammarian of Henllan, Denbighshire, and a
member of a younger branch of the famous Salusbury family of
Lleweni, applauded Henry Herbert in 1593 for the manner in
which he had protected the people's welfare by exercising justice
and mercy in public duty.[95] Maecenas, he continued, was renowned
for his discipline and control and his guardianship bore fruit in the
manner in which he cared for intellectual values. The martial skills
sprang from the traditions associated with the *bonheddig cynhwynawl*
(innate free gentleman), whose primacy was based on lineage.

Status was regarded as being the most explicit form of power.
Official sources occasionally recorded the ambivalence between
'squire' and 'gentleman', as in the case of a Howell James of
Llandeilo Crosenni who was described in the Monmouthshire
Quarter Sessions records as 'yeoman alias Howel Herbert,
gentleman'.[96] Likewise, in the Caernarfonshire court in 1547,
Owen ap Richard ap Rhys of Eiriannws, Arllechwedd Isaf,
gentleman, was 'otherwise known as a yeoman'.[97] It was not at all
times easy to distinguish between various gradations although, in
an age of increasing social mobility, individuals did acquire a new
status if circumstances affected their living standards. After all, it
was the collective decision of the community that, in the last
resort, accorded to the individual his status. It was what his
neighbours thought him to be that counted, and it was considered
vital that a man should maintain his station in the community.
Loss of 'good reputation' for shameful reasons was feared and
deplored. One example is the demotion of Edward Lloyd of
Llwyn-y-maen, Llansilin, near Oswestry who, in 1621, was
publicly branded and deprived of his gentility and coat of arms for
uttering scandalous words against Frederick, king of Bohemia,
and his wife Elizabeth, daughter of James I, and their children.[98]
Moreover, in another context, Viscount Lisle confessed to his wife
in 1607, that his poverty had sadly affected his social position:

For as my state is now . . . I will not say in respect of myne honour and credit, but even for things of necessary maintenance. I have not meanes to pay the interest for my debts . . . I have not money to . . . buy necessary clothes for the winter nor to pay for man's meate or horsemeate, besides for all other sudden occasions which every hower fall upon me.[99]

Loss of status, for whatever reason, would have detrimental effects on the concept of honour as envisaged within each social rank and on the livelihood of the individual. Maintaining that honour involved community reactions to male honour, such as paternity and inheritance affairs, marriage and domestic relations and the preservation of public order. Such factors fell within the pattern and context of male honour as reflected in official records and stereotypical images in literature. The defence of honour often involved the practice of legal chicanery, violence and disreputable conduct in public and sometimes in private life.

Status, therefore, was not measured merely by deference alone but also by a man's worth as expounded in the Welsh laws and related to the individual's sense of honour and propriety. It was essential for the *uchelwr* to protect kinship and lineage but he also forged inextricable links with his family and locality, two factors which contributed significantly to establishing the territorial identity of the Tudor gentleman. Such ties continued to be the most potent feature in identifying the nature and extent of local loyalties as well as determining the way in which status, kinship and territorial affinities were protected in the Tudor and early Stuart periods. Vestiges of earlier social conventions had survived despite the economic transformation, and the Tudor settlement enabled those who obtained offices to adapt themselves to the needs of government at the time. In this respect the defensive system applied to status involved the preservation of the family name as well as the succession and the augmentation of landed property.

Conclusion

Status, as revealed in contemporary sources, needs to be applied to the immediate social environment of the individual squire. The public image of the regional administrator merely reflected his standing within the social and economic circumstances of his age. The situation that governed his movements and conditioned his relationships with members of his immediate and extended family and acquaintances is fundamental in any analysis of the gentry's status and the structured social gradation within which he was placed.

Despite the changes that were gradually eroding the existing structure of society there remained a strong attachment to time-honoured customs and practices. To many gentry the avaricious grasping of land and its defence by litigation were forms of defending their own positions and establishing a firmer foothold in their localities. This was accomplished usually through the exploitation of property and enhancing its value. Their involvement in the land market appears the most powerful manifestation of their intent to defend what they had already acquired, either through inheritance or purchase. It was only gradually that the powers of the law replaced the armed violence that had been a marked feature in the Welsh countryside.

The desire to preserve or defend property was but one aspect of unstable family relations in the countryside for pride and honour were equally important. Such defensive practices entailed manipulating the customary *cymortha*, although it had been abolished by law, to force dependants to recognize a superior power dominating their lives. Another form of defence was the continual competition that existed between rival houses for domination in the countryside. Although Welsh members of parliament by the early seventeenth century had become acclimatized to the surroundings at Westminster they still projected an assertive attitude of mind and revealed basic rural instincts. They may not have been as politically aware as historians in the past, such as A. H. Dodd, considered them to be, but they were doubtless mindful of their own personal skills and qualities which gave them prominence in provincial society.[100] This was displayed in the innumerable clashes between the gentry, such as those in Glamorgan in the 1580s and 1590s, and the disputes between the Owens of Bodowen and Y Frondeg and their satellites in the western and south-western parts of Anglesey and the Bulkeleys of Henblas, Beaumaris.[101] In Merioneth the Llwyn family of Dolgellau opposed the house of Nannau and the Salusburies of Rug were at odds with the Prices of Rhiwlas.[102] In Montgomeryshire rivalry broke out between the Herberts of Montgomery and Powys Castle, religious affiliation being but one reason for the feud.[103] The Montgomery branch had risen rapidly in the social ranks, Sir Richard Herbert (d.1539) having been appointed a steward under Charles Somerset, earl of Worcester, as Receiver of the York and Mortimer estates. His son, Sir Edward Herbert, supported the assimilation of Wales with England, served as a squire of the body to Queen Elizabeth, and was pricked sheriff of Montgomery on two occasions (1557 and 1568). He also performed duties as *custos rotulorum* in his county and was elected member of parliament continually between 1553 and 1588. Many similar cases could be cited, especially in the old Marcher areas where lands had fallen to the Crown and where the impact of faction and religious loyalties was strongly felt in political life.

Whatever the aims of these families actively engaged in advancing their reputations the prime motive was the preservation and enhancement of a family's good name. Those 'gentlemen of good living and reputation' who collected *cymorth*, it was said, 'are commonly of such calling, kindred and friendship in the country that they will have, not according to the will and powers of the givers, but to their own liking'.[104] The *cymorth* exaction was not only a means of extracting unfair payments from tenants on the pretext that the lord was in need of financial support but rather, usually on an annual basis, a formal acknowledgement that 'lordship' was a manifestation of precedence. A defence of one's position at a personal and regional level implied serving one's own interests and protecting the quality of community life. That occurred in the 1580s and 1630s respectively when, on the one hand, Catholic activity threatened to undermine the unity of the realm and, on the other, constant demands for taxation caused difficulties in the regions. In both cases the gentry in office took it upon themselves to protect the state, first of all by punishing recusants and then by maintaining stability, often in dire economic conditions. In both cases the emphasis was laid upon protecting the community essentially as a part of the realm. One characteristic example of the blend of aggression and a sense of personal honour emerged in the misfortunes that befell Sir John Salusbury of Lleweni who succeeded as head of the estate his elder brother, Thomas Salusbury, the conspirator who was implicated in the Babington Plot and executed in 1586. He was accused of disloyalty and corruption and found it hard to live down the embarrassment caused by his brother's treasonable activity. His involvement in the election debacle of 1601, his rivalry with his kinsmen at Bachymbyd and his debts did not aid his cause; yet, despite all this, he strove valiantly to defend his honour. This is amply testified in the corpus of bardic tributes composed in his honour and, in the family correspondence, he was, as Sir Eubule Thelwall appropriately called it, 'he who could change the lion's skin with the fox'.[105] His defence of his position as head of the Lleweni estate was typical of men of his milieu forced by circumstances to dig in their heels. In 1609 he vowed never to subject himself to the will of his adversaries over the matter of debts and was prepared, since his health had been restored, to 'purge' himself in the King's presence.[106] The development of Welsh gentry status in the post-Union period created an awareness of the need to utilize innate defensive skills inherited from the past, applying them in a less military and more legalistic context.

In a stressful year like 1598, when Sir John Salusbury's enemies rallied to overthrow him, he was advised to 'look unto hit . . . and be still, youe haue mighty adversarys . . . if they can plucke youe downe they will . . . they will smyle and cut throts'.[107] They were opponents whose 'malice still encresith more venemous then the stinge of aders'. With the fierce competition for land and property and the increased activity of lawyers in the courts of law, it is hardly surprising that the growth of litigation, according to William Vaughan, had produced 'two-legged asses . . . which doe nothing but wrangle in law the one with the other'.[108] Vexatious litigation often led to prolonged and severe family animosities tending to destroy good order and to impair family or individual status. In contemporary sources such abuses were normally associated with other transgressions characteristic of men of authority. That view is confirmed by that perceptive cleric Huw Lewys of Llanddeiniolen, who attributed the vanities and corruption of the age to false pride and arrogance:

> Pa faint yw rhwysc cybydd-dod, vsuriaeth, chwant, trais, lledrat ac ysbel, in mysc, fe wyr pawb sy yn dal ac yn craffu ar gwrs y byd . . . casineb, llid, gelynniaeth, digofaint, ymrysonau, ymgyfreithiaw, anghariadoldeb ac anudonau sy ry aml, ac agos a gorescyn ein gwlad.[109]

> [How much pomp, miserliness, usury, lust, oppression, robbery and spoliation there is everyone knows who observes and looks intensely at the course of the world . . . hatred, passion, hostility, wrath, contention, litigation, unkindness and perjury are excessive and almost overrun our country.]

Genuine lay people and clergy alike drew attention to the basic reason for the malaise in Tudor and early Stuart society, namely the disregard for legitimate authority in practising law.

Despite the changes that occurred in the social life of the Welsh gentry and the increasing threat to their status, the basic features of their rank and reputation survived. The privileges enjoyed by the landed gentry entailed performing specific duties. Thus emerged the liaison which strengthened the bonds between them and their dependants: their power was built largely on the labours of others on their estates and the income produced by rents. Thereby, the principle of landownership rather than estate profits boosted their prestige. Regardless of their economic plight modest proprietors in Wales still clung tenaciously to what they considered to be their inalienable birthright as stipulated by law. Each successive generation set out to protect what inheritance they had received and to apply their power comprehensively to safeguard the welfare of the family and other dependants. This defence of common interests was central to their role in local government and was allied to political and cultural dimensions normally associated with the activities of squire-administrators.

It is within this framework that the *uchelwyr*, who enjoyed their landed power, are identified with the concept of the public governor in the late sixteenth and early seventeenth centuries. Both, in different fields of activity, were aware of their authority and were regarded as community leaders. Both were protectors of a common cultural heritage. This homogeneity of interests was centred on power structure within families, the chief features being the manner in which individual *uchelwyr* viewed and interpreted their place and role in society. That was largely based on the impact of the Tudor settlement on the privileged class. It formed essentially an economic order, far-reaching in its repercussions and all-embracing in community life. Where it is possible to speak of a 'county community' the concept appears to have assisted in preserving an awareness of a brand of *uchelwriaeth* that stemmed from that blending of obligation, the right to govern and the duty to protect the governed. This fundamental factor in asserting and preserving status formed a recurrent theme through the period and created a distinctive cultural entity. The defence of status in the lives of country gentlemen rendered necessary the aid of academics, antiquarian scholars, genealogists and herald poets in recording the descents of families claiming illustrious ancestries and, in the case of professional poets, in displaying their excellence in the most ostentatious fashion. That exercise presupposed that such families were endowed with qualities that gave status its rightful place in privileged society. It is these qualities that form the theme of the following chapter.

CHAPTER 3

Honour, Order and Authority

O bu Feirion heb fawredd,
Heb iau nag ych bôn i'w gwedd;
Beth a'i dwg i obaith da?
Bod awdurdod i wrda.[1]

[If Merioneth lacks grandeur without a yoke or leading ox for its team;
what shall give it sure hope? That authority be granted a nobleman.]

Thus sang Siôn Phylip, one of the best known Welsh strict-metre
poets at the turn of the seventeenth century, in honour of Huw
Nannau Hen, a prominent Merioneth squire who was actively
engaged in shire administration and in pursuing his family's
advancement. This encomium contains some of the finest lines
composed in strict-metres to describe sturdy patrons of his type as
the ideal administrators of their regions and, in part, reflects
contemporary thought on the auspicious courtier-type leader of
his people. The patron is regarded as a governor responsible for
exercising regional authority; the perfect example, so it is said, of
the native Welshman who had applied his traditional role as an
uchelwr to serve the needs of Tudor government. The inference in
these lines is that Huw Nannau was familiar with the mechanics of
local government, loyal to the Tudor and Stuart dynasties and to
the principles of common law, and highly respected in his
province as a symbol of equity and justice. Doubtless the object of
this eulogy was to portray a man of considerable magnitude in his
neighbourhood. Characteristic of his generation, however, Huw
Nannau was also a lawbreaker and scheming oppressor who was
often made to answer for his infamous deeds. In other words, as in
the case of so many others of his kind who patronized poets and
whose virtues were extolled, authority was often distorted since it
could be justly or unjustly applied; either way usually it served to
enhance the squire's reputation as leader of his community. The
images of honour, order and authority, so highly esteemed by the
Welsh gentry and overtly publicized by social commentators, form
the theme of this chapter. Such concepts add further dimensions
to status as the basic requirement in any claim to gentility, as

examined in Chapter 2. Honour and esteem and the exercise of
authority, as well as the imposition of order were entirely
dependent on status which the leaders, whatever their social
standing, cherished and regarded as the norm for performing
public service.

Justice, Honour and Power

Central to the code of conduct which characterized the gentry
were the virtues of justice and honour, and the presumption that
they would respond to their duties in the post-Act of Union era by
practising the moral principles advocated by Renaissance writers.
It was not equated with fame or magnanimity although firmly
associated with them. It implied an acquired virtue, often
attributed by others to the gentleman, which led him away from
vice towards the good; it contained a significant blend of an
awareness of moral obligation and the skill to perform wholesome
deeds. According to Jacques Hurault, 'the good man par
excellence' was he who was self-assertive and self-expressive.[2] He
was a person who exercised the highest among virtues, namely
justice: 'without justice', Elyot declared, 'all other qualities and
virtues cannot make a man good'.[3] Allied to this virtue was
honour and magnanimity: 'magnanimitie', Hurault again maintained, 'is an ornament unto all vertues, because the deeds of
vertue be worthy of honour, the which are put in execution by
magnanimitie'.[4] The man aware of his honour was he who desired
to preserve his reputation and become a pattern of excellence for
others to follow. It is in this context that the connection between
the code of honour and governorship needs to be examined and
applied to a variety of public offices entrusted to the gentry.

The Tudor period saw the publication of works by a group of
social and educational commentators such as Sir Thomas Smith,
William Harrison, Roger Ascham, Thomas Blundeville and Henry
Peacham, all of whom based their observations on community-
held principles of order and social stratification, rank and status.
The system, as conceived by them, was controlled by families
normally involved in the business of maintaining local
government. According to these social expositors legitimate
authority comprised the exercise of discipline, obedience, justice
and control. The authoritarian nature of Tudor rule doubtless
emerged as its most prominent feature. Society was controlled and
government exercised by that authority, extending from the
highest to the lowest ranks, acting as a binding force and creating

a cohesiveness which served to preserve the realm as an organic entity under the Crown, divinely appointed to wield authority and to delegate it to the central and regional agencies of government. Authority implied that the exercise of control was legitimately imposed on the community of the realm and that an effective amount of discipline was required to maintain an ordered society. It emerged as a distinct entity which assisted in defining the relations between monarchy and subject, landowner and tenant, and master and servant, and which accorded to the *paterfamilias* his rightful authority within the household. Authority was regarded as the chief factor in the preservation of unity and harmony in the state. Its clearest manifestation is found in the homily in 1547 which established the close-knit bonds between different orders in society. The *Homily of Obedience* runs as follows:

> Almighty God hath created and appointed all things in heaven, earth and waters, in a most excellent and perfect order . . . In earth he hath assigned and appointed Kings, Princes with other Governors under them, in all good and necessary order . . . Every degree of people in their vocation, calling and office hath appointed to them their duty and order . . . Take away Kings, princes, rulers, magistrates, judges and such estates of God's order . . . and there must needs follow all mischief and utter destruction both of souls, bodies, goods and commonwealths.[5]

This extract is a key to contemporary views of social stratification emphasizing divine law, the rigidity of human relations, rank and status, the superiority accorded to the most eligible through lineage and landed power, and the destructive consequences of lack of leadership. Older generations of Welsh gentry clung doggedly to these hierarchical principles, evaluating their own positions and defending themselves, hence their attempts to assert power to combat the pretensions of *nouveaux riches*, or 'gent. of the first head', as they were once deridingly called, steadily climbing up the social ladder.[6] The second half of the sixteenth century represented the crisis point in the development of the older established and more conservative heads of families, claiming impeccable descent and eager to maintain their precedence in the shire community. Their resilient spirit is revealed by Sir John Wynn of Gwydir, in one of his more reflective moods in the following extract from his *History of the Gwydir Family*:

> If you ask the question why the succession of Hywel [his ancestor] sped better than the posterity of the other two brethren I can yield you no

other reason but God's mercy and goodness towards the one more
than the other . . . by the goodness of God we are and continue in the
reputation of gentlemen from time to time sithence unto this day . . .
Yet a great temporal blessing it is and a great heart's ease to a man to
find that he is well descended . . . [7]

This section explicitly details the basic features of gentility in a
characteristically Welsh context. The quality of being gentle is
equated with authority since it implied practical leadership, and
without that authority leadership would be void and ineffectual.
The fear among such families that they were losing status and a
grip on power in the localities emerged clearly in periods of social
and economic change and the rise of new families to positions of
authority. This view was amply displayed in the responses of
several commentators, some involved in public administration, to
the condition of law and order in Wales. Dr David Lewis, a firm
supporter of Rowland Lee's vigorous policy of law enforcement,
was essentially conservative in his views, urging the government to
defend and continue good government based largely on what had,
over the previous half-century, been established by law.[8] Lord
Zouche, the newly appointed lord president of the Council in the
Marches in 1601, on the other hand, emphasized the crucial issue
encountered by him at Ludlow: 'I do find the Council and the
whole Court against me,' he observed, 'not for any offence, but
because I would alter that which they have walked in, which, as I
suppose, hath brought credit to som and money to others'.[9]
Several lawyers were offended at a meddling layman questioning
the precedence they enjoyed.[10] Maintaining a position of honour
was the personal responsibility of every gentleman who
considered himself to have a family history and reputation worth
preserving. Despite his alleged malpractices Sir William Morgan
of Pen-coed in Monmouthshire placed his trust in the Privy
Council in 1577 when it refuted the allegation that he was about
to be committed to the Tower for planning an expedition against
Spain in Wales; so that 'it may appear that the gentleman', it was
declared, 'upon his deserts, is well thought of . . . both by her
Majesty and their lordships, and that there is care both for the
maintenance of . . . his reputation'.[11] In 1536 the interests of Sir
Walter Devereux, Lord Ferrers, chief justice of South Wales and
steward of Builth, and Henry Somerset, earl of Worcester, justice
of Glamorgan, were preserved as were those of George Blunt,
steward of Bewdley and Ledbury in 1543. The statutory
requirement that no legislation should be 'prejudicial or hurtful'

to them implied that honour as well as official status was involved.[12] Sir Thomas Smith's reference to the lower orders as those who 'have no voice or authority in our commonwealth and no account is made of them but only to be ruled', revealed how rank created acknowledged divisions between people.[13]

Among the nobler sections in society authority was dispersed between various gradations of officials representing degrees of responsibility within the gentry order. Authority was accorded to individuals more on merit and economic aggrandizement than on lineage alone, and this applied not only to incoming families and professional families but also to yeomen freeholders who, within their respective degrees, enjoyed power in the shire community. All in all, the concept of authority was the most dominant feature in Welsh society in the lives of the gentry whose responsibility it was to maintain the welfare of their communities. It was a major obligation in Elizabethan and Jacobean society that those vested with power should protect the interests of the 'commonweal', an obligation which could only be fulfilled through the exercise of legitimate authority. Those who had 'gentilnes mixte with gravitie' were more than equipped with the virtues needed to combat the situation and to exercise their authority under the monarchy. It was invariably the case that what was considered to be beneficial for the Crown was also regarded as advantageous for themselves.[14]

Although the ideal of the regional governor was set out in bardic convention, a variety of sources placed considerable emphasis on other concepts of authority, enabling Welsh *uchelwyr* to display their qualities positively and thrust themselves to the forefront of Welsh regional society. That authority, referred to in the above extract from Sir John Wynn's *History*, had a long history, and the Welsh administrative class which recognizably emerged during the course of the fourteenth century laid the basis of government in Wales and the Marches. Despite political and economic pressures this pattern survived into the sixteenth century, and those who succeeded in establishing their landed power also developed their potential for wielding authority in the Principality or the Marches. The spirit of the *uchelwr*, in his role as free-born clansman, continued into the Tudor age and his tenacity as well as his family affinities enabled him to thrive and extend his connections. The new breed of gentry that emerged was chiefly characterized by its skill in accumulating wealth based on land and office. These *uchelwyr* were the social climbers who established families and enjoyed regional domination, and their progress signified a range of important features, namely that status was dependent, not on pedigree alone, but on the accumulation of material wealth; that office-holding was regarded as a formative element in consolidating family power and that the nature of authority was associated with the type of office or position acquired. The new gentry and eventually the *nouveaux riches* replaced the native aristocracy of Wales and assumed their role and bore the burdens of government shouldered by their predecessors. Power was not only delegated to them but was also exploited by them; they were aware of the need to use it to maintain public authority and to promote private interests. In that context authority was composed of an amalgam of status and wealth, and the descendants of this gregarious and enterprising class of men who were closely attached to their localities by ties of kinship and dependent on royal favour became the chief representatives of landed power and maintainers of law and order in Wales after the Tudor settlement.[15] Sir William Thomas's words to Sir William Maurice in 1608 appealing to him to attend a meeting of magistrates to discuss military arrangements in Caernarfonshire came very close to explaining the essential role of the individual in local government: 'yo'r p'sence or advise will greatly avayle vs & doe the countrey good: for that woord quality in the lordes letter [i.e. the lord president] will admitt divers constructions, but lett all agree as neare as wee can for the countreys good – *pauca sapienti*'.[16]

As senior magistrate, Thomas was intent on ensuring that his colleagues – the 'select few wisemen' – displayed their loyalty to the Crown to protect the welfare of their communities and their power to maintain peace and security. These features of gentry life are amply illustrated in a variety of sources which, despite their belligerent nature, reveal the manner in which their power functioned in the sixteenth century, and how, in varying circumstances, it was applied to maintain peace, stability and justice. Although the Crown had not succeeded entirely in establishing peace and security in Wales and the Marches in the fifteenth century, developments occurred which tightened royal supervision over the *uchelwyr* who clung to their traditional privileges. During the course of the sixteenth century, particularly after the Tudor settlement, the alliance between the Crown and the local communities was strengthened and became an effective means of maintaining order and government. That relationship varied depending on economic and political conditions. George Owen, however, seemed content with the peace and goodwill that existed in his native Pembrokeshire. He testified that its people enjoyed 'peace, quietnes and neighborly love . . . [being] verye obediente to the magistrates of the Countrey vndertaking willingly to theire power any burden or chardge layed vpon them, for the princes service, or theire Countreys good'.[17]

In his 'Dialogue of the Government of Wales', Owen maintained further that public conduct generally in the county was exemplary with little faction, 'so that it is a rare and seldome thinge to here of an affray or quarrel amonge the Gentlemen of the Cheefest sorte': 'With this', he continued, 'is God pleased, the prince well and carefully served, her Laws duely obeyed and Justice duely ministred.'[18] Owen's account was clearly misleading: his motives had led him to adopt an idealized view of Pembrokeshire society whereas in that county, as elsewhere in Wales, persistent struggles between aspiring families were a dominant feature. What he had to say, however, reflected the attitudes which prevailed among men of his type concerning the growth of stability under a regime highly esteemed for initiating practical methods of administering local government.

The Use and Abuse of Honour

The Council in the Marches was authorized to curb lawlessness, and the abuse of authority that was often the cause of it, for the well-being of the state and the local community. Henry Herbert, second earl of Pembroke, and Lord President of the Council in the Marches, displayed an awareness of obligation in this respect and was deeply concerned in January 1586, for example, since he had become aware that law and order was not being observed as it should in Glamorgan. Piratical activities, which were notorious off the south-east coast of Wales led him to question the trust-worthiness of Sir Edward Stradling and William Mathew of Radyr, two prime administrators in the county, in suppressing these illicit operations.[19] He hoped to make amends for deficiencies in government after Sir Henry Sidney's long periods of absence from Ludlow during his presidency. Herbert came to power at a crucial time in the war between England and Spain. He sought to improve coastal defence, which was a constant source of anxiety (a matter discussed in detail in Chapter 4), he revealed his mistrust of deputy-lieutenants and reprimanded them for their recalcitrance. He feared that both Stradling and Mathew had acted maliciously and in contempt of his position as the govern-ment's chief administrative officer in Wales and the borderland, and in his communication to them raised a fundamental issue:

And when I enter into consideracon of both your accions, I doe not fynd such singularytie in the upright administration of justice that I maye justly thinke you eache way faultles; for it is reported that some ryottes, unlawfull assemblyes, many frayes and bloodshedes . . . have byne not onely unpunished, but bowlester'd by you; w'ch yf it be so . . . you are not in deed what you seeme in showe.

He seriously questioned the nature and use of the authority bestowed upon these deputies in their shire. Moreover, he declared that the abuse of authority could not be tolerated and expressed his eagerness to see that the right to impose it was honourably executed and properly controlled, and that his opinion was appreciated among *uchelwyr* in public office in his day. His attitude on this occasion prompts a further question: what was the intrinsic nature of the public authority that Herbert expected privileged men to exercise in their communities and how was it to be interpreted by them and shared out among them? Moreover, what was the origin of the innate power entrusted to them to enforce obedience and to reprimand when it was violated; and why was it considered crucial that this authority, represented by the lord president's position and their own, should be sustained in the late sixteenth century?

Tudor social commentators insisted that concepts of order and discipline should be accorded the most prominent place when describing community life and the manner in which the individual's awareness of his responsibility over his dependants forced him to conduct himself fittingly in public and private. It was an age when decorum was closely observed. 'I can judge something of men for I have studied many', James Howell pertinently remarked in 1648 when assessing the quality of his own companionship.[20] Similarly, monumental effigies and suchlike remembrances of renowned individuals were erected primarily to draw attention to the deceased person's distinctive contribution to his or her immediate community; only second were they intended as commemorations for future generations to admire. Observers continued to refer to essential hierarchic features. Based on a divine plan, the focus was on precedence and deference. In his attack on the Ket Rebellion in 1549 John Cheke remarked in *The Hurt of Sedicion howe greueous it is to a Communewelth*: 'Have ye not in disordre first greuouslie offended God, nexte trayterouslie risen against your Kynge, and so nother worthy euerlastyng life, as long as ye so remayne, nor yet ciuile lyfe, being in suche a breache of commune quietnes.'[21] He appealed to the rebels to honour the commonwealth and the authority vested in the Crown and its officials. The notion of a structured society based on patriarchalism had survived the Middle Ages signifying good order and government. The contribution of *uchelwriaeth* to the state forms a central feature in the political thought of the age. In any consideration of an organized realm hierarchical concepts dominated with layers of authority vested in men of ability who functioned in carefully arranged positions within a range of government institutions. The ruling families, whether functioning in the higher or lower regions of government, were considered to form an integral part of the organic structure of the state. Regardless of the theories that explained the nature of social inequality it was a common belief that the 'gentleman' was a central component in the links between the monarchy and its subjects. Since that monarchy assumed responsibility for the welfare of its subjects so the *uchelwr* was regarded as the benefactor of his own people. *Uchelwriaeth*, in that context, was essentially regal. The 'coming to power' of the local squire was usually equated with lawful succession to the throne; it involved attaining a prestigious regional status and a degree of personal merit. The hereditary succession was significant in that the *uchelwr* was considered to be one fit to rule, normally a scion of 'royal' blood who, by means of his innate qualities, minimized the possibility of a power struggle. It involved exercising a degree of political cunning which, in turn, placed greater emphasis on effectuality than on personal integrity.

These *uchelwyr* were the protectors of their dependants, preservers of law and order, and the administrators of government in the state; they were thus entitled to all the privileges that their order allowed them. Among those powers was the right to share responsibilities in governing the state, and the duty to defend its independence. The pursuit of official duties was considered essential for the well-being of the individual in power as well as those whom he governed. Gentility and monarchy alike had obligations to fulfil, thus contributing to stability in regional society equally in civil or military government. The qualities of gentility were based fundamentally on the type of service that gentility rendered to the state. Out of it emerged the ideal of citizenship and the qualities associated with Plato and Aristotle; privileged groups in society were most naturally suited to protect and maintain the interests of the state. Despite the instability that increasingly created rifts and changes in the social fabric *uchelwriaeth*, symbolizing the prime qualities of native gentility, strove to embody traditional values.[22] It is not difficult to discover how public office became a goal to be achieved among the most hard-headed of *uchelwyr*. As Bishop John Salcot (or Capon) of Bangor, for example, aptly described it when referring to the nature of the ambitious Welsh squire on the eve of the Tudor settlement:

> for the nature of a Walshe man is ffor to bere office and to be in authorite. He will not let to ru'ne thorow the fyer of hell and to sell and geve all that he can make of his owen and of his ffrends for the same, and also they be very tycle [sensitive] of theym sealfes.[23]

Salcot's observation reveals tendencies that were already dominant well before the time when Thomas Cromwell passed his legislation assimilating Wales with England, elements that had been conspicuous for over two centuries. There was a close association between the concepts of authority and its practice. The holding of Crown offices was considered to be essential in the creation of a new image for the gentry in Wales after 1536. The hierarchy of power survived but was transformed, particularly in the Marcher areas, to form a uniform system in royal employment. In addition to pedigree-hunting and feudal service greater emphasis was placed on the attributes of the modern landowner and governor.[24]

Although emphasis was placed on self-assertiveness and competitiveness, honour was assessed principally in terms of duty and obligation. Honour was defended because it was in the nature of the squire's obligation to be 'well-reputed' or to maintain his 'credit'. Reputation, it was said, 'was the very essence of their ability to govern'. In 1617 Sir John Wynn asserted that he would not have served in the commissions of the peace of three counties had he not been aware of the need to maintain law and order.[25] As a 'pillar of his county' Sir William Maurice was considered to be a person who not only exercised military control over a defined region but who also maintained its integrity by keeping order and dispensing justice.[26] 'The lord hath made yow a pyller of this country', Gervase Babington, later bishop of Llandaf, remarked to Sir Edward Stradling when requesting his support in assessing his literary output, 'and, yf yor godly zeale shall ever make yow soe, allso of his kingdome'.[27]

Many of the public obligations associated with the Welsh gentry were indicative of their growing self-consciousness as individuals privileged to perform duties to the state because of the historic attributes which they claimed to possess. This entailed using what political, social and religious lineaments that were at hand to create an image of public spirit shaped by a diversity of experiences in law, administration and culture. What has been called the 'cultural hegemony' of the gentry is normally linked to the use and preservation of the law. Any attempt to examine 'authority', 'honour' and 'reputation' enjoyed among the gentry normally focused on the institutions considered essential to the survival of an ordered society. A cursory glance at public administrative records in Wales in this period indicates that a sense of honour transcended all attempts to subordinate authority because of the acceptance of law as the basic feature of human existence. This concept was applied in all sections of society, as Oliver Lord St John of Fonmon Castle explained to Sir Edward Stradling in 1578 when deploring the failure of an understeward to govern tenants because of his lack of learning, experience and 'stowtnesse of countenance'. Such duties, he continued, required 'great government and skill in learninge to bringe . . . tenantes to good order'.[28] His response highlighted the fact that honour and reputation were found not solely among a privileged élite but rather among all strands in society. In conduct books it was declared that all, of whatever degree and favour, were subject to the rule of law. The order that law created stemmed from the family and household, regarded as the 'major vehicle of discipline'.[29] Society appeared to be stable despite increasing tensions in the early decades of the seventeenth century that eventually created major upheavals. Ambitious and daunting the gentry may have been but in their respective localities, even though they often discarded the law, they themselves never interpreted their use of authority in such a manner that it might deprive them of their honour. Although they often had to be cajoled into acceding to the wishes of the central government the propaganda of order in Wales lay essentially in the manner in which they maintained key institutions with the least harassment.

Society in Wales, no less than in England, was not totally ungovernable, and when it is considered that the system established to ensure effective government was less than a hundred years old, at a time when society was gradually changing and older concepts of public order disintegrating, it is the more remarkable. Again, attention is drawn to the immense power exercised in turn by the familial entity and the state. Local communities were composed of well-governed households. This phenomenon and the group relationships between families in vills, parishes and hundreds explains the role of the shire as a recognized regional entity. Although the administration of the parish and hundred cannot be ignored, localized power was normally exercised within what has been termed the county community. Authority was dependent on status in an age when the homogeneity of social relationships, as Sir Thomas Smith observed in the 1580s, was beginning to show clear signs of strain and disintegration, and when the hierarchical structure was gradually collapsing before the forces of change.[30]

Although that hierarchical structure had been based largely on past social conventions, the possession and exercise of authority in the sixteenth century was not merely a matter of exhibiting an impressive lineage. It is true that most families prided themselves on their ability to maintain and safeguard their honour, however crudely it might be presented. While some considered honour to be uppermost in family reputation others adjudged it to be an adjunct of divine favour, as revealed in the case of the Wynns of Gwydir. It was in this vein that Sir John Wynn expressed his mind in the *History of the Gwydir Family*:

> I have in my mind . . . compared or likened God's work in that to a man striking fire into a tinder box for, by the beating of the flint upon the steel, there are a number of sparks of fire raised. Whereof but one or two takes fire the rest vanishing away.[31]

In such words he expressed the thoughts of other notables of his milieu. By the early seventeenth century, the code of honour became increasingly identified with an oppressive self-assertiveness and a quest for economic advantage. The exercise of governmental power in the regions was viewed increasingly as the preserve of those who adeptly associated their public interests with a deep-seated desire for economic advancement. Power cultivated links with economic competence, which essentially constituted the chief feature of *uchelwyr* exercising their authority. Not all families succeeded in establishing precedence in regional or shire government; however, in terms of material means, a large group of cadet families continued to enjoy basic comforts and, at the same time, while retaining their regional identity, commanded the allegiance of their dependants and wielded considerable territorial power.[32]

Social cohesiveness among the privileged families, however, did not necessarily imply that the authority which they shared was properly exercised. Ambition and the acquisition of power invited corrupt practice – a constant hazard for successive governments in their attempt to impose order. The dependence on those regarded as worthy governors did incur some danger. The power game was most evident among men in the highest official positions. 'Mr Townshend', the earl of Pembroke declared about Sir Henry Townshend, second justice of Chester, to the Queen in 1600, 'is not by the judges . . . esteemed learned, in the opinion of the country not held incorrupt . . . much suspected to rest often affectionate, and more given to respect his own private fortune than your public service.' The earl defended his own record at Ludlow and feared that decreasing the Council's power had brought more profit to 'some private persons' than to the Queen. His defence, however, was too late to save his reputation: 'For myself', he continued, 'I do loyally affirm that in this office I have not dealt corruptly in matters of justice'. 'I have not used mine authority to private purposes', he proceeded further, '. . . Only I beseech you that I may not be dishonoured by receiving less credit in my office than my predecessors have had.'[33]

The records of Star Chamber and other central courts often refer to the despoliation of lands by the gentry. Common phrases which occur describe the aggressor as 'a man of great power and authoritie', 'turbulent and contentious', 'a man . . . of great kindred, power and authority', bent on grasping all the benefits that material advancement might offer him.[34] With the increase in the land market in the latter half of the sixteenth century it was to be expected that assertiveness and cupidity would characterize those who were busily involved in supplementing their landed power. Those proprietors who were consolidating their landed power were as conservative as they were forward-looking, in the sense that they wished to preserve and consolidate what they had already acquired. For them maintaining order was paramount in an age of rapid social change, and the ways in which estates were built and family influence extended became, in the context of the age, manifestations of that order and stability. It is hardly surprising, therefore, that they were determined to stabilize that which formed the nucleus of their good fortune, hence the authority they exercised was essentially an assertive feature and a means of demonstrating order and safeguarding the existing social structure. That could only be done if the gentry succeeded in consolidating their hold over their respective regions.

In Wales the *uchelwyr* dominated the countryside; source material illustrates that they placed emphasis on performing duties and securing obedience. It is, therefore, hardly surprising that authority was not abused to such a degree that it caused regional insurrection in Wales as occurred in 1536, 1549, 1554 and 1569 in England. After Sir Rhys ap Gruffudd's rising in west Wales in 1529–31, no stir occurred in Wales.[35] Social deprivation partly accounted for that but the fundamental factor was that preserving order was central to the authority imposed by the *uchelwyr* on their people and was also revealed in religious life. The leadership assumed by the privileged order was a major factor in maintaining unity and the cohesive pattern of community life in Welsh regions.

Rioting and general disturbance was a common phenomenon in any society, rural or urban. Commentators, such as Rice Merrick, Dr David Lewis and George Owen, discouraged it and defended unity and uniformity. Precedence was given to those who, in their official capacities, sustained that unity. The response of Hugh Gwynn of Pembrokeshire to the mayor of Haverfordwest (in his capacity as deputy-lieutenant) in 1588 with regard to the mustering of townsmen indicated how legitimate authority could be undermined: 'If I have offended the Lord President', he asserted, 'I am sorry for it, but as for you [the mayor and court officials] that sit there I care not for you, neither do I crave for your good wills.'[36] This example reveals an individual reaction to two types of authority, the one directly responsible to the Crown, which the defendant fully acknowledged, and the other, to borough officials, whom he held in contempt. The spirit of the law was broken in two directions: notably in open rebellion against legally constituted authority or acts of insubordination on the part of those specifically appointed to govern the realm. All offenders arraigned before the courts of law were accused of transgressing the King's peace. Justices of the peace in Quarter Sessions were controlled by the Council in the Marches, the administrative arm of the Privy Council. Authority lay essentially in interlinking these institutions and exercising power by their means.[37]

Honour and Status

The honour associated with the status of *uchelwr* stemmed from a combination of virtues, not the least of which, in an age which was increasingly forsaking medieval concepts of chivalry, were self-esteem and self-assertiveness. They could and often did emerge in the violent manner in which individuals were prepared to defend their status but also in the exercise of authority. That authority at times served to curb desires to assert control in the most despotic manner, and it was in that context that conflict ensued between authority exercised honourably and its illegal use as an act of oppression. Authority, consequently, could be distorted and corrupt. The defence of honour caused friction and hatred; it was to defend his status that Sir Rhys ap Gruffudd of Dinefwr challenged Lord Ferrers in open court in 1529,[38] it was partly to save his good name that Sir John Wynn of Gwydir wrote his *History of the Gwydir Family*,[39] and it was to vindicate his pedigree that Sir Edward Stradling of St Donat's compiled the 'Winning of the Lordship of Glamorgan'.[40] Confronted by the malice of his enemies Owen Salusbury of Holt challenged his kinsman, Sir John Salusbury of Lleweni, to a duel in 1593.[41] The Welsh gentry often identified themselves with that 'honour culture' based on lineage, leadership and householdership, and in which bards were well versed. Individual patrons were often made paradigms of honour: housekeeping, administering the law, defending the realm and establishing cultural relations were all features designed to demonstrate self-esteem and power in Tudor society. However weak their case may have been, it could be argued that aggressive defendants in the Westminster and regional courts intended to maintain their honour. When testimonials were submitted to Quarter Sessions by parishioners in support of an impoverished neighbour who had inadvertently broken the law, it was in defence or protection of that person's honour that this communal act was done. Higher up the social scale, when Anthony Mansel, for example, was described, as were many of his contemporaries, as 'a man . . . of great kindred, power and authority' who made his tenants 'wearie of the occupation of . . . landes and tenementes' his conduct was viewed as an ineffective means of defending his honour.[42] Robert Devereux, second earl of Essex, was also described in such daunting terms which revealed the power which he enjoyed among his contemporaries in south-west Wales: 'Most of those that wears your honour's cloth in this country is to have your honour's countenance and to be made sheriffs, lieutenants, stewards . . . everything is fish that comes to their net'.[43] As this declaration maintains, power was associated with the desire to preserve honour in the constant struggle to acquire influence. It was to prevent the exercise of power from injuring the individuals that Henry Stanley, earl of Derby, defended his son-in-law, John Salusbury in a letter to the Privy Council, against the malicious accusations of his rivals. His friends, it was said in 1590–1, were intent on protecting his credit and reputation. He had never shown any disloyalty or disobedience, it was declared, and should, therefore, not be allowed to become the prey of his enemies.[44]

One of the most notable examples of a man struggling to defend his reputation was Sir John Wynn who, in 1615, wished to be exonerated after being accused (in his absence) in the Council in the Marches of oppressing his tenants and, on the same occasion

when he expected the Lord Chancellor to investigate an accusa-
tion made against him for maladministration. 'I showed him [the
prosecuting counsel] how much I thought my reputation to be
wronged . . . and how hardlie he dealt with me in that he valued
my credit so little in the face of the country.'[45] In entirely different
circumstances, William Morgan, bishop of St Asaph, defended his
honour against the same assertive squire in the following words:
'and my confydent trust ys that God wyll not p'mytt anythynge to
be commytted agaynst me but that which shalbe for my good,
eather in thys world or in the world to com'.[46] This worthy prelate
realized that his primary obligation was to defend the integrity of
the Church and to safeguard his own reputation as the spiritual
leader of his people against the status-conscious layman disposed
to destroy him.

In a broader perspective, Richard Davies, bishop of St David's –
possibly Morgan's mentor in his early days as a cleric in that
diocese – attempted to explain much of the spiritual malaise in his
diocese by attacking those in secular authority who, in his view,
failed to 'observe any good order'. In his report on the diocese in
1570 he blamed the sheriffs for abusing or abandoning their
authority which, in turn, adversely undermined discipline in the
Church.[47] Further, he questioned the integrity of men in power,
and although he expressed some positive criticisms much of what
he had to say only served to clarify his own problems in the
diocese. In his sermon on the death of Walter Devereux, first earl
of Essex (1577), he heavily criticized local government officials
because of their lack of integrity when exercising their authority:

> . . . where they were put in trust and made officers in the commonwelth,
> they haue not iudged rightly . . . but delt parcially and corruptly, agaynst
> law and conscience . . . they neuer thinke of any reconing to be made
> howe they behaued themselues in their authoritie . . . but contrarilie
> unreasonably walke after the pleasures and riches of thys worlde . . .
> How thinke you what is it to committe authoritie to such men? Is it any
> better then to commit a sworde to a madde mans hand . . . [48]

This strongly worded attack followed many setbacks which
Davies had experienced owing to the opposition of some
prominent lay administrators in his diocese, such as Sir John
Perrot and the lawyer Fabian Phillips, but Marmaduke
Middleton, his successor, in 1593 bluntly blamed him for not
attending to the needs of the diocese.[49] Davies's comments on
the impact of misused authority reflect contemporary views on
the desire among administrators to seek the main chance. He

emphasized the central role of the commonwealth and the need to exercise jurisdiction equitably within it. He painted all administrators with the same brush: describing them as constant abusers of authority which rendered their service ineffective and allowed them to pursue their private interests freely. Davies was aware of the neglect of legally constituted authority and his reaction to it was prompted by his contempt for his own enemies. By any measure he considered that the violation of authority was detrimental to the fortunes of the state and that nobility, responsible for maintaining that state, sprang from divine approval and the natural virtues inherited by the governor. Davies's comments on the features of nobility are interspersed with his precepts on moral and spiritual aptitudes:

> First he putteth them in remembrance of a matter comonly forgotten amongst great men, that is, that the rule is given them of God, and that their authoritie is from the most hyghe. Whereupon followeth that they shoulde apply their authoritie to set out his glorie and honour, who placed them in so high a rowme, and who also will trye their workes and search out their purposes.[50]

Davies pertinently commented on obligation in the exercise of authority; it should be impartial and the ennobled privileged to use it were characterized by prudence, justice, fortitude and temperance which were safeguarded by 'true religion'. They were, he observed, echoing the thoughts of his contemporaries on these matters, 'bulwarks and walles of defence of the whole realm', and justice – their prime feature – was 'precious, and commendable in all men, and especially in the Nobilitie, who by reason of authoritie, may also with all his might, succour and comfort the helplesse and oppressed'. The bishop's observations aimed to elevate the concept of authority and the code of conduct associated with it, and his declarations were largely defensive.

This defensive attitude was amply demonstrated in the responses of laymen in power to their equals in local administration. The norm was the 'good governor', a variously interpreted phenomenon in county society. As Owen Salusbury of Rug explained to Robert Vaughan of Hengwrt when excusing his non-attendance at Merioneth Quarter Sessions at a critical time soon after the execution of Charles I:

> . . . I do therefore desire that my indisposition may not be an obstruction of meeting for the countrey's good . . . assuring you that there are many eyes upon the actions of them in commission in this

poor county. I do address myself unto you more particularly in regard you are he that best knows this countrey having longest lived in it, and therefore ought most to study the good thereof.[51]

His directive to Vaughan to conduct the administration of law in his absence reveals several qualities which he considered necessary when attempting to achieve stability.

Administering the courts of Quarter Sessions was regarded as a means of maintaining equilibrium in the local community, protecting its welfare, upholding the powers and prestige of commissioners of the peace who were, in their own right, regarded as men of integrity, acknowledged for their distinguished service and experience in office, and emphasizing the two prime features of legitimate leadership, namely authority and obligation. It was with such a goal in mind that Sir Henry Sidney in 1580 called upon Sir Edward Stradling and his associates, in a period of 'brawls and contentions' in Glamorgan, to settle the country 'and to deale soe by yor wisdomes and discressions . . . for the preventinge of the mischife and inconvenience that otherwise . . . may growe to the disturbance of the peace and disquiet of the countye'.[52] The squire who appealed to his mentor 'to provide for me and my credit' was eager to seek protection in order that 'my family be not forced first to yield for that will turn to my great reproof and shame in the country'.[53] When soliciting the support of Sir William Maurice of Clenennau in the county election of 1620 the wily young lawyer, John Griffith of Cefnamwlch in Llŷn, gave expression to the proper conduct which gentlemen should adopt towards each other so as to uphold their reputations. 'I waygh other mens Creditt in the same ballance wth my owne', he explained, 'I honour and respect you & . . . what yow may worthily doe in my behalfe you shall finde shalbe faithfullye acknowledged.'[54] Despite the personal ambitions of such individuals it is certain that an awareness of personal honour and status combined with experience of power in office would normally be reflected in the social relations between the gentry.

The Theory of Government and the Concept of Order

Attached to these images of honour are the exercise and control of authority. Concepts of authority in Tudor Wales are normally associated with the aim of the administrative settlement imposed on the country in the 1530s. In the preamble to the Act of Union 1536 it is formally stated that the Crown 'by the authority' of

Parliament, had 'ordained, enacted and established' that Wales
was to be assimilated with the realm of England. Moreover, in the
statute of 1576 appointing one additional justice of assize in each
Welsh circuit of Great Sessions, it was declared by the authority of
Parliament that the Queen and her successors were empowered to
exercise 'full power, prerogative and authority' to appoint justices
in Wales.[55] Authority worked downwards from the monarchy and
was delegated to its agencies in the provinces, hence the emphasis
in local administrative records on the authority granted to the
Crown's officials to maintain the 'Queen's peace'. Reference was
made continually on the need to preserve equitable government
under the Crown. Lord Herbert was unyielding in this matter
when comparing the governments of the Low Countries and
England in the 1630s:

> Neither is there any danger our nation should be drawn to approve
> their form of government; the wisest of them find that republics instead
> of one king have many, and we acknowledge His Majesty's government
> so temperate that we are happier than any nation living.[56]

In this context power and justice were vested in the Crown's
representatives even though Herbert was writing in a period of
non-parliamentary rule when tensions in domestic and foreign
affairs were running high.

Authority was all-embracing and had its impact on all ranks in
society. Whatever the nature of local insurrections in England
might be, their leaders never questioned the right of the monarchy
to govern and their duty to obey. These two factors are formative
in any evaluation of attitudes in Elizabethan England and Wales.
By the latter half of the sixteenth century the Tudor policy of
investing authority in the Crown was a major characteristic of the
new Protestant realm. At a time when the old aristocracy was
losing its grip the new nobility emerged to replace it and the royal
court became the chief pivot of power and influence under the
Crown. An aid to the acquisition of power was the accumulation
of wealth usually, but not exclusively, defined in terms of landed
property. Thus emerged the *noblesse oblige*, the obligations which
noble birth placed upon a man of honour or, as Edwart ap Raff
described him: 'Swyddwr a chredans iddo' ('A creditable
official').[57] The power and influence bestowed on Welsh *uchelwyr*
implied that they were aware of what they themselves were
expected, by the very nature of their status and reputation, to offer
the community protected by them. Authority at all levels implied
the acknowledgement and practice of responsibilities and they

were obligatory in a public as well as a private capacity, hence the anxiety expressed by men in prime positions, such as Henry, earl of Pembroke, his successor Lord Zouche and a host of other prominent gentry who felt that their grasp of power was failing when confronted by opposition. Pembroke, for example, was fiercely opposed by Henry Townshend, second justice of Chester, in 1600 because, as he declared, 'I was not willing to forego the presidency of Wales, to weary me out of it . . . [he] plotted to diminish the authority I now have'.[58] Zouche, likewise, feared men in privileged positions in north-east Wales since they often hindered good government, thereby 'wise men have been wearied to seek reformation'.[59] These two examples reflect the pressures on the Council in the Marches when its authority was being seriously undermined and stable administration threatened. In theory, such power was constant and resolute and could not be demolished.

In all its aspects legitimate authority was not a virtue which an individual bestowed upon himself; it was rather acquired, granted and respected by others. Authority was conferred on the worthy, normally by a sovereign power, but in the latter half of the sixteenth century it was usually defined in a delegative capacity as the means by which leading gentlemen, or *uchelwyr* in a Welsh context, justified their existence as men of substance and degree, morally and materially. Fundamentally, it was an acknowledgement of precedence rather than authority that accorded to the public official his primacy. Tied to that were a number of other attributes such as lineage, honour and integrity with their subsidiary qualities, magnanimity, service and leadership. Conspicuous though authority was as a factor in the lives of the Welsh *uchelwyr* it was not by any measure hereditary. While it is true that office did pass on in succession, often ascribing to the heir a position of grandeur and superiority, it is undeniable that lawfully constituted authority entailed exercising acquired virtues, not usually tied to birth. It presupposed the possession of innate qualities, many of which were practised privately, but the prime features of authority were demonstrated in a public capacity. Virtue, in whatever form, was revealed most explicitly in the relationship between the individual and his kinsmen, neighbours and, in a broader context, the Crown and its agencies.[60] So confident was Gervase Babington in 1575 that Sir Edward Stradling was a paragon of virtue that he attributed to him the highest accolade possible that any secular landowner and benefactor could wish for:

The Lorde hathe made you able to doe much good, and, his mercies considered, I doubt not will make you willinge . . . Vertue being furdred maketh her founders famous – famous, I say, in this world, and renowned ever in an other world, neither ever persisteth the memory of the righteouse.[61]

Underlying these factors was the concept of order which, in the opinion of contemporary commentators, could only be preserved if the rigid social stratification was respected. The 'deferential society', as it was called, acknowledged the superiority of divine power and it is richly illustrated in the literary works of the sixteenth and early seventeenth centuries. The emphasis on authoritarianism and stability was a paramount feature in the way in which those positioned in the upper reaches of gentle society viewed themselves. Authority, to them, was an inherent virtue, inbuilt and revealing the most forceful manifestations of their superiority.[62]

The properties of this *uchelwriaeth* presuppose that the essential qualities of leadership sprang from the exercise of authority within the established order. While it normally appeared in the routine manner in which Welsh gentry set about their tasks in keeping public order it was also manifested in those qualities which effective leadership embraced. That leadership was measured in terms of the loyalty that the *uchelwyr* commanded in their native community; it is principally regional or provincial and features a deep-seated conservatism and insularity. In that context authoritarianism implied the cultivation and exercise of bene-volent and courtly virtues within the *llys* or *plasty*, the fount, in the local context, of legitimate regional power. Authority for the Welsh gentleman had always been localized, emerging from the principles that governed sovereignty tied usually to the political patrimony or the medieval Welsh kingdom (*gwlad*/*dominium*). This territorial entity or region derived its importance from the cohesiveness of its social features rather than its political function, an area with which inhabitants could identify historically and culturally. The *gwlad* or province or shire, its sixteenth-century equivalent, was composed of a group of neighbourhoods which formed a focus for stability and continuity. The influence and power of a sizeable proportion of gentry extended well beyond shire boundaries. The power of kinship, however, still reigned supreme in the interrelations between families and gave the distinct impression that the identification with patrimony con-tinued to assume importance in the Welsh regions. In medieval

Welsh law the king (*brenin*) enjoyed paramount authority. The commote was the basic unit of territorial administration, its pivot being the royal *llys* and the jurisdiction exercised was royal. Legal doctrine, as defined in Welsh law, stipulated that the *brenin* enjoyed exclusive royal rights. The claims of the *uchelwyr* to authority extended back to the *priodorion* (free clansmen) of the twelfth and thirteenth centuries who ceased to be nomadic and had settled permanently on the kindred patrimony (*treftadaeth*). Features of their landholding displayed a deference to a direct and unbroken line of descent. They were the nobility (*brëyriaid*) who normally claimed ancestry from the ancient kings of Wales, and they stood within a network of kin relations based on the ties of blood and obligation.[63]

Although it is inappropriate to describe this emergent social group as a 'class' in the later Middle Ages, they formed a vigorous and aggressive section of the kindred community, varying in their material wealth but retaining strong regional affinities and commanding respect among their own people. The most prominent feature in their social and cultural make-up was the acquisition of landed property based on, but remaining essentially outside, the kindred nexus and built upon inheritance, marriage, conveyance and purchase. These kindred affinities were particularly strong and, depending on circumstances, often led to confrontation or a stubborn defence of their interests. Political loyalties were often shortlived down to the loss of Welsh independence in 1282; thereafter, excepting the years of the Glyndŵr Revolt, the emergent *uchelwyr* were characterized chiefly by their support of the Plantagenets and Lancastrians in military campaigns at home and abroad. In their respective regions, however, the ties of patrimony enabled them to reinforce their status by asserting leadership and the acquisition of public office. Their leadership usually involved extending control over the *plaid* or retainers, representing the naked force that *uchelwyr* could use in their localities. The influence and sheer assertiveness of such heads of households enabled them to advance their fortunes, regardless of the strength of their allegiances in the Glyndŵr Revolt, and their business acumen assisted them to survive the depressed economic conditions. In the course of the fourteenth century they had developed a sense of corporate responsibility within shires of the northern Principality but the growth of royal power in the Marches as well as the increasing absenteeism among other independent lords led to law and order being maintained by a new landed order (see Chapter 1, pp. 3–7)

One explanation of the role of regional loyalties is that the ties of neighbourhood were as important as the ties of blood or kinship and their structure was based on patterns of economic life and social relations. It was within this context that law and order was normally maintained, hence the importance of authority as applied to the region governed by a corpus of native legal customs. Thus developed the concept of lordship (*arglwyddiaeth*), the powers granted to an *arglwydd* (*dominus*), which implied a territorial lord in Welsh law. Leading *uchelwyr* of the later medieval and early modern periods were themselves regarded in bardic sources as the descendants of those who possessed regal power. They viewed their territorial possessions as ancient lordships gradually being converted into estates based on a money economy. For them regal status (*brenhiniaeth*), aristocracy (*penaduriaeth*) and gentility (*bonedd*) were, by their very nature, sucessive features of their development. Individual free clansmen asserted their power over dependants, tenants and bondmen, a common feature in the Principality and Marches.[64]

The order of gentility (*bonheddig*), as its origins suggest, regarded those who were of high status as descending from noble stock, and they were usually described as such. This new social rank grew out of family groupings and pedigrees assumed a legal function. By the Tudor period the development in genealogical activity reached amazing, even frenzied, proportions and displayed honour in its most overt fashion. Not only were traditional Welsh families ennobled but the closer ties with England, the Council in the Marches and the royal court led to further researches in heraldry, genealogy and regional and family history. Families became more ostentatious owing to the attention which they gave to their heritage and their accessories, such as titles, heraldry and armorial bearings, and establishing ancestral connections with noteworthy events and similar embellishments was a common feature within their ranks. It was Walter Corbett who requested that Sir Edward Stradling, owing to his expertise in genealogical matters, might instruct him to trace his family's pedigree: 'we cannot as yette come to the marke we shoott at', he declared, 'and soe, by the advise of my owncle . . . [I] writte unto you . . . that you would geve us some instruction, as allso your pettigree, whereby we maye the better come to o'r purpose'.[65]

The status of those claiming *uchelwriaeth* remained and their authority was usually recognized in the less military and more staid atmosphere of courts of law and administrative institutions. One feature which distinguishes Welsh from English pedigrees in the early modern period is that, in England, emphasis was placed primarily on the senior branch and the practice of primogeniture whereas in Wales attention was also given to cadet families, usually established within closely knit community patterns. Collateral as well as agnatic features clearly emerge, and this wealth in Welsh genealogical sources was identified essentially with inalienable birthright (*genedigaeth-fraint*) rather than material ostentation. Blood ties were closely guarded and the *uchelwriaeth* of medieval Wales survived partly because old clan associations were still revered. Nevertheless, with the formal adoption of primogeniture in 1543 (not an entirely new feature in Welsh landholding), families grew in influence and authority and they often claimed to have derived their privileges from those whom they firmly considered to be illustrious forebears.[66]

Although Sir Robert Filmer advocated patriarchalism and paternalism in *Patriarcha* (in manuscript) in the early 1640s, the basic concepts were already regarded as a central feature in the political thought of both the English and Welsh gentry. All authority was established on the familial perceptions of politics. The holder of the Crown could claim absolute obedience and political authority was associated with patriarchal government within the family (see Chapter 6, pp. 203–10). The king could command obedience because he enjoyed power as a paternal prerogative. Parts of this theory were expounded by Sir Thomas Elyot in *The Book named the Governor* (1531), a handbook for rulers where, in the title to chapter 2, he stated that 'our sovereign governor ought to be in a public weal. And what damage hath happened where a multitude hath had equal authority without any sovereign.' He proceeded to explain further in the text: 'For who can deny but that all thing in Heaven and earth is governed by one God, by one perpetual order, by one providence?' The words were similar to those expressed by others, not least Sir John Hayward who, in 1603, wrote as follows:

> The whole world is nothing but a great state; a state is no other than a great family; and a family is no other than a great body. As one God ruleth the world, one master the family, as all the members of one body receaveth both sense and motion from one head . . . so it seemeth no less natural that one state should be governed by one commander.[67]

These views were echoed in many other sources which purported to define and interpret royal power as vested in nobility. It emerged clearly in Sir William Maurice's plea to Justice Richard Barker in 1612 in a dispute involving Maurice brought before the

Merioneth Great Sessions. He feared that his rivals had influenced Barker but, if the suit were to be heard in the Chancery Court of Equity as well as the assizes, he hoped to obtain justice in both, and he continued: 'I desire no more nor deserve no lesse . . . whereupon I ground my greatest title on my sou'aigne Lo. and Master King James who . . . is the fountaine of Justice in whose name, I humbly crave . . . that I may have justice.'[68]

Localism and Particularism in the Defence of Honour

These aspects of honour, authority and the social order had significant repercussions in the provinces. Despite the relative peace enjoyed in Elizabethan England before 1585, when war broke out with Spain, serious problems continued to threaten internal security. Not only did the defence of the realm leave its impact on the provinces; the handling of such matters in the localities themselves also had significant repercussions. Social commentators had become aware of the benefits of peace from the 1560s onwards. Obedience to the sovereign power and loyalty to the authority which it delegated to its agencies in the localities, in turn, preserved the organic unity of the realm (see Chapter 4, pp. 151–3). The danger of revolt caused perplexity and the fear of opposition to royal power after 1534 was increased in the 1580s by the need to enforce civil obedience during the war with Spain. Added to this were economic and cultural factors. In the works of Thomas Starkey and Sir Richard Morison and *The Book of Homilies* (1547), the dangers of sedition, treason and rebellion were emphasized. John Cheke's comment in *The Hurt of Sedicion* also had the same objective: 'some must rule, some must obey, euery man may not bear lyke stroke for euerye man is not lyke wyse, and they that haue sene moste, and beste habyll to beare it, and of iust dealynge beside, be most fite to rule.'[69]

The reprimand issued on a later occasion by the beleaguered Henry Herbert, earl of Pembroke, to the Caernarfonshire deputy-lieutenants echoed similar sentiments (see p. 67).[70] It was in this context, which highlights the role of responsible men in public office, that humanist scholars, who were aware of the need to preserve the realm's best interests, addressed their patrons; prefaces to religious works, written usually in Welsh and Latin, reveal how highly valued were those privileged individuals who maintained the unity of the Protestant state. In the Elizabethan age priority was given to the need for stability. Bishop Richard Davies urged his countrymen to express joy because the Queen's authority in parliament had revived their privileges in Wales.[71] In days of war that devout Roman Catholic Dr John Davies of Brecon drew attention to the benefits of peace and security to the secular world:

A hawdd yw canfod fôd yr heddwch a'r llonyddwch yn achosiol o bôb daeôni o'r a allo bôd ym mysc dynion. Canys heddwch yw y Cyfarwydd a'r Llywiawdr sydd yn cadarnhau pôb glân gyfeillach; ac hebddei ny's gall fôd nêb ryw gydfasnach ym mhlith pobl y byd, na dim cyfrannu meddylieu . . . Yr heddwch, a'r cytundeb y sydd ynn peri pôb elwaidd drapherth, a chyfnêwid rhwng teyrnas a theyrnas, rhwng pobloedd a phobloedd . . . A'r anghytundeb a'r anhêddwch beth a wnâ hitheu, onyd gyrru pawb benbenn; i ymleassu ae gilydd, ac i waethu pawb arr eu gilydd . . . Canys nyni a'n drycanian yn anad neb, sydd ynn rhoi peunyddiol gynhaliaeth i Lys Cynghor Cyphinyddion Cymry, ac ony bei ni a'n llîd a'n cynhen tu ac at eu gilydd . . . ef a allei llawer gwr ynn byw wrth gyfreith, fyned i gylôra, ac o's mynnei i fwyâra yn lle ei gyfreithwra.[72]

[It is easy to find that the peace and quietude are the causes of all good that can be between men. For peace is the guide and ruler which confirms all virtuous fellowships, and without it there can be no co-trading between people in the world, and no sharing of minds . . . The peace and concord and exchanges between kingdom and kingdom, between people and people . . . And the disagreement and instability, what does it do but create conflict to oppress each other and to harm each other . . . Because we and our evil disposition more than anything give daily sustenance to the Court of the Council in the Marches of Wales, and were it not for our rancour and discord towards each other . . . many a man who lives by the law could gather earth-nuts and, if he wished, gather blackberries instead of litigating.]

That hearty colonial pioneer, William Vaughan of Llangyndeyrn, later expressed similar sentiments. Legal entanglements over land matters caused friction among families and kindred but it is equally noteworthy that the exercise of authority in private matters was tempered by the will to maintain cordial relations and avoid unnecessary litigation. 'Law shall not make me dislike with you', Henry Johnes wrote to his father-in-law, Sir William Maurice of Clenennau, in 1607.[73] Moreover, the quarrel between Sir Edward Stradling and Carne of Ewenni ('this boylinge hatred') caused Henry Herbert so much anxiety in 1575 that he was prepared to travel from Wiltshire to Glamorgan to arbitrate between them.[74] Sir Richard Bulkeley of Beaumaris did not consider that a minor land dispute with his kinsman, Sir John Wynn of Gwydir, merited abandoning amicable kindred relations:

'[If] that patch of land', he maintained, 'is the case of unkindnes
. . . in my simple opynion it were no wysdom to loose so good a
kynsman for such a trifle.' 'All men wonder that such trifles should
make us strangers', he ruefully continued, 'w'ch shall not be on
my parte; for whatsoever you have righte to yow shall have w'thout
lawe.'[75] Sir William Jones, the eminent lawyer of Castellmarch,
responded to Wynn's property claims in this matter, indicating the
mood of the time among men eager, in their own personal
interests, to establish amicable relations in family affairs. He
deplored the fact that friction between kindred could cause so
much disruption:

> soe near kinsmen of such discretion as you both be, should be drawn
> by such small variance to separate in love and friendship, and yt cannot
> be w'thout tuche of discredit to him uppon whose p'te the offence is
> offred and greef to those that love you both and contentment to others
> that envie yo'r agreement.[76]

The practice of arbitration had not decayed, for it was
customary in certain areas to employ local gentry, especially those
steeped in genealogy and tradition, to arbitrate in disputes
between heirs over property. Arbitration was a social form of
exerting authority – the personal relations between the arbitrator
and the two parties involved helped them reach an agreement that
would be acceptable in law. It was often regarded as the most
amicable way of dealing with the multifarious problems that beset
landholders without recourse to legal proceedings. 'Kindred'
offences had become common and the Council in the Marches
was criticized for conducting suits unworthy of its status. In
addition to gross maladministration, which was often reported but
not always supported by evidence, in the courts of law and
government institutions the misuse of authority was rife in
personal affairs. Since landed property was doubtless the chief
creator of wealth for the majority of privileged families it was
jealously eyed and every opportunity was taken to benefit from it
by fair means or foul. Hence, the exercise of authority was often
oppressive; it seemed to sever relations and to deepen animosities.
One of the qualities of the worthy gentleman in authority,
according to William Vaughan, was that 'he must be endowed with
mercy to forgive the trespass of his friends and servants', meaning
that he should use his power and authority for the benefit of
either.[77] Sir John Perrot of Haroldston, it was said in 1604, 'has
exceeded his authority' in matters relating to investigating
recusants' lands.[78] So formidable a character had George Barlow

of Llanddewi Velfrey and Lampeter Velfrey in Pembrokeshire
become to his tenants that he attempted to convert their freehold
tenure into copyhold, and later he became involved in a costly
legal battle with his dependants at Narberth which his son was
eventually to discover to his disadvantage.[79] Several other
examples of similar reactions could be cited to illustrate the
devious means employed by *uchelwyr* to advance their own
interests, but not always to their profit. Abused authority revealed
a native gentry who, because of the lack of a native aristocracy,
wielded tremendous authority and exploited a situation that gave
them all the benefits that they received. The English commentator
William Harrison referred to the litigious nature of the Welsh
freeholders and, with some derision, described their avid desire to
defend their interests in courts of law:

> . . . our Welshmen doe exceed of all that ever I heard, for you shall here
> and there have some one odd poor David of them given so much to
> contention and strife that without all respect of charges he will up to
> London, though he go barelegged by the way . . . [80]

The most prominent Welsh gentry were also attracted by
litigation in the expectation that they might benefit at the expense
of tenants and kinsmen, but publicly they exercised their authority
in more auspicious surroundings, especially if they chose to serve
as members of parliament and officials in regional institutions,
and it was in that capacity that they were able to put their
authority to good use (see Chapter 2, pp. 74–85). Gradually,
during the century following the Acts of Union, there was an
increasing tendency to abide by legal procedure in matters of
debate or contention. As members of parliament the most
conspicuous gentry rose to prominent positions within the
political structure of Wales. They not only asserted authority
vested in them by royal consent but also displayed in the House of
Commons that dual brand of regional authority as the elected
representatives in the realm and as leaders of communities
representing their shire and borough constituencies. Although the
awareness of a parliamentary tradition only gradually emerged
among the Welsh members, perceptions of authority influenced
members of the House of Commons from early days. Despite
erratic attendances in the early days the increasing familiarity of
members of well-established families with the House's business,
especially after the 1570s, became an important feature; and their
membership was considered a privilege beyond any other that
Tudor government could offer. It appears that only a few of them

had strong connections at court and that most factious rivalries were locally based. They have been described as 'politically backward, their horizons stretching little further than their own back-yards'.[81] It has also been suggested that their 'political inertia' in their early years in parliament stemmed from the 'racial persecution' they and their predecessors had suffered in the past and that they did not wish to jeopardize their new privileges. It is further suggested that they considered themselves 'a community apart, both in language and temperament'. Such views are partly correct. Doubtless a large proportion of Welsh members of parliament were absentee and conservative in the mid-sixteenth century, yet their new experiences as elected members and officials made them conscious of their obligations to the shire community. The spirit of localism did not necessarily inhibit them from revealing an exuberance in the exercise of many public duties. Although John Griffith of Cefnamwlch explained to Sir William Maurice of Clenennau the value to the community of parliamentary representation, it was evidently a position which individuals regarded as a private means of advancing personal interests. 'You knowe best the experience that is obtained by beinge of parliament', he declared, 'and that every true lover of his countrie should endeavoure to do service therein.'[82] On this occasion he solicited Maurice's support against the Wynns of Gwydir in the county election of 1620, and it is evident that it was the quest for power that spurred him on. The growth of faction and parliamentary contests conducted by a vigorous and ambitious group of families enabled them to manipulate authority purely for private reasons, as in the case of Denbighshire in 1558 and 1601, Radnorshire in 1572, Montgomeryshire in 1588 and Cardiganshire in 1601.[83]

As previously observed power politics and faction were rife (Chapter 1, pp. 40–3). For example, in Anglesey and, in Merioneth in 1571, the contest between the Llwyn and Rug factions, caused the Council in the Marches concern during the election, to the extent that the 'great labour' and 'outward signs and tokens' forced it to authorize the sheriff and justices of the peace to prevent weapons being carried on that occasion and to warn them that they would be responsible for any breach of the peace that might happen.[84] In Anglesey, tension grew between the English Bulkeley family of Cheshire and members of native stocks in 1588. The contest which ensued between Sir Richard Bulkeley III and his enemies involved disputes over land and public authority. The charges brought against him by Lewis ab Owain of

Y Frondeg that he had seriously abused his authority in matters relating to defence, that he had contacts with a 'dangerous' recusant, and that he had colluded with pirates, might have been damaging to his reputation. He was summoned to Star Chamber but, after being censured, was sent back to Anglesey to defend the island. Despite these irritating circumstances and the allegation that he was a man 'void of that godlye fear & zeale of Justice . . . and carried awaie only with ambition & desire of bearinge of the cheifest swaie', Bulkeley retained his power and his position after 1592 was unassailable.[85]

In all these examples the basic features were localism, particularism, bonds of kinship and the ensuing feuds, all displaying crude attempts to defend honour. Where the prize had to be acquired by force there was contention which threatened law and order. Whether legitimate authority, on occasions of this kind or in matters involving land disputes, threatened to cause irreparable damage to stable conditions in the 'county community' is debatable because it is doubtful whether most of the contending factions had sufficient armed support to offset the agencies of local government successfully. Remarkable though the abuse of authority was, it appears not to have reduced regions to any serious disruption at any time during the early modern period. Those commentators who dwelled excessively on the prevalence of disorder exaggerated for a specific purpose. The most notable was Dr David Lewis who, on two occasions in 1576, referred to the evils of retaining, especially in Glamorgan, and the continued abuse of power in the older Marcher areas by then converted into shires. The situation was so critical, Lewis declared, that 'the authority of the Council [in the Marches] there is not regarded as it hath been'.[86] He feared that the pivot of Tudor government in Wales and the borderlands was largely ineffective in combating lawlessness. The problem of corrupt juries there had concerned the government in 1534, as legislation in that year revealed.[87]

The report on conditions in the Marches was echoed in a bill of complaint by Rees Arney of Newry against the staunch Roman Catholic Edward Morgan of Llantarnam concerning the misuse of the jury system, in the Council in the Marches: 'it wilbe hard to get an indifferent Jurye for tryall in this countie ye or any Jurye at all considering ye kindreds, allyances and other causes of affection to me and them'.[88] Such problems were the legacy of a close-knit kindred structure which, despite the change in law, still maintained a powerful hold over community life in most Welsh rural areas. While it is true that administration in this period showed signs of inefficiency and that a network of gentry relationships was created for purely private reasons, nevertheless, the framework of government seemed not to be severely affected and the machinery continued to function adequately when the new Stuart dynasty was installed in 1603. That was largely due not only to the well-established nature of such institutions by that time, but to the authority exercised by the *uchelwyr*, whose leadership and protective qualities were paramount. When Sir Richard Bulkeley was described as a person who 'had powerful friends at Court and had the gentry and commonalty of the county at his service', he was acknowledged as a dominant magnate possessing twin powers which sprang from royal circles and the Anglesey community.[89]

In south Wales the response to the execution of the second earl of Essex and his henchman Sir Gelly Meyrick was by no measure flattering, as Sir Richard Lewkenor's letter to Sir Robert Cecil records:

> The Earl of Essex was greatest in South Wales . . . I assure you the fall of the Earl, in those parts where he was greatest, is not grieved at, because I do generally hear that he was . . . often very chargeable and burdensome with them; and Sir Gelly Merrick himself lived by such oppression and overruling over them that they do not only rejoice at his fall but curse him bitterly.[90]

Lewkenor's view presents two pictures, one of absolute authority brought to bear by landed possessions and territorial aggrandizement; the other of hostility felt as a consequence of the misuse of that authority and the way in which it corrupted others. Corruption in office and all it entailed in the free acquisition of power was deplored by Lord Zouche, who was frustrated by factious dealings in the Council at Ludlow.[91] He came to power at a sensitive time in the Council's history when authority was monopolized by groups of lawyers and when the reputation of the Council in the borderlands was threatened by increased opposition. Essex was often the subject of complaint but George Owen regarded him, Henry Herbert and Edward, earl of Worcester, to be 'chiefe Patrons & carefull conservators & protectors of this poore Contrie of Wales'.[92] Again, in Pembrokeshire, Sir John Perrot of Carew, placed lower down the social scale, was accused in 1578, of 'using great authority, making his luste a law in all things, and to all men, discountenancing the officials and encouraging offenders, not punishing them'.[93] When Thomas Churchyard wrote in 1587 of the gentry of Wales as 'the strength and securitie of the land' in whom 'but trust and credit stand' he was distinctly unaware of the daily routine and real motives of landed proprietors of whatever rank.[94] It was often a harsh and turbulent age when ambition, above all else, ruled men's desires and outlook. The introduction into the commission of the peace in all counties of Wales of inferior magistrates, despite the concern shown by the Council in the Marches, prolonged a situation whereby government was, in part, controlled by unworthy men.[95] It is hardly surprising that Dr David Lewis and others rebuked the government for its handling of affairs in Wales. Individuals had assumed prominence to the detriment of others, some because they were aware that they only could provide effective leadership and were prepared to declare that publicly, others because, if they did not assert their power, they would be supplanted by their rivals. Sir Richard Bulkeley combined both as he explained in a letter to Thomas Cromwell in 1535:

> And further may hit like you to call to remembraunce how yor m't'ship spake unto my s'v'nt . . . at his last beyng wth you. That is to saie that I wold suffer no man to dwell in this cu'trey but my self. Sir I trust yor m't'ship beleveth non suche thinges in me, ff'r I was never abowt to expulse no man owt of this cu'trey nor never intend to doe but wold be gladde from tyme to tyme to s've my sov'aign lord to the utt'most of my symple power.[96]

He was aware of his own abilities but also wished to assert his power in view of the opposition he encountered from Edward Gruffydd of Penrhyn and his allies.

Honour and the Concepts of Lordship, Order and the State

The concept of lordship (*arglwyddiaeth*) played a formative part in the ordered society in Wales and the Marches in the Middle Ages. It was the basis of authority, and when it ceased or was threatened this undermined the framework of social relationships which exercised control in the localities. The close links established between the lord (*uchelwr*) and his dependants made lordship a vital factor in the community structure. If it was abandoned the vacuum that ensued might cause dislocation and turbulence. Similarly, in a late-sixteenth-century situation, in comparison with the patrimony controlled by *uchelwyr*, lordship, as displayed in their performance of public duties, needed to maintain its coherence through the exercise of control and authority. Failure to do this had a greater impact on the dependants of those who, by force of circumstances, gradually estranged themselves from that patrimony that had sustained them and their forebears than it had on government at regional level. It was at once a denial and an acquisition of authority; a withdrawal from the responsibilities that were considered fundamental to the welfare of the family and the cultural well-being of the regional community in the decade following the Tudor settlement.[97]

Humanist sources continually refer to the withdrawal of patronage and a change of attitudes, principally because they were deeply concerned with the lack of vision among *uchelwyr* with regard to raising the language to the level of other Renaissance languages in western Europe (see Chapter 1, pp. 54–7). It was Richard Davies who declared that a sense of honour had been abandoned and had yielded to feckless apathy towards good order and discipline. 'Often in Wales, though the law marks it not', he declared, 'the mansion of the nobleman is a refuge for thieves . . . [and] but for the help and protection of the nobleman there would be but little thieving in Wales'.[98] Competitiveness and self-assertiveness could destroy honour and undermine legitimate authority and make *uchelwyr* unworthy subjects. The Privy Council wrote to the sheriffs lamenting excessive process and unreasonable borrowing rates, which it attributed to greedy commercial dealers and usurers. The Welsh professional poets revealed the basic weakness of governing families; and this was the complaint too of those directly appointed by the Queen to govern Wales and to supervise the efficiency of local and regional government.[99]

The authority that had been prostituted, it was alleged, was that derived from the Godhead and bestowed on the well-endowed members of the community privileged to exercise their Christian citizenship sanctioned by divine overlordship. The obligation to maintain order was based on the inborn qualities of those invested with powers to govern. The royal official was essentially God's representative, and the concept of authority thus emerged as a vital component in the 'nation state', the central political feature in the growth of national independence. Thomas Cranmer declared that 'the gentleman's children are meant to have the knowledge of government and rule in the commonwealth', and it is in that context that the basis of government in Elizabethan Wales needs to be evaluated.[100] Government at the highest level in the regional community was the preserve of the *uchelwr*. The essence of his power lay in liberty to govern, and the latter half of the sixteenth century was characterized by the need to apply that authority under the Crown. The political entity within which this authority was exercised was the realm comprising England and Wales as they were constituted after the political settlement in 1536–43. The nation was drawn within the broader framework of the nation-state which evolved in the 1530s, emerging out of the debris of feudal and kindred structures, and the damaging effects of retaining, diversity of jurisdictions and particularism. Not that the social and political framework ever reduced Wales entirely to a state of law and order. The power of the kindred affinity continued to play a dominant role in the Welsh countryside but, by the latter half of the sixteenth century, it was being increasingly controlled by a government forced to act by internal and external forces, determined to extend the benefits of Tudor order to Wales and to use that country as an effective means of protecting national independence.[101]

These concepts relate also to the conceived images of the nation-state. The basis of the national sovereign state (as G. R. Elton interpreted it) had been truly laid in the Reformation Parliament (1529–36). The powers of the Crown increased as the authority of the papacy diminished. The actions taken to bully the Pope into submission reached their peak in 1534. Two years later, after measures had been taken to lessen the power of independent jurisdiction in Wales and the Marches, the policy of assimilation gave official sanction to social and administrative trends that had been in existence during the previous century. Consequently, the views of Welsh commentators of the Elizabethan era on the nature and success of the system were altogether positive. Their own participation in the administrative sector enabled them to come to terms with it, and to benefit from its most progressive features. By the 1570s Elizabethan government in the Welsh shires had been well established. Despite the discordant note sounded by Dr David Lewis in 1576 the institutions of law and administration were in reasonably good working order.[102] It is true that his views of the condition of the Marcher areas of south-east Wales confirmed the evidence in other official sources that the quality of government left much to be desired, but essentially the mechanism of government was maintained. At the same time authority had caused the more eligible among shire governors to protect their own interests. Office gave them power and their eagerness to maintain their domination led them to exert that power in a dual capacity benefiting themselves and the state.

In 1572 it was reported that corrupt practice among sheriffs had led to their 'forgetting their duty and trust' and using 'their office to their own private gain' to 'the harm of the Commonwealth'.[103] The term 'commonwealth' was identified with the 'political nation', the articulate actions of the communities aware of the needs and obligations of the government. When the proposed move of the Council in the Marches to Shrewsbury was discussed in 1590–1 the gravity of the matter required that 'for the good of the Commonwealth you may sende such persons of credite to solicite the cause'.[104]

Care was taken to protect the image of governmental control in public affairs, even though its agencies often failed to grasp what the Privy Council was eager to promote. The need to maintain solidarity was reflected in the manner in which individual governors were esteemed in private correspondence and other sources. For example, Sir Edward Stradling was described in terms that demonstrated his external posture as a man of good reputation in public affairs as well as a man of honour in the company of his equals. In 1574 reference was made to 'the greate care yow have alwaye had to equitie and justice respectinge rather thestimacon of yor worshipp and credit than anie waise bente by will in the behalfe of anie to wronge the leaste'.[105] It was his service to the state, it was declared, that elevated his willingness to serve his people and made him a figure to be admired. The workings of Tudor government gave men of his calibre the power to project an image of being just. Sir Thomas Elyot emphasized justice as the prime factor in the career of the ideal governor. The virtues of 'equity and justice', as attributed to Stradling, made him able to apply law himself as a beneficiary of the Tudor dispensation. The 'empire' claimed by Henry VIII in 1533, in local government terms, entailed that the power of the state was applied to the microcosm of the regional unit of administration, especially the shire.[106] The 'empire' envisaged by Elizabeth was independent, self-governing, self-sufficient and unhampered by external authority. It underlined the need to maintain sovereign rights. These rights, applied within the county community controlled by eligible gentry, gave them vestiges of what, in theory, they might claim for themselves of regal power. In that context they were not only delegates but also a corporate embodiment of the state. To Dr David Lewis, 'commonwealth' implied the regional community or the 'neighbourhood' which was normally identified with a populated area enjoying legal protection. 'Good and lawful men of the neighbourhood' were those chosen to represent their areas in courts of law under the legal authority of resident gentry.[107] Such was the method used by humanist scholars to expose the chief characteristics of gentility in individual families and regions. Their intellectual prowess enabled them to advance themselves as the prime expositors of the Elizabethan and Jacobean state. Sixteenth-century commentators made similar declarations which identified power with the region or location where it was, in fact, exercised. Geographical location helped to strengthen the use of power within defined boundaries. In the Middle Ages it was normally identified locally with the *gwlad* (*dominium*) or political entity where the king exercised exclusive jurisdictional rights, the 'cantref' or 'commote', depending on the nature and extent of the authority enjoyed by the *uchelwr*.[108]

Conclusion

In the post-1536 period, therefore, the identity of gentry power was associated principally with the shire or hundred and only occasionally extended to the larger region or province. It was reasonable, therefore, that the personal correspondence of gentry should refer to the community power entrusted to them. Moreover, that power was linked to a diversity of factors that attributed the principal virtues to the 'perfect' governor. What Tudor legislation did was to reinforce in the gentry those qualities that the state, through them, could exploit essentially for its own benefit. The state, in that respect, constituted those essential features that supported the structure of legal authority. If it can be said that the authority of the central government was developed it is then a natural corollary that its power in the locality should be vested in those best able to wield it and to benefit by it.

In view of these conventions, attempts to preserve an established social structure in Elizabethan Wales were doomed to failure. While it is true that those who had prospered as a result of social advancement maintained their precedence by acquiring pedigrees and adopting coats of arms, they utilized that exhibition of grandeur to advance their enterprising schemes. The basic distinction in the social structure lay between the gentry and the non-gentle orders who, between them, owned or held land and those who worked on it. To be regarded as landed gentry families had to prove that they had achieved the required standard – independence, substance, *gravitas* and ability to govern their localities efficiently on behalf of the Crown. The chief characteristics of the medieval *uchelwyr* survived into the Tudor period, emphasizing that gentility, despite social change, still retained the fundamental features which drew together a heterogeneous and extensive order of freemen as responsible agents of public order.

Although varying in their economic means they were united in their adherence to a mode of conduct overtly manifested in all fields of activity, private and public, in war and peace. The emphasis laid on the bonds of kinship arose out of the interplay of lineage and marriage and the connections between families based on such foundations that were usually projected in the exercise of communal authority. They gave the *uchelwr* the right to use that skill and exert political power.

Such bonds of loyalty and affinity had their disruptive features but they also gave the Tudor and Stuart governors the opportunity to display how strong and cohesive kinship ties were and how essential to the concept of unity in the state. It is evident, on the one hand, that the relationships between lineage, marriage and the nexus of family affinities were often vital ingredients in provoking a rising or revolt.[109] It is equally true, on the other hand, that they signified those qualities absolutely necessary to maintain organized government. A kin-conscious society often strengthened communal leadership in the arts of peace. The Welsh gentry, regarded as the pillars of society, enabled the Tudors and early Stuarts to entrust experienced men, by the very nature of the innate properties, with the authority to exercise control. They had their faction or 'followers', as did their predecessors in the previous centuries, and that, on occasions, could be extremely destructive. But that was not the only feature of their power. The distinctive qualities of government emerged from the skills that were exercised by them in the localities. 'Gentlemen', William Harrison informed his readers in *The Description of England* (1577), 'be those whom their race and blood, or at least their virtues, do make able and known'.[110] The ability to develop those virtues was considered to be implicit in the conduct of the gentry, their interpretation of their role in society and their common interests in relation to political affairs in the early Stuart period.

These common interests were interpreted in an essentially territorial manner in the period spanning the reign of Elizabeth I and extending into that of James I. This chapter has sought to discover the Welsh gentry's self-perceptions on honour. What was distinctive about them within the realm, particularly on the accession of James I, was their assertiveness based on a surviving native kindred system as well as a prophetic tradition (see Chapter 4, pp. 134–40). Honour was regarded as a robust out-growth of the pride taken by them and generations of *antecessores* in their inalienable birthright. As the poets and genealogists demonstrated, they were worthy descendants of the forefathers of a unique race amply displayed in their pride and national awareness. In due course these features were broadened so as to interpret the role of *uchelwyr* within the concept of the whole of Britain as a political entity. Sir William Maurice, much against the will of parliament, advocated that James I should be called 'Emperor' and his realm 'Great Britain'.[111] Genealogists linked Henry Tudor and James with Brutus of Troy and Cadwaladr, King of Britain (d. 664 AD) who, according to Galfridian traditions, was destined to reappear to lead the Britons against the Saxon usurpers. George Owen Harry was the most explicit exponent of this myth. James I, he declared,

> . . . beganne his raigne ouer this Land the foure and twentyeth day of March Anno, 1602 [old style] bringing with him Vnity, Peace, and Profite to all these Realmes, by vniting and knitting together all the scattered members of the British monarchy, vnder the gouernment of him, as one sent of God, to fulfill his diuine predestinate will.[112]

He was to become the restorer of the realm's unity, and the Welsh gentry found such a myth congenial to their political aspirations, priding themselves on the honour bestowed on them as latter-day leaders of the Cambro-British under the Crown within the isle of Britain.

In Wales of the period *c.*1536–1640 emphasis in the exercise of public office was placed on reputation and substance. These features were based essentially on honour, order and authority and, in the early Stuart period, they had a broader constitutional dimension. Although ownership of land and officeholding were not essential they were still considered significant in any attempt to promote the interests of individual families and to claim gentility.[113] In an age when the state was inextricably identified with the Protestant establishment, legitimate authority was geared to ensure its preservation. In its regional context it was manifested in three spheres of activity; in public office, in the *llys* or *plasty* and in the community. They formed the principal features of early modern Welsh society. Authority exposed how government developed, controlled by those qualities that were for the most part inherited. The Welsh gentry, even on the eve of the Civil Wars, relied almost exclusively on the skills mastered by them as well as the opportunities offered them before and after the Tudor settlement.[114] These skills, as applied to matters relating to defence affairs, religious dimensions of gentry life and activity, and the role of the family will be subject to examination in Part II of this study.

Part Two

THE EXERCISE OF AUTHORITY

CHAPTER 4

The Defence of the Realm

'Besides, while we keep the superiority of the sea not all the World can offend us.' These words were written in April 1635 by Lord Herbert of Chirbury in a holograph copy of a 'brief discourse on the state of . . . [the] . . . kingdom in relaytion to others'.[1] In it he assessed the strategy and resources of Spain, France and the Low Countries in the Thirty Years War. Fear of Spanish aggression had long been a matter of serious concern for England.

> From the Sea, the Spaniard, and the Devil, the Lord deliver me. I need not tell you who preserves him from the last, but, from the Spaniards, his best Friend is the sea itself . . . Water may be said to be one of their best Fences; otherwise I believe they had not been able to have borne up so long against the gigantic Power of Spain.[2]

Thus wrote James Howell in April 1617 echoing the sentiments of many others of his generation regarding the dangers posed by Spain to the independence of the 'island empire'. Tensions had arisen at that time for James I was intent on strengthening the links with Spain. He had hoped for a Spanish marriage between his heir Henry and a Spanish princess and, after Henry's death, between Charles and the Infanta. Howell's words focused on anti-Spanish feelings which continued to exist in Wales, particularly in maritime areas.

Such sentiments illustrate the close surveillance kept in Wales in years of foreign threat, and this chapter aims to reveal the impact that different aspects of the defensive structure and strategy had on the attitudes of Welsh gentry in times of crisis towards the security of the realm and their localities. Aspects of this theme have already been given some attention, chiefly in relation to concepts of honour and status, but further consideration is needed in view of the dangers which beset the English and Welsh coasts and the impact of impending invasion in a period of political and economic unrest. A cursory look at administrative and private sources for all Welsh shires, particularly the maritime ones, in the early modern period indicates the time and labour expended to maintain defences and how occupied justices of the peace and other official colleagues, however inefficient they might have been, were with training soldiers, shire levies and the levying of taxes for defence purposes. Defence against the Roman Catholic threats from Spain and Ireland in the Elizabethan era and the continuing dangers from France and Spain in the years which followed created much anxiety among those appointed to maintain the independence of the realm and who were concerned for their own private interests.

This chapter, in accordance with the main theme of this volume, attempts to place the role of defence in the context of Welsh political thought as observed in the administrative correspondence and memoranda of the gentry and other commentators on Welsh affairs. The obsession with preserving the liberty and character of regional communities had wider intellectual repercussions than might be supposed, stemming from a deep-rooted identity with ancient British traditions and the concept of the 'imperial' status of the 'isle of Britain'. Since the earliest times the sea had been both a source of sustenance and danger to Welsh identity, because its cultural heritage had been enriched and reinforced via the western routes from Cornwall, Ireland and the continent and, at the same time, the coasts were exposed to invasion. Despite conquest and economic strains, Wales survived the Middle Ages with its cultural traditions intact, and the accession of Henry Tudor saw the culmination of the powerful myth of the 'son of prophecy', based on ancient prophecies and the traditions associated with the twelfth-century chronicler Geoffrey of Monmouth who, in his most famous work, *Historia Regum Britanniae* (*c*.1136), by using the prophecies often attributed to Merlin, accorded to the Britons an illustrious past extending back to Brutus, reputedly a great-grandson of Aeneas of Troy. Although native Wales had lost its political autonomy in 1282 and never fully recovered it, national consciousness and cultural identity survived and continued to be powerful forces in the post-Glyndŵr era. The chief mouthpieces of this tradition in the Tudor and early Stuart periods were the professional bards who, even in an age when a movement away from native cultural associations gathered pace, particularly among the more powerful gentry families, continued to identify community leaders with noble forebears, kings and *arglwyddi*. Within a new political infrastructure imposed in the 1530s the *uchelwyr*, in their regional communities, were still regarded as descendants of mighty leaders. In the context of the historic myth, therefore, honour and good lineage continued to be fundamental in any attempt to define status, authority and reputation.[3] The mid- and late sixteenth century saw a restatement of this national literary and religious heritage and a small but dedicated band of humanist scholars, both Catholic and Protestant, contributed significantly to it.

The two and a half centuries between the Glyndŵr Revolt and the mid-seventeenth century denoted the last stages of a significant social and economic transformation in Wales. Out of the decaying structure of the Middle Ages emerged a modern society which eased the growth of a new money economy and a gentry order whose power, after 1536, was based formally on the ownership of land as well as administrative and legal powers which tied it firmly to the Tudor state. In Wales, the main features of this development were the attempts made by descendants of the traditional 'nobility' to consolidate their position as loyal servants of the new regime. This new order was not wholly Welsh because, since the Edwardian conquest and settlement, new families of Anglo-Norman origin had resided in castellated boroughs in the Principality and, despite the colonial nature of the conquest, gradually a more racially integrated community structure emerged, particularly in the urban areas, and was firmly established by the mid-fifteenth century.[4]

Myth and the Historic Past

Long-cherished traditions and ideals came to the fore in the post-Glyndŵr era and during the dynastic wars between York and Lancaster, in which the rising Welsh nobility were closely involved. Regardless of their prominence in English political faction and later Tudor government and administration, the gentry, when their own interests were at risk, would retreat, as the Glyndŵr Revolt revealed, into another world which identified them, at regional level, with the type of leadership characteristic of old clan forebears and their descendants. During the last two centuries of the Middle Ages, when Anglo-Welsh political relations grew increasingly tense, sections of the *uchelwyr* developed a yearning for older concepts of gentility which safeguarded their reputation and independence. Thus emerged again the age-old millenarian tradition which conceived of the deliverance of a people, the dawn of the 'golden age', after a long and gruelling period of oppression. In times of crisis there still existed a deep-seated feeling of aristocratic separatedness, a hankering after old values symbolized by the bardic order, and a firm belief in the glorious British past. During his campaigns Glyndŵr had cited Merlin's prophecy and Geoffrey of Monmouth's interpretation of British history but, at the same time, far from clinging to the inspiration of the past, he based his policies on the practical methods of government initiated by the Princes of Gwynedd. In that respect he vigorously expressed Welsh consciousness, but the dual loyalties that characterized the Welsh *uchelwyr* were too strong, support for his cause was short-lived among many families and political independence, as he conceived it, consequently was not achieved. That did not imply, however, that the Welsh myth was abandoned for, in a period of political crisis and ensuing dynastic struggles in England in the years *c.*1450–85, old ideals were invoked by vaticinatory poets who attributed the role of 'deliverer' to the most prominent Welsh military leaders, Yorkist and Lancastrian, such as Sir William Herbert of Raglan Castle and Jasper Tudor, the uncle of Henry Tudor.[5]

The myth was again revived at a time when the Arthurian legend became popular in England; it was proclaimed in a deliberately obscure manner that the 'son of prophecy' would arrive to take his rightful place as ruler over Britain. That leader, identified in the 1480s as Henry Tudor, emerged in years of political tension when England was divided by civil war. The myth was associated with a privileged social order which, despite its different origins, possessed similar features to those of the emerging gentry in English society. This paradox became a remarkable feature in the history of Wales on the accession of the Tudors: the emergence of progressive families intent on achieving political ascendancy and adopting English values but who, in political crises, clung desperately to their awareness of a common origin and historical development. The *uchelwyr* of Wales eventually claimed their inheritance but chiefly as hard-headed political realists bent on pursuing the main chance and not in the manner in which vaticinatory bards would have wished.[6]

The Acts of Union ended the medieval duality of the Principality and the Marches and assisted the development of a Welsh squirearchy which dominated the social and political scene for the following three centuries and more. Wales saw the emergence of newer perceptions of *uchelwriaeth* which were adapted and established to function in the new and eventually Protestant sovereign state. Old prophetic aspirations were blended with a strong Machiavellian ambition which assisted in forming the character and temperament of the *uchelwyr* in their native environment. In that respect the long-term ambitions of Welsh leaders were fulfilled since they emerged to assume a leading role in Tudor government, principally by being allowed the opportunities to apply their acquired skills to maintain a new governmental organization. They retrieved what they considered to be their birthright within the 'British' context and were granted authority, as George Owen put it, to function as direct representatives of the ancient leaders of their own race.[7] The Tudors gave governors, scholars, commercial adventurers, lawyers and churchmen the opportunity to further their own interests, especially after the religious settlement of 1559, and those of the new Protestant state. The duality, however, persisted; the social withdrawal into the cultural enclave cherished by their predecessors often appealed to the more conservative among the *uchelwyr* (who were diminishing in numbers by the early seventeenth century), hence the patronage still accorded to poets and scholars and the contribution of a handful of squires to the advance of humanist scholarship in the vernacular. The most prominent among the Welsh gentry, through marriage ties, education and a broadening social environment, involved themselves increasingly with the civility of English court life, but they maintained contact with what was traditional while gradually introducing Renaissance culture into Wales, a factor that deserves due recognition in any examination of social development in early modern Wales. They were all aware of their history even though, owing to social change and adaptation, their identity had become less evident. In the latter half of the sixteenth century, particularly the years 1576–85, the celebrated Dr John Dee gave publicity to the historic myth in a political context as the basis of his concept of the 'British Empire', after he had read Sir Humphrey Gilbert's *Discourse* (1576) on a north-west passage to America.[8]

The Elizabethan age has been described as the period of early 'British imperialism' and, in 1583, a tract was written drawing attention to the legendary Madog of Gwynedd (fl.1170) and the discovery of America to accompany the founding of the Virginia Company at a time when Spanish power was increasing in the New World. To promote England's claims and interests in America, an appeal was made to early British traditions based largely on the writings of Geoffrey of Monmouth and the theory of early Christian missions in Britain and the establishment of the apostolic church. The early history of Britain was crucial in any understanding of the role of Wales in the formation of the 'empire' which Dee and others had conceived. It is hardly surprising that the influence of these British traditions reached their peak of popularity in the 1580s when war with Spain became imminent.[9]

It was Dr John Dee, in his *General and Rare Memorials Pertayning to the Perfit Arte of Navigation* (1577), who eagerly undertook to publicize 'British imperialism' and to advocate the concept of *pax Britannica*. In his view England had a rightful claim to be the centrepiece of an empire; he was aware of the dangers of invasion and urged that precautions needed to be taken to develop the navy by devising an advanced system of defence. Dee was influential at court and a close acquaintance of Richard Hakluyt, Ralph Holinshed and William Camden. He expounded the view that Britain had discovered the New World well before Columbus and Americus Vesputius, and in 1578 he discussed it with Sir George Peckham and Hakluyt. In *A True Reporte* (1587), dedicated to Sir Francis Walsingham, Peckham produced a treatise claiming that England had colonization rights in the west and he set out to prove the Queen's 'title to the New Worlde based, not only upon Sir Humphrey Gilbert's discourses but also those of Madoc', reputedly the son of Owain Gwynedd who, according to tradition, discovered America in the late twelfth century.[10] Dee believed that King Arthur had discovered lands in the north-west but placed greater credence on the Madog tradition. He believed that Elizabeth could lay claim to Atlantis because Madog had inhabited Terra Florida. He therefore urged the Queen 'both to renew the Premisses and likewise by Conquest to enlarge the Bonds of the foresaid Title Royal'.[11] It was an effective piece of propaganda designed to undermine Spanish colonial interests in the New World. The tradition was based on this son of the ruler of Gwynedd who, it was said, sailed with his brother Rhiryd, lord of Clochran in Ireland, from Abercerrig near Abergele to seek a better life away from fratricidal encounters. There is no evidence that Madog ever existed but, in later generations, the legend became popular as the basis to the tradition of the survival of white Mandan Indians of Welsh stock in the upper Missouri. In the latter half of the sixteenth century antiquaries favoured Madog's existence because it seemed to promote British patriotism at a critical time in Anglo-Spanish relations.

The myth became popular in a period of intense antiquarian activity. In Wales, Dr David Powel, in his *The Historie of Cambria* (1584), referred to the legend, attributing it to Humphrey Llwyd, another eminent Welsh antiquary who took the slight and doubtful evidence supplied by Gutun Owain, Caradog of Llancarfan and

Maredudd ap Rhys into account.[12] There were several traditions, including Flemish and Icelandic sources, but it was Dee, with his belief in the 'Brytish Empire', who gave the legend its prominence.

Wherein lies the significance of this myth in any examination of the practicalities of English foreign policy in the 1580s? In the first instance it revealed that Welsh antiquaries, caught up in the Renaissance spirit, in their eagerness to delve into the Welsh past drew upon material, spurious or otherwise, which emphasized the richness of Welsh antiquarian tradition. Moreover, it assisted in promoting Welsh antiquity and Hakluyt was to use it in his famous *The Principall Navigations, Voyages, Traffiques and Discoveries of the English Nation*, published in 1589. The military situation in 1585 was also an important factor. The Madog legend was used to further the imperial interests of Elizabeth when hostilities broke out with Spain. What the invention of the 'Protestant Church Theory' sought to accomplish for the Protestant Reformation in Wales the Madog legend did in the secular context.

To what extent this legend was embraced by the Welsh gentry and how far it influenced their attitudes in the latter half of the sixteenth century it is difficult to judge but doubtless the antagonism felt towards Catholic Spain and its imperial ambitions formed part of their mentality. There does not appear to be any direct impact; the Welsh bards remain silent on the subject and pursuing a claim to the Americas based on an unfounded Welsh tradition seems to have been a less urgent proposal than ensuring that government legislation against Roman Catholics was being enforced at home. The task of frustrating Spanish hopes of a successful invasion of England and Wales and curbing Roman Catholic activity in the hinterland was considered to be more important, especially in view of the increasing incidence of recusancy in the 1570s and 1580s. It was an age, down to the eve of the Civil Wars, when the defence of the Protestant settlement and the independence of the realm became matters of primary urgency. Having said that, it is evident that, in this context, the governors of the Welsh shires, in periods of political and religious pressure, were distinctly aware of their historical prestige. In the first instance they wished to preserve their distinguished identity and thus clung tenaciously to that version of British history upheld by the poets and antiquaries. Since the coming of the Tudors dispensed with prophecy as a political force, the claims of the gentry to rule and exercise authority in their respective regions and to defend the realm from the opposition of other nations was fully manifested in the statutory powers which upheld that authority. The fact that they held the reins of government and, as George Owen stated, became 'magistrates of their own nation', signified that the concept of a political partnership had eroded the old prophetic tradition, although its spirit survived.[13]

The Mechanics of Defence

Regardless of the concepts of the new British 'imperialism' that emerged in the latter half of the sixteenth century, in practice all matters concerning the defence of the realm were ultimately the responsibility of local administrators to whom successive governments entrusted this key role. The manner in which the right to rule was applied to defence affairs unravels many features of self-perception and attitudes among the gentry. How did concepts of government and routine administration apply in practice, and how did they relate to Welsh literary interpretations of monarchical authority and royalist symbolism? Doubtless the anti-Spanish feeling was gathering strength in mid-century and had increased significantly in the reign of Elizabeth. Efforts were made to place men of known integrity in key posts in the maritime shires. Anglesey's defence in 1588, for example, during the war with Spain, was placed in the charge of William Herbert, earl of Pembroke, 'in whom', it was said, 'we have special trust', and magistrates of the counties of Gwynedd.[14] In pursuing his duties Sir William Morgan of Pen-coed, Monmouthshire, when required to lead an army to Ireland in 1579, anxiously reported that his troops were substandard and poorly equipped. Shortage of money, he considered, would mean that 'they may perish for want'.[15] He considered that entrusting the defence of the realm to such an insufficient band of soldiery might be dangerous. He was concerned about the condition of his troops but equally aware of the damaging potential impact on the country's welfare. Inefficiency in military service was regarded as a major factor in increasing tensions and anxiety in government circles, and local administrators were more eager to safeguard their own reputations as leaders of their communities than to function as government agents. In the last resort, preserving their independence within those communities meant most to them. There were three potential sources of danger: external invasion from France and Spain, with Ireland as a useful launching base, and the Massacre of St Bartholomew's Day (1572); internal rebellion, especially in 1569 (the Rising of the Northern Earls) and during the Catholic plots of the 1570s and 1580s; and the possibility that periodic economic stringency might intensify the existing instability. The most urgent threat was the exposed nature of the Welsh coastline, hence the constant occupation with routine matters concerning the recruitment of soldiers, especially in maritime counties.[16] Gradually during the sixteenth century the Tudors had become aware of the need to attend to military affairs and to use a system consisting of the old and inefficient county militias whereby men between the ages of sixteen and sixty were expected to serve in the defence of the mainland. Private retinues were also recruited and used on a contract basis for service, usually overseas. The militia was the responsibility of the chief landowners in each county who were to ensure that forces were raised to meet requirements, particularly for coastal defence.[17]

In Elizabeth's reign emphasis was placed on protecting the realm from internal dissension and defending the maritime counties against potential Catholic threats. Regular training of the militia – which was a new creation in Wales – became a more common feature and increased interest was taken to ensure that the defensive structure in critical times was sufficient. Precautions were taken to set up beacons and coastal defences were reinforced. Attempts were made to reform the military organization of the realm and overseas service was also reshaped. Trained bands were made more selective and expected to perform military service on the continent until the crisis of the Tyrone Rebellion in 1598 demanded that they should be sent to Ireland. That directive caused problems because, owing to the unpopularity of the service, there was marked absenteeism in the musters, eligible soldiers 'hiding in rocks and caves, some flying into foreign countries, so that they [deputy-lieutenants] were fain to hunt them by the pole like outlying deer'.[18] As baronial levies became scarcer (although they did not disappear altogether), the militia and trained bands served as main agencies for defensive purposes. It was reported that the earl of Essex kept a retained army with 'many honest gentlemen in Wales',[19] and Star Chamber records constantly refer to retaining as a common feature amongst recalcitrant gentry.[20] The militia adapted the military structure of each county to the needs of the times in preparation for war and the defence of the localities when it broke out. This system was largely inefficient and amateurish, devoted mainly to home defence but, because of the need to exercise regional military control, the militia was frequently used. Its functions and the degree of success it had achieved varied because so much depended on a number of factors, ranging from local finance, the assumption of responsibility and a constant awareness of impending crisis.

Despite the survival of 'retaining' soldiers, the use of trained bands and the militia placed greater responsibilities on the localities to defend their own interests and keep their territories free from external pressures. Because the late Tudor navy was unable to defend the coastline effectively the maritime counties took it upon themselves to reorganize their resources so as to relieve the situation. Regardless of inefficient organization and lack of co-ordination between counties, it is in this respect that Tudor government gained most success since it could depend on local gentry to rise to the occasion in so far as they were aware of the problem and were committed to solving it. Despite the stubborn pro-Catholic stance taken by some families, the majority of Welsh families were palpably aware of the need to defend the political realm and their own heritage.

Welsh administrators became increasingly conscious of the dangers that Spain and the Catholic faith posed, perils which increased an inbred hatred of all foreign influences. In February 1570 Pope Pius V's bull *Regnans in Excelsis* excommunicated Elizabeth: it was followed by plots which ended only with the execution of Mary Queen of Scots in 1587. The position assumed by Philip II as Mary's successor in her claim to the English throne intensified attacks on Catholic priests from the continent, and intentions to recover the realm for the Old Faith were frustrated. There was a determined and forceful campaign to repossess the realm for Rome and Spain. In this respect Mary's death had bred more danger than Mary alive. Threats to Elizabeth's life had serious repercussions on the security of the state and drew attention to the dire condition of defence organization generally in the localities. A combination of factors, including Catholic missionary campaigns at home and seafaring ventures attacking Spanish shipping on the high seas, jeopardized relationships between England and Spain. It was clear that the new Elizabethan state could not survive unless the Reformation settlement was safeguarded and the Queen, making what use she could of Protestant support elsewhere, tried to aid the cause where it was threatened on the continent. This accounted for her support of the Netherlands, to prevent Philip from using it as a base from which to attack England. The pro-Spanish Guise faction in France was another source of danger. Eventually, in 1585, war with Spain broke out and continued until 1604. Elizabeth tried to nurture the resistance of Protestant minorities in France and the Netherlands, which strengthened the alliance between Spain and the Guise family. It was indeed a tense period but, despite economic and religious problems, England was far more united in 1588 than it had been in 1558; the resistance to persistent Spanish naval attack revealed how solidly loyal the country was to the monarchy.[21]

The basis of this loyalty had been well laid in Henry VIII's reign, following the momentous changes in the 1530s and the wars in Scotland (where the Guise connection was strong) and France, wars which continued into Edward VI's reign. The recruitment and organization of armies were not as efficient as they might have been and the threat of war abroad and rebellion internally demanded a major review of the situation, the prime innovation being the appointment of lord lieutenants to supervise military affairs in the counties in Edward VI's reign and at critical intervals thereafter. In Wales and the Marches William Herbert, earl of Pembroke, the Lord President at Ludlow, assumed similar powers, and a rudimentary system was set up in each county with a view to establishing a more efficient defence structure.

Improvements had been introduced in weaponry and the organization of musters in Mary I's reign. Further changes in the use of weapons were introduced under Elizabeth and, with impending crisis in the 1580s, commands were issued that musters were to be more disciplined, the fortification of defences more impregnable and organization of trained bands made more effective. For foreign service the county militia was utilized to supply foot soldiers, which caused a great deal of trouble for the local gentry. Since baronial retinues were no longer, as in the past, the main source of military service, greater reliance was placed on individual gentlemen-soldiers who had served their apprenticeship under noble leadership.

In Wales, particular emphasis was placed on the *uchelwyr* as military leaders which, although their achievements were not at all times given the attention they deserved, offered the basis of disciplined control. Hugh Gwynn of Berth-ddu, Llanrwst, for example, a scion of a younger branch of the Gwydir family who served in armies on the continent, was described in the following words by Wiliam ap Raff:

> A'r wlad a ddaw draw i'r drin
> I'th law a phawb i'th ddilyn.[22]

[And the country will come yonder to the fray and follow you.]

These lines, which are echoed in many other similar poetic adulations of the day, signify the co-operative spirit of defence in the neighbourhood and the title of protector accorded to the local governor. The vulnerability of the Welsh coastline, in times of war, especially in Pembrokeshire, Caernarfonshire and Anglesey, caused concern for the authorities. Many sources disclose how prominent a feature the local defence mechanism really was. It empowered gentry, who were otherwise occupied with administering their estates and attending to a diversity of routine matters appertaining to the localities, to lead men in matters of grave concern to the state. The period from the French wars of Henry VIII to the Bishops' Wars in 1639 and the preparations for royal service in the Civil Wars has, as its chief feature, in war and peace, the need to protect the realm from external threat. Despite the deficiencies in the Welsh defence structure during general musters and the equipping of soldiers, the Welsh gentry were aware of the urgency and the need to attend to such matters. Although they often lacked the will to act, the need to defend their territory drove them to attend to their duties.[23]

The Privy Council, through the agency of the Council in the Marches, was constantly concerned with the dangers of invasion and Catholic intrigue. Among the gentry one of the most eager to draw attention to the danger of recusancy was Sir James Perrot who, in 1611, declared Haverfordwest to be vulnerably placed. He feared the influence of 'recusants of the marcher shires [who have] . . . come to settle themselves in these remote parts of Wales'. He also suspected the activities of Jesuit priests who had close connections with border shires.[24] In 1627, he again reported the influx of 'strangers coming out of other parts of Wales and England that reside there' so that the Old Faith might survive.[25] George Owen had drawn attention to the defensive weakness of Milford Haven in his 'Dialogue of the Government of Wales', at a time when the county was 'sub't to great perill of invasion' (from Ireland and the continent) and should be 'stronger to defend itself against any sodaine invassion'.[26] In 1617, the Council in the Marches reported that it had ordered the suppression of St Winifred's Well in Holywell, thus ending there 'the great concourse of people'.[27] Dr William Griffith of Caernarfon, a scion of a younger branch of the Penrhyn family and deputy vice-admiral of north Wales, in his letter to Archbishop John Whitgift concerning papist activity at Rhiwledyn in Creuddyn in 1587, observed that he had entrusted the matter to Sir Thomas Mostyn of Gloddaith, the local magistrate, but was eager to suppress the use of a cave for printing of subversive material: 'if my self had not bene trobled in th other end of the Shiere with Marine Causes I would have bene more privie to the qualitie of the persons & their doeinges & when I cann meete with anye of the watch will learne and knowe more'.[28]

Anxious minds often expressed fears about the spread of Roman Catholicism. The Merioneth magistrates, headed by Cadwaladr Price of Rhiwlas, on spotting a Spanish galleon on the coasts in November 1597, were charged by the lord lieutenant 'to use all means procurable to suppress the Spaniard', but they failed to do so, 'leaving us most sorrowful that our care and diligence took not better successes',[29] and four years later Richard Lewkenor, chief justice of Chester, in a letter to Sir Robert Cecil, was concerned at the 'backsliding in religion' in the border areas of Wales: there were 'many runners abroad', and he feared that the threat would increase unless parliament took measures to suppress it.[30] He sternly rebuked Church leaders for their remissness, declaring that bishops should investigate the problem rather than allow their chancellors to use presentments 'to gain and profit rather than reformation'. The defence of Milford Haven in 1592 led Henry Herbert, earl of Pembroke, to refer slightingly to the Welsh whom he distrusted in the local trained bands and to deploy troops from Somerset and Gloucester, who were 'better disposed than many of the inhabitants', to relieve the Pembrokeshire port.[31]

Three factors emerge in these responses that reflect the dangers from Spanish attack: the need to defend strategic urban centres, the widespread Catholic practices that hindered the advance of Protestantism and Catholic activity abroad. So acute had the amount of recusant activity become in the early years of the seventeenth century that Richard Parry, bishop of St Asaph, despairingly reported to Cecil that there had been an 'unfortunate and ungodly' increase among them in the diocese.[32] Whereas in 1602 a total of 140 were reported, his visitation three years later saw the number rise to 400 and 'with their number their courage is increased'. 'They little fear the words', he continued, 'until they feel the smart of the laws.'[33] There was a strong feeling among county governors as well that recusancy was a problem, particularly in view of a period of war with Spain, and steps were taken to prevent the sons of gentry sympathetic towards the Old Faith from travelling abroad for their education and being influenced by papists. It was reported in 1589–90 that some 'toward youths' from Wales, particularly Y Fan, Tredegar (Newport), Llantarnam and Bedwellte (mostly scions of the Morgan family), might have been sent abroad for learning 'where they should edify themselves to their comfort and service of their country hereafter'.[34] The Privy Council in 1593 was eager for Pembroke to investigate how many sons of gentlemen had been sent by their parents overseas 'under colour of languages to be learned' and who were influenced to become seminary priests and 'unsound subjects'. Suspect houses were to be searched for Jesuit seminary priests, and all closets, chests, desks and coffers opened and examined for seditious books, letters, writings and other material.[35] Early in 1603 it was ordered that rumours concerning the Queen's death were to be suppressed and officials were to 'govern themselves with such discretion and judgement as is meet'.[36] They were expected to safeguard the welfare of the state so that 'we and you and all others that truly love the state may, in unity and common amity, join together in all such courses as may preserve, both in public and private, the peace and tranquility of the same'. In such dire circumstances, when the Spanish war dragged on and the Irish rebellion erupted, another Armada was planned in 1597. The weather on that occasion, however, prevented it from proceeding further than the north-western coast of France.[37]

Problems at home also caused the government many difficulties: parliamentary attacks on royal prerogatives, disputed monopolies, the Essex Revolt (1601), bankruptcy, corruption in high places, religious conservatism, threats to law and order and the economic crisis that characterized Elizabeth's last years. It was against that background that the efforts made to offset any Roman Catholic reaction and to curb Spain's intention to invade must be viewed. It was known to the government that Roman Catholicism was still traditionally practised, especially in remoter areas, but it was arguable that the influence of Catholic missionaries from the continent on local society was minimal and that they failed to make any effective breakthrough even after the papal bull had been issued in 1570 and the Jesuit mission in the 1580s. Nevertheless, the challenge persisted and the government remained intransigent in its opposition to Rome and Spain.

Literary Reflections on Defence

Welsh literary sources in the 1580s and 1590s reflect firm anti-Spanish sentiments. In Siôn Tudur's view Sir Ieuan Llwyd of Iâl, who was responsible for two companies of soldiers at Nijmegen in Flanders, was the 'cur Sbaen' ('the bane of Spain'),[38] and Edwart ap Raff applauded Queen Elizabeth in 1594 for allowing the translation of the scriptures into Welsh, for her victory against the Armada and for her constant opposition to Roman Catholicism.[39] Despite her tribulations she maintained her dignity and God defended her realm in critical circumstances. The poet's opposition to the Old Faith knew no bounds. The Jesuits, described as the 'Pope's men' ('gwŷr y Pab'), he believed, were false and perverted and unworthy of being called the Queen's subjects.[40] In its opening section the Latin dedication of the Welsh Bible in 1588 described Elizabeth's triumph over her enemies, and regarded her reign as the culmination of the Protestant mission in Wales. According to William Morgan it was God who gave her the success which she achieved, as well as

> that happy peace which you enjoy above your neighbours, and that divine protection which can never be sufficiently acknowledged, whereby you have both lately put your savage foes to flight and have ever most fortunately escaped many great dangers, but also, most of all, by that distinguished piety, famous all the world over . . . and that most forward zeal for both the propagation and the defence of true religion.[41]

This section of the preface refers to a number of fundamental features of Her Majesty's reign: the intervention of divine power in government, esteemed leadership, the successful defence of the Protestant settlement and, in Wales, the statutory provision of the scriptures. Compared with the rivalry between France and Spain, and the turbulence in France and the Netherlands, Morgan saw the realm's stability and the Queen's care for the spiritual welfare of her subjects as achievements to be highly valued. The defeat of the Armada, which had occurred some months before Morgan wrote his dedication, in his view reinforced God's hand in advancing the new Protestant faith to which Wales had significantly contributed through the scriptures. Contemporary verse in Welsh revealed the same attitude, depicting the Queen as a magnificent figure commanding her subjects' allegiance. Despite her problems there was a feeling of greater security, confidence and optimism which helped to create the image of the Queen's grace, elegance and authority.

In a long poem entitled *Cân am y waredigaeth a gâdd y Brytaniaid o law y Spaeniaid cynhennys yn y flwyddyn 1588* (a song commemorating the deliverance of the Britons from the contentious Spanish in the year 1588), Thomas Jones, vicar of Llanfair Cilgedin near Llanofer in Gwent, joyfully celebrated the defeat of the Armada, glorifying in each verse the realm's liberation and the nation's resources.[42] He observed the need to defend its independence, its religion and its government. The poem is divided into six sections, and the emphasis is placed on the emancipation of the isle of Britain by divine sanction. The themes appear as follows: (i) the planning and actual invasion with references to the policies of Philip II and the papacy; (ii) Philip II's claim to the English throne as successor to Mary Queen of Scots and Spanish and French arrogance intent on subjugating England; (iii) the Queen's response and defence arrangements under Lord Howard of Effingham, lord high admiral, the exploits of Sir Francis Drake, and the stormy conditions which caused disasters to the Spanish fleet; (iv) the joy expressed with the outcome (if the Spaniards had succeeded in defeating England, the cleric declared, the country would have flowed with blood and the people been afflicted by the 'branding iron'); (v) the continued opposition of Spain and the danger caused by many traitors who sought to further the Catholic cause; (vi) an eulogy to commemorate the Queen's serene leadership and to express jubilation owing to the survival of the island of Britain. References appear to the 'Spaeniaid cynhennys' ('the contentious Spanish'), 'Gelynion cas' ('hateful enemies'), 'hil gynhennys' ('contentious race') and 'Y bleiddiaid blin twyllodrus' ('the deceitful evil wolves'), indicating that although the Armada had been defeated the poet still considered the Spanish threat to be a reality and the world to be dangerous ('mae'n fyd peryglus'). The fear of Jesuit priests, and the need to suppress them, is also hinted at, which echoes the apprehension expressed by moderate Catholics in 1605:

> [Jesuits] have nothing in their mouthes but the sworde, the sworde and wars . . . they bragg much that they shall have assistaunce from the kinge of France and the kinge of Spaine. In respect of which perswasions many Catholicks in Wales are in greate feare and doe wishe the Jesuites with all their adherentes out of the land.[43]

Soon after occurred the Gunpowder Plot (1605) and the conspiracy planned by Hugh Owen of Plas-du in Llŷn to organize a Spanish and Irish invasion of England and Wales. In another of his poems Thomas Jones welcomed the translation of the scriptures. As expected, this is intensely Protestant invoking the theory of the apostolic church and the value of the scriptures as a guide to 'gwir athrawiaeth' ('true doctrine') for the Welsh. It is an attempt to come to terms once more with Spanish threats by stressing the value of God's Word to the people in their own language.[44] Two other poems addressed to 'Sydanen' ('the silken one') refer specifically, as did English literary and sources and portraits, to the splendour of the royal authority wielded by Elizabeth at court.[45] She is regarded as a 'British' queen; in faith, nature and gracious bearing, the poet adding that she is the ultimate good ('o ffydd o greddyf a gras / o ddaioni yr dyrnas').

Another anonymous poem applauded her defence of the government and Church:

> yn kadwr iawn lyfodreth
> i gyd a chwbwl or gyfreth.

> ac a gadw[o]dd i chyrefydd
> gida dvw kadwedic fydd.[46]

[maintaining good government and the law in its entirety . . . one who
kept her faith and who shall be with God the saviour.]

Similarly Maurice Kyffin, a friend of Dr John Dee, who was
appointed surveyor of muster rolls in the Netherlands in 1588, in
his poem *The Blessednes of Brytaine* (1587), magnified Elizabeth,
in the prophetic tradition noted at the start of this chapter, as a
gift to the Welsh people since she had descended from the 'blessed
branch of Brutus Royall race'.[47] It was a spectacular eulogy
composed on Elizabeth's government and designed to support the
Queen's cause after the Babington Plot in 1586. Similarly, Edwart
ap Raff, composing in 1594, emphasized the peace and good
order that came in the wake of the Armada.[48] The situation was
not as settled as these expressed sentiments assumed, of course,
since Spanish threats continued to trouble the government. What
is important, however, is that this singular triumph revealed the
urgency of the need to preserve national independence and to
defend the realm. The 'mortal moon', which referred to the third
eclipse in 1588, when the end of the world was expected, also
symbolized the crescent-shaped formation of the Armada in the
English channel. Kyffin, on this occasion, graphically describes
Spain's doom in *The Continuation of The Blessednes of Brytaine*
(1588):

> This was the year wherein by fire and sword,
> Our foes forethought to work the kingdom's wrack . . .
> The fatal year of fearful Eighty Eight,
> Forethreat'ning falls of empires, realms, and kings,
> Out-breathing bale to every early wight
> By pest'ring plagues and dreadful dreary things,
> Is now nigh spent, and yet our realm and Queen,
> Through God's great pow'r, secure in safety seen.[49]

The poem's theme is similar to that contained in Thomas Jones's
poems, forecasting the peace that would follow the downfall of
Spain. The emphasis is on the impending tragedy and the
peaceful outcome. Likewise, Edwart ap Raff, after praising the

publication of the Welsh Bible, referred briefly to the earlier deliverance:

> Fo luniwyd hwnt, flina' taith,
> I Suwsanna siâs unnwaith,
> Duw Tad a fu geidwad hon,
> Duw'n gwared y dyn gwirion.[50]

[Yonder, a wearisome chase was once contrived for Susanna [the lady of beauty described in *The Apocrypha*]; God the Father was her saviour; God delivering the virtuous.]

Divine providence had preserved Elizabeth and the nation in crisis, a declaration which Siôn Tudur referred to in a different way when he applauded the Queen's grace and honourable bearing as means of combating the threats of outlaws and traitors:

> Â mawredd Duw ni 'myrrir
> Mae gras i'ch teyrnas a'ch tir . . .
> Troi'r cledd a'i rinwedd oedd raid
> At herwyr neu draeturiaid,
> Os bradwyr Ynys Brydain,
> Na bo rhwydd i neb o'r rhain.[51]

[With God's magnitude there will be no intrusion; your kingdom and land are graced . . . It was necessary to use the sword righteously against despoilers and traitors. If there be betrayers in the isle of Britain not one of them is to be treated favourably.]

The poem was composed in 1594 and in it the 'Ceidwad, amddiffyniad ffydd' ('Custodian and Defender of the Faith') was regarded as standing resolute against a variety of threats and conspiracies to her life. The most serious were those which occurred between 1569 to 1588, since they had Welsh associations and implicated individual Welshmen, such as Thomas Salusbury of Lleweni, William Parry, the Catholic conspirator and double agent from Northop, and Hugh Owen of Plas-du in Llŷn. An anonymous poem composed on the triumph over the Armada considered external factors to have been largely responsible.[52] It was God's intervention that saved the day and the nation from the treachery of Philip II and Parma. The 'prince', the embodiment of the national sovereign state, in a David and Goliath situation had avoided defeat owing to external forces beyond its control. In 1583 Sir Thomas Smith observed that 'the Prince is the life, the head and the authority of all things that be done in the realm of England'.[53] In Edwart ap Raff's view, Elizabeth was 'the wise Prince in a perfect state' ('Prins doeth mewn purion ystad'), symbolizing the highest authority in the commonwealth.[54] The unique rights of the Crown formed its prerogatives, and although the monarchy had beneath it a hierarchy of institutions, in the nation's eyes Elizabeth ruled and it was that fact that featured most prominently in contemporary thought. One long free-metre poem in praise of Elizabeth – 'ein gwir Frenhines' ('our true Queen') – denounced the Babington conspiracy and deplored the fact that the Queen's life and the realm's safety should have been threatened in this odious manner.[55] The poet named the conspirators, including Sir Thomas Salusbury of Lleweni and Edward Jones of Plas Cadwgan near Wrexham, who, with others were regarded as the 'diffeithwyr Babilon' ('the scoundrels of Babylon') and 'traytwyr creulon afles' ('cruel and evil traitors').

The critical 1580s and 1590s, as the literary evidence shows, produced distinct expressions of loyalty and attitudes to royal authority. In purely regional terms this was overtly declared in Sir Richard Bulkeley III's response to Spanish threats in the summer of 1599: 'for so longe as the Spanishe navye is upon the coast, I maye not com owt of this Ile wch wth godes healpe I will kepe or make it my grave'.[56] His concern to maintain the independence of the isle and safeguard his own reputation underlies his fervent awareness of his responsibility to the state and his duty to defend it as well as his local community. The irascible Sir John Perrot and his son, Sir James, were equally troubled by Spanish danger and the fear of Catholic influences, emphasis being placed on the vulnerability of Milford Haven.[57] Their pleas contained a mixture of loyalty to the Protestant realm and local sentiment and their desire to avoid dissension and upheaval, although they themselves were often embroiled in factional quarrels that exposed their intentions in public administration. In the 1580s and 1590s the imminent danger from Spain and Ireland was foremost in the minds of officials. Several Welsh commanders and soldiers served with distinction in the wars in the Netherlands and elsewhere, such as Ieuan Llwyd of Yale, William Thomas of Caernarfon and Sir Thomas Morgan of St George's (Glamorgan) and Pen-carn in Monmouthshire, and some of them returned with amazing tales of their exploits to tell.[58] Spanish pretensions and Irish Catholic support ('kythrel Gwyddelic') were deplored and the Queen's person elevated as a symbol of independence and virtue in the Renaissance atmosphere of the royal court. It is in this context that literary sources commenting on wider issues need to be closely evaluated.

The writings of George Owen reveal a variety of contemporary views on the cult of monarchy and its bearing on the defence of

Wales. Despite its shortcomings the Tudor settlement, he maintained, 'now being governed by these good laws . . . in time . . . will grow to a perfect well-governed commonwealth'.[59] When referring to the traditional game *cnapan*, being played in Pembrokeshire in the summer of 1588 at a time when the 'invincible' army of Spain was on the coasts and the hard and 'bloody' encounter was about to take place, he observed a response to the question of how these aggressive players could be pacified:

> 'Well', said one, 'this is all in play, and will be taken in good part'. 'If this be but play', quoth the other man, 'I could wish the Spaniards were here to see our play in England [i.e. Wales], *certes* they would be in bodily fear of our war'.[60]

In the opening section of his 'Dialogue' he described the imaginary Barthol as a German lawyer from Frankfurt who visited England after the sack of Antwerp by the duke of Parma in 1585 where his wife and two sons had been murdered by the 'Spanish sword'. He described the damaging effects of the Spanish war on Pembrokeshire, in that the county was expected to train far more soldiers than any two counties in Wales and 'thereby have greatlie impaired themselves in wealth so that of later years her Majesty's subsidy in that shire is decayed half in half & more of that it was heretofore'.[61] In 1597 300 troops were also maintained by the shire for service in Ireland before they were dispatched from the county, and seventy-five Spanish captives were maintained for over four months to their 'intolerable charge'.[62]

Whatever the misgivings, the impact of government was regarded as beneficial. In 1578 Rice Merrick of Cotrel, the antiquary whose work has been cited above, declared that the unity of the realm was created by the rule of law. 'What was then [i.e. pre-1536] justifiable by might, although not by right is now to receive condign punishment by law', he declared, emphasizing that only legitimate government could maintain order and justice.[63] The need to establish peace and unity was identified with a powerful monarchy ruling in accord with the wishes of its subjects through the hierarchical structure of its institutions. Forces were ranged against the realization of such sentiments; symptoms of disorder were in evidence, such as a devalued currency, religious disunity, isolation in Europe, dynastic problems, economic instability, lack of a central military control, unrest in parliament and combating foreign threats. It was the exploitation of the Queen's role in such circumstances that could create unity out of diversity and restore peace in unstable conditions. Government was not at its most efficient but Elizabeth achieved her aim of preserving the realm's independence. She prevented the Habsburgs from benefiting from her weakness and her political expediency helped to maintain her security, particularly during the Anglo-Spanish war.

The Defence of the Faith: Puritan Observations

The period of peace before 1585 enabled the Queen to boost her self-confidence. Given her weakness, however, some writers were less assured that the Queen offered the realm her best service and expressed the concern that Spanish power might yet again revive, not only because of military and naval strength but because of God's judgement on the realm and its monarch. This is amply reflected in the works of John Penry, the Welsh Puritan agitator, who passionately believed that, since the government had failed to introduce a preaching ministry into his native country, the moral condition of its inhabitants had been seriously damaged. In his three main treatises on Wales, published in 1587–8 with regard to the need for spiritual regeneration, he ponderously referred to the Roman Catholic threat as a divine instrument used to reconvert the people, and he urged the Queen and the government to attend to this critical situation by establishing what he regarded as God's Church on earth. His outlook, therefore, highlights another aspect in which the realm might be defended. Penry's attitude was both frank and cautious for he used the consequences of the Spanish Armada as a means of forcing the Queen's hand.[64] He was aware that the Old Faith was gaining ground on the continent and urged the Queen to attend to the need for Church reform before it was too late. His intransigence and harsh comments on the clergy, especially the bishops, revealed the intensity of his plea. The ignorance and superstition of the Welsh people, in his mind, revealed moral degeneracy and the survival of the 'blasphemous mass' and its traditions, among other things, caused the 'utter ruin of our land, the raising of our names from under heaven, that we shall be no more a people'.[65] It was the government's responsibility to destroy heresy, to improve the moral standards of the nation and establish the true Church of God as he envisaged it. Penry's ardent plea was made in a period of impending crisis: it was not only intended to safeguard the realm faced by Spanish aggression but also to protect Puritanism which was under threat. Despite his contempt for the Spaniards and his belief that they were militarily inferior to England, he saw them as divine agents whose military and naval preparations would punish 'sins within the land'. In his view, Spanish hostility was less to be feared than moral degeneration. Penry used Spain as a means to alarm the Queen and her government into positive action after the defeat of the Armada. Owing to more favourable circumstances he had been forced to adopt a different but equally persuasive line of argument.[66]

After stating his case in the *The Aequity of an Humble Supplication* (1587) John Penry proceeded to particularize on the evils that could undermine unity and the reformed Church. Had it not been that God

> in mercy chocked with their owne raging spirits, their vnsatiable blood-suckers Babington and his adherentes, that we should haue had in this kingdome the hand of the vile, against the honorable, the base against the noble, the indign against the woorthiest of the land?[67]

Had the circumstances been more favourable the 'heathen popish traitors' might have destroyed the monarchy. This is Penry's first attempt to use external affairs to frighten the Queen into positive action. The 'crew . . . of obstinate idolaters [persistent priests and recusants] that would fain be again in execrable Rome . . . that sacrilegious nest' were supportive of Spanish designs and the 'forces of Rhomish Caine' and 'Rhomish Antichrist'.[68] They were the enemy's agents in residence; given the appropriate circumstances, they would be prepared to strike against what Penry considered to be an ineffective monarchy. The first treatise, submitted to the Queen in parliament in February 1587, revealed Penry's detestation of Roman Catholicism which he considered to have been among the chief causes of spiritual malaise in the kingdom.

Penry's attack on Spain in that work was more restrained than in his third treatise, which appeared soon after the Armada. The *Aequity* was intended to cajole rather than to coerce the Queen into shaping a new reforming policy. He concentrated on presenting the Welsh case rather than on reprimanding the Queen. In his view it was God, not the Queen nor her government, that had rescued the realm from catastrophe in the period 1569–87. He did not overstate the case but rather suggested methods by which reform might be achieved despite external threats. Spanish designs were far too serious to be used at that time to chastize the Queen. By reforming the Church, Penry believed, she would advance her policy significantly to counteract foreign threat and fortify her own kingdom. As God's instrument she might prove herself to be an agent whereby the spiritual regeneration of the Welsh people might be secured. As a member of a revered royal line and a descendant of the ancient British she was regarded as a power within her own realm which, provided she searched her conscience and fulfilled God's will, Philip II could not challenge successfully. Thus, if success were to come his way, the king of Spain, despite his pretensions, would have no part in achieving it.[69]

It was the imminent preparations for the Armada that forced Penry into adapting a different and more radical outlook in the second treatise, *An Exhortation unto the Governors of Wales*, because religious conditions, in his opinion, were rapidly deteriorating. Penry had realized that Spain's crusade, especially since the death of Mary Queen of Scots, demanded urgent attention. The circumstances could be used to chastize and compel the Queen and the Council in the Marches to take action. His message to Henry Herbert, lord president of the Council in the Marches, at Ludlow was clearly aimed at expounding the essence of Christian 'governorship':

> Gouernors, my Lorde, must gouern vnder God. They haue no allowance to be rulers, wher the Lord is not serued, where he hath no acknowledgement of superioritie, there man hath no commission from him to beare rule. Satan hath a kingdome my Lord, where Christ ruleth not . . . If you would declare vnto the world (which thing you ought to be careful of) that the power of the worde hath touched your verye soule, with a conscience to serue your God, you can neuer doe this as long as you haue no care that the Lorde bee glorified in as many as he hath committed vnto your gouernment.[70]

Spain is not specifically mentioned in this treatise but the above extract reveals the emphasis Penry placed on the central role of the governor, in this case the lord lieutenant of Wales, in the advancement of the 'true faith'. Emphasis is placed on government and the place of secular magistrates in the task of defending God's Church against forces which upheld 'public idolatry and the false worship of the true or false God'.[71] The exercise of legitimate government as 'honourable magistracy' was founded on divine appointment. Pembroke was described as the agent designated by God to initiate what exclusive powers he had 'so necessarily and fatally laid' upon him. People committed to his charge should be 'fed with knowledge' to offset the forces of evil.

It is in the third treatise, *A Supplication unto the High Court of Parliament*, published after the defeat of the Armada, that Penry pressed his argument most forcefully. In the last sections of the treatise he passionately deplored the dire condition of Wales in

view of the continued Roman, Spanish and Guisian threats. The
'late deliverance' in 1588, he maintained, would not have occurred
if God had intended to punish the nation for its ignorance 'and
wicked ecclesiastical constitutions'. Although God had not called
the sins to account, circumstances did not augur well for the future
unless parliament attended immediately to the reforming pro-
gramme. 'The lord, by that deliverance', he stated, 'gave us
warning that he passed by us, but so . . . unless the corruptions of
his service be clear done away with speed . . . meaneth to pass by
us no more.'[72] He believed that God favoured the nation when the
Armada was dispersed as he was at times disposed to treat the
Israelites, for he would not wish the Spaniards to believe that it
was they not he who had acted high-handedly. God, Penry
continued, could use the same instruments to destroy the nation.
'The same Lord that wrought our deliverance', he maintained,
'will surely be the cause of our ruin.' Unless the gospel be granted
'free passage . . . the navy of the Spaniard . . . shall come again, and
fight against the land, and waste it with fire and sword'. They
should not deceive themselves by believing that the 'discomfited'
Spaniards were weakened to such an extent that they were unable
to fulfil their intentions. When that invasion took place God would
strengthen them a thousandfold more and would 'send a tremor
into the heart of our valiantest and stoutest men'. He continued on
this theme in his most rhetorical manner:

> It is not therefore the Spanish furniture and preparations: but the sins
> within the land, which we are most of all to feare. For although the army
> of the Spaniard were consumed with the arrowes of famine: although
> the contagious and deuouring pestilence had eaten them vp by
> thousands: although their tottering shipps were dispersed, and caried
> away with the whirlwinde and tempest, although madnesse and
> astonishment were amongst them, from him that sitteth in the throane,
> vnto her that grindeth in the mill: although the Lords reuenging sword,
> in the hand of our valiant captaines and souldiers, had so preuailed
> against them . . . a navie of winde and weather beaten ships, a refuse of
> feeble and discomfited men, shalbe sufficiently able to preuaile against
> this lande; vnlesse another course be taken for Gods glory in Wales . . . [73]

This section marks the peak of Penry's anti-Spanish stand. Percept-
ively, he attributes to Spain the power that God might use to reduce
the realm to submission. Despite all its afflictions Spain would
conquer since God's favour to England would have been lost. It is a
powerful section aimed at bringing the Queen finally to the point of
recognizing and undertaking her most urgent obligations.

Defence Concerns in Early Stuart Wales

John Penry's pleas were powerfully presented and provided food
for thought for a government beset by severe economic and
political problems. In less critical times it was this attitude of mind
that prevailed in the seventeenth century, although, during the
period to the outbreak of Civil War, firmer attempts were made to
secure peace in Europe, as is signified in the works of Sir John
Stradling of St Donat's whose view of the Anglo-Spanish War in
1624 seems not to have been clear despite his expressed loyalty to
the Crown.[74] In *A political discourse or dialogue between a knight of
the Commons-house of parliament and a Gentleman his friend being a
moderate Roman Catholic* in 1625, the Catholic argued against an
anti-Spanish alliance while the knight (who aired Stradling's view)
believed that Spain had forced England into war.[75] In attempting
to remedy all abuses, as the eccentric William Vaughan of
Llangyndeyrn recognized them while preparing the way for the *The
Golden-fleece*, he composed a long poem in which Apollo
pronounced an Oracle to deliver the realm from such detestations
as 'Spanish pensions and their Spies . . . Spanish Sallets . . . Spaines
gallies . . . all State Reason hatcht in Spaine . . . the Spanish
Inquisition'.[76] When surveying overseas plantations with a view to
establishing a colony in the East Indies, of all the difficulties he
considered that 'the malise of the Spaniards' was the most
obstructive factor – 'who being like the Dogge in the Manger doe
want people to plant and yet they will not permit others to plant'.[77]

   The ill-fated journey of Charles, Prince of Wales, to Spain to
seek the Spanish Infanta in marriage in 1623 was viewed with
much trepidation in England and even among those who
accompanied him.[78] James I's plan formed a part of the grand
scheme to establish peace in Europe. The proposed marriage
would yield a substantial dowry which could be used to restore
the Palatinate to his son-in-law, the Elector Frederick. Sir James
Perrot, fully in support of the sovereign's policy, also considered
the defence of Protestantism to be a crucial issue. In 1621 he
reminded the Commons that supporting the Elector Palatine
implied involving themselves and their estates legitimately in
'Defence of Religion', a striking reminder that he and his fellow
gentry in Wales still clung steadfastly to traditional principles.[79]
He also envisaged that peace would be restored and that James,
who wished to be regarded as the 'arbiter' of Europe, would
improve his reputation on the continent and preserve his honour
at home. This plan, however, was impracticable because the match

was unpopular in England and the proposal came at a time when
the reformed faith was being threatened on the continent. Spanish
diplomacy at the time frustrated James for Spain was unprepared
to go to war against the Emperor. However, a Spanish alliance still
appealed to him. Parliament, which was summoned for the third
time in 1621, urged the King to declare war on Spain and seek a
Protestant wife for Charles but, in his view, such proposals
threatened his prerogatives. Sir Richard Wynn, gentleman of the
privy chamber to the Prince of Wales, had misgivings about his
intended journey to Spain with Prince Charles:

> It is my ill fortune to be commanded by the king to be one of those that
> are shortly to follow the Prince into Spain, a dangerous and ane
> expensfull iorny, but being a subiect and a servant I am tied to obaie; if
> I can possibly avoid it I will, if not I will with patience under go it.[80]

Lack of correspondence from Spain on this venture was caused
largely by the interception of private letters and papers to prevent
any serious intelligence leak. Moreover, the landscape of Castile
and Aragon did not match that of Wales for 'our barrenesse [is]
most frutfull to thers'. Rhys Prichard, the puritan vicar of
Llanymddyfri, composed forty-four free-metre verses to welcome
Charles back from Spain. Fear of Spain still remained strong and
the following two verses by Prichard indicated that:

> Spain a fynnai, mewn cyfrwysder,
> Gadw'n Prins dros ddyddiau lawer;
> Duw a gwlad a fynnai, er hynny,
> Fyrr ymchweliad Prins y Cymry.
>
> Duw 'mddiffyno rhag bradwriaeth,
> Cadwed Crist ef rhag Pabyddiaeth,
> A rhag pawb sydd yn amcanu
> Drwg na speit i Brins y Cymry.[81]

[Cunningly, Spain was determined to detain the Prince for many days;
God and the realm demanded, however, the quick return of the Prince
of Wales. God defend him from treachery: May Christ keep him from
Papistry and from all who aim to harm and spite the Prince of Wales.]

This opinion was not shared by all: James Howell, writer,
traveller and historiographer royal, for example, wrote as follows
in 1624:

> I hold the Spanish Match to be better than their Powder; and their
> Wares better than their Wars; and I shall be ever of that mind, That no

country is able to do England less hurt, and more good than Spain, considering the large Trafic and Treasure that is to be got thereby.[82]

Howell also declared that England was then better esteemed by Spain because of the prospect of a Spanish match although the upper classes did not favour it. Commercially, it would be an asset and, despite the strong opposition to it, it was welcomed by the nobility and the gentry.[83] Howell was a perceptive observer; his travels abroad had taught him much about the characteristics of Europeans, and had enabled him to make shrewd comments about them, but he was insensitive to the continuing anti-Spanish feeling in the country. The Madrid visit was a fiasco and the duke of Buckingham, who accompanied Charles, became extremely unpopular in England and among the Spaniards. Charles was hailed a hero on his return because the marriage, if it had gone ahead, might have achieved for Spain what the series of Armadas had unsuccessfully attempted, namely to make England and Wales Roman Catholic. War was eventually declared against Spain in 1624 and the abortive Mansfeld expedition and the collapse of the Cadiz raid made Buckingham an object of ridicule in the House of Commons. The Irish threat and Charles's marriage to the French princess, Henrietta Maria, aroused suspicions which were not alleviated by a more stringent enforcement of the Penal Laws. By 1627 England was at war also with France, which led to Buckingham's disastrous attack on the Isle of Ré in 1627 in an attempt to relieve pressure on the Huguenots at La Rochelle.

During the wars, the danger of a Franco-Spanish-papal alliance arose and anxieties concerning the inadequacies of coastal defence again came to the fore. Danger also came from recusant activity at home and Irish support for Spain. Threats were posed by the recalcitrant earls of Worcester at Raglan and the Herberts of Powys Castle who were prepared to advance the Catholic cause in the traditional breeding grounds. The fear of popery and the threat that a Welsh popish army might be raised continued long after the Gunpowder Plot. The Catholic Irish rebellion in Ulster in 1641 intensified the situation in the same way as it had created anxieties in the past. Hugh Owen of Plas-du, whose years in Spanish service caused the government to suspect his loyalty, projected a plan which entailed using Spanish and Irish troops who would land on the coasts of England and Wales pretending that bad weather conditions had forced them to take shelter on their way to Flanders. They were to capture the fleet at Rochester and reinforcements from Flanders were expected to join them from Dunkirk to overrun the country.

From 1595 onwards about a thousand men a year left for military service in Ireland, which proved unpopular for a variety of reasons. In 1599 the Privy Council complained that the choice of men for service, their unruly behaviour, and their mutinous spirit and desertion had caused much concern. It appeared that men were chosen for service chiefly to 'disburden' the country of vagrants and the like.[84] Such a situation, it was declared, led to inefficiency and dissatisfaction, which advantaged the Irish. Ieuan Llwyd Sieffrai, a contemporary north Wales bard, in his poem entitled 'Yr Hydd o Essex' ('The Essex Stag') described Devereux's feats, the death of Sir Henry Bagenal, related to the Penrhyn family, and Spanish designs in Ireland during the Tyrone rebellion:

> Llosgi rhongddo'r wlad, a'i sbeilio;
> Lladd a mwrddro'r Saeson:
> Cael y Spaenwyr ar i dir,
> A'u bryd ar gefnu'r Werddon.
>
> Y siwrne a fu atgas, gwanychu yn teyrnas,
> Marfolaeth a gafas llawer gŵr tal:
> Sawdwyr Cymru, llwyr gwae ni
> Oedd ladd Syr Harri Bagnal.[85]

[Together they razed to the ground and despoiled the countryside, killing and murdering Englishmen. The Spaniards descending on its land intending to support Ireland. Hateful was the journey and crippling to the realm; many a fine man met his death. Soldiers of Wales, woe, woe to us by Sir Harry Bagenal's death.]

Conclusion

The theme of Spanish aggression and opposition is particularly relevant in any examination of the reactions of Welsh gentry, antiquaries and litterateurs to the external issues confronting the Tudors and early Stuarts and to the concept of authority and methods of exercising and maintaining it within the sovereign realm. It is also a factor that has not received the attention it deserves and needs to be examined as an integral part of the political and social environment of the *uchelwyr*. Foreign threats had, over the centuries, caused constant concern, regardless of whether the realm was prepared to meet them or not. The coasts were exposed to attacks from east and west and, in the sixteenth century, the rise of the Habsburg and Valois powers in Europe led to the creation of further pressures in economic and religious as well as political affairs. Twenty years earlier England would not have been capable of surviving Spanish aggression and, in 1585, the theatres of war on land and sea placed heavy demands on her resources. Spain's opposition exposed many weaknesses in the realm's defensive mechanism: the lack of a standing army and manpower, a smaller population compared with France and Spain to finance the war, naval inadequacies, the increase in war expenditure as well as the danger posed by Mary Queen of Scots.

It is in this broad context that the strength of Spanish power against England must be evaluated. It gave rise to imperial claims to the New World because hatred of Spain was fostered by commercial rivalry as well as political aspirations. It also served to expose concern over security and the unity and survival of the Protestant realm. Danger also sprang from rebellions and plots: legislation and royal proclamations increasingly dealt with regional religious and political grievances from the Rising of the Northern Earls (1569) onwards to the end of Elizabeth's reign. In religious matters the involvement of Catholic priests in conversion missions abroad continued after the Armada. The proclamation that commanded that priests should be detected and punished in 1591 criticized Philip II for allowing seminaries, such as Valladolid in Spain, to be established to provide for English students. Moreover, further provisions ordered local governors to inquire into religious practices and to investigate the activities of any persons who had returned from the continent as Catholics. Philip II had

> no good success with his great forces against our realm, yet if now he will once again renew his war . . . there shall be found ready secretly within our dominion many thousands . . . that will be ready to assist such power as he shall set on land.[86]

The opening section of the proclamation referred to continued opposition on behalf of Spain although Philip's mission had waned: 'after his continuance in seeking to trouble our state . . . so many years have waxed faint and decayed in him'. Since he continued to threaten the realm action had to be taken against those who assisted him in the name of religion.[87] Since dangerous rumours (noted above) had spread concerning the Queen's ill-health in her last months – a situation which might have spurred ardent Catholics on to conspire – the Privy Council urgently commanded local county officials to suppress them as 'p'sons of cheife authority and reputacon . . . and of entyre affection to the preseruacon of the state'. At Ludlow, Lord Zouche, lord president of the Council in the Marches, reinforced this urgent plea in 1602:

... for I protest the desire of a peaceable gov'm'nt and due execucon of Lawes is all I seek w'ch to neglect wilbe the ov'throw of comon wealthes, and p'vate estates . . . the State p'sent wherein we have all receiued wonderfull blessinges is the cause of o'r care . . . all men ought to take to hart if god should so punish us, as to make our tymes vnhappie by dep'ving us of so most p'cious a Jewell [i.e. the Queen].[88]

Considering all these factors relating to the use and abuse of authority, practically and symbolically, in preserving the realm's independence of foreign interference it needs to be asked: how do those who wielded that authority fit into the picture of maintaining the realm's sovereignty? The answer lies fundamentally in the fact that the Welsh regarded themselves, by virtue of their racial distinctiveness, as being inextricably bound to it and part of it. That is how they perceived themselves to be and any declaration of loyalty would certainly appeal to the Welsh gentry for to them the bonds between Church, state and the establishment of good order sprang from their historical awareness and national identity, usually termed *yr iaith* – the community of people or race (*natio*) – which implied, for the gentry, that inalienable birthright inherited from a highly privileged native aristocracy. It was linked with the ancient traditions of the ancient British united within the bonds of race, religion and culture. The 'undefiled' religion, as defined by Welsh Protestant humanists, had its roots in that civilization. The concept of 'Great Britain' for Sir William Maurice, one of its chief advocates, implied that James I was 'wedded to the old widow Britaine',[89] and in a letter to a kinsman he expatiated at some length on the British prophecy in its relation to the Tudor and Stuart monarchies:

I meane the prediction or prophesye of *coronoge vabann*, and heerin I will rejoine a littell with you sensiblye on that pointe and stand uppone the maxime of all our propheseys which is that out of the Bryttishe line shold descende one that sholde restore the kingdoom of Brittaine to the pristine estate. This did Kadwalader, the last kinge of the Brittaines, prophesye at his departure. Thence cometh all our propheticall predictions and oracles.[90]

Some fifty years earlier Sir John Price had regarded Edward VI as descended from 'one of the most primitive and notable pedigrees of British kings'.[91] It was the restoration of the primitive Christian Church, the revival of ancient learning and the union in 1603 of the crowns of Britain which, in Protestant opinion, gave credence to the imperial claims of the Crown (see pp. 112–13).

The humanist Humphrey Prichard, in his preface to Dr John Davies's *Cambrobrytannicae Cymraecaeve Linguae Institutiones et Rudimenta* (1592), drew attention to Elizabeth as a descendant of ancient lineage in the spirit of other writers of his time among English and Welsh scholars.[92] In that context the Reformation and what it represented in terms of national solidarity was regarded as the fulfilment of ancient prophecies that the historic identity of Britain would again be restored.

For the Welsh gentry steeped in these traditions, however, the Tudor monarchy stood not so much as a symbol of the ancient prophecies and national prestige but, more realistically, through the agency of the law, parliament and the Church, as a bulwark against anarchy. Each was linked to form the composite structure for the government of the realm of Britain. The pacification of Ireland and establishment of Protestantism there were regarded partly as a means of consolidating political lordship and defending the realm against Spain. Thus, in the gentry's view, politics and religion were integrated; the Church assumed its political function and was interwoven into the fabric of government as an essential component in maintaining order. As early as 1625 Sir John Stradling of St Donat's, an unyielding royalist, expressed concern that power in the realm had declined because of the sharp and irreconcilable divisions within it:

> . . . let Unitie us in one bundle binde
> That all may be of one heart, and one minde.[93]

Fundamentally, it was support for this alliance between the gentry and the Church and a desire to defend it and maintain unity in the realm that accounted principally for the measure of support given to Charles I in Wales during the Civil Wars.

CHAPTER 5

The Protestant Church

Attention has been drawn in earlier sections of this study to the position of the Protestant Church as one of the bastions of unity and uniformity in the Elizabethan and early Stuart periods. An examination of the exercise of authority in the state uncovers the firm alliance between the ecclesiastical and secular spheres of government, and it is in keeping with the central theme of this study to inspect more closely the nature of the authority the Church exerted in relation to the gentry, who had benefited so much by plundering it, and in community life generally. One leading issue that emerges is how Protestant ecclesiastical leaders, most of whom enjoyed gentry status through their lineage, viewed their obligations in the Church and, as agents of the Crown engaged in maintaining the integrity of the Protestant establishment, how far they were prepared to go to control the ambitions of lay gentry, some of whom stood at nothing to despoil ecclesiastical property. At the basis of this theme lies a fundamental issue, namely the degree to which the Elizabethan Church, despite deepening divisions within it by the mid-seventeenth century, was able to impose its authority and uphold its credibility as a state institution, again with particular reference to the ruling gentry.

The Gentry and the Religious Order

The authority exercised by Church leaders in the careers of lay gentry in this period is well attested, but in order to establish further the role of the gentry in community life it is necessary to consider the degree to which a close alliance was established between the Church and the ruling families in an age when uniformity and internal security were priorities. This section aims to examine their contribution to religious affairs in the context of their role as regional governors and as a preliminary survey to a more detailed investigation of issues regarding the fortunes of the Protestant Church and adherents of the Old Faith.

The preservation of the social order was identified by the majority of gentry, who were beneficiaries when the religious houses were dissolved and friaries and chantries abolished, not only with secular institutions but also with the Protestant Church establishment of 1559. The majority, who adhered to the national Church, were not able to distinguish between royal authority in Church and state. To them, the Church and institutions of government shared the same authority which sprang from the same divine source. Though they were firmly committed to upholding the main agencies of Tudor regional government, some uncertainty occurred in religious allegiances. The introduction of Protestantism in the reign of Edward VI, followed by the reversion to Roman Catholicism under Mary I, created confused loyalties among families that had supported the creation of the Henrician nation-state and had benefited immensely from it. The years c.1550–70 constituted a bewildering period for some, although the majority, hard-headed and ambitious as ever, followed government guidelines and accepted the new Elizabethan settlement after Mary's death. To what measure strong Protestant feelings were formed among the gentry in general is difficult to assess on Elizabeth I's accession. Public records and private correspondence are often silent on such matters. What is evident, however, is that the die was cast after the Queen's excommunication in 1570, when Catholics were absolved of their allegiance to the Queen and urged to oppose her and her government. Whereas opposition to the religious settlement had hitherto been heretical, it was thenceforth treasonable.[1]

Despite the tense political implications of the religious situation a select band of gentry, varying in their material means and well-distributed throughout Wales, clung fearlessly to the Old Faith and commanded the support of their kinsmen and tenants. Sir Thomas Stradling of St Donat's was imprisoned in the Tower from 1558 until 1561, having been accused of causing pictures of the cross to be made in the grain of a tree at the castle and for hearing mass.[2] Among other powerful recusants were the Pughs of Penrhyn Creuddyn, Owens of Plas-du, Edwardses of Plasnewydd and Chirk, Herberts of Powys Castle, the earls of Worcester at Raglan, Morgans of Llantarnam and Turbervilles of Pen-llin in the Vale of Glamorgan and their cadets. In matters of income and territorial power they represented a varied group of gentry who commanded the full support of their tenantry. They interpreted their authority in a dual capacity, as adherents of the papacy as the spiritual head of the Church and as secular administrators who, despite their convictions, clung to office as fast as they could. In that respect they exercised their powers on two separate yet inter-related bases: in the Elizabethan era, while they remained loyal to the Old Faith, in secular affairs most of them continued to maintain their allegiance to the Queen. It is hardly surprising, therefore, that some of them confidently exercised official positions under the Crown. Despite his deep religious convictions Robert Pugh of Penrhyn Creuddyn, for example, served as member of parliament for Denbighshire in 1559 and as sheriff two years later. Sir Thomas Stradling of St Donat's was also a prominent administrator, and William Morgan of Llantarnam, although he benefited handsomely from the dissolution of religious houses, served as sheriff of Monmouthshire in 1568 and member of parliament for the shire in 1559 and 1571, and his descendants were equally active. Edward Herbert of Montgomery and Blackhall, a kinsman of the Raglan family, was regarded as late as 1585 as a supporter of Mary Queen of Scots although he was squire of the body to Elizabeth and reputed to be a keen suppressor of thieves in mid-Wales. Members of the Edwards family of Chirk and Plasnewydd, particularly John Edwards senior, who was imprisoned in 1579 for having mass said in his home, and his son and namesake, were equally actively engaged in local affairs. The third John Edwards was also outwardly conformist, but when recusancy laws were imposed after 1605 he failed the sacramental test and refused to take the new oath of allegiance. Consequently he was fined two-thirds of his estate and regarded as a 'dangerous recusant'. Such a duality explained attitudes in that family towards the political and religious situation in the realm after 1559.

The majority of Welsh gentry, however, with varying degrees of enthusiasm decided to defend the New Faith. Individual members of gentry families responded according to their private circumstances or to the political pressures exerted upon them. Gauging the extent of Protestantism in Wales by the close of Elizabeth's reign is an impossible task: it was a period of transition, not only in religious allegiances but also in social trends and dynastic affairs. What can be said, however, is that Roman Catholic practices continued to linger on in the hinterland and that Jesuit priests, few though they were, were still active in the Welsh countryside. Although the number of recusants was relatively small, fear of plots and invasions persisted and Welsh bishops were increasingly concerned about the degree of recusant activity in their dioceses.

To what extent the Old Faith was a potent force in parts of Wales in the late sixteenth and early seventeenth centuries is not altogether clear but, judging from the sparsity of Catholic priests, it does not appear that the Jesuit mission had much impact, particularly in the heartland. What is certain, however, is that the early decades of the seventeenth century saw the deeper rooting of the Elizabethan Church in Wales. Despite difficulties, a firm base was established by first- and second-generation bishops and inspired humanist scholars among the priesthood. The peak of achievement was reached in 1588 when the first translation of the Bible into Welsh appeared. Not that the Bible in Welsh was welcomed by all: in the long period between 1563 and the appearance of the complete version no enthusiasm was invoked among the gentry generally to see the statute enforced, most concern being expressed by the puritan John Penry. It was he, it is argued, in his first pamphlet addressed to the Queen in parliament, persistently calling upon the government in 1587–8 to ensure that the scriptures were made available in the vernacular, who was partly responsible for spurring Archbishop Whitgift and William Morgan onwards to complete the work. There was indeed some hostility towards the language and opposition to the decision to translate the scriptures for, in 1595, Maurice Kyffin reported that a cleric, possibly Bishop William Hughes of St Asaph, had remarked that there was no need for a Bible or any other books in Welsh and that the Welsh people should be instructed to learn the English language.[3]

Despite the frustration that hampered Morgan's progress with the translation, the Bible did appear in 1588 and the Church increased its pressure to offset Catholic threats, particularly in the border areas. With the growth of a Protestant tradition it naturally followed that the Elizabethan Church was regarded by the majority of the gentry as a bastion of unity and uniformity alongside the Crown, the law and parliament. With regard to the majority of these conforming gentry, some of whom were more devoted to the Protestant faith than others, they believed that authority in the Church could not be separated from authority in the state and their exercise of power on behalf of the Crown in the localities. 'What really counted with most of the Welsh gentry', Sir Glanmor Williams declared, 'was the security of the political and social order from threats internal and external. Its stability was guaranteed in their eyes by the successful liaison between their pre-eminence in the locality and royal jurisdiction at the centre.' It is in this context that the ethos of gentility in the century following the assimilation of Wales with England, as it was applied to public life, needs to be understood. 'This close-knit unity between squirearchy and church', he maintained further, 'is the key to

understanding much of what happened in Stuart Wales',
particularly at the time when the Civil Wars broke out.[4] By that
time a significant minority of puritanically inclined gentry had
acquired some prominence in public life, such as Edward
Downlee (or Dunn Lee), member for Carmarthen boroughs, who
presented John Penry's first treatise to the Commons in 1587. The
speech delivered by Sir William Herbert of St Julian's, member of
parliament for Monmouthshire, in the House of Commons
against Mary Stuart in 1586, appears to be the first one recorded
by a Welsh member in the House's Journals.[5] Others among them
were Sir Richard Trefor, soldier and administrator, of Trefalun in
Denbighshire, Sir James Perrot, illegitimate son of Sir John Perrot
of Haroldston, and Sir Thomas Middleton of Chirk Castle[6] and
London who, together with Rowland Heylin, a native of Llanymynech, Montgomeryshire, and a London merchant, sponsored
the pocket-size edition of the Welsh Bible in 1630.[7]

These individuals, in different walks of life, were sufficiently
prominent and highly regarded to impose their authority on
society. They all emerged from the social ranks which had tasted
power and had exerted influence, and religion was considered to
be yet another potent force which consolidated their reputations
as public governors. The Reformation had so much to offer the
gentry whatever their religious pursuasions. It enabled them to
augment their estates by purchasing or leasing Church properties
and tithes that increased their landed powers, a practice that
caused much anxiety to Church leaders. Serious though recusancy was, it was not as deep-seated a threat as that posed by the
rapacity of those gentry families who busily impropriated tithes
and livings. William Morgan, bishop of St Asaph, furiously
opposed his one-time patron, Sir John Wynn, concerning the
leasing of church lands in Llanrwst parish in 1601, declaring that

> . . . one thynge moveth me agaynst all these, vz. my conscience w'ch
> assureth me th[a]t your request ys such th[a]t, in grauntyng it I sh'd
> prove my self an unhonest, unconscionable and irreligiouse man, ye a
> sacrilegeous robber of my church, a p'fydiouse spoyler of my diocesse
> and an unnaturall hynderer of preachers & good Scholers.[8]

Such bitter words were intended to show some retaliation on the
part of the most conscientious prelate of his generation (see
Chapter 3, pp. 77–8). The gentry sought, even in days of a change
in the value of Church properties, to exploit the market with
exceptional shrewdness. Although the Church, as an institution, on
the one hand, represented order, it was, on the other, vulnerable to

exploitation. Bishop Richard Parry, Morgan's successor at St Asaph, commented on the ruthless activities among lay gentry when he reported the miserable state of the diocese in 1611, focusing on persistent recusancy and the poor quality of the clergy and stressing the bad effects of lay impropriation. The diocese failed to sustain a powerful preaching ministry because stipends were low and insufficient to support a learned and dedicated clergy. He was forced to lease episcopal lands to prominent lay squires because the livings of bishops had not kept pace with the rise in prices. Bishop Francis Godwin, in his injunctions for the diocese of Llandaf in 1603, drew a very bleak picture of its condition owing to its impoverished state. He was aware that more than half the benefices were impropriate, churches in disrepair and morale very low among the clergy.[9] Despite the Crown's attempts to recover Church lands and rights in the early Stuart period, the gentry's hold on ecclesiastical property remained strong. In 1605 pluralism was denounced;[10] in 1632 the Crown tried to recover the patronage of livings[11] and, in 1634, steps were taken to curb the long leases on Church properties.[12] Nevertheless, the gentry were still firmly established and the alliance between the gentry and the Church was reinforced. It is a relevant factor when assessing the extent and nature of the support that Charles I obtained in 1642 and the character and development of the landowning families in the eighteenth century.

The above examples show that leading ecclesiasts were not backward in demonstrating their authority when confronted with hard-headed landowners intent on their own private interests. Bishops were aware of the central problems besetting the Church, namely economic malaise, the secularization of properties and, gradually in the 1630s, the growth of a vigorous brand of Puritan nonconformity. They were also adept at using their positions to counter the ambitions of the most unscrupulous among pro-prietors, some of whom, as has been illustrated, were prepared to go to any lengths to maintain their reputation and the good name of the institution they served. Where they failed was in defending their position chiefly from a position of weakness, since the Protestant establishment which they represented was largely based on a Church impeded by its medieval structure. In this context it is necessary to examine the evidence which suggests that serious attempts were made to establish the Elizabethan Church as a solid bastion of order and tradition in the Tudor state, despite the reverses which it experienced in an age of guarded allegiance and split loyalties.

The Role of the Protestant Church

When Richard Davies, bishop of St David's, submitted his report on the diocese to the Privy Council on 25 January 1569 he was particularly concerned about the condition of his clergy. In conclusion he appealed to the Privy Council:

> To become protectors and defenders of the church . . . that it be no further troblede, spoyled or impoverishede. But that smale patrymony of the church which is yet remayning to the maintenance of goddess s'vice, may so styll co'tinue to the sustentacon . . . of preachers and teachers . . . [13]

Richard Davies desired the Council to assert its authority to ensure that the Church, despite its shortcomings, maintained its role in society by providing a preaching and teaching ministry, a need that Davies considered to be essential. He was aware that the Elizabethan Church, in its first generation, faced serious problems of definition and adaptation, and he interpreted its role to be that of a defending and promoting institution designed to consolidate the Protestant settlement (1559) after a period of insecurity and uncertainty. Indeed, he and other Welsh bishops in the Elizabethan and Jacobean Church were aware of the underlying difficulties but set about defending the doctrine and organization of the new Protestant Church. They also attempted to strengthen the Church by protecting the Protestant establishment and by reforming the most glaring abuses in the Church. Within the ecclesiastical structure, they viewed their responsibilities as being twofold: establishing the New Faith in their respective dioceses by seeking to destroy its less attractive features, and suppressing vestiges of Roman Catholic recusancy and Puritanism, particularly in the borderlands of Wales. [14]

Doubtless the main deficiency in the religious life of Wales was the backward social and economic conditions hindering the Reformation from making an effective breakthrough. If the Reformation was to succeed then the Church needed to overhaul its defensive and offensive mechanisms and, in that respect, much depended on the quality of the clergy and ecclesiastical leadership and the attitude of governing families. The Protestant Church's authority after 1559 was designed to uphold the tenets of the New Faith as well as defend the integrity of the Elizabethan state. In that context both prelates and clergy were expected to share a political role essentially geared to discharging a wider obligation than is normally recognized. To succeed in maintaining that role the Church had to ensure that the quality of its clergy was sufficient to combat the real dangers encountered in the latter half of the sixteenth century. The decisive breakthrough of the Reformation depended on a number of factors which invite comparisons with the fortunes of the Protestant Church on a broader European scale. Fundamental to maintaining the Church's prestige was the exercise of authority which could only be fully asserted after the Church had adequately reformed its clergy.

It is argued that the Church in England, by the pre-Civil War period, had made some advance owing to improved educational facilities, a greater degree of mobility regarding promotion and a marked improvement in stipends.[15] Comparisons between a moribund Church in Wales and a more prosperous counterpart in the more richly endowed dioceses of southern England, however, would be unrealistic. The Welsh Church was impoverished because of its social environment and handicapped by the shortcomings of its clergy, and its problems were insuperable for its leaders. Although it inherited a coherent administrative structure under the jurisdiction of the archiepiscopate of Canterbury within which to advance the Reformation its chief weaknesses lay in its personnel, from the highest to the lowest in the ecclesiastical hierarchy, and the widespread illiteracy and ignorance that had gripped the vast majority of parishioners in dispersed rural communities. In the depleted diocese of St Asaph, for example, shortly after his appointment as bishop, Richard Parry declared that its condition was deplorable.[16] He earnestly requested Robert Cecil, lord treasurer, for assistance to enable him to come to terms with the dire situation unfolded in his letter. Among other things he referred to the fact that, of the 130 livings within his jurisdiction, thirteen of them either had no vicar or rector or were badly served by poor curates whose educational standards left much to be desired. He appealed for his diocese to be given assistance in order that livings might be improved to attract quality clergy, hoping that lay impropriations of Church properties might thereby be curbed. The number of livings held *in commendam* by Parry and his fellow bishops revealed how depressing the situation really was. Moreover, dilapidated church buildings, poor preaching skills and pastoral care, and low moral standards caused much apprehension among Church leaders. The 'frozen age', to which Lewis Bayly, bishop of Bangor, once referred, pointed to the less commendable aspects of ecclesiastical life whereby an impoverished Church lay at the mercy of grasping gentry.[17]

In the latter half of the sixteenth century the clergy seemed to have became more adept at fulfilling a pastoral vocation, but to what extent that was a common feature in Wales it is difficult to tell. It does appear, however, that increased educational training made a larger proportion among them more aware of the positive role they were expected to play in ecclesiastical affairs. The Church was attracting younger sons of gentry on an increasing scale: they, for the most part, had benefited by receiving education and had become aware of that authority which they, particularly the high-ranking clergy, were expected to impose so as to defend and advance the Protestant state. Doubtless social conditions were unfavourable but the ultimate responsibility for the Reformation's success within the Church lay essentially with episcopal leadership. It is not easy to decide the extent to which the bishops confined exercising their authority merely to seeking uniformity after 1559 rather than correcting abuses in the Church. An effectively governed episcopate could maintain the Church's prestige and promote the advance of Protestantism, but in Wales, owing to the conditions they had inherited, the response of prelates was consistently disheartening.

Within the jurisdictional and pastoral framework it is nevertheless evident that a succession of bishops attempted to advance the New Faith, but even the most praiseworthy faced considerable difficulty in combating long-term problems. Elizabethan bishops in Wales lacked the material resources to perform their functions, such as enforcing ecclesiastical discipline, emphasizing hierarchy and order, conducting regular visitations and offering hospitality. In England there was greater variety in material resources enjoyed by bishops than some historians are prepared to concede, but in Wales the situation was critical. The bishops endeavoured to maintain modest standards of living which were appreciably lower than those in the majority of English bishoprics. Even less reputable bishops like William Hughes and Marmaduke Middleton, who followed two highly esteemed predecessors at St Asaph and St David's respectively, in some respects revealed a keen awareness of the need to establish a Protestant tradition.[18] Church leaders were also aware how close the alliance was between the Church and the government and how positive a part that Church played in creating uniformity and a national awareness among the Welsh people.

Safeguarding the Protestant Tradition

One fundamental feature of the Elizabethan religious settlement was the emphasis in the Church on the Word of God and the teaching of the New Testament. It demanded personal devotion based on justification by faith. By promoting knowledge of the Bible the new Church was expected to fill the void in the spiritual life of a superstitious and ignorant peasant folk. That Church, however, was frequently harassed because uniformity was not in fact achieved. A compromise was reached with regard to doctrine, organization and ceremonial but it failed to satisfy two extreme groups in the Protestant and Catholic camps. The authorities were increasingly concerned about persistent recusant activity among families drawing their support principally from among kindred and tenants, the Jesuit mission from 1580 onwards and the ignorance and superstition of the peasantry. The first two groups were regarded as being potentially more threatening to the Church's mission than a conservative peasantry whose Catholic sentiments, strongly persistent in some areas, would in due course be subsumed into the New Faith. The circumstances which bedevilled the Welsh Church, however, revealed how unsatisfactory its situation was and how critical was the challenge facing its leaders in the period down to the Civil Wars.

Whilst the Catholics accused the government of having strong Calvinist leanings, ardent Protestants believed that reforms in the Church had not gone far enough. Elizabeth's own position was difficult because, on the international scene, despite the Peace of Câteau-Cambrésis (1559) between England, France and Spain, the threat of a Catholic League and persistent religious intrigue dogged most of her reign. At home, the situation was equally frustrating because she either had to revert to the Roman Catholic policies of Mary or accept the Church reforms introduced in Edward VI's reign. It might have been easier for her to take the former path because the Old Faith was still cherished by the mass of the peasantry, and taking such a course would also have solved many international problems.

Although Elizabeth's basic aim was secular, to maintain a united and independent realm, she also assumed the role of the pious Protestant prince. She was the symbol of the independence of the realm and personified the nation's common interests. She linked government and nation and the monarchy was the focus of national unity. Her religious settlement in 1559 revealed in what direction she intended to go: it was characterized by comprehensiveness and based legally on the Acts of Supremacy and Uniformity, a modified second Book of Common Prayer, the Royal Injunctions, and the Thirty-Nine Articles, based on the Forty-Two Articles of 1553, passed in convocation in 1563 and in parliament in 1571. The Queen, therefore, enjoyed full authority over the Church which doctrinally embraced Lutheran, Zwinglian and Calvinist teachings but, as time passed, it became more Zwinglian and Calvinist and, after 1570, was Calvinist, although the Church still clung to Roman Catholic features in discipline and ceremonial. Bishop John Jewel's *Apologia Ecclesiae Anglicanae* (1562) and Richard Hooker's *The Laws of Ecclesiastical Polity* (1593–1600) defended the Church establishment on a legal basis, which avoided civil war in England over religious matters in Elizabeth's reign. It was not a *via media* settlement but rather the creation of a national institution based on 'pragmatic political considerations'. The Church, with the 'supreme governor' at its head, was regarded as 'the most powerful motor of Tudor domestic stability'.[19]

This religious settlement was subject to attack by Catholics and extreme Protestants, the first group determined to reinstate the direct authority of the papacy and the second desiring further doctrinal and organizational reforms and denouncing recusants and priests as 'idolaters' and principal agencies of the papacy. Of these two sources of opposition it was the Catholic threat that chiefly occupied the Welsh bishops during the period down to the Civil Wars. On the continent Roman Catholic moves to regain lost ground threatened further the survival of the national English Church; the bull *Regnans in Excelsis* (1570) served to clarify the position of Catholics in relation to the Queen; the Council of Trent took a stand on liturgy and organization; the activity of the Inquisition and the introduction of militant Jesuits was intended to spread the message of reconversion to all parts of the world. Catholics at home needed to reconcile the claims of the papacy with Elizabeth's authority which was almost exclusively recognized in the realm.[20]

The Queen's problems increased following the missionary activity abroad, and the movement of seminary priests into the country in 1574 intending to convert souls caused further concern because they were regarded as Spanish agents, and persecution seemed only to strengthen their will to continue the mission. Difficulties lay in deciding who among them would stop at conversion of souls and who would be prepared to plot the Queen's death. Pope Gregory XIII, who launched the Jesuit mission, was eager to see the country converted by missionary work and more militant methods, and suggested a Spanish attack on Ireland, assuring Catholics in England that political assassination was justified. Consequently, efforts to reinstate the Old Faith were identified with treachery and treason; it threatened the new Protestant Church as well as the unity and independence of the realm. Catholics who suffered persecution were regarded as martyrs but secular authority viewed the conflict with Jesuits as being essentially political and a means of suppressing traitors.

Against such a background the Protestant bishops of Wales set out to safeguard both the new Church establishment and their own interests. From the outset they were aware that both tasks were aspects of the same challenge, the aim being to maintain the Queen's authority and domestic stability. The introduction of the religious settlement into Wales was not hindered by social or political opposition and proceeded undisturbed. Only one Marian bishop, Anthony Kitchin of Llandaf – a remarkable survivor but underrated as a prelate – was prepared to subscribe to the Act of Supremacy.[21] Other first- and second-generation Elizabethan bishops used what resources they had to promote the Church but were hindered by the social inadequacies cited above. They often found it difficult to cope with, although their correspondence does reveal that they attempted to impress the government with their determination to advance the faith and their efforts to come to terms with their problems. The most ardent among them, Richard Davies, desired the Privy Council 'for godd's sake to consider all the sp'uall sores and diseases of the dioces and to remedy the same'.[22] The appeal detailed most of them and suggested proposals aimed at eradicating some of them. It also drew attention to Davies's inability to remedy the most glaring weaknesses in his diocese. He was intent on defending a system which served as the basis of his own authority in the Church. The pressures upon that Church before 1559 were to persist in new circumstances, for the Elizabethan Church inherited many of the problems which had blighted its counterpart in the later Middle Ages.

Elizabethan bishops were responsible for governing the Church with a view to advancing the Protestant faith as well as supporting the political establishment. Among the most serious threats to the Church's integrity was the increasing secularization of Church property and tithes. Although leading laymen mostly represented families loyal to the monarchy and the New Faith, they considered the Church to be a prime means of extending their landed power in the localities. Their ambitions often led to serious confrontation between the most aggressive gentry, and the nature of the problems occasionally emerged from the responses of bishops and higher clergy to government intervention in ecclesiastical affairs.

Concern was expressed as well that ignorance and superstition seriously undermined the aim to improve the quality of religious life, particularly among the lower orders. What is uncertain is the extent to which bishops concealed their own shortcomings in these matters.

Although Church leaders did not consider it to be an insuperable task to solve such problems, they realized that ignorance and illiteracy seriously hindered the advancement of the Reformation and the exercise of their own authority. Greater concern was expressed about practical problems. At St Asaph and St David's Richard Davies experienced serious setbacks which he considered to have impeded his mission. His response to Archbishop Parker's request for information on the condition of St Asaph and its clergy in 1560 referred to the low standard of the priesthood which stemmed from absenteeism, pluralism and an inadequate preaching ministry.[23] Those who preached had sought to improve spiritual life but he, like Thomas Davies, his successor at St Asaph, was forced to accept the grim situation.[24] Davies drew attention to the widespread survival of relics and practices arising out of centuries of tradition that would take a long time to eradicate. Such strictures attributed the situation to the clergy's ineptitude. 'Ye dregs of superstition . . . ye blindness of the clergy . . . and also . . . ye closing up of God's word from them [the peasantry] in an unknown tongue' were also considered to be matters of grave concern before and after 1588, which thwarted effective pastoral leadership.[25]

From a reading of Davies's *Funerall Sermon* (1577) and his successor Marmaduke Middleton's onslaught on superstitious practices, it emerges that the Church's major problems continued to trouble the bishops. Among lay commentators who were equally concerned about illiteracy Richard Price, son of Sir John Price of Brecon, pertinently commented on the lack of instruction among the peasantry. His comments echoed the complaints made by his father in the short preamble to *Yny lhyvyr hwnn* (1546).[26] Sir John Price, eager to improve the moral condition of the people, considered that, if they were properly instructed, they would make use of the 'ample gifts of wit and understanding which God has given to them' and seek 'a taste for the sweet and pure will of God and for the salvation of their souls'.[27] That explained his desire to provide a translation of the Lord's Prayer, the Creed and Ten Commandments in Welsh. The depressed spiritual condition of the peasantry also caused concern to William Salesbury, doubtless the most erudite Welsh layman of his generation, as was revealed in the preamble to *Oll Synnwyr Pen Kembero Ygyd* (1547) which advocated the promotion of the Welsh language as a vehicle of Renaissance learning:

> ... Ac e vyddei haws i Cembro ddeall y pregethwr, wrth pregethy gair Deo. E vyddei haws o lawer, ir prechethwr traythy gair Deo yn ddeallus.[28]

> [... it would then have been easier for a Welshman to understand the preacher who preaches the Word of God. It would be much easier for the preacher to proclaim the Word of God with understanding.]

Salesbury's preamble to *A Dictionary in Englyshe and Welshe ...* (1547), dedicated to Henry VIII, reveals what his intention was: to assist the Welsh to learn English, not because he desired the extinction of the Welsh language but in order that they might, by learning English, become acquainted with the contents of the Bible and adhere to Protestant teachings which were available in that language. His words emphasize the role of the monarchy within a united realm and the central position assumed by a common language within that realm to reinforce unity and uniformity within it. Salesbury acknowledged the authority of the realm based on the scriptures and the Protestant establishment:

> Your excelle't wysdome ... hath causede to be enactede and stablyshede by your most cheffe[s]t heghest counsayl of the parlyament that there shal herafter be no differe'ce in lawes and language bytwycte youre subiectes of youre principalytye of Wales and your other subiectes of your Royalme of Englande mooste prudently consyderynge what great hatred debate [e]t stryffe hathe rysen emongeste men by reason of dyuersitie of language and what a bonde and knotte of loue and frendshyppe the comunion of one tonge is, [e]t that also by the iudgement of all wyse men it is moost conueniente and mete that they that be under dominio' of one most gracious hedde and kynge shal use also one la'guage and that even as theyr hertes agree in loue and obedie'ce to your grace so may also theyr tongues agree in one kynd of speche [e]t language.[29]

In these words Salesbury manifests the three major features of a sovereign realm, particularly in his references to the monarchy. The first is the English language as a bond of unity and the benefits gained from acquiring such a vehicle since the scriptures were already available in it. In other words, Salesbury underlines the authority of the Crown within a Protestant state and the role of language in sustaining it. He mentions two other contributory factors that consolidate that authority, namely the peace which the Crown had assured within its realm compared to the 'greate

displeasures and disturbaunce' which others have suffered, and
the legislation which assimilated Wales with England, thereby
strengthening that authority even further. Other works of his,
especially the *Baterie of the Popes Botereulx* (1550), are manifestations of his firm attachment to the New Faith. This piece of
Protestant propaganda aimed to destroy the altar as the buttress of
the Roman Church and, despite attempts to force his argument,
emphasized the tenets of the Protestant faith and the authority of
the scriptures.[30] In his preface to *Kynniver llith a ban* (1551)
Salesbury appealed to the bishops of Wales and Hereford to use
his translation into Welsh of the liturgical Gospels and Epistles if
they were approved by six scholars in each diocese since it was
they, he added in conclusion, who had the authority to do so. 'I
wrote this to you', he declared, 'because you are, after His Majesty
the King, governors overall in such matters.'[31]

Salesbury had already drawn attention to Edward VI's
responsibility in advancing the cause of Protestantism. His mild
rebuke of the bishops suggests that sufficient attention was required to publicize the cause of the faith in the Welsh language.[32]
The authority vested in Elizabeth I to defend the religious
settlement in her realm is also referred to by William Morgan in
his Latin preface to the 1588 Bible (see pp. 146–7). He considered
that the Queen's personal attributes complemented her role as a
national governor prepared to defend the sovereignty and
independence of her realm. The introduction to this preface
signifies the authority which the Queen rightfully possessed to
govern her people, and it is that authority that had been
transmitted to the leaders of her Church in Wales to enable them
and their associates to provide the scriptures in the vernacular. He
referred to a delegated authority, explaining why he is gratified by
the Queen's support for the venture:

> For . . . what an affectionate care your Majesty has for your British
> subjects this alone is sufficent to testify through all time, that you have
> not only graciously permitted, but have anxiously ratified it with the
> authority of the High Parliament of this most famous realm . . .

He immediately added his deep regret that the statute had not
been acted upon with greater urgency, as if to confess that the
benign authority of the sovereign had been rudely disregarded, an
admission that may well reflect unfavourably on the attitudes of
clergy and laity alike towards the task.[33]

Such comments drew attention to an embarrassing situation,
particularly because so much time had lapsed since the measure

providing the scriptures had been placed on the statute book. Penry emphasized Elizabeth's obligations as 'supreme Governor', ruling the Church as a lay person and exercising her authority through parliament. Maurice Kyffin translated John Jewel's *Apologia Ecclesiae Anglicanae* (1562) in 1595 (entitled *Deffynniad Ffydd Eglwys Loegr*), which constituted a stalwart defence of the Protestant settlement. His first paragraph in the preface presented to the 'general Christian reader' declared the authority possessed by the newly established Protestant Church and the manner in which it was exercised by the Queen and her prelates:

> Dymma i ti ar les d'enaid, yn hyn o lyfr, sylwedd a chrynodeb y Ffydd wir Gatholic; ith hyfforddi a'th berffeithio yn llwybr gwasanaeth Duw, ag Iechydwriaeth dyn. Wrth ddarllen hwn y cei di wybod hanes, a dealld gwirionedd y Grefydd Gristnogawl, a chyda hynny ddanghossiad a dat-guddiad amhuredd crediniaeth Pâb Rhufain. Rhoed y Goruchaf Dduw iti ochel y drwg, a chalyn y da.[34]

> [Here, for your soul's welfare. in this book, is the substance and abstract of the true Catholic Faith to instruct and perfect you in the path of God's service and man's salvation. By reading this you shall know the history and understand the truth of the Christian religion, and with that the appearance and revelation of the Roman Pope's impure belief. May God Most High enable you to avoid the evil and follow the good.]

His words testify to the authority of the new Church as conceived in the *Apologia*. It was a strict definition of creed and an attack on the Puritan concept of the primitive Church by declaring that it had been established on apostolic principles and the teaching of the Church fathers, based on scriptural authority. Kyffin considered it essential to translate this extensive work, so well received in English Protestant circles, so that the leaders of Church and state in Wales might become apprised of the authority and distinctive individuality of the Elizabethan Church.

The Condition of the Church

The anonymous writer who commented in 1586 on the religious life in the archdeaconry of Brecknock explained why ignorance had persisted among the people: there were 'very few spiritual livings or parsonages but are impropriate and in those few not one preacher'.[35] Most preambles to religious texts translated into Welsh refer to similar deficiencies. Among the most ardent critics were Maurice Kyffin, who scathingly attacked the clergy and laity alike in his preface to *Deffynniad Ffydd Eglwys Loegr* in 1595 and, in the same year, Huw Lewys, later to be appointed rector of Llanddeiniolen, Caernarfonshire, who provided a Welsh version of Miles Coverdale's translation of Otto Werdmüller's *A Spiritual and Most Precious Pearl* (*Perl mewn Adfyd*). Both authors referred to the lack of Welsh books (excepting the Bible) of any value to teach and instruct the ignorant, and feared that the authority vested in the new Protestant establishment might not be imposed on peasant folk who most needed guidance to accept and respect it. Huw Lewys more explicitly attributed the ignorance to the inadequate supply of Welsh books and the defects of prelates and clergy who were

> ... yn ddiog yn ei swydd ai galwedigaeth, heb ymarddel a phregethu ac a deongl dirgelwch gair duw i'r bobl, eythr byw yn fudion, ac yn aflafar, fal cwn heb gyfarth, clych heb dafodeu, ne gannwyll dan lestr ... [36]

> [... most slothful in their office and calling, not cherishing the task of preaching and interpreting the mystery of God's word to the people but rather living mute and unmelodious like unbarking dogs, bells with no clappers or candles beneath a vessel ...]

Lewys believed that that was why there was so much spiritual ignorance among the Welsh and many 'grey-haired sixty year olds ... so ill-endowed that they could not account for the articles of faith of the Christian religion no more than new-born children'.[37] His following comments referred to idolatry, oppression and superstition. In his view neglect of Protestant principles accounted for the serious spiritual malaise in Welsh society. The nation's woes, he believed, were caused by a self-indulgent and oppressive gentry, a factor that is seized upon also by Richard Davies and Richard Price. Besides the fact that the gentry arguably were not serving the fundamental needs of the communities as they might, but rather took advantage of the Church's debility to line their own pockets, such an argument points to its failure to come to terms with its responsibilities in the Protestant realm. In the undated suit heard in the Exchequer Court concerning the dire conditions in Churchstoke parish in Montgomeryshire and Shropshire it was claimed that the defendants had failed to provide a proper minister but had installed stipendiary ministers who were 'unlearned, poor, bare, and needy fellows ... unable to preach'. The complainants also alleged that such a situation was 'a mischeif & inconvenience'. Although they dwelt 'in Wales, amongest the mountaynes, yet they hope they are Christian people ... and their auncestors in auncient tyme gave

and yelded of their free will the tenth of all their lyvinge to be
rightlie and truelye instructed and taughte . . . in the true and
Catholike Religion'.[38]

To what extent were the bishops, as leaders, aware of their role
as defenders of the new order and of the Church as a buttress of
law and uniformity and how conscious were they of their authority
as governors of the Church? It was essentially the responsibility of
the Queen's principal secretary and the Privy Council to maintain
unity in the realm in conjunction with regional councils and other
local government institutions. It could, therefore, be said that
bishops and other senior officials in the Church were regarded by
secular authorities as servants of the state employed, like their lay
colleagues, to maintain stability in the realm.

In another related context the Church was viewed as a bastion
of the moral order enforcing discipline and obedience among the
Queen's subjects. Richard Davies saw a connection between the
support the Church required as a state as well as a religious
institution and the need to deplore unworthy, even irreverent,
conduct towards it by negligent laity. They were described as
'God's chosen officers who had acted, in all things, contrary to all
that God and the government expected, applying all their power
to further and continue the kingdom of Anti-Christ'.[39] In his
preface to the translation of the Welsh New Testament Davies
expounded at length the theory of the apostolic Church and the
'privileges and honour' which, it was said, the Welsh people had
inherited through the restoration of their 'Old Faith', allegedly the
pristine form of Protestantism.[40] That implied not only the need
to spread religious propaganda but also an attempt to establish
uniformity in the Church. When Davies referred to the need for a
knowledge of the 'eternal will of God, what religion, what
commandments and what conduct he deserves', he interpreted
order in society essentially as a manifestation of God's law as
exposed in the scriptures.[41] Neglecting God resulted in a decline
in moral standards and led to greed, oppression and violence. In
other words, disregarding or disobeying the Word created
disharmony and instability. Office-holding, legal practice and
leadership in the communities had been seriously abused. The
creation of order in society meant obedience to God's Word and
observing his commandments. William Morgan went a step
further in 1588 when he emphasized the benefits which the
Queen brought to Wales by law and providing the scriptures in the
vernacular. It was the statute of 1563 that made the translation
possible and, despite the long delay that occurred, it is certain that

it would not have been achieved without it. Thus, statute law provided the Welsh nation's greatest need, a deepening of spirituality among the people in their own tongue:

> . . . there can be no doubt that unity is more effectually promoted by similarity and agreement in religion, than in speech . . . For, unless religion be taught in the vulgar tongue, it will be hidden and unknown. For, where one is ignorant of the thing itself, he cannot know its use or sweetness, or its worth, and he will undergo no trouble to acquire it.[42]

To attend to the spiritual needs of the people through legislation was a matter of urgency. The above statement underlined the position of the state as having the sole legal authority to expedite the propagation of the gospel, and to exercise that authority by risking to forsake one of the main principles of the Act of Union. The Bible appeared as a consequence of the royal will and formed an essential part of the drive to create uniformity in the Protestant state. Morgan stressed the need for unity but considered harmony in religious affairs to be of greater importance than unity in speech: 'there can be no doubt', he asserted in his dedication, that unity in the realm was fostered more successfully when there was harmony and unity in religious faith, and he proceeded to advocate the need for piety, expediency and 'external concord'.[43] Admittedly Morgan's prime motive was religious and more attention needs to be given to the manner in which he and other Protestant writers in the Church interpreted religion within a wider political context.

In another direction Morgan, as bishop of St Asaph (1600–4), firmly defended the Church against the aggressions of powerful landed proprietors like his arch-enemy Sir John Wynn of Gwydir. On this occasion he was assertively conscious of his authority as a bishop and protective of the Church's moral welfare and integrity. He considered that allowing Wynn the right to present to a benefice was 'p'iudiciall to preachers . . . & to the church yt self w'ch wanteth competent mayntenance for p'chers'.[44] His defence even went further to declare unequivocally that he rested his case on conscience which prevented him from being made a 'stave . . . to dryve preachers partryges to hys' opponents' nets.[45] He stood steadfastly by his principles although often confronted by fierce opposition. He was aware of Archbishop John Whitgift's support and endeavoured to make the Church an institution worthy of the Protestant state. Morgan, of course, had to protect his own private interests as well as the welfare of his diocese and of Protestantism. His correspondence clearly revealed his resentment of lay impropriators who selfishly abused the authority with which they had been entrusted and indeed the authority divinely bestowed on him as bishop. For Morgan and his fellow prelates the Church symbolized the authority of the Protestant order. It stood as a buttress which, like parliament and the law, safeguarded the unity and independence of the realm. Nevertheless, the threat to the Church was a reality: 'but covetousnes raignes soe generallye . . . amongst men at this day', William Fleming, a poor priest who had been offered a chaplaincy at a price, informed Sir Edward Stradling in *c.*1580, 'that the doore w'ch leades men to any preferment, be yt never soe meane, can not be opened w'thout the sylver or goulden key'.[46] His appeal for patronage, in the first instance, revealed the difficulty of obtaining positions in the Church without adequate financial means, as well as his dependence on the goodwill of enlightened rectors. Since his days at Oxford he had attempted unsuccessfully to obtain a preferment and he relied on Stradling, whom he called 'one of the chiefest authors of my wellfare', to assist him.[47]

Aside from purely spiritual considerations, the availability of the scriptures and an improved clergy were regarded as a means to an end, namely to consolidate the realm. The poet Owain Gwynedd regarded Morgan as a 'pearl' among bishops ('Perl ydych i'r preladiaid'), not because of his erudition and glowing moral qualities alone but also because of his unyielding defence of the establishment.[48] Despite his relatively short period as bishop Morgan was concerned about lapses in clerical discipline, the dangers of nonconformity, safeguarding the Church's property, providing and administering God's Word and maintaining its integrity. Emphasis was placed on clerical residence, regular episcopal visitations, the quality of preaching and hospitality. Owing to two major weaknesses, attempts to improve episcopal control were not always successful: both the impoverishment of the Church and the interference of lay gentry forced prelates to exercise powers *de jure divino*. In that respect Morgan wished to advance the New Faith in three directions, namely by providing a dedicated ministry, by maintaining a resolute defence of the Church's position, and by acknowledging the role of monarchy and the law in promoting its scriptural foundation. In his dedication of the Bible he essentially stressed discipline, loyalty and uniformity.[49] His contribution was more extensive than that of any of his contemporaries in Wales. It entailed more than merely translating the scriptures, for his main task was to implant Protestant values more securely among his fellow Welshmen, and in the last section of his dedication where he referred to the need for unity in piety and godliness, he expressed that aim in the context of the Protestant state and the authority given him to maintain it.

Political Pressures and the Puritan Tradition

The motives underlying Elizabeth I's policies at home and abroad were similar and were often dictated by the threat of foreign invasion. In the 1580s the increasing dangers from Habsburg Spain caused the Queen and her government much anxiety. She was politic and aware of the need to achieve a balance of power in Europe between the Habsburgs and the Valois in order to prevent a Catholic alliance against her. When she took the initiative it was designed to assert her independence and preserve her sovereignty. In Wales that independence was interpreted by William Morgan and others in a more positively spiritual context. The poems composed in his honour relate chiefly to the role of the Bible as the nation's main power-house because it represented the unity of the 'British' people within the Protestant tradition. In that context the Queen is addressed by Huw Machno:

> Rhoes inni o'i gras uniawn
> Ffydd dda i'n mysg, dysg a dawn;
> Ordeiniodd wŷr da enwawg
> Gwaith rhwydd, i bregethu rhawg.[50]

[Of her just grace she gave us a fortuitous direction, learning and skill; she ordained good and famous men expeditiously for a long time to come.]

The Queen, as the fount of authority in the Church, it is said, is the giver of the true faith through her grace and propriety, and worthy men were ordained to preach this faith that would perpetuate divine favour and protect sovereign power. In the preface to *Rhann o Psalmae Dafydd Brophwyd* (1603), Edward Kyffin, while praising the Queen for her enlightened outlook on Wales, also drew attention to the need to take advantage of the stability to promote Wales's cultural interests.

A chan eyn bôd yn byw yn yr Oes honn dann ardderchokaf Vrenhines o'n gwlâd eyn hunain . . . tra fo duw yn canhiattau i ni, y rhwydd-deb, yr heddwch, a'r rhyddid y rydym yrowron yn ei gael . . . dangoswn i'r byd, eyn bôd yn prisio mwy am Ogoniant Duw, am Orchafiaeth a derchafiad eyn Gwlâd a'n hiaith . . . [51]

[And since we live in this age under the most excellent Queen of our
own country . . . while God affords us the facility, the peace and the
freedom that we now have . . . let us show the world that we value more
God's glory and the supremacy and ascendancy of our country and
language.]

The author associates what he considers to be a stable realm with
the opportunity that the Queen has given the Welsh, by divine
grace, to improve their moral status and repossess their past glory.
The humanist scholars showed concern not only to foster spiritual
regeneration among the Welsh people but also to establish a new
religious and cultural genre, usually associated with securing
political stability in the realm. With the strains and tensions
imposed on the Elizabethan economic and political as well as
religious settlement in the late sixteenth century, it is doubtful
whether this stability became a reality. Maurice Kyffin (the
brother of the above-mentioned Edward), however, viewed the situation from an angle that was losing much of its relevance in the
country, namely the partnership established between the Crown
and its subjects to maintain the 'commonwealth of interest'. The
interaction in Wales was viewed chiefly as a personal bond
between a nation afforded the opportunity to achieve a spiritual
uplift and a sovereign power whose descent incorporated within
itself the essence of the 'British' myth. Thomas Salesbury, the
London publisher, for example, proclaimed James I to be the
'excellent monarch who springs from Brutus's line' ('ardderchawg
frenin yr hwn sydd yn dyfod o lin Brutus').[52] This was but one
example of the ways adopted to combine religion, politics and
antiquity as one force designed to expedite the exercise of royal
authority stemming from ancient Christian tradition. Darker
clouds, however, were cast in the late 1580s when the Queen's
authority was condemned for being misapplied or misdirected.

Alongside the arguments advanced by John Penry on the need
to liberate the realm from the 'wrath of God' and its chief instrument, Spanish naval aggression, he and his fellow Presbyterians
advocated an oligarchic rather than a democratic structure of
Church government. They were much in agreement with the
desire to maintain the Protestant tradition and reform the Church,
but interpreted it from an entirely different angle. In the 1580s
they aimed to change the religious settlement in parliament, the
institution that had created it. They emphasized personal piety
and discipline and insisted on the need for a 'moral reformation'.
They feared that the existence of what they considered the

'unreformed' Church imperilled the political and spiritual welfare of the realm, hence the opposition voiced to the survival of popish practices, the episcopal system and ecclesiastical abuses and the use of vestments, as well as the inadequacy of the preaching ministry and the poverty of the clergy. Some of Penry's ideas were not wholly rejected by those who considered that reform was possible within the existing framework. Vicious attacks on the episcopacy revealed violent Puritan opposition to the hierarchy of the Church.

The Presbyterian campaign reached its peak in 1586–7 when Sir Anthony Cope presented to parliament a second 'bill and book' advocating a Genevan form of worship. Harsh measures were taken by Whitgift to suppress the *classes* – conferences of local Puritan clergy meeting in secret to discuss the scriptures and other matters – because they seriously jeopardized the fabric of the Church. His eager suppression of seditious literature, insistence on conformity in religious practice and the use of the Court of High Commission guaranteed his success and, among others, he was ably assisted by Richard Bancroft, bishop of London, Dr John Bridges, dean of Sarum and Richard Hooker, who laid the intellectual foundations to the Church's authority in the erudite *The Laws of Ecclesiastical Polity*. He appealed to Puritans to revere the Church's traditions and restrain their zeal so as to avoid disruption in the realm. What is surprising is that no intellectual figure of the calibre of Maurice Kyffin undertook a translation of Hooker's work into Welsh to deepen further the Protestant tradition.

In *The Aequity of an Humble Supplication* (1587), his first treatise concerning Wales, John Penry, while fully acknowledging the Queen's authority, emphasized her responsibility to initiate reform.[53] He was concerned about the 'state of the commonwealth and her Majesty's', and wished that 'the lord in mercy deliver from all foreign and domestical treasons'.[54] He also respected the Crown's secular institutions, especially Parliament and the Council in the Marches of Wales, as a means of introducing reform in the Church, and he dutifully recorded his loyalty to the Queen, wishing to secure 'the safe estate of this kingdom and our sovereign' and provide that 'the government may be according to the Lord's own laws'. Penry's allegiance to the Queen, however, could only be maintained if she acceded to God's laws; indeed, he considered that her own authority was in danger if she failed to do so.[55] His ardent message on this point spurred him on to desire God

... to blesse our vertuous Queene Elizabeth with the blessinges of a regenerat heart, and a prosperous quiet gouernment: when I call to mind what an earnest and ardent affection, a true Christian beareth vnto his Prince ... I cannot in duty but beseech hir Maiestie not to be wanting vnto her owne safety euen in this one thing ... For what will our children that rise after vs and their children say when they shal be brought vp in gross superstition, but that it was not Queene Elizabethes will that we their Parentes should haue that true religion she professed, made knowen vnto us.[56]

Penry feared that the Queen was not prepared to undertake what he considered to be her principal duty in the realm. Her Protestantism was not in question: rather it was thorough reform of the ecclesiastical structure which she upheld as 'supreme Governor' and the need for an effective preaching ministry that forced the issue. The responsiblity to safeguard the moral welfare of her subjects lay entirely on her shoulders. Institutions of government, Penry continued, should be utilized to further that 'Godly reformation', a point that emerged more poignantly in his second treatise, *An Exhortation unto the Governors of Wales* (1588), in which he came to the heart of the matter concerning institutional responsibility. Henry Herbert, earl of Pembroke, ruled Wales directly from Ludlow on behalf of the Privy Council and was concerned to improve the moral standards as well as to maintain the material welfare of his subjects in Wales and the Marches. In his appeal to him and local government officers in Wales John Penry requested that they should diligently attend to the matter of ecclesiastical reform before any other administrative tasks. Governorship, or the exercise of authority in a public role, in his opinion, assumed an essential role in the task of establishing a preaching ministry. Penry's address to Herbert matched his plea to Queen Elizabeth:

Hath the Lord called you to be lord president of Wales vnder Her Maiestie, to this ende you should sit still when you see your people runne vnto hell, and the Lord so notably dishonoured under your gouernement? ... So, my Lord, with reuerence be it spoken vnto your Honour, if it lie not in you to bring Wales vnto the knowledge of God, or if your leisure will not serue thereto, then bee not the Lorde president thereof.[57]

Penry's words struck at the very roots of Herbert's authority. Included among the Council's responsibilities were maintaining the established order, religious uniformity and the Queen's government in Wales and the borderland. As the administrative arm of the Privy Council in Wales it used its authority to defend the realm against all subversive activity, and the safety and honour of the monarchy was linked to the defence of the state represented by the Protestant Church. Penry went further, emphasizing Herbert's moral and spiritual duties, not only to preserve what had already been established but also to promote God's Church as Penry conceived it. 'Governours, my lord', he asserted, 'must govern under God', and he proceeded to counsel him that his 'governorship' (or 'lieutanancy') was inadequate if he failed to accomplish his mission in God's name.[58] It appears that Penry was far more concerned to advance 'Christ's Holy Government' than secular authority, although he was fully aware of the necessity for the Queen's government to carry through the reform. What he wished to avoid was having to declare how moribund and ineffective the Church had become under royal governorship. In secular society the 'magistrate' had the duty of maintaining God's honour; if that was not fulfilled then Penry doubted his integrity as a public servant and commitment to defending 'conformity and obedience', the foundations of the religious settlement.[59]

The monarchy, Penry declared, did not deny true religion to any of its subjects and vowed to destroy all heresies. Any subject who claimed to have been deprived of his privileges should be allowed to present his case in parliament. That right was upheld by law and Penry cautiously wrote his treatises in the spirit of the law. Parliament had the choice either of rejecting Christ's reign over his people or of establishing God's government in the Church for the good of the 'commonweal'. He solicited parliament to legislate to ensure that Church reform be executed by law: magisterial powers should be impelled to rear the Welsh nation 'in instruction and information of the Lord'. In the last resort, he declared, it is the responsibility of a preaching ministry not any political laws to save the nation from destruction.[60]

Penry introduced concepts of authority into his text: secular authority wielded by the Crown to maintain law and order and spiritual authority or mandate granted to that Crown to establish God's law. In both cases civil authorities or magistrates had a significant role, although Penry is vague as to how they might proceed with their task of seeing 'all within Wales taught by the Word preached'.[61] What he does state in the *Exhortation* is that Henry Herbert is obliged to act on the Queen's behalf to pursue his duties because he was 'governor over all'. He firmly declared his definition of the restrictions imposed on the funcional duties of local magistrates: 'They [i.e. the governors] haue no allowance to be rulers, wher the Lord is not serued, where he hath no acknowledgement of superioritie, there man hath no commission from him to beare rule.'[62] He called upon the civil authorities to protect God's Word, the administration of the sacraments and the externals of Church government. Such a directive led the author to provide specific definitions of authority in the state as applied in literature seeking the advancement of the Reformation. Although ministers and magistrates did not enjoy equality of status they had been appointed to administer divinely approved laws. Magistrates linked their office with the 'outward' calling and had skills to discharge their duties. The office was granted to persons capable of exercising their responsibilities and they were associated with those authorized to appoint them to office. The minister was ordained by God who used his prerogative to appoint ministers enjoying a privilege similar to that exercised by the Queen in ordaining magistrates. If the minister is unworthy he has no right to exercise authority in the Church; similarly an incompetent 'magistrate' can be legitimately deprived of his office. To allow a nation to 'perish for want of knowledge' implied that governors had neglected their most urgent duties.

Penry accepted that the Church was 'governed' by the Queen and the convocation of bishops: their reluctance to initiate further reform revealed how unworthy they were of acting 'for the glory of God and the good of his Church' by using parliament for that purpose. Only in the true Christian commonwealth, where the Church of God (as Penry defined it) functioned, would God's will be realized. Although the Queen and her parliament and officials were the means by which reform might be achieved, it was God's authority that would care for the spiritual welfare of the people. Penry harshly deplored the inadequacies of government officials in these matters so that 'not one family or one tribe; but a whole nation should perish for want of knowledge . . . governors unto whom of trust he hath committed inferiors, discharge not their duties in his sight'.[63]

Penry's message was proclaimed loud and clear: the authority exercised on behalf of the Elizabethan state would continue to fail to fulfil expectations unless it was made aware of God's will, and all Puritan writings from Thomas Cartwright's lectures on the Book of Acts advocating Presbyterianism and John Field and the anti-episcopalianism of Thomas Wilcox in *An Admonition to the Parliament* (1572) expressed the same belief. Authority rested with God's Word:

To desire the free passage of the Gospell in this land, together with the
speedie remoouing of all that hindereth the same, is to plead the cause
of that God who hath controlled kings and great Monarches, yea quite
ouerthrowne, them & their kingdomes, for denying the free vse of his
seruice within their dominions.[64]

The Church was handicapped by continuing Roman Catholic and
Puritan threats but struggled to consolidate its authority in the
early seventeenth century. The unfeeling and spiritless age, as
Bishop Lewis Bayly described it in 1626, exacerbated an already
impoverished institution.[65] Bayly's appeal for support to refurbish
his cathedral church drew attention to the basic weakness, the fear
that papist criticism of the Church's dilapidated condition might
well be justified and would initiate further attacks on it. Economic
recession had severely impaired efficiency in the Church, with a
marked drop in clerical residence, hospitality and licensed
preachers. The Church was fettered by dire poverty and its mission
impeded by problems that had dogged it over the centuries.

Although there were traces of Puritan activity in Wales in the
1580s, especially on the eastern borders, there was no great
danger that the established Church would be overawed by it.
Aside from the translation of the scriptures, efforts were made to
reinforce the Church's authority as a godly institution governed by
the state, and the literary works of Maurice Kyffin, Huw Lewys,
Robert Llwyd, David Rowlands and Rowland Vaughan sought to
counteract Roman Catholic threats and to promote the Protestant
faith by advocating the publication of more religious books in
Welsh.[66] Huw Lewys deplored the fact that the Bible was locked
in parish churches and used only once a week, and, as mentioned
above, he translated *A Spiritual and Most Precious Pearl* into Welsh
so as to assist in the interpretation of biblical text and content.[67]
Emphasis was placed on the role of the gentry in supporting and
promoting the New Faith and improving the moral standards of
the nation through the publication of books and manuals, and the
negligent manner in which this task was undertaken was severely
criticized. In his preamble to *Llwybr hyffordd yn cyfarwyddo yr
anghyfarwydd i'r nefoedd* . . . (1630) Robert Llwyd refers to the
appeal of Rowland Vaughan's translation of Bayly's *The Practice of
Piety* (*Yr Ymarfer o Dduwioldeb*), and applauded his example to
others:

Dyna ŵr bonheddig yn treulio ei amser yn weddol, ac yn ganmoladwy,
gan wneuthur gwasanaeth i Dduw, daioni i'w wlâd, a llesâd mawr iddo

ei hûn drwy gyfieithu y llyfr godidog hwnnw. Pe cymmerai foneddigion ieuaingc ein gwlad ni ryw gyffelyb orchwylwaith duwiol, a buddiol, i dreulio eu hamser arno, ni byddei anllywodraeth, a rhysedd yn cael cymmaint rhwysc: Na gwir Grefydd uniawn-grêd yn cael cyn lleied brî, a chymmeriad.[68]

[There goes a gentleman spending his time fairly and praiseworthily in the service of God, doing good for his country and to his own benefit by translating that excellent book. If the young gentlemen of our country proceeded to undertake a similar godly occupation, profitably to spend time on it, there would not be ill-government and excess would not be displayed: and true orthodox religion would not be undermined.]

Again emphasis is placed on the need to protect the Anglican Church and safeguard its authority. Owing to the lack of a strong Puritan tradition in Wales that authority was not publicized to a great degree except in prefaces to Protestant works designed to advance the faith. It was exemplified, for example, in the works of Richard Parry, bishop of St Asaph, Edward James, vicar of Cadoxton-iuxta-Neath and chancellor of Llandaf, Robert Llwyd, vicar of Chirk, David Rowlands, vicar of Llangybi and Llanarmon and Robert Holland, a native of Conwy who held the livings of Llanddowror and subsequently of Robeston West in Pembroke-shire. Parry's Latin preface to the revised edition of the Welsh Bible (1620) emphasized the authority which God had delegated to James I to defend the faith:

Y mae dyn yn estyn ei ddeheulaw, ond Duw sydd yn ei rheoli hi . . . A chwithau, Eich Mawrhydi, yr anrhydeddusaf ymhlith brenhinoedd a'r gorau ymhlith dynion, nid wyf yn gwneuthur yn annheg â chwi wrth roi yn uwch na chwi y Duw a'ch gwnaeth ac a'ch gosododd mewn awdurdod.[69]

[Man extends his right hand, but it is God who controls it . . . And you, your Majesty, the most honoured among kings and the best among men, I do you no injustice by placing above you the God who created and placed you in authority.]

The new edition of the Bible was yet another attempt, in the third and fourth generations of the Elizabethan Church, to establish alongside secular works the authority of the scriptures and, in conjunction with divine will, to endorse the temporal power vested in the Crown used to enforce that will.[70] In the anonymous preface (probably written by Dr Michael Roberts, principal of Jesus College, Oxford) to the small edition of the Bible in 1630, 'y

Beibl bach coron' ('the small five-shilling Bible'), as it was called, priority is given to the authority of the Bible in the process of redemption:

> . . . mae'n rhaid iddo drigo yn dy stafell di, tan dy gronglwyd dy hun . . . mae'n rhaid iddo ef drigo gyda'th ti fel cyfaill yn bwytta o'th fara, fel anwyl-ddyn a phen-cyngor it' . . . fel y gallech ti fod yn gwbl barod, i bob gweithred dda, a dyscu o honot gadw dy ffyrdd yn ol gair Duw.[71]

> [. . . it must reside in your room, on your hearth . . . it must reside with you as a friend eating your bread, as a dear man and chief counsellor to you . . . so that you can be fully prepared to accomplish all good deeds, and to learn how to keep the faith according to God's word.]

There is a strong Puritan ring to such words, stressing the ultimate authority of the scriptures and the means of obtaining salvation through pious thoughts and deeds.

Deepening a knowledge of the faith was one thing; ensuring that it was not corrupted by surviving Roman Catholic practices was another, and both factors were not entirely unrelated. Richard Parry was particularly concerned about the incidence of Roman Catholic practices in his diocese, his report in 1605 referring to 'an unfortunate and ungodly increase of papists' whose influence was undermining the Church's authority. Most of the recusant activity in the early seventeenth century, however, occurred in south-east Wales and the borders.[72] Medieval customs survived and pilgrimages continued to be popular in all parts of the country.[73] An undated contemporary account referred to the popularity of older practices among the peasantry of north Wales:

> The people . . . doe still in heapes goe one pilgrimage to the wonted wells and placs of supersticon, and in the nights after the feasts when the ould offrings weare used to be kepte at anie idolls chappell albeit the church be pulled downe; yet doe they come to the place where the church or chappell was, by great jorneys barefoote vearie sup'sticiouslie . . . [74]

While the authority of Rome was acknowledged by this diverse group of pilgrims it was still not understood; visits to shrines in the seventeenth century signified the dying embers of medieval religious traditions which had formed a noteworthy feature of popular culture. Any study of that culture in relation to concepts of authority must take into account that not all, even among the peasantry, were 'practising' Christians in the sense that they assiduously attended the parish church, nor were they knowledge-able in the doctrines of the faith. None the less, although in the eyes of many the Church did not stand for orthodox teaching and authoritarianism, it did assume a crucial role in community life.

Much weight was placed on religious control and conformity stemming from the central authority of the state. It was virtually impossible, however, to impose uniformity or orthodoxy. Although religious commentators and divines seriously attempted to explain to simple parishioners their status and role in life, religious instruction *per se*, which contained solid social teaching, could not guarantee that the lower orders would appreciate the moral values associated with their superiors.[75] The holy wells and springs of Wales survived, although shrines, images and relics had long since been destroyed, and the reports of Bishops Nicholas Robinson, Richard Davies and Richard Parry deplored practices which perpetuated superstitious beliefs. The image of Derfel Gadarn in mid-Wales, for example, had been a centre of pilgrimage for centuries and, in 1538, when the government decided to destroy shrines, Dr Ellis Price informed Thomas Cromwell of the power possessed by the image in the eyes of peasant folk: 'whosoever will offer anie thinge to the saide Image', he declared, ' . . . he hathe power to fetche hym or them that so offers oute of hell when they be dampned'.[76] Other fears of recusancy were expressed, such as Sir James Perrot's report that incoming recusant families into Pembrokeshire tainted people's minds,[77] and Lewis Bayly's concern about the activity of the turncoat Roman Catholic agent, Hugh Owen of Gwenynog, Anglesey, and his followers.[78] Houses, such as Plas-du, Plas Newydd, Powys and Raglan castles and Llantarnam, became citadels of recusant activity challenging the authority of the Protestant state. Fundamentally, the persecution of Roman Catholics was a political matter, the state imposing its common law and religious uniformity, with a view to sustaining the Protestant ethos and safeguarding its role in the Tudor state.

Would all these challenges with which the Church contended be intensified and its authority undermined by the emergence of Puritanism in Wales? Religious dissent in England had stirred the religious waters for generations before it had any impact on Wales. Puritan thought and activity in early-seventeenth-century Wales appeared largely in the manner in which individual priests interpreted their personal faith and the purpose of their ministry among illiterate parishioners rather than through the growth of any sect. In their view authority in the Church was still based on royal supremacy, and personal piety was essentially regarded as a private matter. Conviction arising out of prayer and meditation on the Word of God deepened a sense of godliness in the individual, reflected chiefly in moral conduct. Godliness, in that respect, characterized those clergy in the Church most ardently concerned with improving the spiritual qualities of the individual. The Word of God manifested the authority which declared the essentials of belief deemed suitable for the Church.

The different preaching techniques used by Anglicans and Puritans reveal that the main purport of Anglican preaching was to preserve uniformity in the Church while Puritans concentrated on 'saving souls', a feature that became more evident as the century progressed. There were no seriously threatening religious issues in the early seventeenth century that might erupt in civil war as there had been in Elizabeth's reign. The Catholic problem was not as menacing as it had been and the Puritan challenge within the Church in Wales not as acute. Attempts, however, to set up a new structure within the Church were not successful.[79] There was a continued emphasis on Puritan zeal but it remained chiefly within the established Church where the laws were accepted supplementing their own form of worship based on sermons and prayers. They placed considerable importance on piety and private meditations, particularly in the household, supported by well-meaning clergy who were themselves aware of the need for deeper spirituality (see Chapter 6, pp. 205–21). John Penry had indirectly drawn attention to this deep spiritual need, and it was in this context also that Robert Llwyd made one of his most perceptive remarks:

Oni wnei ddaioni i dylwth dy dŷ, na wna gam a hwynt am ymborth eu heneidiau, ac os gwnei, ti a gei atteb am dano . . . Canys er porthi o honot gyrph dy blant, a'th deulu, a gadel ar hynny heb ymorol a'm eu heneidiau, beth yr wyt ti yn ei wneuthur iddynt chwaneg, nac a wnei i'th farch, i'th ŷch, ie i'th gi? Darllein hwn gan hynny, i'th wraig, ac i'th blant.[80]

[If you do not do good to the family in your abode do not wrong them regarding feeding their souls, and if you do so you shall answer for it . . . For, although you feed your children's bodies and family and leave it at that not seeking after their souls, what do you do for them more than you do for your horse, your ox, yes for your dog? Read this therefore to your wife and children.]

This was the purport of *The Practice of Piety*, the verses of Rhys Prichard of Llanymddyfri, and *Car-wr y Cymru* (1631) by Oliver Thomas. Prichard drew attention to the centrality of the Protestant Church and the saving of souls, and his Puritan traits become apparent in the manner in which he demonstrated the authority of the Church in aiding private prayers and meditations. He defined the spiritual progress of the sinner in the context of social conditions which often obscured the meaning of religious principles for the peasantry. He emphasized the importance of prayer – 'Dros bob 'stad o'r Eglwys' ('For all estates in the Church'), for monarchs so that they might govern their people 'in grace, peace, and with probity and bliss', for churchmen, to enable them to preach God's Word 'fluently'; for officials so that they might punish wrongdoing and maintain the faith and virtue; for scholars, to enable them to fill the country with light, maintain moral standards and conduct themselves in a religious manner, and for the poor and common people in order that they might live according to their station and so that God might sustain and comfort them.[81] In accordance with the rights of the Church, he also focused on the divinely ordained hierarchy in the social structure.

> Dilyn gynghor doeth bregethwyr,
> Ymddarostwng i'th reolwyr,
> Bydd gariadus i'th gym'dogion
> Ac heddychol â phob Cristion.[82]

[Follow the counsel of wise preachers; Submit to your rulers; esteem your neighbours; and be peaceful to all Christians.]

The need for Christian discipline within the social order emerges distinctly in this verse whereby the individual is called upon to act devoutly in all spheres of activity. Rhys Prichard pronounced God's authority in the Christian life as demonstrated in the scriptures. His emphasis is consistently on divine power, the sanctity of the Word, the all-embracing authority of the Church, the role of the clergy in ministering to the essential spiritual needs of the people, the necessity to exercise spiritual discipline in all aspects of human existence and the inevitability of death and the Day of Judgement. These features provide the cornerstone for Prichard's message to humble parishioners and disclose his prime motive for composing such an extraordinarily large corpus of popular religious verse. His theology draws attention to the *paterfamilias* who has a responsibility to God, his family, his community and himself. An unrighteous man brings disrepute on his whole family ('Dyn anneddfol . . . A bair anghlod i'th holl dylwyth').[83] What the *paterfamilias* was expected to accomplish within his household compared to the monarch's obligation as head of state (see Chapter 6, pp. 205–7). Authority within the household was considered to be a microcosm of the head of state's responsibility for the welfare of the commonweal. The anonymous writer of the preamble to the popular edition of the Welsh Bible in 1630 called on his readers to allow the scriptures 'to dwell in your heart, which is the main piece of furniture of your soul, and it is essential as well that it dwells in the house'.

Maintaining the Faith: the Early Stuart Century

Whatever the condition of the Elizabethan Church in Wales on the threshold of the seventeenth century, it had obviously failed to maintain the absolute uniformity that the government expected of it, to ensure an effective ministry or to restrain the rapacity of lay gentry. Such a harsh judgement, however, tends to obscure some of its more salutary contributions. The quality of its clergy by the end of the sixteenth century showed significant signs of improvement; its bishops, for the most part, were enthusiastically prepared to defend its spiritual and material interests, and aside from the persisting Catholic threat and emerging Puritan opposition in the 1630s, the Church more than upheld its authority. By the eve of the Civil Wars it had consolidated its hold over the vast majority of the population who followed the natural leadership imposed upon them despite the widespread illiteracy, superstition and ignorance that dogged the spiritual life of the Welsh countryside. It is true that the authority of Church leaders sagged when confronted by that enduring malaise but it is remarkable how the institution strengthened its hand as one of the bulwarks of order which maintained its firm alliance with the ruling classes at the appropriate time.

The Elizabethan Protestant Church was reinforced by its adherence to Calvinist doctrine and its emphasis on order and discipline. The appearance of prose works, mostly in translation, defended its tenets and liturgy, promoted its well-being, and underlined its all-embracing authority. Among them were Edward James's *Book of Homilies* (1606), the new version of Bishop Morgan's Bible revised by Dr John Davies of Mallwyd (1620), Edmwnd Prys's *Salmau Cân* (1621), a metrical version of the Psalms in Welsh and the *Llyfr Plygain* (issued in 1607, 1612, 1618, 1633). Greater weight was placed on the need for preaching, and the number of graduate preachers gradually increased. That Church, however, still suffered many setbacks. Bishops in Welsh dioceses – some of them English-born – faced the same problems arising out of impropriations, pluralism and non-residency. All the Welsh bishops were particularly concerned about the material condition of their clergy, and priests, such as Rhys Prichard (Llanymddyfri), Robert Powell (Cadoxton-iuxta-Neath) and Robert Llwyd (Chirk), overtly expressed the need to abandon frivolities and vain practices and adhere to a stricter moral code, but in a less censorious manner than John Penry.[84] These admonitions were made within the Church, moderately Puritan in tone, in an attempt to safeguard its reputation and authority. When William Wroth was accused in 1635 of 'leading away many simple minds' and Erbery and Cradock of preaching 'very schismatically and dangerously to the people' they were considered to have proclaimed to ignorant parishioners views contrary to the teachings of the Church.[85] *The Book of Homilies* emphasized the role of discipline and good order in the home and in public life as being fundamental in the life of the Christian (see Chapter 6, pp. 218–20). Edward James, the translator, drew attention to the homilies as an 'aid for clergymen' when conducting services, expounding clearly the doctrines of the Church and declaring the authority by which that Church performed its spiritual duties.

. . . yr homiliau duwiol ymma: yn y rhai y cynhwysir y prif byngciau o'n ffydd ni ac o'n dlyed tu âg at Dduw a'n cymydogion: fel y galle yr offeiriaid a'r curadiaid annyscedig, y rhai ni fedrent yn amgen etto wrth adrodd a datcan a darllen yr homiliau hyn, bregethu i'w pobl wir athrawaeth . . . Etto er nad oedd rheitiach i vn wlad wrth y fath gynhorthwy nac i wlad Cymru am fod pregethwyr mor ambell ynddi, ni ewyllysiodd Duw ini gael neb o'r Homiliau hyn na'r fath eraill yn yr iaith Gymeraeg hyd yr amser hyn.[86]

[. . . these godly homilies, in which are contained the main principles of our faith and our debt to God and neighbours: so that our ignorant priests and curates, those who cannot preach to their people true doctrine other than by reciting, declaring and reading these homilies . . . Yet, although it was not necessary for one country to obtain such assistance more than the country of Wales because preachers were scarce there, God did not will it that we should receive these Homilies or others in the Welsh language until this time.]

These short sermons were to be read in parish churches every Sunday and in time their influence was bound to be widespread. James considered his work to be laborious rather than pleasurable. His work was complementary to what William Morgan had accomplished in 1588, followed by Maurice Kyffin, his brother Edward and Huw Lewys, namely to expose God's authority as it

unfolded in the scriptures and was manifested in the role of the
Church as an expounder and defender of the true faith.[87]

In 1603 Edward Kyffin emphasized the freedom which the
Tudors had allowed his countrymen to enrich their spiritual
experiences in their own language. He adapted some of the psalms
of David into Welsh free verse, and in his preface to *Rhann o
Psalmae Dafydd Brophwyd* . . . applauded the translation of the
scriptures and the opportunity they were afforded by Elizabeth I
to embellish the language while, at the same time, expounding the
truths of the Protestant to the people. His words seem to extol the
virtuous ancestry of the 'British' nation and Tudor policy enabled
the Welsh to redeem a lost heritage:

> A chan eyn bôd yn byw yn yr Oes honn dann ardderchockaf Vrenhines
> o'n gwlâd eyn hunain, yr honn sydd yn canhiadu i ni gael y Scrythur
> lân yn eyn hiaith eyn hunain, ag oll gyfreidiau eraill ar a ddamunem ei
> cael tu ag at amlhau Gogoniant Duw, a mawrhâd eyn hiaith . . . na
> chollwn yr amser presennol, ond yn hytrach gwaredwn yr hir-amser a
> gollasom yn barod . . . [88]

> [And since we live in this Age under the most excellent Queen of our
> own country, who allows us to obtain the Holy Scriptures in our own
> tongue, and all other necessities we desire to increase God's Glory, and
> the magnitude of our language . . . Let us not lose time at present, but
> rather let us redeem the long-time which we have already lost . . .]

Authority within the Church was reflected in its ancient
traditions, a trait that was exposed also in contemporary religious
tracts. 'Hospitality', George Wheler remarked, 'is an excellent
Christian practice' for it signified the assumption of benevolent
tutelage or guardianship.[89] In the Church that benevolence was
reflected in the exercise of God's benign authority over his people.

The Arminian teachings of William Laud, particularly during
his years as Archbishop of Canterbury, initiated the policy of
suppressing Puritanism. They emphasized the need to reform the
clergy and ceremonial of the Church. More emphasis was placed
on sacraments than sermons, and on the return of the Court of
High Commission and Star Chamber, the introduction of
Catholic reforms in Church organization and ceremonial, and
strengthening the episcopacy. Laud used episcopal visitations,
censorship of the press and the suppression of sermons among
other means to achieve his gaol. Puritans objected, some violently,
accusing him of popery.[90] The Arminians did not go as far as to
advocate transubstantiation; their advocacy of liturgical changes,
the positioning of the communion table to the east of the church

and isolating it by erecting rails, the *juro divino* episcopacy and belief in the apostolic succession were all contrary to the tenets of the Church. Laud's relations with the Puritans were inflexible, not because of their suspected disloyalty to the Crown but because they differed on matters of conscience. The power granted the bishops created much resentment among Puritans with regard to its nature and the way it was wielded. To Puritans the bishop was not a ruler but rather a spiritual guide. In their view the principal authority lay within the Crown, parliament and the magistracy who shared authority in Church and state. The jurisdictional power granted to the Church exposed the rights inherently vested in the Crown but which had been granted to the bishops. The Puritans also considered that the Church had betrayed the laws of the realm. They based their concept of authority and political obligation on God's will, and they questioned passive obedience to the Crown. Its authority was not doubted in matters relating to ecclesiastical affairs but Puritans did seek further reforms as the law allowed. More radical thinkers, however, were prepared to resist a monarch who refused to accede to their demands. Their opposition to the monarchy as supreme governor was based largely on conscience which undermined any belief in passive obedience.[91]

In a Welsh context these factors played relatively little part because the impact of Puritanism, with the exception of John Penry's invective, before the 1630s was largely orthodox. Erbery and Cradock were accused of refusing to read *The Book of Sports* publicly; tainting the minds of simple folk with their 'schismatical proceedings', as stated in the indictments against them, deserves further consideration. So does Laud's report to the King concerning these two dissidents in 1636 that 'both [of] them persist in their by ways and their followers judge them faultless'. The impressively strong group of Puritans and Quakers in Cardiff suggests that it was chiefly through Erbery's influence that it was initially formed.[92] The evidence connecting Erbery's influence with earlier sixteenth-century examples of nonconformity, however, is very sparse indeed. It is known that the Herberts, earls of Pembroke, and the Lewises of Y Fan had strong Puritan leanings in the early seventeenth century, but more evidence needs to be elicited to prove that their influence was formative.

Despite the dearth of evidence it is not unreasonable to suggest that Erbery was quite popular among a minority group in Cardiff and the surrounding district. Although he expressed orthodox views in a second-hand version of a sermon delivered at

Burrington and Chew Norton in Somerset, he revealed his
support for an 'independent' church consisting of members,
pastors and the administration of God's ordinances which were to
be dispensed by the pastors only to 'those who are saints by
calling'.[93] In the same spirit but with a more positive outlook
William Wroth went further to establish an 'independent' church
at Llanfaches which held close connections with the Broadmead,
Bristol fraternity.[94] It was set up initially as a reaction against royal
absolutism and Laudianism, and as a church which did not
altogether sever ties with the Church of England. Wroth minis-
tered to the congregation there and, in 1642, Walter Cradock, who
had succeeded as pastor, and whose congregation had fled to
Bristol, drew both congregations together. This church, better
known as the Antioch 'in that gentile country', was settled at
Llanfaches where it accommodated both separatists who
considered the Elizabethan Church to be unscriptural and
congregational independents who were prepared to conform. In
short it was an *ecclesiola in ecclesia* and its foundation was based
on the authority of the scriptures. Although both groups agreed on
matters regarding the nature of the Church and its ministry,
conforming independents considered that it had features which
enabled them to adhere to it. Llanfaches was established on the
'New England pattern' and was heavily influenced by John
Cotton, the Puritan divine of Massachusetts Bay.[95] Its members
had united to follow in Christ's path; they covenanted and
brothers came from other churches to witness its foundation, but
the links with the Church of England were not broken, thereby
enabling Wroth to minister to members of a new church and those
who adhered to the old. At Llanfaches there was a pastor, a
governing elder and a teacher, and it was declared to be the
government's duty to establish a pure church in doctrine, worship
and governance based on God's Word. It was also the government's task to urge Church leaders to punish those who challenged
uniformity within the Church and who propagated the view that
authority in the Church lay in God's Word and that it was the
secular government's responsibility to establish the purified
Church of God.[96]

Conclusion

The state Church established by Elizabeth based its authority
essentially on royal governership. The concept of the *via media* is
no longer tenable: the Church was not based on a compromise

between Rome and Geneva; the Church was placed in that position owing to political circumstances, and the framework of the Church eventually evolved owing to the uneasy relationship between Elizabeth and her prelates. With the organization of the Church well in hand, however, it braved political and economic storms and, in Wales in the early seventeenth century, showed far more progress than Roman Catholics would have wished since it enjoyed the overwhelming support and loyalty of all ranks in society and saw an increase in the numbers of its preachers.[97] Impropriations lowered income but this might not have had the depressing effects that it is considered to have had in all dioceses. At Bangor, for example, most impropriated parishes were vicarages, and incumbents may have shared the tithes rather than accepting a fixed stipend. This did give some of them a higher income, but obtaining only part of parochial income, which was already low, meant very low stipends.

Although lay control was strengthened by rights of presentation to rectories, episcopal patronage was widespread, and efforts were made to appoint qualified clergy;[98] among them appeared many dedicated clergy of high calibre who catechized privately. According to the few visitation articles that have survived for Welsh dioceses in the early seventeenth century – 1603 (Llandaf), 1621 (Llandaf) and 1627 (St David's) – it is clear that discipline in the Church was rigidly adhered to in the chapter houses and parishes. A comparison reveals that the problems referred to in 1603 still remained a major cause of concern in 1622, and the injunctions are amply borne out in contemporary English and Welsh commentaries, disclosing the inertia of clergy and laity in the task of improving standards in the diocese. The use of devotional and didactic works in the 1630s enabled the Church to consolidate itself and provided it with teachings to 'remedy the soul' ('r[h]oddi meddyginaeth i'th enaid').[99] *The Practice of Piety* by Lewis Bayly is a work of religious instruction as well as a manifestation of Protestant doctrine, and it is hardly surprising that Rowland Vaughan, who translated the work, was a true royalist and Anglican when the call to arms came in 1642. In 1650 he proceeded to translate *Eikon Basilike* into Welsh (part of which has survived), the meditations reputedly composed by Charles I on the eve of his death. Bayly's 'epistle dedicatory' to Charles, Prince of Wales, observed that he, as heir to the throne, was best distinguished by godliness, which is the basis of his authority: 'But without Piety', Bayly maintained, 'there is no internall comfort to be found in Conscience, nor externall peace to be looked for in the World'.[100] By the 1630s the instructive features of Protestant vernacular literature in Wales had become more readily available in print. By then it had the basis to advance further: thus, despite its shortcomings and the dark days of rebellion and Puritan rule that lay ahead, the organization and authority of the Protestant Church in Wales had been firmly established and accepted by the native gentry by the eve of the Civil Wars, enabling it to recover in the Restoration era.

CHAPTER 6

Family and Household

In recent years historians and sociologists have devoted attention to the study of the family in the social structure of western Europe. It has been examined chiefly within the context of economic and political changes and readaptation. Whereas in the past emphasis was placed on the wider kindred group, the nuclear family, retaining part of its medieval character, has been accorded more prominence and defined as having made a more significant contribution to the structure of community life. The family unit was essentially an economic entity and was considered to be the foundation to an ordered and disciplined society. It was also regarded as a bulwark of law, order and good government and maintained well-established conventions tied to accepted social and political structures. The family reinforced bonds established between itself and the notion of the well-ordered society manifested in the state, and was associated closely with the concepts of 'regionalism', 'locality', 'rank' and 'gender'.[1]

Lawrence Stone has argued that changes occurred in the family structure from the 'open lineage' type to the 'patriarchal nuclear family' between the mid-sixteenth and early eighteenth century.[2] He maintains that loyalties to the kindred circle and the local community were superseded by a strengthening of ties with the state and its institutions which, owing to the developing power of the central government, served to increase authority in public affairs. Such a theory is questionable, especially with regard to the position of more conservative and poorly endowed families in less favourably placed economic circumstances. In Wales, for example, the social and economic climate demanded that time-honoured features continued which indicated that several families clung to ancient customs and concepts of honour. This background was fittingly associated with the very nature of Welsh kindred structure, distinct features of which survived into the early modern period. In that context, as Chapter 1 has revealed, nobility was based essentially on inherited status, and a freeman in Welsh medieval society was a *bonheddig (nobilis)*. If he increased his prestige by obtaining land or by becoming head of a household he was regarded as a member of the *optimates* order (*uchelwr* or *breyr*).

He was also described as a *bonheddig cynhwynawl* (gentleman by birth and descent), enjoying supremacy in his *bro* or *cymdogaeth* (neighourhood or region). In Welsh society, therefore, there were two grades of nobility, each claiming free status despite the differences in their material resources. Regardless of the Edwardian settlement (1284) and its impact on the status of *arglwydd* (lord) in relation to the old royal houses of Wales, the *uchelwyr*, new landed proprietors and office-holders in the Principality and the Marches, and founders of illustrious country seats, emerged to assume ascendancy. The qualities of gentility (*bonedd*) that went with it were judged not, as in England, by economic competence and official status but rather by blood affinities within the family group and its claim to have descended from a common ancestor. Lordship, in sixteenth-century terms, was applied to signify the *uchelwr* exercising territorial authority over his *cymdogaeth*, *bro* or *gwlad*, his neighbourhood, kingdom or region of jurisdiction. Close relations were established between the kindred chieftain and his neighbourhood and the tradition was maintained. 'I dwell among my own people', Richard ap Hywel, an ancestor of the Mostyn family declared when declining an invitation to serve Henry Tudor at court after the battle of Bosworth, thereby considering his associations with his native region in north-east Wales to be more appealing to him than the benefits of office in more sumptuous surroundings.[3] Despite the gradual withdrawal from permanent residence by an increasing number of heads of households, the lure of the countryside still continued to be a dominant feature of life for the privileged order.

The squires of Tudor and early Stuart Wales were fully aware of their power in their respective regions and the jurisdiction which they claimed, and any persons, including kinsmen, who attempted to rival them or deprive them of their rights stood to be severely reprimanded. This was clearly manifested, for example, in the response of William Somerset, third earl of Worcester, in 1583 to his inefficient agent Sir Edward Mansel, concerning the records of the court of Swansea. 'God willing', he declared, 'I will be lord of my own. I shall be enforced to discharge you not to meddle with anything that is mine'.[4] Dispute or contention was often used as a means of acquiring or preserving ascendancy. Whatever credence can be given to George Owen's declaration regarding late Elizabethan Pembrokeshire that its gentry were 'striveing to exceede in curteisie and kindenes the one to the other no one faction side or quarrell amonge them', there is no doubt that kindred stock and lordship did create and perpetuate animosities and often disrupted family unity.[5] Sir Edward Stradling, one of the most prominent Tudor squire-genealogists, was described as a person 'of great antiquitie and worship [who has] . . . a mynde to maintayne and prefer such p'sonages as are like unto yor selfe'.[6] So preoccupied were Welsh freemen with their stock that, in Humphrey Llwyd's estimation, they became subject to apt comment on their use of 'nobility' and their desire to enter households of the English aristocracy:

> ouermuch boastyng of the Nobilitie of their stocke, applying them selues rather to the seruice of noble men . . . So that you shall finde but few noble men in England, but that the greater parte of their retinew . . . are welshmen borne . . . Besides, beyng somewhat high minded, and in extreame pouertie, acknowledgyng the nobilitie of their famely . . . [7]

Family bonds were not necessarily associated with political affiliations but the power they asserted in their neighbourhood certainly had an impact upon the development of public relations, and the emphasis on continuity and inheritance was essentially dynastic. Alongside the ambitions of prominent gentry to serve the Tudor state the close-knit structure of the kindred and the power enjoyed by the head of the household continued to exert considerable influence. All sources of authority exercised within familial groups displayed the degree to which kindred relations managed to strengthen or weaken the family unit. Genealogical sources for the sixteenth and early seventeenth centuries, especially the compilations of Gruffudd Hiraethog, Lewis Dwnn, Simwnt Fychan, 'Sir' Thomas Wiliems and John Jones, Gellilyfdy, revealed in detail the importance of blood affinities in the structure of family relations.[8] The 'temporal blessing' that good descent accorded to auspicious gentlemen indicated that, although kindred could stifle development, it also served as an effective means of reinforcing the bonds which the bards – one of whose obligations was to preserve family stability – considered essential to give the family its structural coherence.[9] Besides the cohesiveness of family, its broader attachment to the local community is also a matter for consideration for, despite its inbuilt deficiencies, the family revealed a deference to authority in its distinctively provincial context and to the divine order that sanctioned it.

Essentially, the family, in a Welsh context, had three fundamental features: initially it was regarded as an institution designed to perpetuate the name and fortune of a particular group of relatives: secondly, in the period down to the Civil Wars, it served as a social entity to improve and maintain moral standards, a buttress to the highest conduct values. Thirdly, it was symbolically identified with the state; whereas the Crown governed the realm the *paterfamilias* maintained order and good government within the family circle directly under his authority. In 1599 James VI of Scotland published his *Basilikon Doron* in which he advised his heir on how to apply the skills needed to practise kingship and he emphasized duty towards God, obligation in office and just exercise of authority in relation to his subjects. The work was essentially paternal and designed to remind Henry that, as heir apparent, he was born to serve. In 1604 it was translated into Welsh by Robert Holland who, in his preface, referred to the king as 'governor' and the translation as a guide to Welsh gentry and clergy who valued their heritage.[10]

Authority in the conjugal family stemmed from the status enjoyed by the *paterfamilias*. He was responsible for safeguarding the welfare of his dependants within the extended family but, above all, for fostering harmonious relations with kindred or clan. Although loyalty to the broader familial structure was exhibited in the voluminous corpus of private correspondence and other sources that have survived and overtly demonstrated in the factions and vendettas that persisted throughout the sixteenth century, the contribution of kindred should not be overestimated in assessing the constructive role of individual families in the social history of Wales. Their part in creating communal structures was based essentially on the primogenitural and patrilineal features of inheritance. In an official capacity heads of households, both Catholic and Protestant, shared common principles in this respect and were regarded as governors; within their own residences they were normally assumed to be paternal benefactors, although one observer in the 1570s strongly denied that to be so in the case of avaricious and self-seeking landed and professional heads of families: 'Then shall appeare that whereas by reason of their offices they should haue bene *Patres patrie*, fathers of the countrey, they became spoylers of the countrey.'[11]

This was perhaps a somewhat exaggerated statement but, in an age of growing prosperity, power, even within the family unit, was increasingly identified with a display of local domination. Family correspondence shows how far this power was exerted. In 1620 William Wynn, one of the sons of Sir John Wynn of Gwydir, feared that, owing to lack of resources to maintain himself in his London office, he 'should bee heartely sorry to conceive that yow [his father] make mee more inferiour then anie of my bretheren in your loue who cannot better affect yow then I doe'.[12] He was not the only scion of that house to grieve over this and express his concern about his father's reluctance to give ample financial support but his situation was critical at the time: 'if my father withdrawe his hand from me now in my greatest necessitie', he continued, 'I must be fayne to fall off from my seruice w'th shame'. Heads of families often used their political influence to make their views known to their sons. Sir Roger Mostyn, for example, being fully aware of his own position in county affairs, cared constantly for his sons' welfare and preferred to see his eldest remain at home managing the estate than seeking a political career in London and leaving his wife in the country. He also believed that the younger son would be forced to contest fiercely for the county's parliamentary seat which would not be worth the having.[13] This sheds some light on the nature of the Mostyn family, whose estate extended into different areas of north Wales but was not as concentrated as that of the Bulkeleys or the Wynns of Gwydir. They clung to traditional values and were closely rivalled in public affairs by the more outward-going Hanmers in Flintshire.

Care was taken in all households to encourage the educational pursuits of their younger members, to give them instruction befitting their birth, and to improve domestic comforts in line with their social status. John Penry greatly valued the education that had been provided for him by both his parents at Cambridge and Oxford, and also expressed his anxiety that, owing to the Queen's reluctance to reform the Church, it could affect 'our children that rise after vs and their children' who might resent that the true faith, owing to this neglect, was not 'made knowen vnto them'.[14] James Howell, litterateur and later historiographer royal, expressed his appreciation of his parents' bounty in allowing him the best education which enabled him to travel and experience European culture and become a cultivated gentleman.[15] Edward Lord Herbert of Chirbury admired his grandmother, heiress to Sir Thomas Bromley, for her devout conduct and example. She was endowed, he declared, with

> rare testimonies of an incomparable piety to God, and love to her children, as being more assiduous and devout in her daily both private and public prayers, and so careful to provide for her posterity . . . she continued still unmarried and so provident for them that . . . she delivered up her estate and care of housekeeping to her eldest son Francis.[16]

The Welsh humanist scholars often applauded the good services of their patrons on the hearth as well as in public service; so also did the poets who were largely dependent on their hospitality. The houses of Mostyn, Lleweni, Gwydir, Plas Mawr and Penrhyn, on or near the north Wales coast, for example, often welcomed government officials from Ireland or London travelling via Chester, Shrewsbury or Ludlow, and were, in their locality, symbols of regional grandeur. They granted hospitality to those state officials who enjoyed in them the best comforts and convivial company. Similarly in south Wales the houses of Tredegar and Raglan, St Donat's, Oxwich and Carew castles, and Margam Abbey also stood for all that the privileged had come to expect. Sustained by their armorial bearings and heraldry the heads of such families – native and English – exhibited the emblems which they conceptually considered to reflect their true value. In the north, the fact that 'Caernarfon flourished as well by trade of merchandise' and that Beaumaris and Conwy were equally substantial urban centres with a strong sense of history gave added impetus to families within reach to consider themselves privileged and to benefit from their available resources.[17] Similarly, towns like Cardigan, Carmarthen, Brecon and Abergavenny, with growing populations, had strengthened their economic resources. The growth of commerce and trade and the increase in the movement of officials to and from Ireland following the tightening of Tudor policy, led to the most accessible houses being centres for such visits.[18] Sir John Wynn drew attention to the qualities of hospitality and good householdership in his *Memoirs*. He regarded Henry Rowland, bishop of Bangor, as the greatest 'in housekeeping and hospitality' in his time,[19] his predecessor Richard Vaughan as 'a worthy housekeeper and a liberal minded man',[20] and William Glynn of Glynllifon, another high-ranking ecclesiast, as 'a great housekeeper'.[21] Among his lay kinsmen he admired two of his uncles, Robert and John Wynn, younger brothers of his father Morus Wynn, as the most bountiful of householders.[22] Wynn considered honourable householdership as a prime manifestation of 'good living' and 'credit' as defined by men of his milieu in rural and urban communities.

'Everyman is a king in his own house', Juan Luis Vives declared in 1550, 'and therefore as it beseemeth a king to excell the common people in judgement and in example of life and in the execution and performance of the thing that he commandeth, so he that doth marry must cast off all childishness'.[23] His privileges demanded that, on acquiring his inheritance and leading a family life, he should assume a mature approach to estate management. The power exerted by the *paterfamilias* over his immediate family was still regarded by lay and ecclesiastical authorities as a prime factor in undertaking regional responsibilities and independence because, in a society lacking a police organization, discipline had to be fostered and imposed largely within the household. In all aspects of domestic life the father was the dominant figure: in a strictly patriarchal society the best interests of the family and the community were based on obedience and moral integrity.

The private correspondence of the more opulent among gentry families, such as that of the Salusburys of Denbighshire, Herberts of Montgomery or Stradlings of St Donat's, reveal how close-knit, though not necessarily amicable, family connections could be. Although relations often became strained, care was taken to supervise the activities and attitudes of the kindred as well. Essentially, authority within the community – the parish, hundred or shire – lay with the head of the 'nuclear' family. Underlying this acquired or inherited status was the concept of hierarchy, a historic feature which served to reinforce the authority exercised as a means of subjecting subordinate members of the family to strict patriarchal control. In the intricate structure of the family unit hierarchy is normally associated with the use and abuse of power, discipline and authority. It is identifiable with the aristocratic features of *uchelwriaeth* which were prominent in all households purporting to be of gentle origin. The deference that characterized such families fostered a pride in heritage and showed a stubborn resistance to change. Although the imposing of one's will within the household was authoritarian, it was recognized as an expression of benevolence and moral guidance. It stemmed from the inalienable birthright enjoyed by heads of families, and regarded as the foundation of the right to impose government on others. In the domestic context that government was equal to the power and control exercised in public administration. When Sir John Wynn of Gwydir, for example, sought a suitable wife for his eldest son he directed his agent to consider the position and good reputation which a prospective father-in-law would be expected to enjoy:

> fyrst a man of what life and conversation he and his family are of & of what birth & present living & what future hope there is of his preferment, how esteemed in his country, what ys his credit with the King, upon what friends & faction he doth & hath depended . . . [24]

Doubtless Wynn's expectations were high, for an appropriate father had to be an estimable person of influence and good credit in his region and possibly at Ludlow, at court and in parliament. He would need to be a person wealthy enough to assume the role of a worthy father-in-law to Wynn's son and heir. Authority was essentially a reflection of good credit: consequently, the ideal father-in-law had to be a man able to govern his own house and affairs, to rear his family in strict moral surroundings, to offer them the highest social and moral values and enable them to cultivate the most favourable connections. Noble ancestry was a prime requisite for any gentleman desiring to achieve ascendancy, and the *plasty* was the principal physical manifestation of that eminence (see Chapter 1, pp. 24–8). Jealousy and rivalry, of course, accounted for much of the opposition to successful proprietors and entrepreneurs. Increasing prosperity as a direct consequence of business acumen and good fortune enjoyed by the few were usually the factors which caused resentment among contentious kindred and other competitors eager to undermine the good fortune of neighbours. He who attempted to 'keep things upright' within his own neighbourhood also desired to exercise his authority at all costs.[25]

Disinheritance of land implied loss of status and authority in the community, hence the increasing number of suits in courts of law, such as Chancery and Exchequer Courts, all of which protected the rights and interests of the Crown and defended or claimed the subject's rights in property affairs. A family seat and landed possessions enabled a family to enjoy security and was a public manifestation of status; hence the emphasis on the revered escutcheon and its coat of arms and title. It was when others, appreciably less worthy, claimed gentility and were prepared to pay for status that the threat became imminent, because rank and authority were then jeopardized. The Welsh *uchelwr*, steeped in the traditions of his region, was, in time – especially towards the end of the seventeenth century – no longer considered to be exclusively the representative of his social order. Far-sighted and resolute *noveaux riches* boldly projected themselves forwards into the ranks of the gentry; they desired and acquired the power that older generations of gentry had imposed on their community and gradually rose to positions of authority and public responsibility. Consequently, the social and economic circumstances of the traditional landed gentry, of whatever rank, changed significantly during the Civil Wars and the Puritan regime.

Hospitality and the Country Residence

Since the term 'county community' is not universally recognized by historians as an apt description of regional unity in the early

seventeenth century, centred on the county town or the court of
Quarter Sessions and signifying local patriotism, it is perhaps
more appropriate to regard the cohesive structure of the family
embodied in the family residence (*plasty*) as the most overt
manifestation of loyalty.[26] The country seat, sustaining the family
unit, doubtless represented regional power so that it is not
surprising that the traditional Welsh poets, for example, identified
in their paeans those bonds of affinity that existed between the
house, as an institution, and its symbolism as a pivot from which
authority sprang and where it was sustained. The hospitality
offered and enjoyed within it represented more than the maintaining of cordial relationships between people sharing similar
privileges, social conventions and attitudes, because it stood for
perchentyaeth – which is essentially benign householdership –
described as the mainspring of authority. That was the domestic
equivalent of the concept of 'good lordship', a concern for the
moral propriety of the family and the kindred, the extension of
patronage and the declaration of loyalty to the state (see Chapter
1, pp. 27–9). It entailed receiving as well as giving, principally a
recognition of status and an acknowledgement of decorum as
the handmaid of power and influence. Fundamentally, hospitality
was the hallmark of the 'ideal' gentleman, and within the house
conviviality and friendship stemmed from a strong sense of communal obligation. Dispensing hospitality had become a growing
commitment, sufficiently weighty to be mentioned in royal proclamations urging gentry to return to their respective residences to
govern their regions as a prerequisite of order and defence, to halt
the 'decay' of hospitality, to promote community feeling and to
administer relief to the poor.[27] It was not a new feature for it was
given priority in the medieval grammars as 'gwrdahaeth' (nobility)
and 'cynhalyad' (support and maintenance).[28] This form of
magnanimity was considered essential in any attempt to maintain
stability and good order. When Sir Thomas Mansel wrote to Sir
Edward Stradling, appointing him supervisor of his estate during
his absence in London, he directed Stradling to ensure that 'the
riche shall not oppresse the poor', and that, at the same time, the
rights and privileges of the well-endowed were safeguarded.[29]
Hospitality was regarded in contemporary writings as central to
any examination of the role of gentry in community life. It
amounted, in fact, to being their *raison d'être*. In *A Summons for
Sleepers* (1589), which was translated into Welsh by John Conway
III, Leonard Wright wished to see men of lesser means than
affluent gentry being able to offer the hospitality and inspired

leadership expected of them according to their rank.[30] All these concepts, of course, are readily addressed in alliterative poetry and the private correspondence of the gentry. In the minds of the poets, no eulogistic verse was considered worthy and meaningful unless the recipient was fully recognized in his community as a governor, a person of authority renowned for maintaining good order within his household, a promoter of Christian charity and dutiful servant of the Crown.[31]

In any estimate of the fundamental features of *uchelwriaeth* attention needs to be given to what amounted to an obsessive desire to preserve lineage. Initially, birth and wealth took precedence over the qualities promoted by Renaissance thinkers, namely virtue, education and skill. When older concepts began to lose their impact it became clear that authority was an amalgamation of both good pedigree and virtuous living. The authority of the state was expounded from the pulpit, reinforcing the innate authority and virtues exercised within the household. The *Homily on Obedience* (1547), for example, emphasized the right order in society. Without 'rules . . . and such estates of God's order . . . there needs must follow all mischief and utter destruction of souls, bodies, goods and commonwealthe'.[32] Other efforts were made to maintain the hierarchical features of society, such as the Statute of Uses (1529), sumptuary legislation, the Act of Precedence (1559) and the educational system. Moreover, in the 1630s the Privy Council reinforced the principles that maintained authority at all levels and governed the social order.

Despite this gradual shift of emphasis in a society engaged in the throes of economic change, status, in the domestic environment, was a distinctive feature. Evidence shows that the patriarchal tradition was still supreme. The concept of the *uchelwr*, with its old and new features, was adhered to well into the seventeenth century regardless of cultural changes which eroded the time-honoured relationships between the gentry and their locality. The honour accorded to the head of the household, however, was being subtly challenged. Although the image of gentility survived distinct signs emerged of cultural alienation between governing and governed in the native community. It became particularly apparent in the Elizabethan era when the accolades of humanist scholars to high-ranking gentry matched the assertive pride often reflected in private correspondence and religious sources. In fifteenth- and sixteenth-century Wales the proliferation of landed estates had created a new cultural environment; thereby, an inspired concept of leadership emerged and was gradually disseminated among the new, educated squirearchy. Authority was enshrined in the medieval *breyr* or *uchelwr*, as described in the traditional laws of Wales, which marked the second rank in the hierarchy of privileged folk in the Middle Ages. The importance of birth and descent, as Gerald of Wales explained, was valued greater than 'anything else in the world'; for they were prepared to 'avenge with great ferocity any wrong or insult done to their relations'.[33] This, he continued, often led to fratricidal jealousies and encounters. 'It is also remarkable', he declared further, 'how much more people love their brothers when they are dead than they do while they are still alive', and one way of creating deep divisions between the Welsh, he said, was by sowing 'dissension in their ranks . . . and stir[ring] them up against each other'.[34] The author dispassionately drew attention to the fundamental weakness in Welsh society which formed an interesting paradox, namely that the kindred, which appeared to be the most cohesive entity in the social structure of Wales, was more likely to perpetuate discord than maintain unity and good order.

A freeman's status determined his worth in his community ('A bonedd a'th wna'n bennaeth').[35] Despite the social and economic trends of the later Middle Ages it was a concept that survived. In fact, it is most eminently represented in bardic tributes down to the mid-seventeenth century. The bonds of affinity are closely adhered to and safeguarded in the copious eulogies preserved in manuscript. These features of Welsh nobility were eagerly public-ized in what emerged as the chief manifestations of gentility in the period *c*.1540–1640. What was regarded as 'nobility native' ranked higher than 'nobility dative' despite the privileges, as repres-entatives of a civil nobility, with which both were endowed.[36] Commentators such as Sir Thomas Smith and William Lambarde emphasized the qualities required of the 'most sufficient persons' to engage themselves in public office and considered landed wealth to be the chief characteristic, whereas in Wales gentry who wished to aspire to similar positions as their counterparts over Offa's Dyke, did so usually by invitation and clientage. Humphrey Llwyd drew attention to this phenomenon when he described social trends among the more opulent Welsh freeholders in the 1570s, and the niceties of the day often appealed to those who were themselves privileged to have either served the wealthy or who had enjoyed their hospitality. Not all householders were disposed to offer such beneficence but their leadership was never in doubt, and it was this attachment to a broader cultural environment that promoted Llwyd to make his remark.[37]

That culture was not solely identified with the patronage of the bards but, more extensively, with sustaining the basic features of a 'way of life' that enabled the gentry to assume leadership on a local or national scale. The authority that went with it was indeed remarkable and unchallenged. It appears that, in any examination of regional power structure regarding the domestic scene, some major aspects require consideration, each interrelated and exposing the fundamental features of *uchelwriaeth* as it appertained to the family circle and to the immediate community.

The first factor is the role of the country residence as the principal manifestation of power and authority. The period 1570–1640 has traditionally been labelled as the age of the 'great rebuilding' and, despite arguments in favour of this title, based on the rise in population and improvement in material means across the social framework, it is evidently too rigid (see Chapter 1, pp. 24–8). Houses were erected by the gentry where and when they considered it convenient and appropriate, and not all of them lavishly displayed the external and internal grandeur that some sources would have historians believe. Some halls were very modest indeed, especially in the more conservative native areas where the unit system predominated, giving rise to two or more houses close to each other on the estate, such as Clenennau, Henblas (Beaumaris) and Penrhyn. Within their respective regions, however, they are of sufficient style and appearance to merit attention.[38] In other areas, such as Brecknockshire, house-groupings of this type did not exist and the buildings at Aberbrân Fawr and Porth-aml were independent and not designed on the basis of the family settlement or unity system.[39]

The country residence was the matrix of regional ascendancy and prestige, concentrating on the 'credit' which the house enjoyed and maintained. By building, the gentry, of whatever rank, 'wished to provide posterity with tangible and enduring evidence of their achievements'.[40] It was 'the capital of the family and the repository of its traditions' as well as an institution which enabled gentry of varying degrees to display their opulence and authority in rural areas.[41] Moreover, it enhanced a claim to deference and reinforced patriarchal supremacy, an image projected by Dr John Davies of Brecon in his address to Sir Edward Stradling in his preface to the *Cambrobrytannicae Cymraecaeve Linguae Institutiones* (1592).[42] That credit was derived from honour which gave the squire an estimate of his own value and others a standard by which to position him and measure his worth in the social hierarchy. It was focused to assess all attributes of gentility: frequent references to the house's 'fortunes' highlight the centre from which leadership sprang, where authority and benevolence were shared on equal terms. Doubtless the most impressive description of a castellated residence was that by Dr John Davies when adulating his patron at St Donat's:

> . . . cadarn ei amddiffynfeydd – y safle mwyaf cymwys am ymhell ac agos . . . Yno y mae'r mor llidiog yn berwi ac yn rhuo yn y fath fodd nes bod y tonnau cynddeiriog . . . yn hyrddio creigiau o faint anghredadwy yn erbyn muriau'r adeiladau hyn – ond i ddim pwrpas.[43]

> [. . . sturdy in its defence – the most suitable site near and afar . . . There the wrathful sea boils and roars in such a manner that the mad waves hurl rocks of incredible size against the walls of these buildings – but to no purpose.]

The symbolism in this extract signifies how the power exercised by Stradling was portrayed by this impregnable fortress. Generations previously, Guto'r Glyn eagerly recorded the dignity accorded to the *plasty* as a manifestation of munificence and pre-eminence and its reputation as the edifice elevated high above the abodes of others ('Uchel yw'r llys uwchlaw'r llaill').[44] Similarly, his contemporary Dafydd Nanmor, as Saunders Lewis aptly illustrated, declared that the residence represented a stable civilized existence.[45]

Nobility, as represented in such adulations, was the source of order and authority and was designated as such. The compositions in honour of noblemen's houses revealed a concern to expose 'an admired and gracious culture' for it was not possible for those properties to be revered 'except where there lies heritage and tradition and an ancient nobility'. Sir Richard Bulkeley III of Henblas and later Baron Hill, Beaumaris, was renowned for his hospitality. His house at Baron Hill was built (*c.*1618), it was said, to entertain Prince Henry on his way to Ireland:[46] Bulkeley was regarded principally as 'a great Housekeeper & Entertayner of Noblemen & had the Gentrie & Com'onaltie of the Countrey att his service'.[47] In that context Sir John Wynn of Gwydir asserted unequivocally that he had 'by honest means brought hit [his house] to the greatest estate of any house in northwales above Conway'.[48] He was not far off the mark either, because the 'house', in this context, referred also to the landed property for which the residence was the fulcrum. Like so many similar dwellings the mansion was the edifice or institution that replaced the castle as the symbol of power. John Leland recorded that new houses appeared in all parts of Wales in the 1530s, thus echoing bardic testimony which glorified the well-placed and well-defended *plasty* owned by a hospitable and well-connected Welsh *uchelwr* who also built and enjoyed his parks, fishponds, dovecotes and richly embellished interiors.[49] In the late sixteenth century George Owen remarked that gentry houses had been utilized to conduct legal proceedings and to attend to routine matters of administration.[50] Richard Davies, on the other hand, accused some of the gentry of keeping dishonourable houses which were virtually dens of thieves:

> Amyl ynghymru, ir nas craffa cyfraith, i ceir neuadd y gwr bonheddig yn noddfa lladron . . . oni bai fraych ac adain y gwr bonheddig ni bydday ond ychydig ladrad ynghymru.[51]

> [Often in Wales, though the law pays no heed to it, the gentleman's hall is a refuge for thieves . . . were it not for the arm and wing of the gentleman there would be but little theft in Wales.]

Both these comments were indicative of trends, the first aimed more positively to show progress and the second signifying how some recalcitrant gentry continued to adhere to older and less commendable forms of self-assertion. In George Owen's time there were new exciting trends in progress within the household (see Chapter 1, pp. 24–7) and symbolically the more prosperous houses in the Welsh countryside were regarded as microcosms of the royal household. Following the reforms initiated by Thomas Wolsey in 1536–40, which made that household more manageable, it became more efficient, thus attracting some comparisons between the court and the most opulent country residences. Architectural innovations in country and town houses reflected a rise in standards of living and status as much as a greater degree of ostentation. Increasing wealth and added prestige often accounted for the rebuilding of gentry houses. 'Houses are built to live in, and not to look on', Francis Bacon declared, 'Therefore let use bee preferred before uniformitie.'[52] He proceeded to modify that view immediately but what he did say was fundamentally correct. Houses, of whatever appearance, were essentially representations of class, and some were lavishly adorned in contemporary style such as St Donat's and Old Beaupré in Glamorgan. At Conwy, Robert Wynn built Plas Mawr, the Herberts resided at the magnificent Powys Castle at Welshpool and William Mostyn and his successors lived at Mostyn and Gloddaith. Plas Mawr was designed in typically Tudor Renaissance style, consisting of a mixture of the classical and high medieval: it was ambitiously constructed and was compared favourably, for example, with the New Place built at Swansea by the Herberts. As a younger son with no sizeable estate to administer, Robert Wynn of Conwy probably prospered through his connections with Sir Philip Hoby, which explains his desire to erect a worthy edifice in the centre of one of the most noteworthy of northern boroughs.[53] In Anglesey, Hugh Hughes of Plas Coch (d. 1609), the lawyer and Queen's attorney, extended his residence in 1588. He was representative of the new families in Tudor Wales who strengthened his business connections by marrying into the Montague family of Brigstock, Northamptonshire, established his legal career and laid the foundations of his estate in Crown lands in his native county.[54]

What this upsurge of building activity proved is that men had more leisure and means to improve their public standing and that their increased standing in their community had stimulated them to adorn that reputation in a more substantially visible manner. There were those, of course, who overstretched themselves, but most did reasonably well and displayed some prosperity in the Welsh towns and countryside. In this context it is hardly surprising that George Owen, in *The Description of Penbrokshire*, regarded the stability enjoyed under the Tudors as reflecting the peace and good order found among the law-abiding inhabitants of the county. Law and order, represented in medieval institutions of government, were described as 'the greatest benefitte that wee of wales enioye above all others the subiectes of this realme to haue lawe and Justice sent home to our howses, and powred into our bosomes'.[55] The consequences of stronger contacts with the royal court, visits abroad and the impact of a broader education and culture introduced them into a new social environment in which less weight was placed on military pursuits. Although a military career continued to attract a proportion of younger gentry England was not involved in any large-scale warfare. Therefore, the desire to uphold status led to honours being given in spheres of activity other than on the battlefields of Europe, and efforts were made to substitute munificence in peacetime for glory in war. There was a changing way of life and, at each stage, new architectural techniques reflected a growing familiarity with the intellectual trends of the age.

The image projected by the *plasty* was sustained also in immediate relations within the family. The authority exercised within the household identified it essentially with a form of government. Social and religious commentators constantly reminded their readers of the importance of obedience and discipline and the need to exercise strict control. Increasing emphasis in the latter half of the sixteenth century was placed on the nuclear family and the interraction between individual members and the personnel of the household – maids, servants, chaplains, stewards and bailiffs. A good marriage within the family served to increase the prestige and power of the landlord. That was also reflected in the dowries, some of them very handsome, that came as a result of propitious marriages. It is not surprising, therefore, that William Lloyd, Sir John Wynn's agent employed in seeking suitable brides for some of his sons, advised his master that the best portion always provided the most lucrative marriage,[56] and that the master himself was rumoured to say in 1615 that he had proposed to 'sell' his second son Richard in marriage to the 'highest bidder'![57] On occasions arranged marriages were considered to be means of strengthening a family's standing, and it was usually the case that marriage contracts were drawn up between families of equal status within the same region, despite the growing tendency to seek brides and husbands in other Welsh regions and over the border. In any event close family ties were maintained; when a widow remarried her inheritance would be reduced, and younger sons would be placed in the heir's care or, in the case of a minority, under the supervision of a guardian.[58]

Disciplinary procedure in the household was revealed in the manner in which children were treated: they were expected to be obedient towards their parents, to care for their mother, and to be on good terms with each other. Although the squire-gentleman was the master of the household, his wife enjoyed equal status, shared the same code of conduct and contributed significantly to household management. Although different circumstances might dictate otherwise there are several examples, especially among well-off families, where prescriptive evidence aids in exposing the nature of familial relations. About 1635 Lord Powys's steward informed Lady Powys that he had 'proud' children but that he was unable to 'bread' them as he might have wished. He exercised discipline like any other father but to no avail because his wife – reputably a stubborn, self-willed woman – succoured them.[59] Lady Sydney Wynn and her daughter-in-law Grace Wynn (the niece of Archbishop John Williams) were powerful figures in the Gwydir household[60] as were Elizabeth Craven and Elizabeth Somerset, the wives of the second and third Lord Powys respectively at Welshpool, both of them being actively engaged in running estate affairs in the late seventeenth century.[61] Thus remarked Henry Smith in his treatise on marriage in 1591: 'The duties of Marriage may be reduced to the duty of man and wife one toward another, and their duty towards their children and

their duty towards their servants.'[62] This statement presupposed
that authority stemmed from the priorities observed by the
gentleman and his lady. Although their household duties differed
they were fundamentally united within the bonds of matrimony. It
was once considered that choosing a wife was like a strategem in
war; if the estate was sizeable and substantial a match should be
arranged 'near home and at leisure'; if, on the other hand, ill-
endowed, a partner should be sought from afar and the marriage
quickly arranged because one 'can buy nothing in the market with
gentility'. Thus was implied that the virtues of good ancestry, in
themselves, were inadequate resources and more material substance was required.

In a more intimate context Rhys Prichard, the famous poet-
priest of Llanymddyfri, revealed the religious ethos of family life
as it was formulated in the mid-seventeenth century. His verses
abound with references to social etiquette and deference as
applied to the heads of households. His aim was to stress the
spiritual needs of the individual and the way in which Christian
conduct assisted in achieving them. His prime texts were the
Bible, Book of Common Prayer and Book of Matins in which he
discovered the devotion, prayer, grace and spirituality regarded as
the main components of the truly religious life. These factors he
associated with the doctrine and authority of the Protestant
Church. The teachings of that Church, coupled with a deeper
awareness of sanctification, would guide the individual to a
knowledge of God whose supreme authority was exemplified in
biblical texts and safeguarded by the Church:

> Bydd reolwr, bydd offeiriad,
> Bydd gynghorwr, bydd yn ynad
> Ar dy dŷ ac ar dy bobol,
> I reoli pawb wrth reol.
>
> Gwna di gyfraith gyfiawn, gymwys,
> I reoli'th dŷ a'th eglwys;
> Pâr i'th bobol yn ddiragrith
> Fyw yn gymwys wrth y gyfraith.[63]

[Be a governor, be a priest, be a counsellor, be a magistrate in your
house and over your people, to govern all by rule. Exercise just and
proper law to govern your house and church. Ensure that your people
live unhypocritically and properly by law.]

These two verses contain the essence of Prichard's concept of
propriety and the way in which it should be displayed within the

household. The *paterfamilias*'s authority in public affairs, as 'governor', 'counsellor' and 'magistrate', is applied to maintain discipline within that household and uphold the teachings of the Church. Weighting is given to law and the exercise of government, among those who resided in that household or who were their guests. A distinct comparison can be drawn between Prichard's works and the authority accorded to the *paterfamilias* in Bayly's *The Practice of Piety*:

> . . . if thou be called to the government of a Family, thou must not hold it sufficient to serve God, & live uprightly in thine owne person, unles thou cause all under thy charge to do the same with thee. And God himselfe gives a special charge to all Householders that they do instruct their Family in his Word, and traine them up in his feare and service . . . and the service of God in a Family, is the best building, and surest entailing of House and land, to a man and his posterity . . . call every morning all thy family to some convenient roome, and firste either reade thy selfe unto them a Chapter in the Word of God, or cause it to be read distinctly by some other.[64]

Such qualities were nurtured in the home. Sir William Maurice of Clenennau, for example, was regarded in 1620 as 'a piller of your countrie',[65] a description that not only contained political overtones but also indicated how notable a figure he was reputed to be within his household and community. Dr John Davies considered that Sir Edward Stradling's best qualities were demonstrated at home:

> Quod praeterea e regionibus transmarinis regressus, tanta cum laude tandiu domi egeris, vt liquido eluceat quam tui sis semper simitis . . . Nae tu quidem fuisti semper verae virtutis custos, rigidusque satelles; semper inter omnes extitisti pacis fabricator.[66]

> [In addition, with regard to your history after you returned from foreign regions, it is seen that you conducted yourself at home with such honour, and that for so much time, that it is absolutely clear that you were at all times a completely steadfast person . . . certainly, you have always been a custodian and unbending follower to true virtue; and you have always excelled every one as a maker of peace].

As such sources overtly reveal, the role of the *pencenedl* (*caput gentis* in the Latin texts of the Welsh laws) or *paterfamilias* was central in maintaining authority.

Attempts were made to avoid any circumstances that might cause disharmony between close and more distant kin relations, given the surviving kindred structure in Wales, but that was no easy task. Within the household hospitality would be a marked feature. 'Good Sir Edward', Arthur Basset wrote to Stradling in 1582, 'I do yield you my hearty thanks for your great courtesy and entertainment at my late being at St Donat's.'[67] That house had a reputation for its sumptuous reception of visitors because many had seen that Sir Edward had 'sundry commodities . . . few or none hath the like in Wales'. Those who gave 'courteous and friendly welcome and entertainment' and who received 'all most kindly . . . according to their degrees' were regarded as ideal hosts. The etiquette adopted was not only an indication of good manners but also a manifestation of that superior position the head of the household enjoyed and the authority that accompanied it in his house. By fulfilling their role as respected hosts or by visiting the Stradlings and their compeers they were simply drawing around them members of other families which recognized mutual codes of conduct. This also applied to specific visits to London or Ludlow or the local shiretown where the qualities of gentility were amply demonstrated. One indication of this was the intention of William, Lord Compton, earl of Northampton, Lord President of the Council at Ludlow, to establish in 1618 a riding school for the gentry:

> . . . an academy for the instruction and training up of young gentlemen in that worthy and commendable exercise of horsemanship. For I hold that horsemanship is a necessary and useful part in every gentleman's breeding and a thing of high estimation throughout the most flourishing and best governed parts of the world and may induce gentlemen to breed and train horses fit for their own practice and the service of the country.[68]

The letter was addressed to deputy-lieutenants and appeared to combine vital aspects of government: the need for good breeding on the part of eligible gentry, the acquiring of expertise in riding and the practical use of horse-riding for defence purposes. The content of this letter was but a further manifestation of the need to extend the use of the code of conduct in the domestic environment.

Conduct, Misconduct and the Family

It was chiefly in the role of public administrator and counsellor that a man's code of conduct was fully exposed and put to the test. Family correspondence often reflects this. For example, in the Clenennau household Sir William Maurice was regarded by a distant kin as 'a man of . . . calling and credit' who, through his courtesy, had made his correspondent, 'a poor gentleman born to nothing', aware of the esteem accorded to the 'head and honour of so ancient a house'.[69] 'I have always accounted so well of you', James Turberville of Llantwit Major maintained in a letter to his superior Sir Edward Mansel of Margam, 'that I have wished myself absent from that place where I might not seem to pleasure you nor displease you.'[70] Favours were often sought of superior gentry, not in order that they might be repaid but rather to elicit a firm declaration of the superiority of status:

> . . . I ame assured by soundrye credible gentlemen in these p'ts of the greate care yow have alwayes had to equitie and justice, respectinge rather thestimacion of yo'r worshipp and credit than anie waise bente by will in the behalfe of anie to wronge the leaste.[71]

Such a statement involved safeguarding one's pride and integrity, particularly in the presence of the family and in retaliation against deceitful kinsmen. If a man's honour was at stake he immediately defended himself. This often led to petty rivalries which occasionally led to serious confrontation. Men, Sir John Stradling remarked, would be 'imbrac't with one hand, stabbed with the other'.[72] Sir John Wynn solemnly cautioned his heir Sir Richard Wynn in 1623 to value friends and beware of jealous kinsmen: 'I have ever more accounted of a true friend than a kinsman, for many kinsmen there are, but few friends.' And he continued later in the same letter:

> You must lerne to know your frends from your enymyes who to take, who to leave & to harken after . . . for be assured the envyous hatefull man feire not & wyle do yow myslike when he is able; as I shall leave yow frends so also enymyes whose cheife motive ys that I prosper.[73]

Although the landed gentry were aware of their role in maintaining the political and economic structure of society they were equally concerned to use kin relations to reinforce their claims to superiority. Whereas kindred could and did, as the above extract reveals, hinder a family from achieving supremacy, it often proved to be an asset, hence the weight placed on the continuity 'in the reputation of gentlemen' by 'the goodness of God' that sustained what Gerald of Wales described as the drawbacks arising out of kindred animosities or stubborn adherence to *gwaedogaeth* (blood affinities).[74] Pedigree, he maintained, was the title-deed which proved a man's descent through nine generations as a legitimate member of the clan (*gwelygordd*) and part-owner of clan or kindred territory (*tir gwelyog*). The terms *bonedd* and *bonheddig* constantly referred to in the verse of late medieval and early modern poets underline the importance of blood affinity. Strength lay in unity, as Siôn Tudur amply noted in some of his most telling compositions: animosities between kindred caused serious disruption, detrimental to the welfare of the regional community, hence the desire to ensure that the kindred remained firm in its allegiance to itself.[75]

The causes of kindred dissension, which proved detrimental to family unity, were closely examined by Richard Price of Brecon and Dr David Lewis, and both believed that a swift solution was required. 'I say', Lewis declared, 'I followe thexample of the good phesision who in a sharpe disease dothe geve a sharpe medyson'. He was an advocate of Rowland Lee's drastic methods and, among other factors, considered that the persistence of retaining and the existence of 'foster brothers loyteringe & ydle kinsmen & others hangers on . . . Maisterless men . . . and ydle persons' to be root causes of disorder.[76] Legitimate and illegitimate consanguineous relations were harmful, and consequently obtaining impartial justice in the courts was often almost impossible. Government in the 1530s showed grave concern for this matter because 'divers adherents friends and kinsfolks . . . have resorted to the . . . Jurors and have suborned them to acquit divers murderers felons and accessories openly and notoriously known contrary to equity and justice'.[77] Status, of whatever rank in Welsh society, was defended by all means possible; where claims to it were dishonoured or transgressed contention ensued. A perceptive comment was made in that context in a petition to Henry VIII by Sir Richard Herbert of Montgomery and other gentry in the Marches in 1536 seeking unity with England. They drew attention to an increase in law-breaking among Welsh freeholders who attempted to assert their status and dwelled on the dire effects of partible inheritance:

> the kynges subgettes there have ev[er] lyved in mouche pov[er]tye and in small reputacon and yet estemyng theym silfes so great gentlemen bicause of their kynred and their landes (thoughe it be verey litle). [They resorted to] theftes, robryes and extorcons [to] beare furthe a gentlemans porte and countyn[a]nce.[78]

It was largely his awareness of his ascendancy among his kinsmen that led Sir John Wynn to declare publicly his determination to pursue his main interests. 'I take hit as a dysgrace', he observed in 1610, 'to attempt owght that I do not performe; nether wyll I attempt but what in reson I am lyke to cumpase'.[79] To save face or avoid any family humiliation others of his rank shared similar aspirations. Bold assertiveness of this kind concealed an immense pride in the organic structure of the family and the need to preserve it. His son Owen Wynn, however, cautioned him not to consider standing for parliament in 1623 following the heavy defeat which his house had suffered three years earlier at the hands of the Cefnamwlch faction in Llŷn. 'I find the countrey distastfull of us', he declared, 'and therfore noe wise parte to put our selves into their hands, for matters of credditt anie more.'[80] To maintain one's 'credit' was considered essential in a close-knit as well as a broader environment. A consciousness of 'region' and 'neighbourhood' became an extension to a feeling of kindred unity. The blood network still remained a powerful element in relations and, within the context of communal obligation, the privileged individual was at its centre, dispensing justice, providing leadership and maintaining hospitality.

For several reasons government agencies feared the proliferation of family feuds. When considering the appointment of lawyers at Ludlow Henry Herbert believed that it was best for them to be strangers because 'friends, alliance and kindred occasion partiality in judgements'.[81] Kindred was involved in perpetuating the unpleasant dispute between Sir John Salusbury and Sir John Lloyd and Sir Richard Trefor in the 1601 Denbighshire election. Sir Richard Lewkenor, chief justice of Chester, had attempted to arbitrate but disagreement had again occurred. He feared that it would 'breed dissension in the shire where the people are found ready to follow those they do affect in all actions without respect to the lawfulness or unlawfulness thereof, as justice will hardly be administered or the people kept in quiet'.[82] He who was 'greatly friended and allied and of many great kindred' to support him in a court of law had the advantage. Lord Zouche, Lord President of the Council in the Marches, was equally concerned a year later, following the murder of a freeholder in the Llanrwst area for which members of Sir John Wynn's kindred were allegedly responsible, and he declared to the squire:

> I pray you lett me intreate yow to consider how mutch it concerneth the breach of peace of the land what a plague it threatneth to the contrye where sutch vipers are harbored and what dishonor it will be to yow besides discredit and the plague of god both to yow and your posteritie.[83]

Zouche identified internal disruption as the chief threat to unity and prosperity within the realm and warned Wynn that his 'credit' might well be smeared unless he, as sheriff of Caernarfonshire, undertook to root out the evil of harbouring felons.

The use and abuse of kindred in supporting the family also caused, or threatened to cause, disruption. Roland ap Maredudd ap Rhys of Bodowyr and William Gruffudd of Porth-aml, Anglesey, employed kinsmen and other followers brandishing a variety of weapons to create insurrection at Caernarfon.[84] Similarly, in Merioneth in the 1570s, and Glamorgan in the 1570s and 1590s, family matters led to the involvement of kindred and retainers to settle differences between seemingly irreconcilable families.[85] The image of an esteemed *paterfamilias* emerges evidently in an appeal for forgiveness because of his 'disordered tongue' which the ageing Owen ap John made to Sir William Maurice in 1612. He sought 'mercy and comfort' and couched his appeal in a manner which revealed the recipient as the true benevolent householder:

> . . . he that showeth mercy, mercy shall finde . . . to forgeve is the noblest kynde of revenge, blessed is he that beareth a revengles harte and that will melte into comiseracion att his neighbour's extremity . . . sett your harte juste and righter towards me and ende all differences in the courte of your owne good conscience unto which I appeale . . . The remembrance of a good name shall never perishe from the earth.[86]

This passage illustrates the principal features of the disciplined and benevolent gentleman, his mercy, compassion and magnanimity, and the qualities of justice and credit which he purported to possess. Doubtless Sir Thomas Elyot would have enthusiastically assented to such an applause and challenge. Sir William Maurice's credit was at stake since he was expected, in difficult personal circumstances, to prove his worth as a charitable householder, to apply his authority to his more immediate needs within the household and to prove that *uchelwriaeth* had been elevated as a manifestation of personal conduct.[87] To the bardic fraternity, it was maintaining a patron's integrity ('gair da') that counted more than anything. Where kinsmen were involved, the obligation was considered to be greater. Humphrey Salusbury expected Sir Thomas Salusbury to respect him, as he had his ancestors, much more than he might respect any hired servants.[88] Sir Edward Stradling's aid was sought in 1578 to maintain an unfortunate kinsman by advancing his fortunes 'w'th yo'r countenance and credyt amongst suche of yo'r frends as will geve'.[89] It was the internal security of the family as well as the welfare of the region that compelled the earl of Pembroke to offer to intervene in the Stradling–Carne disputes which threatened the welfare of the rural community. He wished to 'set' them 'at unity', and if he could assist to quell animosity he was prepared to visit the county for that purpose.[90]

The concern to maintain unity between families and the use of official channels of government to that end was essential in any demonstration of loyalty to the regional community. It reflected a deference to authority at home, and an extension to the domestic culture so highly valued in the early modern period. The relationship between the gentlemen and the immediate family and kindred signified the need to maintain order among gentry of all ranks that claimed gentility and attended to their responsibilities in the household, hence the attempts made at different levels to follow the example of superiors, offer noble patronage and provide public service. The aim of the ideal householder was to undermine vestiges of discord in the family and to cherish the best of what remained of the old kindred spirit in public and private affairs. 'The humour of my tenants', the squire of Gwydir maintained in 1616, 'were ever to take my word, or my mood, because they trusted me.'[91] Such assurances, however, were not always honoured and mistrust between gentry and their tenants often caused contention. For example, it appeared that Thomas Glynn of Glynllifon suspected Wynn and his political motives about four years later on the eve of the famous Caernarfonshire county election. In a letter to Sir William Maurice, Wynn's kinsman, he cautioned the squire of Clenennau not to be

> drawn by those who I feare, neyther love your creditt nor esteeme the countreys [i.e. region's] quiet to be content to observe your owne glory and the honour heretofore truly attributed unto yow and that only for the private endes of those w'ch make show of fidelity for the cause thereof.[92]

Glynn attempted to dissuade Maurice from being deceived by the 'show of fidelity' and advances of faithless friends and kinsmen (the Wynns in this case) who had only their own selfish interests at heart.

The Paterfamilias *and the Religious Ideal*

The landowner, as businessman or supervisor of his household, provided the essential moral ingredients making for harmony between the privileged and unprivileged and the powerful and the weak. Edmwnd Prys admitted so much in his poem on oppressive

officials; in an epigrammatic couplet he drew attention to the
injustice suffered by the weak who had to maintain the strong
merely to increase their power:

> Rhaid i'r gwan ddal y gannwyll
> I'r dewr i wneuthur oer dwyll.[93]

[The weak must hold the candle for the bold to commit his betrayal.]

Such a telling assertion uncovers the callous features of business
life and public service, a factor which the poet-priest considered it
essential to publicize. Those who were forced to admit that the
opposition of rivals was damaging to their reputation also
confessed that 'the malice of others . . . seeking to work division
betwene us and therby make us a pageant to laugh at' threatened
the reputation of the family and powerful men in public office. It
is evident that the links between the head of the household and his
community were fundamental in any examination of the exercise
of the moral code in the Welsh countryside.[94]

The extent to which amicable relations were established
between the head of the household and his immediate family is
not easily determinable. Despite the acrimony which arose
between the houses of Mostyn and Gwydir at the turn of the
seventeenth century, Sir John Wynn advised his son-in-law, Roger
Mostyn 'to submit your self in all resonable matters unto him [his
embittered father, Sir Thomas Mostyn], as thus being an obedyent
child to the father' and to accept his 'fatherly aucthoryty'.[95]
Lawrence Stone argued that family relations before the eighteenth
century were characterized mainly by an 'emotional coldness'
caused by the natural hazards that often shortened human
lifespan, such as disease, death in childbirth and infant
mortality.[96] Pictorial and literary evidence, however, does reveal a
more optimistic picture, closer unity of family identity and a belief
in the continuity of life after death.[97] Life was naturally hard for all
sections of the community, especially at times of economic
distress, and, in view of bad harvests and foreign threats, Thomas
Churchyard's rosy picture of the gentry in 1587 is untenable:

> In any soyle, where gentlemen are found,
> Some house is kept, and bountie doth abound . . .
> Their glorie rests, in countries wealth and fame,
> They have respect, to blood and auncient name . . . [98]

When the place of honour in the household is assessed, value
judgements which emphasize the general rather than the specific

features of fundamental issues must be avoided. The 'turbulent and contentious man' was, in another context, often regarded as the benevolent householder.[99] Men reacted differently in different circumstances and exercised their gentility accordingly, but essentially they considered that the home was the 'centre of gravity' where gentility was nurtured. While John Penry was mainly concerned about the exercise of royal authority in reforming the Church he was also eager to project the patriarchal tradition and its role in defining moral responsibility.[100] In his address to Henry Herbert at Ludlow, while acknowledging that God's Word had been introduced to his family, Penry cautioned him that his duty lay principally in ensuring that 'the power of the Word hath touched your very soul' so that he might serve God by means of his government. Government, in his view, was an extension to disciplined conduct within the household and was indeed recognized as the cradle of probity and honesty.[101]

One formative Welsh source which reveals the role of the master in instructing his household 'in the ways of God' is the preface by Robert Llwyd to his translation of Arthur Dent's *The Plain Man's Pathway to Heaven (Llwybr hyffordd yn cyfarwyddo yr anghyfarwydd i'r nefoedd . . . (1630))*. He addressed his monoglot fellow-countryman, reminding him, for his soul's sake, of the Day of Judgement and of the need to prepare himself to meet his Creator. If he should neglect his own condition then, at the least, he should consider his family's spiritual welfare. The head of the household's chief responsibility was to his family and dependants, and in Llwyd's work spirituality and the imposition of moral discipline were the principal needs. In his address he upbraided the reader for attending more to material comforts than to moral requirements:

> Ai anhawdd gennit dreulio amser yn y gorchwyl hwn, nid rhaid i ti golli dim amser a waethygo arnat, neu a rwystro dy orchwylion bydol yn eu prŷd: y mae'r nos yn hîr y gaiaf, a'r Suliau ar gwiliau yn hîr yr hâf; gad ymmaith y twmpath chwareu, a'r bowliau, ar tafarnau, a'r bêl-droed, a'r denis, a'th negeseuau.[102]

> [Is it difficult for you to spend time in this work; you need not waste any time which harms you or which hinders you in fulfilling your worldly tasks in their season: the winter night is long, and the summer and Sundays and holidays are long; leave the dancing tump, and the bowls, and taverns, and football, and the tennis and your errands.]

If the head of the household or any other among his family could not read then, Llwyd declared, that error should be corrected. He went on to decry the common but irreverent customs of his day

and commended Rowland Vaughan for serving God for his
countrymen's spiritual well-being by preparing a translation of
Bayly's work that was about to be published. If younger generation
Welsh gentry like him did the same, Llwyd added, there would be
less disorder, over-indulgence, money-lending and greed for property as well as less abuse of alehouses and addiction to tobacco.

It was in the sphere of the ordered society that both Anglican
and Puritan divines addressed their audience in the works that
appeared in the early years of the Protestant Church settlement.
As previously cited (see Chapter 5, p. 192–4) the place accorded
to piety and the household was fundamental in any understanding
of the authority which the patriarch enjoyed among his people.
The increasing emphasis on the need to strengthen the Protestant
establishment, as exposed in a small but significant crop of
literature in the century after 1546, led to an increase in the
awareness of spirituality within the household, and piety became
the keyword in the private devotions of members of many
Protestant and Catholic families. The Protestant interpretation of
this kind of outlook where devotions assumed a major part of the
family's daily routine, is well-documented.[103] When referring to
the need to publicize the new pocket edition of the Bible in Welsh
(1630) among the Welsh, the anonymous author of the preface
aptly remarked:

> Ac lle y dylai yn bendifaddeu breswylio yn y galon, yr hon yw
> dodrefnyn pennaf yr enaid, Etto mae'n angenrhaid iddo hefyd
> breswylio yn y ty . . . mae'n rhaid iddo drigo yn dy stafell di, tan dy
> gronglwyd dy hun.[104]

> [And it should especially reside in the heart, which is the principal
> ornament of the soul. Yet it is necessary for it to reside in the house . . .
> it must reside in your room, under your own roof.]

He declared that God's authority, as exposed in the scriptures, lay in
the heart: it is the individual's responsibility in the divine presence
to acquaint himself with the truth as revealed in the Word of God.
This was the image of the honest Christian gentleman often
illustrated in contemporary sources in the early seventeenth
century; the man of virtue who reflected in his domestic conduct
the ideal way in which to govern the secular realm within the
context of his own locality. Sir Thomas Middleton, the puritan
landowner and entrepreneur, charged his chaplain 'to teach my
children, read service every morning and evening, instruct my
familie, and preach twice every month', duties which were similarly

performed in several other households.[105] The pious 'lady of the household' is also given prominence, as in the case of the redoubtable Lady Brilliana Harley of Brampton Bryan in Herefordshire.[106] She and many others of her rank emerged as the godly and benign gentlewoman portrayed in contemporary classical Welsh poetry. Lady Margaret Lloyd, wife of John Lloyd of Rhiwedog, who commissioned Rowland Vaughan of Caer Gai to translate Bayly's *The Practice of Piety* into Welsh, was regarded publicly as a devout person,[107] and Catherine Anwyl, wife of Robert Anwyl of Parc, Llanfrothen, and daughter of the celebrated royalist commander Sir John Owen of Clenennau, was also characterized by her piety, and known for her patronage for which she was presented with a theological book, translated by Ellis Lewis of Llwyngwern, Merioneth, to engage her attention during her leisure hours.[108]

In an era of increasing tension between parliament and the first two Stuart monarchs, the majority of the Welsh gentry supported the Crown. Since increasing pressures, especially financial ones, in the Welsh localities led to sharp criticism of the extravagances among favoured royal officials their participation was a guarded show of loyalty. It was an age when modest Anglican gentry revealed a profound sense of piety and disclosed their interest in aligning themselves in defence of the Protestant establishment.[109] These traits were set alongside the concept of justice and its subsidiary qualities. There were positive connections between them for authority was entrusted to the *paterfamilias* and was transmitted through him in the manner in which he governed his region. The Puritan preacher Oliver Thomas highlighted the essential link as an important factor in his own generation in the decade before the Civil Wars:

O Dâd a Meistr Nefol ti yr hwn ydwyt Benna Pen pob teulu, Rheola a llywodraetha yr holl deulu hwn, a goswng yn calonnau i vfuddhau ith Reolaeth ath lywodraeth di, ac fel ein gwnaethost yn dylwyth vn tŷ, dyro i ni vn feddwl ac vn galon ith wasnauthu di . . . [110]

[Oh Father and heavenly Master, you are the highest *paterfamilias*. Rule and govern all this family, and humble our hearts in obedience to your rule and government, and as you made us a family in one house, give us one mind and one heart to serve you . . .]

Conclusion

It is against this background that the position of the household and the role of its head should be evaluated on the eve of the

Civil Wars. In Wales it was an institution which, despite its shortcomings, had come to represent the firm alliance between the governing classes and the Crown. It was supported not only because of its abiding loyalty to two dynasties and its interaction with government at the centre but also because of its strong Protestant ethos. It established a powerful liaison between the native gentry and their social inferiors; by its very nature the wholesome household gave them an incentive to respect law and order. That law was often flouted or undermined by privileged and unprivileged alike, but it existed and could not be ignored or destroyed. That law was a means of maintaining discipline and governors and governed alike gave it priority when seeking to preserve peace inside and outside local courts. The example of the Church, the control exercised by the household, the application of the Poor Laws and related duties, were accompanied by an increased awareness that respect for authority, in the last resort, provided for people what modest benefits they could expect to receive in an age that was often described, in days of economic crisis, as harsh and unfeeling. In that context the principle that advocated the exercise of law and law enforcement drew all sections of Welsh society together in a bond of unity.[111]

Wales has often been labelled a 'royal fortress' during the 1640s when it is calculated that the majority of Welsh privileged families, either in principle or militarily, supported Charles I in his struggle with parliament. In practical terms that was certainly the case, regardless of the pockets of Puritan opposition in some well-defined areas of the country, but the monarchical tradition was a deep-seated factor in determining the choice of sides, actively or otherwise, in the wars. The royal court was similarly looked upon as a fortress in the sense that it acted as an extension to the cultural stronghold of the native *llys* in the countryside, maintaining a moral stand against treason, disobedience and infidelity. The King was seen as a national figurehead and the fount of justice under whom all subjects within the realm enjoyed privileges according to status. John Jones of Gellilyfdy, in one of his manuscripts, gave this phenomenon its clearest definition, describing the government of Britain as a round tower, five storeys high which, in turn, represented the honour of the land, its justice, its peace, its wealth and its religion. He then continued:

If this piller be cutt downe all the greate beames of the buyldinge supported by ytt . . . fall downe to the ground . . . This great Towre is the kingdome: the great piller is the Certes [sic] thereof is the kinge which sustayneth the Machine of the whole . . .

It was Charles Price of Pilleth, member of parliament for Radnor, who stated unequivocally in 1628 when the Petition of Right was being discussed in the chamber: 'Wee sitt here as the body and the king is our head . . . if any blow be given to the body the head will feele it, and if there be any violation of the priviledge of this house it will concerne the whole kingdome.'[112] These words offer the clearest exposition of the concept of the national *paterfamilias*, the fount of the nation-state and its institutions but also the source of the familial hierarchy, its authority and its bonds of affinity.

Conclusion

The Roman Catholic scholar Gruffydd Robert, in his dedication of *Dosbarth Byrr ar y rhan gyntaf i ramadeg Cymraeg* to William Herbert, earl of Pembroke and lord of Cardiff, written in Milan in 1567, exalted his patron in lavish style and offered the following tribute:

> ... gan fod yn eglur, nid o feụn loegr yn unig, eithr ymhob mann y mae son am dani, nad oes dim a phrụyth ynḍo yn perthynu at stad y deyrnas meụn heḍụch, a rhyfel, ond a luniuyd trụy'ch cyngor, ag a ụnaethbuyd trụych grym a'ch cymorth, a'ch anorphụys lafur.[1]

> [for it is clear, not only within England but rather in all places where there is mention made of her, that there is nothing which bears fruit relating to the state of the realm in peace and war, but that which is formed by your counsel, and done through your power and assistance and indefatigable labour.]

The words are fulsome praise of a prominent figure in mid-Tudor politics and administration who was applauded also by Wiliam Llŷn and the notable lexicographer 'Sir' Thomas Wiliems of Trefriw. For a Catholic exile in Italy to offer adulation to such a personage, however, is indeed remarkable. Although Gruffydd Robert was a self-imposed Catholic exile in Italy he, like other litterateurs of his generation, attributed to Herbert those virtues common to gentry of all religious persuasions because he was a person who could command much respect at court and in governmental circles. Herbert's conscience was flexible; he survived four reigns and was regarded among Catholics as a fervent supporter of the Old Faith, which may well be why his patronage was sought on this occasion. The chief features in the eulogy, however, are the virtues and worthiness exemplified by Herbert as a public-spirited person. He is regarded as the central figure in the Elizabethan state and as a firm and trustworthy royal counsellor in times of war and peace. His example gave others a lead to follow.

The tribute underlies much of what was declared by other humanist scholars and commentators about the English and Welsh gentry in the sixteenth and early seventeenth centuries. It

appeared that their position was assured: strongly allied to the
Crown and equally loyal to the institutions of government.
Honour, justice and a deep sense of responsibility to their
respective communities appeared to be the basis of their authority,
and squires and gentlemen in power were constantly aware of the
obligations delegated to them. Such attributes, however, did not
guarantee the effective performance of their duties, nor did they
consider that service to the Crown was an obstacle to satisfaction
of personal ambition. The prefaces of humanist scholars, dedicated to dignitaries whose practical contribution to the Welsh
administrative scene was marginal, go part of the way to
explaining the essence of gentility 'in action'. Qualities in the
exercise of authority were universally publicized in contemporary
social commentaries and were usually applied to the most
prominent in local or central administration and in royal and legal
circles. This reassured such people that, together with their Welsh
ancestral traditions, they continued to maintain a strong hold over
their patrimonies and regions of jurisdiction.

The qualities possessed by the Welsh gentry were normally
those identified with the early medieval aristocracy. Members of
some families, such as the Vaughans of Golden Grove, Mostyns of
Flintshire, Pryses of Gogerddan and Griffiths of Penrhyn, were
eulogized because they had illustrious roots, but the circumstances of most gentry houses were not as auspicious as those in
the more privileged regions of England. In their own environment,
however, by the very nature of their heritage, the Welsh gentry
enjoyed considerable prestige. They were entrusted with the
custodianship of their shires and hundreds, and it was their task to
ensure that the administrative machinery worked effectively. Not
that all their aims were achieved. In fact, their reputation was
often besmirched either by inefficient attention to duty or by
economic difficulties that hampered their control. That control,
however, was not wholly lost or abandoned; in fact, it was revived
at critical times to show that the gentry still had at their command
the skills, particularly of leadership and administrative management, to advance their own interests and command the loyalty of
their social inferiors. They adhered closely to the factors that were
regarded foremost in their gentility, namely lineage, heraldry,
landed property and the country residence, as well as the honour
and authority that such privileges granted to them.

Public records and private family correspondence abound with
examples of the fears and desires, the advance, decline and
pretensions of these regional leaders who conveniently combined

traditional features of *uchelwriaeth* with the social manners and the world of the cultivated courtier, which became evident by the latter half of the Tudor period. The century between the Acts of Union and the Civil Wars saw the Welsh gentry maintain their chief characteristics, principally their continued residence in their country seats and the support they gave to the bardic order. What light does this traditional concept of *uchelwriaeth* throw on the image projected of the public figure in action and how far can it be regarded as a guide to true gentility? Whatever the influences of external factors on Welsh gentility may have been, medieval notions of *uchelwriaeth* survived well into the seventeenth century and identified the *uchelwyr* with *yr iaith*, the ethos of Welsh social, territorial and cultural entities.

Private virtues were often exemplified in practical terms because concepts of the Welsh gentleman had underlying practical as well as moral features, and the abuse of virtue and innate skills usually led to a neglect of authority. His public image could be distorted and the abuse of authority for private advantage often besmeared his reputation. The evidence of court records, in London, Ludlow and in the shires demonstrate the frequent litigation and family animosities caused by the desire to establish, sustain or defend men's reputations, usually in matters concerning land and property. In this respect influence and power were predominant and the sources used in this study palpably illustrate how powerful and sustaining that factor could be. In many ways acquiring or defending one's rights over property was a key issue in maintaining power and prestige. The gentry were well informed about the characteristic features of their milieu and were also sensitively aware of their misdoings although anxiously prepared to defend their actions. Further traditional methods were also used to save one's face, such as armed retainers, the exploitation of corrupt juries, malicious litigation, open hostilities and persistent family squabbles. Such features usually propped up their authority, maintaining their credibility, but they also often tainted their reputation in the countryside. These features marked the development of all ranks of gentility from the most prestigious to the most modest, for they all had one prime quality to defend, namely reputable lineage and social standing. Such a defence often generated a spirit of competitiveness which bred corruption and a disregard for the legal rights of others. In an age when the survival of the fittest seemed to be the accepted means of advancement the unscrupulous always gained at the expense of the less fortunate who became a prey to those more able to weather the economic storms or adapt themselves to benefiting from propitious circumstances. Although the Renaissance introduced new features of gentility into Welsh households prominent traces of the old survived, especially the defence of honour. In earlier times that would have been achieved principally by appealing to the force of arms but, in the sixteenth century, it was defended increasingly and formally in a court of law.

The gentry have to be studied in their natural environment among their equals and dependants. It was within their respective shires or provinces that these governors usually exercised their authority. Nevertheless, the Tudor age after the 1530s introduced them to two contrasting but not necessarily incompatible concepts, the British dimension – the *pays legal* of the Tudor state – and the *patria* which comprised the ancient inheritance of the isle of Britain. It was a key image that emerged among a group of Welsh gentry following the accession of James I to the throne. Simultaneously, there appeared views of the 'prediction or prophesye of coronoge vabann', as Sir William Maurice, a keen advocate of Britain's heritage described it: 'and heerin I will rejoine a littell with you sensiblye . . . and stand uppone the maxime of all our prophesyes which is that out of the Bryttishe line shold descende and that sholde restore the kingdoom of Brittaine to the pristine estate'.[2] In some of his correspondence and tiresome parliamentary speeches Maurice heralded the unity of 'Great Britain' under the new Stuart dynasty, but the concept of Wales in England had also appealed to an increasing number of gentry from senior and cadet families. The idea of the 'independent nobility' had persisted. They and their ancestors had, over many centuries, maintained the aristocratic spirit which characterized the favoured class as conceived of in the Middle Ages. Pride in ancestry and a sense of community identity survived and out of the old nobility emerged a changed brand of *uchelwriaeth* which prided itself on its independence in a newly fashioned political environment. It was this group which, in due course, failed to maintain its leadership, and it is in this context that order and authority in the early modern period to the Civil Wars must be evaluated. The rising Welsh gentry, attached to new concepts of conduct and government, were anxious to secure for themselves a position in the new social structure that had already been acquired by Marcher and English gentry who, like their predecessors, obtained rewards for faithful service to the Crown and its government.

Within this framework the Welsh gentry were closely linked to the main institutions of Tudor government, a significant proportion of which enjoyed the benefits of a world beyond the boundaries of Wales. Crown, parliament, common law and the Protestant Church settlement were combined to form the chief pillars of the Tudor state in the Elizabethan age. Attached to these features were the lineaments of a new cultural tradition which brought into Wales and England an invigorating spirit of rebirth and regeneration. Other institutions grew up to attract the educated sons of gentry and to broaden their insight and extend their authority. The growing popularity of schools and colleges and the Inns of Court, as well as the appeal of the royal court and diplomatic and military service, together with the attraction of the 'Grand Tour', introduced the gentry into circles of acquaintances and influence that affected their attitudes towards their native communities. Travelling on the continent, particularly in France, the Netherlands and Italy, became almost a necessity for some such as James Howell:

> Believe it Sir, that one year well-employ'd abroad by one of mature judgement . . . advantageth more in point of useful and solid Knowledge than three in any of our Universities. You know running Waters are the purest, so they that traverse the World up and down have the clearest understanding; being faithful eye-witnesses of those things which others receive but, in trust, whereunto they must yield an intuitive consent, and a kind of implicit Faith.[3]

His words conveniently summarize all that characterized the views of young gentry on the benefits of European culture. From the latter half of the sixteenth century onwards foreign travel became more popular because of the ambitions of an inspired younger generation. Honour and prestige were not only demonstrated in the courts of law or in parliament but also in broadening cultural horizons, enhancing the ambition and enterprise of the Welsh *uchelwr* in his new environment.

What assessment, therefore, can be made of the Welsh gentry in the context of their public image, and how are honour and authority, as conceived in the gentry residence and the locality, to be properly valued? In several respects they adhered more closely to their counterparts over Offa's Dyke with a view to advancing their own ambitions and adapting their habits to current codes of conduct. That was due to the close relations established between them for generations before the Tudor settlement and their common passion to associate themselves with Renaissance culture. Examining this theme, viewed from both conceptual and practical angles, has been the prime object of this study. The *plasty* was evidently the fulcrum of power and was symbolic of discipline and control, leadership and hospitality. In this institution, in town and country, qualities were fostered and enhanced and features of piety subsequently emerged. With changes in the religious climate more emphasis was placed on spiritual as well as secular attributes, and that was manifested chiefly in the religious manuals that appeared in the years before the Civil Wars when small Puritan groups began to appear in different parts of Wales, particularly the south-east.

Despite social change the bonds of unity between governors and governed survived, sustaining a feeling of common heritage. It was not as potent a force in the reign of Charles I as it had been half a century earlier, perhaps, but it was observed in the defence by individual gentry of their community values in times of economic hardship and increasing demands for royal taxes. This bond, however, did not at all times achieve its aim of ensuring that the prestige and good example of the father was passed on to the heir, with experience in leadership enhanced and hospitality maintained. Although a *coterie* of families governed the localities in successive generations, in times of hardship many were increasingly harassed by not being able to achieve what their more prosperous counterparts more easily obtained, namely immense profits from land and other possessions and substantial marriage contracts. In more prosperous times patronage, power and property were equal prerogatives of the privileged but attached to them was the sense of obligation. The duty to maintain defences was not restricted to military organization but extended to protecting status in an age of increasing political tension and the fiscal demands of an impoverished government.

The true value of status, based on the legitimate exercise of authority, became obscured with the inflation of honours in the early seventeenth century, when more knighthoods were granted to Welsh gentry. Despite the public honour conferred on such individuals, purely in the native context status continued to be associated with lineage and ties of kindred, both of which claimed precedence. This gave Welsh *uchelwyr* their distinctive character and made them objects of derision among their English peers. An undated and anonymous report of Welsh rural custom in the late sixteenth century revealed how addicted people of all ranks were to their pedigrees: 'and then doe they ripp upp [i.e. open up] their petigres at lengt how eche of them is discended from those theire ould princes'.[4] In an age when financial inflation, economic distress and social mobility were, in different proportions, affecting the quality of gentility, it was only to be expected that social standing would be defended and the political loyalties that characterized men in power would become more pronounced. This situation had long-term repercussions, for they were obliged to ensure that their credentials were correct to reaffirm their regional identities and to exercise authority within them. These factors centre on five major considerations that have received attention in the foregoing chapters and are essential in any examination of the world of gentlemen in authority in the century between the Acts of Union and the Civil Wars.

1. Given that the gentleman of quality was fully assured when displaying his innate virtues it could be argued that the Tudor settlement, contrary to most accepted views, served to weld him and his peers together as resident landowners in a firm alliance with their communities. Granting them the authority formally to govern and to enjoy the benefits of equal citizenship did not necessarily draw them permanently away from their localities. The authority which they enjoyed strengthened the bond of unity between them and their dependants, although economic stress and property disputes did increasingly cause hostility.

2. Authority was not granted in order that the gentry might demonstrate unrestrained power as administrators and landed proprietors, since its exercise entailed honouring an obligation. It was rather interpreted as being what the gentry, in their administrative capacities, were able to provide for their communities with a view to sustaining political stability; and as a service which assisted in maintaining, on a broader level, the unity of the national sovereign realm and promoting a new brand of loyalty. To their Welsh consciousness was added a firm allegiance to the united realm. For them being 'British' was a generic term, because the *uchelwr* was distinctly aware that his roots lay in the 'island empire', a concept that extended to the centuries before the Saxon invasions.

3. The exercise of authority implied defending status against new economic forces which threatened the supremacy of the privileged order. In maritime counties it involved dealing with matters other than the routine needs in periods of foreign threats. Gentlemen used the institutions of government to defend the corporate unity of their shire or region in its relation to the state.

4. An awareness of regional unity presupposed that 'good lordship' (*arglwyddiaeth dda*) was respected, implying that the resident *uchelwr* was expected to attend to the needs of the whole

community. Householdership survived as a major feature in the
Welsh community structure and the essence of lordship survived
in the territorial role assumed by many heads of families.
Gradually, godly and pietistic elements were introduced to
reinforce the moral obligations tied to lordship, thus adding new
and significant dimensions to traditional *uchelwriaeth* in a
changing environment.

5. Although community life was subject to challenges that
gradually undermined old hierarchical principles and new Renaissance ideas were seeping into gentry households, *uchelwriaeth*
continued to make a deep impact on the structure of society.
Although the harsh realities of the gentry's world dominated
much of their activities in the social scene, the community ethos
continued to survive and kindred relations, combined with a
profound respect for the family, helped to create and sustain this
feeling. In addition, bonds of neighbourhood tied people together
according to kin structures. Although the early decades of the
seventeenth century revealed features of a growing social hiatus
and the emergence of two distinct cultures, the role of the *uchelwr*
was still identified with the dispensation of justice, governorship,
moral leadership and 'good lordship'. In practice, it was the
qualities displayed by them in courts of law and in the country
residences that truly revealed the Welsh gentry in action.

Factors that preserved unity among the gentry assumed a
significant role in community life down to the Civil Wars,
sustaining the power of ambitious heads of families such as Sir
Rice Mansel and his heir Sir Edward of Margam, Sir Richard
Pryse of Gogerddan, Sir Edward Herbert of Montgomery and
Blackhall, Sir Roger Mostyn, Sir John Perrot of Haroldston and
Sir William Glynn of Glynllifon and their successors. Their
achievement, measured in different spheres of activity, was
dependent on the degree to which they were able to maintain
equitable relations with their peers and inferiors. The prominence
given to *yr iaith*, the awareness of corporate unity based on
cultural uniformity, gave their authority a meaning other than to
exercise personal power under the Crown. It was the fear that
innate authority might be abandoned that accounted largely for
the assertiveness of individuals in courts of law and their desire to
maintain vestiges of *uchelwriaeth*. Richard Davies, who had so
much to fear from the malice of the gentry in his diocese,
expressed in his *Funerall Sermon* on the death of Walter Devereux,
first earl of Essex, in 1577 that desire on the part of the most
honourable to rule as expeditiously as possible: 'For such valiaunt

and couragious Noble men are the bulwarks and walles of defence
of the whole realme . . . expert to gouerne and rule . . . aswel in
warre as peace, the strong towers of defence, both of hir Maiestie
and hir highnesse realme.'[5]

It is necessary to examine further the degree of success achieved
by the gentry in exercising control. While the five aspects noted
above suggest that the situation was reasonably satisfactory, others
remain which indicate that government in Tudor Wales was not yet
as stable as historians generally have been led to believe. On the
credit side it appears, first, that surviving records reveal that the
machinery of government, despite symptoms of lax and inefficient
administration, developed apace and was in good working order;
second, that far less credence needs to be given to the judicial
evidence suggesting widespread lawlessness with a view to
defending honour or promoting private interests; and, third, that
after Sir Rhys ap Gruffudd's execution in 1531 and the
subsequent Acts of Union Wales generally experienced a more
stable era in social, political and religious affairs.[6] That might
partly be explained by the lack of any staunchly conservative
aristocratic leadership attempting to cause opposition and disruption in Wales and partly by the firm hold that the institutions of
Tudor local government had on Wales.

On the contrary, the restless and competitive spirit of the past
prevailed and was often reflected in government agencies
responsible for the smooth running of Tudor local administration,
namely the shire system and its officialdom, as well as in the need
to defend one's reputation. These aspects are revealed in the
following three factors.

1. To impose English common law in areas familiar with the
'custom of the March' where traditionally the 'king's writ did not
run', or in the Welshries, where native kindred law had survived,
was no easy task. Many of the abuses associated with the borders
were survivals from a past age, such as retaining and *cymortha*,
customs which had a serious impact on conditions in the
Principality as well. As has been shown Richard Price, Dr David
Lewis and others deplored the continued use of the illegal
exaction of monies or taxes.[7] Sir Henry Herbert, for example,
reprimanded the Caernarfonshire deputy-lieutenants in 1590 for
attending more to their own private affairs than to the urgent
needs of the state: 'You have ever been forward in *cymortha* for
your own private gains', he asserted in a well-known letter,

'wherefore I conceive you will be much more forward in this *cymortha* for the public good of the whole state.'[8] The failure of the Tudor settlement to resolve these problems reveals a fundamental incapacity to meet one of the basic requirements of sound efficient government.

2. Office-holding as well was subject to abuse on a large scale and evidence indicates that offices were often used purely for private gain. George Owen was severely critical of inefficient sheriffs and their deputies. The Merioneth deputy-lieutenants, for example, were charged in 1598 with embezzling £1,000 out of the artillery and munitions at Harlech Castle and of making 'their said office means of great riches to themselves'.[9] It is undeniable that private interest took precedence over public duty when circumstances demanded it and that officials were given ample opportunity to line their own pockets.

3. Family vendettas were common, many of them arising from property disputes and office-holding. To neglect good government, Lord Zouche, President of the Council in the Marches, declared in 1602, would mean 'the overthrow of the commonwealth and private estates', and he later added that when 'men's affinities can hinder the prosecution of justice: when blood [i.e. kindred loyalties] calleth for vengeance, the commonwealth suffers'.[10] These strong words were used initially to protect Zouche's vulnerable position in the borderlands as much as to control the aggressive temperament of the most vociferous heads of gentry families.

In all, however, the quality of government in the Welsh shires appeared to be reasonably commendable. Much depended on the initiative shown by the landed and mercantile classes – a blend of the traditional families and the *nouveaux riches* – in creating stable conditions to serve their own ends as well as those of the state. Emphasis was placed on establishing control, obedience and discipline within a restrictive social structure that was essentially hierarchical and patrilineal. In an oft-quoted passage the earl of Pembroke made this point clearly in 1591:

> For how can your mynds be united in publique defence when they are devyded by pryvatt quarrells. And what hope of succour in the field may any man have from him who is his professed enemie at home. Or how shall Her Majesty's service . . . in this tyme of danger go forwards yf one of you crosse the same because the dealinge therein is comytted to another . . . some must governe, some must obey.[11]

The lord president was referring to two fundamental social features affecting the gentry in power, namely privilege and obligation, which all sections of the community shared in the hierarchy. The prominence accorded to status based on lineal descent, and the authority which heads of families hoped to acquire by being 'well-descended' (Sir John Wynn), is reflected in a variety of sources, including contemporary verse in praise of individuals. 'It is a temporal blessing and a great heart's ease to a man to know that he is well descended', Wynn again confidently remarked when reflecting in this oft-quoted sentence on his own good fortune and the circumstances which hindered the advance of his ancestors in Eifionydd and Nanconwy.[12] It was a statement, not only of pride in ancestry but also of defence and indeed of relief when social mobility was becoming a marked feature of Tudor life. A link was forged with the past through lineage, landownership and officeholding. The Tudor battle for status involved the Welsh gentry as much as it did their counterparts elsewhere, and the basis of the authority delegated to them lay essentially in the manner in which they interpreted their privilege and fulfilled their obligations.[13]

Tudor and early Stuart rule in Wales, therefore, appeared to be reasonably successful, chiefly it seems, because the gentry were identified with a flexible administrative organization that was at once partly innovative and partly conservative. The Tudors were skilful in adapting existing institutions of government into a new framework which could easily be applied to the needs of regional government. It was the effective interaction between the Crown, parliament, the law, the Protestant Church and regional communities that chiefly accounted for the success of the Tudor settlement in Wales.[14]

The alliance between Crown and gentry eased the establishment and consolidation of the Protestant tradition based on the new Church settlement in 1559. That settlement was essentially political in that it consolidated political unity within the state.[15] The Elizabethan Church buttressed the realm and the Protestant faith and eventually served to reinforce a political settlement which relied heavily on the twin loyalties of the native gentry order to the Tudor Crown and to its communities. In religious affairs these governing families, for the most part, identified their interests with that Crown and the well-being of the commonweal.

The Protestant faith was interpreted by its chief supporters as an essential part of the myth regarding the nation's destiny.[16] Its propaganda was based on the belief that the New Faith was a restoration of the Old Faith of the Britons to counter the ill effects of the medieval Catholic Church. Thus it fostered a belief in a common religion and cultural heritage which inspired literary works penned by Welsh Protestant humanists and which gave Wales a new identity within the Protestant tradition. The writings of William Salesbury,[17] Richard Davies,[18] Maurice Kyffin[19] and others invoked an appeal to the ancient apostolic Church in Britain and sought to create a unity in religion as well as secular affairs in the realm. It was the gentry's responsibility to exercise their authority so as to maintain that bond of unity. This interpretation of history, projecting belief in the nation's unique heritage, has prompted a new generation of scholars to conclude that the Welsh cultural dimension, with its concept of nationhood in the Tudor period, survived because of rather than despite the extension of the English state into Wales.[20]

It is evident that the focus in any evaluation of law and order and uniformity in Tudor and early Stuart Wales needs to be placed on the three main factors that sprang chiefly from the Tudor settlement itself: constitutional unity, social and economic advancement and the imposition of law and good government. All three were dependent initially on the establishment of political and institutional harmony, stability within the community structure and powerful sense of pride in the past. The focal point was the governing families which, despite social change, created and preserved the ethos of an ordered, stratified and well-governed community structure. The integration of such forces established an organic political entity in Wales in the decades following political assimilation in 1536–43.

The success of Tudor government in Wales depended essentially on the co-operative spirit and willingness of the gentry to align themselves by common consent with a monarchy whose interests were exclusively devoted to achieving legal and administrative uniformity. Those Welshmen who welcomed the Stuart succession were not only aware of the Welsh lineal connections binding the two dynasties but were also conscious of the common political heritage which linked both and attached the ruling classes in Wales to a sense of loyalty and obedience to the Crown. It was William Vaughan, that eccentric squire from Llangyndeyrn in Carmarthenshire, who, in 1630, identified and gave the most overt expression to Welsh aspirations in his day:

> I rejoice that the memorial of Offa's Ditch is extinguished with love and charity; that our green leeks, sometimes offensive to your dainty nostrils, are tempered with your fragrant roses. God give us grace to dwell together without enmity, without detraction.[21]

He placed his adulation within the context of the Cambro-British tradition that was prevalent among prominent Welsh gentry of his day, but the meaning of his words to his generation is abundantly clear. In his Latin preface to Dr John Davies's *Cambrobrytannicae Cymraecaeve Linguae Institutiones* (1592), Humphrey Prichard, a contemporary of Dr John Davies at Oxford and rector of Llanbeulan in Anglesey, offered a more realistic sideline on the benefits of the Tudor settlement than that provided by George Owen:

> Caeterum quid laudabilius, aut magis honorificum: quam diuersas nationes diuersitate linguarum distinctas, sub eiusdem Principis ditione missas videre . . . Eâdem omnes comoramur Insulâ, eisdem Reipublicae ciues; eadem vtrisque lex; eademque illustrissima Princeps; negotiationes, amicitiae, conciones, coniugia, forum, fanum, & omnia denique; decôra & honesta nobis cum anglis sunt comunia.[22]

> [Whatever, what is more praiseworthy or more honourable than to see different nations, divided by differing languages, brought under the rule of one prince . . . We live on the same island; we are citizens of the same state: the same law exists to all of us, and the same very renowned Queen, business matters, associations, joint-assemblies, marriages, legal and religious matters – in a word, all that is seemly and honourable – are common to us and the English.]

Such words clearly testify to the desire of men of Prichard's calibre to foster a sense of unity between the two peoples on constitutional grounds. The chain of command in Tudor Wales, extending as it did from the Crown and the Privy Council down to the most humble of local officials, depended largely on the loyalty, ability and initiative of those who were eligible and who chose to serve that Crown. The amount and nature of service depended largely on the opportunities that the Crown had to offer for social advancement. William Camden, although his interest in Wales was chiefly topographical and antiquarian, attempted to place the country and its ruling order in context when he described the long-term effects of the assimilation of 1536:

> And since they were admitted to the Imperiall Crown of England, they have, to their iuste praise, performed all parts of dutifull loyaltie and allegeance most faithfully thereunto; plentifully yeelding Martiale Captaines, iudicious Ciuillians, skilfull common Lawyers, learned Diuines, complete Courtiers, and aduentrous Souldiers.[23]

Like George Owen, Camden had fully realized that social advancement was in progress in Wales by the close of the sixteenth century.

Thus the government of Wales in the Tudor age, by its very nature, touched upon virtually all aspects of Welsh life, the key to its success being popular participation by its leaders who desired of their own accord to become involved. These administrative leaders were unified by their will to prosper, to serve, to assert their independence and to guarantee their security in a world of competition and threats of foreign invasion. Although the Welsh *uchelwyr*, in terms of their public activities and personal attributes, corresponded closely to the image of the typical English Tudor squire, some underlying characteristics survived which guaranteed for them a distinctive, if not unique role. The equality of status which they had achieved gave them added impetus and resilience to survive as citizens of a national Protestant state and to benefit by it. Wales, as an integral part of the independent realm established by Henry VIII and consolidated by Elizabeth, was expected to play a vital role in maintaining internal security and defending the nation's honour abroad. This common identity introduced the Welsh gentry into spheres of activity which ultimately broadened their outlook as Cambro-Britons, deepened their understanding and appreciation of issues which affected affairs well beyond the confines of Wales, matured their approach to national exigencies and enabled them to cope with a new and exciting situation, enhancing their prestige. Despite the problems which beset the progress of Tudor rule in Wales after 1536 the period which separates the career of Rowland Lee from the Civil Wars does indeed represent an era of growth, prosperity and stability in the history of Wales.[24] It is in that context that the ethos of the authority exercised by the Welsh gentry must be viewed and interpreted.

Notes

Notes to Introduction

[1] Thomas Elyot, *The Book named the Governor* (1531), ed. S. E. Lehmberg (London, 1962), p. 241. See also pp. 95–7, 99.

[2] Ibid., p. 99.

[3] *The Book of the Courtier*, ed. J. H. Whitfield (London, 1975), pp.17, 18.

[4] *Gramadegau'r Penceirddiaid*, ed. G. J. Williams and E. J. Jones (Cardiff, 1934), p. 132.

[5] *Book of the Courtier*, p. 3.

[6] Fritz Caspari, *Humanism and the Social Order in Tudor England* (Chicago, 1954), p. 86.

[7] A. H. Dodd, *Studies in Stuart Wales* (Cardiff, 1952), p. 1.

[8] *Rhagymadroddion a Chyflwyniadau Lladin, 1551–1632*, ed. Ceri Davies (Cardiff, 1980); Ceri Davies, *Latin Writers of the Renaissance* (Cardiff, 1981); R. Geraint Gruffydd, 'The Renaissance and Welsh literature', in Glanmor Williams and R. O. Jones (eds.), *The Celts and the Renaissance: Tradition and Innovation* (Cardiff, 1990), pp. 17–39.

[9] Gwynfor Evans, *Land of My Fathers* (Swansea, 1974), p. 304 et seq.; W. Ambrose Bebb, *Cyfnod y Tuduriaid* (Wrexham and Cardiff,1939); Saunders Lewis, *Tynged yr Iaith* (London, 1962). For a reappraisal of the historiography of the Acts of Union see Glanmor Williams, *Wales and the Act of Union* (Bangor, 1992).

[10] David Powel, *The Historie of Cambria, now called Wales* (Amsterdam, 1969 edn.), pp. 390–1.

[11] Rice Merrick, *Morganiae Archaiographia*, ed. Brian Ll. James (Barry,1983), pp. 67–8; Humphrey Llwyd, *Commentarioli Descriptionis Britannicae Fragmentum* (Cologne, 1572), tr. by Thomas Twyne as *The Breuiary of Britayne* (London, 1573), fo. 60b; George Owen, 'The dialogue of the government of Wales', in *Penbrokshire*, III, pp. 36–40, 55–7; Rice Lewis, *A Breviat of Glamorgan, 1596–1600*, ed. William Rees, *South Wales and Monmouth Record Society*, 3 (1954), 96.

[12] *Penbrokshire*, III, p.57.

[13] For general and detailed studies of the Acts of Union see William Rees, *The Union of England and Wales* (Cardiff, 1948); W. Ogwen Williams, *Tudor Gwynedd* (Caernarfon, 1958); Glanmor Williams, *Renewal and Reformation: Wales c.1415–1642* (Oxford, 1993 edn.), pp. 253–78; idem, *Wales and the Act of Union*; Peter R. Roberts, The "Act of Union" in Welsh history', *TCS* (1972–3), 63–72.

[14] Glanmor Williams, *Henry Tudor and Wales* (Cardiff, 1985), pp. 9–41; idem, 'Prophecy, poetry and politics in medieval and Tudor Wales', in *Religion, Language and Nationality in Wales* (Cardiff, 1979), pp. 71–86.

[15] *Penbrokshire*, III, p. 55.

[16] J. Beverley Smith, 'Crown and community in the principality of north Wales in the reign of Henry Tudor', *WHR*, III (1966), 145–71. For the political and administrative background see Glyn Roberts, 'Wales and England, antipathy and sympathy, 1284–1485', in A. H. Dodd and J. Gwynn Williams (ed.), *Aspects of Welsh History* (Cardiff, 1969), pp. 299–318.

[17] *Tudor Gwynedd*, pp. 5–37; Peter R. Roberts, 'The union with England and the identity of "Anglican" Wales', *Transactions of the Royal Historical Society*, XXII (1972), 49–70.

[18] John Leland, *Itinerary in Wales*, ed. L. Toulmin Smith (London, 1908), p. 53.

[19] Peter R. Roberts, 'Union with England', pp. 55–60.

[20] HMC, *Calendar of the Manuscripts of the Marquis of Salisbury (Hatfield House MSS)* (London, 1933), XVI, p. 364.

[21] J. Goronwy Edwards, *The Principality of Wales, 1267–1967: A Study in Constitutional History* (Caernarfon, 1969), pp. 23–6.

[22] Ibid., pp. 37–9.

[23] W. Ogwen Williams, *Tudor Gwynedd*, pp. 35–7.

[24] Peter R. Roberts, 'Union with England', pp. 55–60; idem, 'The "Henry VIII clause": delegated legislation and the Tudor principality of Wales', in T. G. Watkin (ed.), *Legal Record and Historical Reality* (London, 1989), pp. 37–49.

[25] Peter R. Roberts, 'A breviat of the effectes devised for Wales, c.1540–41', *Camden Miscellany*, XXVI (1975), 31–45.

[26] Ralph A. Griffiths (ed.), *The Principality of Wales in the Later Middle Ages: The Structure and Personnel of Government*: I. *South Wales 1277–1536* (Cardiff, 1972), intro., xv–xix, pp. 1–72 passim; Glyn Roberts, 'Wales and England', pp. 304–18; W. Ogwen Williams, *Tudor Gwynedd*, pp. 22–37.

[27] Glanmor Williams (ed.), *Glamorgan County History*, IV. *Early Modern Glamorgan from the Act of Union to the Industrial Revolution* (Cardiff, 1974), pp. 92–9.

[28] Glanmor Williams, *Renewal and Reformation*, pp. 342–57.

Notes to Chapter 1: The Gentry Order

[1] Cited in A. L. Rowse, *The Elizabethan Renaissance: The Life of the Society* (London, 1971), pp. 109–10.

[2] *The Gentleman's Magazine*, LV (1785), 32; NLW MS 465E.247.

[3] A. D. Carr, *Medieval Wales* (London, 1995), pp. 89–107; R. R. Davies, *The Age of Conquest* (Oxford, 1993), pp. 412–30.

[4] Ralph A. Griffiths, *The Principality of Wales in the Later Middle Ages: The Structure and Personnel of Government*, I, *South Wales 1277–1536* (Cardiff, 1972), xv–xix, pp. 1–72; Glyn Roberts, 'Wyrion Eden: the Anglesey descendants of Ednyfed Fychan in the fourteenth century', in A. H. Dodd and J. Gwynn Williams (eds.), *Aspects of Welsh History* (Cardiff, 1969), pp. 295–318.

[5] John Leland, *Itinerary in Wales*, ed. L. Toulmin Smith (London, 1908), p. 14.

[6] John Wynn, *History of the Gwydir Family and Memoirs*, ed. J. Gwynfor Jones (Llandysul, 1990), p. 34.

[7] Ibid., p. 21.

[8] Glanmor Williams, *Renewal and Reformation: Wales c.1415–1642* (Oxford, 1993 edn.), pp. 39–54; W. Ogwen Williams, 'The social order in Tudor Wales', *TCS* (1967 ii), 167–78.

[9] *History of the Gwydir Family*, pp. 39–41.

[10] A. D. Carr, 'Gwilym ap Gruffydd and the rise of the Penrhyn estate', *WHR*, XV (1990), 1–20.

[11] *History of the Gwydir Family*, pp. 50–2; J. Beverley Smith, 'Crown and community in the Principality of north Wales in the reign of Henry Tudor', *WHR* III (1966), 154–7.

[12] Francis Jones, 'Welsh pedigrees', in *Burke's Genealogical and Heraldic History of the Landed Gentry*, ed. L. G. Pine (London, 1952), lxix–lxxvi; idem, 'An approach to Welsh genealogy', *TCS* (1948), 303 et seq.

[13] William Harrison, *The Description of England*, ed. Georges Edelen (New York, 1968 edn.), p. 416.

[14] *History of the Gwydir Family*, p. 26.

[15] *APC*, IX (1575–77), p. 159.

[16] Lord Mostyn and T. A. Glenn, *History of the Family of Mostyn of Mostyn* (London, 1925), p. 126.

[17] *DWB*, s. n.; C. A. J Skeel, *The Council in the Marches of Wales: A Study in Local Government during the Sixteenth and Seventeenth Centuries* (London, 1903), p. 82.

[18] Ifan ab Owen Edwards (ed.), *A Catalogue of Star Chamber Proceedings relating to Wales* (Cardiff, 1929), p. 136.

[19] G. J. Williams, *Traddodiad Llenyddol Morgannwg* (Cardiff, 1948), p. 82.

[20] NLW MS 9053E.429–30.

[21] George Owen, *The Description of Pembrokeshire*, ed. Dillwyn Miles (Llandysul, 1994), p. 40.

[22] William Camden, *Remaines concerning Britaine* (London, 1623), p. 27.

[23] *Rhagymadroddion*, p. 3.

[24] Ibid., p. 53.

[25] See for example B. R. Parry, 'Huw Nanney Hen (c.1546–1623), squire of Nannau', *JMHRS*, V (1972), 185–206.

[26] Glanmor Williams, 'Rice Mansell of Oxwich and Margam (1487–1559)', *Morgannwg*, VI (1962), 33–51.

[27] R. R. Davies, *The Age of Conquest*, pp. 114–20.

[28] William Vaughan, *The Golden-grove* (London, 1600), III, cap. 16.

[29] William Rees, 'Metal-mining in the XVIth and XVIIth centuries', in *Industry Before the Industrial Revolution* (Cardiff, 1968), I, chap. 3: pp. 134–227; Frank Emery, 'The farming regions of Wales', in Joan Thirsk (ed.), *The Agrarian History of England and Wales*, IV *1500–1640* (Cambridge, 1967), pp. 113–60.

[30] Rees, 'Metal-mining', I, pp. 74–5.

[31] Ibid., I, pp. 312–17.

[32] Ibid., II, pp. 389–400.

[33] B. R. Parry, 'Huw Nanney Hen', 185–206.

[34] W. J. Lewis, *Leadmining in Wales* (Cardiff, 1967), pp. 40–73.

[35] L. & P., X (1536), no. 453, p. 182; *The Statutes of Wales*, pp. 67–9.

[36] W. Ogwen Williams, *Tudor Gwynedd* (Caernarfon, 1958), p. 22.

[37] L. & P., XVII (1542), p. 68.

[38] R. R. Davies, 'The twilight of Welsh law 1284–1536', *History*, LI, 172 (1966), 143–64.

[39] *Statutes of Wales*, pp. 122–3.

[40] L. & P., X (1536), no. 453, p. 182.

[41] R. Stephens, *Gwynedd, 1528–1547: Economy and Society in Tudor Wales* (Ann Arbor, MI, 1979), pp. 39–107.

[42] Leonard Owen, 'The population of Wales in the sixteenth and seventeenth centuries', *TCS* (1959), pp. 99–113.

[43] For further details see Glanmor Williams, 'Glamorgan Society, 1536–1642', in Glanmor Williams (ed.), *Glamorgan County History: IV. Early Modern Glamorgan* (Cardiff, 1974), pp. 84–5; W. Ogwen Williams, *Tudor Gwynedd*, pp. 44–6.

[44] For the English background to this theme see J. Barry and C. Brooks, *The Middling Sort of People* (London, 1994). See also Glanmor Williams, 'Glamorgan Society, 1536–1642', in *Glamorgan County History*, IV, pp. 84–5; idem, *Renewal and Reformation*, pp. 103–4.

[45] George Owen, *Description of Pembrokeshire*, p. 38. B. Stevenson (ed.), *The Home Book of Quotations* (NY, 1967 edn.), p. 68.

[46] Glanmor Williams, 'Rice Mansell', pp. 37–51; idem, 'The Stradlings of St Donat's', in Stewart Williams (ed.), *Vale of History* (Cowbridge, 1960), pp. 85–95; Ralph A. Griffiths, 'The rise of the Stradlings of St Donat's', *Morgannwg*, VII (1963), 15–47; N. W. Powell, *Dyffryn Clwyd in the Time of Elizabeth I* (Ruthin, 1991).

[47] George Owen, *Description of Pembrokeshire*, pp. 47–8.

[48] W. Ogwen Williams, *Tudor Gwynedd*, p. 47; R. Stephens, *Gwynedd*, pp. 27–31, 79–80; A. H. Dodd, *Studies in Stuart Wales* (Cardiff, 1952), pp. 14–15.

[49] Thomas Smith, *De Republica Anglorum*, ed. Mary Dewar (Cambridge, 1982), pp. 71–2.

[50] Thomas Pennant, *Tours in Wales*, ed. John Rhys (Caernarvon, 1883), I, pp. 17–18; Lord Mostyn and T. A. Glenn, *History*, p. 83; A. D. Carr, 'The Mostyns of Mostyn, 1540–1642', *FHSJ*, XXVIII(i) (1977–8), 17.

[51] NLW MS 464E.189.

[52] G. D. Owen, *Elizabethan Wales: The Social Scene* (Cardiff, 1962), pp. 12–13.

[53] PRO, Court of Requests 82/46. See *The Stradling Correspondence*, ed. J. M. Traherne (London, 1840), CCXLVIII, p. 317; John Stradling, *The Storie of the Lower Borowes of Merthyrmawr*, ed. H. J. Randall and William Rees (Cardiff, 1932), pp. 62–9; Gareth E. Jones, *The Gentry and the Elizabethan State* (Swansea, 1977), pp. 64–7; idem, 'Local administration and justice in sixteenth-century Glamorgan', *Morgannwg*, IX (1965), 11–37; idem, 'A case of corruption', in Stewart Williams (ed.), *Glamorgan Historian*, V (Cowbridge, 1968), pp. 121–32.

[54] Colin A. Gresham, *Eifionydd: A Study in Landownership from the Medieval Period to the Present Day* (Cardiff, 1973), p. 115; *Calendar of Star Chamber Proceedings*, p. 155.

[55] *Calendar of Salusbury Correspondence c.1553–1700*, ed. W. J. Smith (Cardiff, 1954), intro., pp. 13–17.

[56] For background material see J. Gwynfor Jones, *The Morgan Family of Tredegar: Origins, Growth and Advancement c.1340–1674* (Newport, 1995), 28 pp.

[57] *Calendar of Letters Relating to North Wales*, ed. B. E. Howells, (Cardiff, 1967), pp. 6–7.

[58] Ibid.

[59] Cardiff City Library, MS 4.329, 11 (old Hafod MS 12); Glenys Davies, *Noddwyr Beirdd ym Meirion* (Dolgellau, 1974), p. 107.

[60] Carr, 'Mostyns of Mostyn', *FHSJ*, XXVIII (1977–8), 17–37; XXX (1981–2), 125–44.

[61] Rice Merrick, *Morganiae Archaiographia: A Book of the Antiquities of Glamorganshire*, ed. Brian Ll. James (Barry, 1983), pp. 147–64; Ralph A. Griffiths, 'The twelve knights of Glamorgan', in Stewart Williams (ed.), *Glamorgan Historian*, III (Cowbridge, 1966), pp. 153–69; G. J. Williams, 'The early historians of Glamorgan', ibid., pp. 69–70.

[62] J. M. Howells, 'The Crosswood estate', *Ceredigion*, III (1956), 70–3; H. A. Lloyd, *The Gentry of South-West Wales, 1540–1640* (Cardiff, 1968), pp. 40–3. See also Gerald Morgan, *A Welsh House and its Family: The Vaughans of Trawsgoed: A Study of the Vaughan Family and Estate through Seven Centuries* (Llandysul, 1997), pp. 21–43.

[63] Francis Jones, 'The Vaughans of Golden Grove', *TCS* (1963), 137–9.

[64] *DWB*, s.n.; N. Palmer, *A History of the Old Parish Church of Gresford* (Wrexham, 1905), p. 101.

[65] Peter Smith, *Houses of the Welsh Countryside* (London, 1980), pp. 222–63; M. W. Barley, 'Rural housing in Wales', in Thirsk, *Agrarian History*, pp. 788–813.

[66] *Rhagymadroddion a Chyflwyniadau Lladin*, p. 71. All extracts selected from this source are translated from Latin into Welsh by the editor and from Welsh into English in the present volume by the author.

[67] Davies, *Noddwyr Beirdd*, pp. 97–8.

[68] Ibid., pp. 55–6.

[69] R. Gwyndaf, 'Sir Richard Clough of Denbigh c.1530–1570', *TDHS*, XIX (1970), 24–65; XX (1971), 57–101; XXII (1973), 48–86.

[70] *Royal Commission on Ancient Monuments in Wales: Caernarvonshire East* (London, 1956), pp. 58–64; R. Turner, *Plas Mawr, Conwy* (Cardiff, Cadw (Welsh Historic Monuments), 1997).

[71] Ibid., *Merioneth* (London, 1921), pp. 75–6

[72] Ibid., *Caernarvonshire East*, pp. 185–9.

[73] *Inventory of Ancient Monuments*, VII: *County of Pembroke* (London, 1925), pp. 50–7.

[74] Ibid., *Inventory of Ancient Monuments in Glamorgan*: IV(i), *The Greater Houses* (London, 1981), pp. 63–76.

[75] A. H. Dodd, 'The civil war in east Denbighshire', *TDHS*, III (1954), 87–9.

[76] *Stradling Correspondence*, p. 66; J. Nichols, *The Progresses and Public Processions of Queen Elizabeth . . .* , I (London, 1788), p. 408.

[77] Arwyn Ll. Hughes, 'Rhai o noddwyr y beirdd yn sir Feirionnydd', *Llên Cymru*, X (1969) (3–4), 161–2; E. D. Jones, 'The family of Nannau (Nanney) of Nannau', *JMHRS*, II (1953), 11–12. For further background information see B. R. Parry, 'Hugh Nanney Hen', pp. 185–206.

[78] R. Gwyndaf, 'Sir Richard Clough', *TDHS*, XXII (1973), 55–85; Smith, *Houses*, passim; Leland, *Itinerary*, pp. 27, 43.

[79] *Glamorgan County History*, IV, pp. 122–41.

[80] Saunders Lewis, 'The essence of Welsh literature', in A. R. Jones and G. Thomas (eds.), *Presenting Saunders Lewis* (Cardiff, 1973), pp. 154–8.

[81] NLW MS 9059E.1186.

[82] *Salusbury Correspondence*, no. 154, p. 78.

[83] *Studies in Stuart Wales*, pp. 16–23.

[84] NLW 9054E.627.

[85] L. & P., IX, no. 841, p. 283.

[86] John Penry, *Three Treatises concerning Wales*, ed. David Williams (Cardiff, 1960), pp. 41–2.

[87] William Vaughan, *The Golden-fleece* (London, 1626), Part III, p. 33.

[88] Glanmor Williams, *Religion, Language and Nationality in Wales* (Cardiff, 1979), pp. 160–3.

[89] Smith, *Houses*, passim; W. G. Hoskins, 'The rebuilding of rural England', *Past & Present*, IV (November 1953), 44–59.

[90] *Stradling Correspondence*, LXXXIV, p. 100.

[91] R. R. Davies, *The Age of Conquest*, pp. 421–30; Glyn Roberts, 'Wales and England', pp. 304–18.

[92] Gareth E. Jones, *The Gentry*, pp. 47–52.

[93] W. Ogwen Williams, *Tudor Gwynedd*, pp. 24–7; Penry Williams, *The Council in the Marches of Wales under Elizabeth I* (Cardiff, 1958), pp. 120–1, 122–4.

[94] *Penbrokshire*, III, pp. 58–9.

[95] William Lambarde, *Eirenarcha* (London, 1581), ed. P. R. Glazebrook (London, 1972), p. 371.

[96] *Statutes of Wales*, p. 113.

[97] Ibid., p. 69.

[98] Smith, *De Republica Anglorum*, p. 106.

[99] *Statutes of Wales*, pp. 4–9; W. H. Waters, *The Edwardian Settlement of North Wales in its Administrative and Legal Aspects, 1284–1343* (Cardiff, 1935), pp. 44, 59.

[100] *Penbrokshire*, III, p. 52.

[101] *Statutes of Wales*, p. 113.

[102] Ibid., pp. 57–8; L. & P., X (1536), no. CLIII, p. 182.

[103] PRO E.163/11/34, f.9v. I am grateful to my research student, Mr Michael Jones, for drawing my attention to this reference.

[104] Henry Ellis (ed.), *Original Letters Illustrative of English History*, III (2nd series, London, 1827), CC, pp. 41–4.

[105] *Clenennau Letters and Papers*, no. 106, p. 31.

[106] D. Ll. Thomas, 'Further notes on the Council in the Marches', *Y Cymmrodor*, XIII (1899), App. B, pp. 128–33; *CSPD* (1547–1580), CVII, no. 4(i), p. 514.

[107] *Penbrokshire*, III, p. 316.

[108] For the administrative background see *Calendar of the Caernarvonshire Quarter Sessions Records*, I, *1541–1558*, ed. W. Ogwen Williams, (Caernarfon, 1956); J. Gwynfor Jones, *Law, Order and Government in Caernarfonshire, 1558–1640: Justices of the Peace and the Gentry* (Cardiff, 1996).

[109] *Penbrokshire*, III, p. 90 et seq.; *CSPD* (1547–80), no. 10, p. 514; XLIV, no. 27, p. 301; (1581–1590), CLIX, no. 1, p. 98. See Glyn Parry (ed.), *A Guide to the Records of Great Sessions in Wales* (Aberystwyth, 1995), intro.; N. W. Powell, 'Crime and the community in Denbighshire during the 1590s', in J. Gwynfor Jones (ed.), *Class, Community and Culture in Tudor Wales* (Cardiff, 1989), pp. 261–94.

[110] *Penbrokshire*, III, p. 56.

[111] *CSPD* (1547–80), XLIV, no. 27, p. 301; David Mathew, 'Some Elizabethan documents', *BBCS*, VI (1931), 77–8.

[112] For more information on the Council's fortunes down to 1641 see Penry Williams, 'The attack on the Council in the Marches, 1603–42', *TCS* (1961), 1–22; idem, 'The activity of the Council in the Marches under the early Stuarts', *WHR* I, (1961), 133–54; R. E. Ham, 'The four shire controversy', *WHR*, VIII (1977), 381–400.

[113] G. D. Owen, *Wales in the Reign of James I* (London, 1988), p. 51.

[114] Ibid., p. 49.

[115] Thomas Elyot, *The Book named the Governor*, ed. S. E. Lehmberg (London, 1962), p. 241; Fritz Caspari, *Humanism and the Social Order in Tudor England* (Chicago, 1954), pp. 76–109, 132–56.

[116] NLW MS 9051E.9.

[117] Ibid., MS 106.

[118] Ibid., MS 144.

[119] *CSPD* (1611–18), LXVII, no. 1, p. 84; (1627–8), LXXXVIII, no. 23, p. 487.

[120] William Lambarde, *William Lambarde and Local Government*, ed. Conyers Read (New York, 1962), p. 95.

[121] W. Ogwen Williams, 'The social order in Tudor Wales', *TCS* (1967 ii), 177–8.

[122] *Stradling Correspondence*, LXXXII, p. 97.

[123] A. H. Dodd, 'Wales's parliamentary apprenticeship (1536–1625)', *TCS* (1942), 8–72.

[124] S. T. Bindoff, 'The Stuarts and their style', *EHR*, LX (1945), 204–5; J. Gwynfor Jones, 'The Welsh poets and their patrons, c.1550–1640', *WHR*, IX (1979), 250–2; E. N. Williams, 'Sir William Maurice of Clenennau', *TCHS*, XXIV (1963), 92–7; A. H. Dodd, 'Wales under the early Stuarts', in A. J. Roderick (ed.), *Wales Through the Ages*, II (Llandybïe, 1960), pp. 54–6.

[125] H. G. Owen, 'Family politics in Elizabethan Merionethshire', *BBCS*, XVIII (1959), 185–91.

[126] J. E. Neale, *The Elizabethan House of Commons* (London, 1955), pp. 80–1; *Calendar of Star Chamber Proceedings*, p. 140.

[127] Emyr Gwynne Jones, 'The Caernarvonshire freeholders and the Forest of Snowdon', in 'The Caernarvonshire squires, 1558–1625' (unpublished MA University of Wales dissertation, 1936), pp. 233–54.

[128] Neale, *House of Commons*, pp. 99–108.

[129] Penry Williams, 'The political and administrative history of Glamorgan, 1536–1642', in Glanmor Williams (ed.), *Glamorgan County History: Early Modern Glamorgan*, IV (Cardiff, 1974), pp. 181–3; idem, 'Controversy in Elizabethan Glamorgan; the rebuilding of Cardiff bridge', *Morgannwg*, II (1958), 38–46.

[130] Penry Williams, 'Faction in Wales, 1588–1603', in *The Council in the Marches*, pp. 229–48.

[131] H. A. Lloyd, *Gentry of South-West Wales*, pp. 101–2, 111–12.

[132] Emyr Gwynne Jones, 'County politics and electioneering, 1558–1625', *TCHS*, I (1939), 40–6; J. K. Gruenfelder, 'The Wynns of Gwydir and parliamentary elections 1604–40', *WHR*, IX (1978), 123–41.

[133] J. Gwynfor Jones, 'Sir John Wynn, junior, of Gwydir and Llanfrothen and the "Grand Tour" (1613–14)', *JMHRS*, XI iv (1993), 379–413; Ceri W. Lewis, 'Syr Edward Stradling, 1519–1609', in J. E. Caerwyn Williams (ed.), *Ysgrifau Beirniadol*, XIX (Denbigh, 1994), p. 155. The authoritative work on education in Wales in the early modern period is William P. Griffith, *Learning, Law and Religion: Higher Education and Welsh Society c.1540–1640* (Cardiff, 1996), chap. 1, pp. 1–57.

[134] Humphrey Llwyd, *Commentarioli Descriptionis Britannicae Fragmentum* (Cologne, 1572), tr. Thomas Twyne, *The Breuiary of Britayne* (London, 1573), fo. 60b.

[135] *Clenennau Letters and Papers*, no. 444, pp. 126–7; J. E. Griffith (ed.), *Pedigrees of Anglesey and Caernarvonshire Families* (Horncastle, 1914), p. 21.

[136] G. D. Owen, *Elizabethan Wales*, p. 94; J. McCann and H. Connolly (eds.), 'Memorials of Father Augustine Baker and other documents relating to the English Benedictines', *Catholic Record Society Publications*, XXXIII (1933), 56.

[137] NLW MS 9052E.271.

[138] *Penbrokshire*, III, p. 56.

[139] Llwyd, *Breuiarye of Britayne*, fo. 60b.

[140] *DWB*, s.n.; D. Aneirin Thomas, *The Welsh Elizabethan Catholic Martyrs: The Trial Documents of Saint Richard Gwyn and of the Venerable William Davies* (Cardiff, 1971), p. 101 et seq.

[141] *The Notebook of John Penry*, ed. A. Peel (Camden Society), LXVII (1944), vii.

[142] *DWB*, s.n.

[143] NLW MS 9054E.572.

[144] Henry Lewis (ed.), *Hen Gyflwyniadau* (Cardiff, 1948), p. 52.

[145] Emyr Gwynne Jones (ed.), 'History of the Bulkeley Family' (NLW MS 9080E.)', *TAAS* (1948), 21.

[146] NLW Llanstephan MS 133,85; J. Gwynfor Jones, 'Governance, order and stability in Caernarfonshire c.1540–1640', *TCHS*, XLIV (1983), 25.

[147] NLW MS 9054E.572.

[148] *Clenennau Letters and Papers*, no. 48, p. 15.

[149] Ibid., 162–3.

[150] *Penbrokshire*, p. 56.

[151] *CPSD*, X, no. 453, p. 182.

[152] J. Gwynfor Jones, 'The Welsh language in local government', in Geraint H. Jenkins (ed.), *A Social History of the Welsh Language: The Welsh Language before the Industrial Revolution* (Cardiff, 1997), pp. 181–206.

[153] W. R. Williams, *The History of the Great Sessions in Wales, 1542–1899* (Brecknock, 1899), p. 16.

[154] NLW MS 9055E.725.

[155] *History of the Great Sessions in Wales*, pp. 16, 57, 93, 133, 169.

[156] J. Gwynfor Jones, 'Welsh language in local government', pp. 190–6.

[157] J. C. Morrice (ed.), *Barddoniaeth Wiliam Llŷn* (Bangor, 1908), p. 73; *Rhagymadroddion*, p. 114.

[158] *Rhagymadroddion a Chyflwyniadau Lladin*, pp. 72–3.

[159] Cited in J. Gwynfor Jones, 'The gentry of east Glamorgan: Welsh cultural dimensions, 1540–1640', *Morgannwg*, XXXVII (1993), 11.

[160] Ibid.

[161] Ibid.

[162] Peter R. Roberts, 'Tudor legislation and "the British Tongue"', in Geraint H. Jenkins (ed.), *Welsh Language*, pp. 136–52.

[163] *Clenennau Letters and Papers*, no. 444, pp. 126–7.

[164] NLW MSS 9053E.429–30.

[165] J. Gwynfor Jones, *Beirdd yr Uchelwyr a'r Gymdeithas yng Nghymru c.1536–1640* (Denbigh, 1997), pp. 128–61; idem, 'Welsh poets and their patrons', 269–71; Ceri W. Lewis, 'The decline of professional poetry', in R. Geraint

Gruffydd (ed.), *A Guide to Welsh Literature*, III, *c.1530–1700* (Cardiff, 1997), pp. 48–51. For further discussion of the culturo-intellectual background to sixteenth-century Wales see R. Geraint Gruffydd, 'The Renaissance and Welsh literature', in Glanmor Williams and R. O. Jones (eds.), *The Celts and the Renaissance: Tradition and Innovation* (Cardiff, 1990), pp. 17–39; J. Gwynfor Jones, *Concepts of Order and Gentility in Wales 1540–1640* (Llandysul, 1992).

[166] Anthony Conran, *The Penguin Book of Welsh Verse* (London, 1967), pp. 197–9.

[167] W. Ogwen Williams, 'Social order in Tudor Wales', pp. 167–78.

[168] *Penbrokshire*, p. 55.

[169] *Rhagymadroddion a Chyflwyniadau Lladin*, pp. 72–3.

[170] NLW MS 9058E.1005; *Clenennau Letters and Papers*, no. 474, p. 135.

[171] Peter R. Roberts, 'The "Act of Union" in Welsh history', *TCS* (1972), 70.

[172] Glanmor Williams, 'Some Protestant views of early British history', in *Welsh Reformation Essays*, pp. 207–19.

[173] *Rhagymadroddion*, p. 33.

[174] Ibid., pp. 52–3.

[175] Ibid., p. 88.

[176] Ibid., pp. 114–15, 117.

[177] For an example of cultural affinity among modest gentry in hinterland Wales see the interests of Huw Llwyd of Cynfal, Merioneth. Davies, *Noddwyr Beirdd*, p. 56; J. H. Davies (ed.), *Gweithiau Morgan Llwyd o Wynedd*, II (Bangor and London, 1908), p. 311.

[178] Dodd, 'Wales's parliamentary apprenticeship', 8–72; idem, 'The pattern of politics in Stuart Wales', *TCS* (1948), 20–2. See also the same author's 'Wales under the early Stuarts', in *Wales Through the Ages*, pp. 54–61. For the Irish dimension see S. G. Ellis, *Tudor Ireland: Crown, Community and the Conflicts of Cultures, 1470–1603* (London, 1985); S. G. Ellis and S. Barber (ed.), *Conquest and Union: Fashioning a British State, 1485–1725* (London, 1995).

Notes to Chapter 2: Status and Reputation

[1] Thomas Elyot, *The Book named the Governor*, ed. S. E. Lehmberg (London, 1962), xiii.

[2] *The Two Books of Homilies Appointed to be read in Churches* (London, 1859), pp. 105–6.

[3] UCNW Penrhos MS II, 19. Cited in W. Ogwen Williams, 'The survival of the Welsh language after the Union of England and Wales: the first phase 1536–1642', *WHR*, II (1964), 68, 82–5.

[4] Emyr Gwynne Jones (ed.), 'History of the Bulkeley family (NLW MS 9080E)', *TAAS* (1948), 22.

[5] *William Lambarde and Local Government*, ed. Conyers Read, (New York, 1962), p. 95.

[6] Fritz Caspari, *Humanism and the Social Order in Tudor England* (Chicago, 1954), pp. 1–27, 132–56.

[7] *Penbrokshire*, III, p. 54.

[8] Henry Peacham (the younger), *The compleat gentleman fashioning him absolute in the most necessary & commendable qualities concerning minde or bodie that may be required in a noble gentleman* (London, 1622).

[9] Richard Pace, *De Fructu qui ex doctrina percipitur liber* (Basle, 1517), p. 98. Cited in Caspari, *Humanism*, pp. 150, 264.

[10] Francis Jones, 'Welsh pedigrees' in *Burke's Genealogical and Heraldic History of the Landed Gentry*, ed. L. G. Pine (London, 1952), lxix-lxxiii. For a detailed study of genealogical matters see Anthony Wagner, *English Genealogy* (Oxford, 1960).

[11] Gerald of Wales, *The Journey Through Wales and the Description of Wales*, tr. Lewis Thorpe (Harmondsworth, 1978), p. 251.

[12] For a comprehensive study of heraldry in Wales see M. P. Siddons, *The Development of Welsh Heraldry*, 3 vols (Aberystwyth, 1991 and 1993).

[13] Francis Jones, 'Welsh pedigrees', lxix.

[14] Idem, 'An approach to Welsh genealogy', *TCS* (1948), 375–7. See also Anthony Wagner, *Heralds of England: A History of the Office and College of Arms* (London, 1967).

[15] T. K. Rabb, *The Struggle for Stability in Early Modern Europe* (Oxford, 1975).

[16] W. H. Greenleaf, *Order, Empiricism and Politics: Two Traditions of English Political Thought, 1500–1700* (Oxford, 1964), chaps 2–5, pp. 14–94.

[17] Ibid.

[18] J. Donne, 'An anatomy of the world', in *John Donne: The Complete English Poems*, ed. A. J. Smith (London, 1971), p. 276.

[19] J. Hayward, 'An answer to the first part of a certain conference, concerning succession', cited in G. J. Schochet, *Patriarchalism in Political Thought* (Oxford, 1975), p. 49.

[20] Emyr Gwynne Jones, 'A Llandegai pew dispute', *TCHS*, IX (1948), 109–17.

[21] See P. L. Abraham, 'Contrasting Cultures? Cultural Propagation of the Concept of Order in Early Stuart England c.1603–1648' (unpublished University of Wales MA dissertation, 1995), chap.1, pp. 1–18.

[22] *Clenennau Letters and Papers*, no. 48, p. 15.

[23] *Penbrokshire*, III, p. 39.

[24] HMC, *Salisbury MSS.*, VIII, p. 233.

[25] Thomas Pennant, *Tours in Wales*, ed. John Rhys (Caernarfon, 1883), III, p. 132.

[26] *Penbrokshire*, III, p. 57.

[27] William Lambarde, *Eirenarcha or the Office of Justices of Peace* (1581–2), ed. P. R. Glazebrook (1972), pp. 63–5.

[28] *Basilikon Doron, The Epistle*, [vi–vii].

[29] PRO, St Cha. 8 James I 207/32.

[30] PRO E.134 8 James I (Mich. 3).

[31] BL Harleian MS 6997 fo. 74.

[32] PRO SP 12 252/42.16.

[33] St Cha. 8 James I 202/23; *Calendar of Star Chamber Proceedings concerning Wales* (Cardiff, 1929), ed. Ifan ab Owen Edwards (Cardiff, 1929), p. 216.

[34] Ibid.; G. D. Owen, *Wales in the Reign of James I* (London, 1988), pp. 165–6.

[35] *A Funerall Sermon* (1577), *The Epistle* [3].

[36] NLW Llanstephan MS 144.31. Cited in J. P. Jenkins, *A History of Modern Wales 1536–1990* (London, 1992), p. 39; *The Stradling Correspondence*, ed. J. M. Traherne (London, 1840), CXXXIX, pp. 167–8.

[37] Philip Styles, 'Politics and historical research in the early seventeenth century', in Levi Fox (ed.), *English Historical Scholarship in the Sixteenth and Seventeenth Centuries* (Oxford, 1956), p. 50. The best modern discussion of historical scholarship in the early modern period in England is found in F. Smith Fussner, *The Historical Revolution, 1580–1640* (London, 1962), especially pp. 29–59, 92–116, 250–2. For the background to antiquarian studies see T. D. Kendrick, *British Antiquity* (London, 1950).

[38] Cited in Ruth Kelso, *The Doctrine of the English Gentleman in the Sixteenth Century* (Boston, MA, 1954), pp.141–2.

[39] Cited in G. J. Williams and E. J. Jones (ed.), *Gramadegau'r Penceirddiaid* (Cardiff, 1934), xci.

[40] Francis Jones, 'An approach to Welsh genealogy', *TCS* (1948), 378–86.

[41] Graham C. G. Thomas, 'From manuscript to print I. manuscript', in R. Geraint Gruffydd (ed.), *A Guide to Welsh Literature*, III, *c.1530–1700* (Cardiff, 1997), pp. 241–4.

[42] NLW Peniarth MS 327, ii. 35. Cited in D. J. Bowen, 'Y cywyddwyr a'r dirywiad', *BBCS*, XXIX iii (1981), 492–3.

[43] Ca. MS 4.76,13. Cited in T. E. Parry, 'Llythyrau Robert Vaughan, Hengwrt (1592–1667), gyda Rhagymadrodd a Nodiadau' (unpublished University of Wales MA dissertation, 1960), p. 306.

[44] *Stradling Correspondence*, LXXVII, p. 90.

[45] *Rhagymadroddion a Chyflwyniadau Lladin*, p. 94.

[46] *Pembrokeshire County History*, III, pp. 140–1; H. A. Lloyd, *The Gentry of South-West Wales, 1540–1640* (Cardiff, 1968), pp. 130–1.

[47] *Calendar of Star Chamber Proceedings*, p. 40.

[48] Ibid., pp. 184, 186.

[49] Ibid., p. 22.

[50] Ibid., p. 23.

[51] P. Redwood, 'The Games family versus the borough of Brecon 1589–1606', *Brycheiniog*, XXV (1992–3), 67–75 (esp. 71).

[52] Penry Williams, 'The political and administrative history of Glamorgan, 1536–1642', in *Glamorgan County History*, IV, pp.150–2; Gareth E. Jones, *The Gentry and the Elizabethan State* (Swansea, 1977), pp. 60–2.

[53] NLW MS 9055E.710.

[54] J. Gwynfor Jones, 'The Welsh poets and their patrons, c.1550–1640', *WHR*, IX (1979).

[55] *Clenennau Letters and Papers*, no. 437, p. 124.

[56] NLW MS 9051E.9.

[57] William Harrison, *The Description of England*, ed. Georges Edelen (New York, 1968), p. 118.

[58] PRO E.134 8 James I (Mich. 3). See n. 30 above.

[59] J. Gwynfor Jones (ed.), *History of the Gwydir Family and Memoirs* (Llandysul, 1990), p. 63. See also J. Gwynfor Jones, 'Bishop William Morgan's dispute with John Wynn of Gwydir in 1603–04', *Journal of the Historical Society of the Church in Wales*, XXII (1972), 49–78.

[60] 'Bishop Morgan's dispute', pp. 75–6.

[61] *Penbrokshire*, III, p. 56.

[62] Ibid., p. 58.

[63] *CSPD* (1547–80), CVII, no. 4(i), p. 514; D. Ll. Thomas, 'Further notes on the Council in the Marches', *Y Cymmrodor*, XIII (1899), 130–3.

[64] *Calendar of Wynn of Gwydir Papers, 1515–1690*, ed. John Ballinger (Cardiff, 1926), no. 1075.

[65] *Penbrokshire*, III, p. 24.

[66] *A Calendar of the Register of the Council in the Marches of Wales, 1569–91*, ed. Ralph Flenley, (London, 1916), pp. 102–3.

[67] *Stradling Correspondence*, CLX, p. 196; CCLVII, pp. 317–18.

[68] UCNW Baron Hill MS 6720. For further discussion of poor law issues see A. L. Beier, *The Problem of the Poor in Tudor and Early Stuart England* (London, 1983); idem, *Masterless Men: The Vagrancy Problem in England, 1560–1640* (London, 1985); A. J. Fletcher, *Reform in the Provinces: The Government of Stuart England* (London, 1986), pp. 183–228.

[69] Fletcher, *Reform in the Provinces*, pp. 3–11, 55–62.

[70] *Clenennau Letters and Papers*, no. 106, p. 31.

[71] NLW MS 9052E.324.

[72] *Stradling Correspondence*, no. 70, pp. 80–1; *Glamorgan County History*, IV, p. 186. See also *APC* (1587–8), pp. 88–9.

[73] NLW MS 9052E.245.

[74] J. E. Neale, *The Elizabethan House of Commons* (London, 1955), pp. 119–28.

[75] *Calendar of Star Chamber Proceedings*, p. 90.

[76] Ibid., p. 40.

[77] W. Ogwen Williams, 'The social order in Tudor Wales', *TCS* (1967ii), 167–78.

[78] *Calendar Council in the Marches*, p. 67 et seq.; Penry Williams, *Council in the Marches*, pp. 195–7.

[79] George Owen, *The Description of Pembrokeshire*, ed. Dillwyn Miles (Llandysul, 1994), p. 38.

[80] Gwynedd Archives Service, X/QS 1615; *Clenennau Letters and Papers*, no. 129, p. 38.

[81] J. Gwynfor Jones, 'Welsh poets and their patrons', pp. 245–60.

[82] *Statutes of Wales*, p. 113.

[83] G. J. Williams and E. J. Jones (eds.), *Gramadegau'r Penceirddiaid*, p. 132; E. M. W. Tillyard, *The Elizabethan World Picture* (London, 1960), pp. 7–15, 23–67; A. O. Lovejoy, *The Great Chain of Being* (Boston, MA, 1936); J. Huizinga, 'The hierarchic conception of society', in *The Waning of the Middle Ages* (London, 1955), pp. 56–66.

[84] *Gwaith Siôn Tudur*, ed. Enid Roberts, (Cardiff, 1978), I, nos. XIV–XVI, pp. 52–65.

[85] John Lyly, *Euphues. The Anatomy of Wit . . .* (London, 1581). Cited in Kelso, *Doctrine of the English Gentleman*, p. 135.

[86] *The Winter's Tale*, Act IV, sc. 4 (l. 831); *Troilus and Cressida*, Act I, sc. 3 (ll.108–9). See Caspari, *Humanism*, pp. 99–101.

[87] Thomas Elyot, *The Book named the Governor*, p. 13.

[88] Ibid., pp. 2, 3–4. See Caspari, *Humanism*, p. 249.

[89] Caspari, *Humanism*, p. 86.

[90] A. O. H. Jarman and G. R. Hughes (eds), *A Guide to Welsh Literature*, II (Swansea, 1979), pp. 198, 270; Saunders Lewis, 'Dafydd Nanmor', *Y Llenor*, IV (1925), 135–48. See also Bobi Jones, 'Beirdd yr uchelwyr a'r byd', in *Ysgrifau Beirniadol*, VIII, ed. J. E. Caerwyn Williams (Denbigh, 1974), pp. 29–42.

[91] Lawrence Stone and J. C. Fawtier Stone, *An Open Elite? England 1540–1880* (abridged version Oxford, 1986), pp. 45–9; *Clenennau Letters and Papers*, no. 75, p. 22.

[92] *Rhagymadroddion*, p. 115; Ceri W. Lewis, 'The literary history of Glamorgan from 1550 to 1770', in *Glamorgan County History*, IV, pp. 594–7; Glanmor Williams, 'The Stradlings of St Donat's', in Stewart Williams (ed.), *Vale of History* (Barry, 1960), II, pp. 92–5; Ralph A. Griffiths, 'The rise of the Stradlings of St Donat's', *Morgannwg*, VII (1963), 37–47.

[93] *Rhagymadroddion a Chyflwyniadau Lladin*, p. 48.

[94] Ibid., pp. 48–9.

[95] Ibid., p. 94.

[96] NLW Tredegar MS 148. Cited in Benjamin Howell, *Law and Disorder in Tudor Monmouthshire* (Cardiff, 1995), pp. 42, 55.

[97] *Calendar of the Caernarvonshire Quarter Sessions Records*, I, *1541–1558*, ed. W. Ogwen Williams, (Caernarfon, 1956), p. 43(9).

[98] NLW MS 9057E.954,957; Owen, *Wales in the Reign of James I* , pp. 183–4.

[99] *Report on the Manuscripts of Lord de L'Isle and Dudley preserved at Penshurst Place*, III (London, 1936), pp. 431–2.

[100] Dodd, *Studies in Stuart Wales*, intro., v; idem, 'The pattern of politics in Stuart Wales', *TCS* (1948), 8–9, 20–1. For a contrary view see H. A. Lloyd, *Gentry of South-West Wales*, pp. 111–12.

[101] *Glamorgan County History*, IV, pp.178–91; Emyr Gwynne Jones (ed.), *Exchequer Proceedings (Equity) concerning Wales Henry VIII–Elizabeth* (Cardiff, 1939), pp. 17, 20, 23, 25, 74–5; J. Gwynfor Jones, 'Concepts of continuity and change in Anglesey after the Acts of Union, 1536–1603', *TAAS* (1990), 46–57.

[102] H. G. Owen, 'Family politics in Elizabethan Merionethshire', *BBCS*, XVIII (1959). 185–91.

[103] *Herbert Correspondence: The Sixteenth and Seventeenth-Century Letters of the Herberts of Chirbury, Powis Castle and Dolguog*, ed. W. J. Smith (Cardiff, 1978), pp. 2–5.
[104] Henry Ellis (ed.), *Original Letters*, pp. 21–2.
[105] *Calendar of Salusbury Correspondence c. 1553–1700*, ed. W J. Smith, (Cardiff, 1954), nos 23, 26, pp. 30–1.
[106] Ibid., no. 59, p. 42. See *Gwaith Siôn Tudur*, I, nos. XIV–XVI, pp. 52–65.
[107] *Salusbury Correspondence*, no. 52, p. 39; no. 91, p. 54.
[108] William Vaughan, *The Golden-fleece*, Pt. II, Chap. VI.
[109] *Rhagymadroddion*, pp. 101–2.

Notes to Chapter 3: Honour, Order and Authority

[1] Arwyn Ll. Hughes, 'Noddwyr y Beirdd yn Sir Feirionnydd' (unpublished University of Wales MA dissertation, 1969), I, p. 387.
[2] M. Jacques Hurault, *Politicke, moral, and martial discources*, tr. A. Golding (London, 1595), cited in Ruth Kelso, *The Doctrine of the English Gentleman in the Sixteenth Century* (Boston, MA, 1954), p. 94.
[3] Thomas Elyot, *The Book named the Governor*, ed. S. E. Lehmberg (London, 1962), p. 159.
[4] Kelso, *The Doctrine of the English Gentleman in the Sixteenth Century*, p. 94.
[5] J. Griffiths (ed.), *The Two Books of Homilies, Appointed to be read in Church* (Oxford, 1859), p. 105. See also W. R. D. Jones, *The Tudor Commonwealth, 1529–1559* (London, 1970), pp. 86–9.
[6] John Wynn, *History of the Gwydir Family and Memoirs*, ed. J. Gwynfor Jones (Llandysul, 1990), p. 35.
[7] Ibid., pp. 15–16.
[8] D. Ll. Thomas, 'Further notes on the Council in the Marches', *Y Cymmrodor*, XIII (1899), loc. cit.
[9] HMC, *Salisbury MSS.*, XII, p. 163.
[10] Penry Williams, *The Council in the Marches of Wales under Elizabeth I* (Cardiff, 1958), pp. 302–3.
[11] *APC*, X (1577–78), pp. 19–20; A. C. Miller, 'Sir William Morgan of Pencoed: "a man much to be accounted of"', *WHR*, IX (1978), 1–31.
[12] *Statutes of Wales*, pp. 93, 132.
[13] Thomas Smith, *De Republica Anglorum*, ed. Mary Dewar (Cambridge, 1982), p. 76.
[14] Kelso, *Doctrine of the English Gentleman*, pp. 31–41.
[15] For general studies of the concept of order in public life see F. Heal and C. Holmes, *The Gentry in England and Wales, 1500–1700* (London, 1994), pp. 166–214; A. J. Fletcher, 'Honour, reputation and local office-holding in Elizabethan and Stuart England', in A. J. Fletcher and J. Stevenson (eds.), *Order and Disorder in Early Modern England* (1985), pp. 92–115; Gareth E. Jones, *The Gentry and the Elizabethan State* (Swansea, 1977), pp. 20–41.
[16] *Clenennau Letters and Papers*, no. 236, p. 70.
[17] *Penbrokshire*, I, pp. 43–4.
[18] Ibid., III, p. 98.
[19] *The Stradling Correspondence*, ed. J. M. Traherne (London, 1840), LXX, pp. 79–80.
[20] James Howell, *Epistolae Ho-elianae (The Familiar Letters of James Howell)*, ed. J. Jacobs (London, 1892), II, Bk IV, XIII, pp. 581–2.
[21] John Cheke, *The Hurt of Sedicion howe greueous it is to a Communewelth* (1549; London 1971 edn.), [50, 51].
[22] Kelso, *Doctrine of the English Gentleman*, passim; J. P. Cooper, 'Ideas of gentility in early-modern England', in idem, *Land, Men and Beliefs: Studies in Early-*

Modern History, ed. G. E. Aylmer and J. S. Morrill (London, 1983), pp. 43–77; Joan Thirsk, 'The fashioning of the Tudor-Stuart gentry', *Bulletin of the John Rylands Library*, LXXII (1990), 69–85; J. Corfield, 'The demographic history of the English gentleman', *History Today*, XLII (Dec. 1992), 40–7; P. Mason, *The English Gentleman: The Rise and Fall of an Ideal* (London, 1982).

23 BL Harleian MS 283 fo. 153. See Edward Owen (ed.), *Catalogue of Manuscripts Relating to Wales in the British Museum* (London, 1900–22), II, p. 125.

24 M. Gray, 'Power, patronage and politics: office-holding and administration on the crown's estates in Wales', in R. W. Hoyle (ed.), *The Estates of the English Crown, 1588–1640* (Cambridge, 1992), pp. 137–62.

25 NLW MS 9056E.813.

26 *Clenennau Letters and Papers*, no. 398, p. 113.

27 *Stradling Correspondence*, CCXVII, p. 277. Cited in J. Gwynfor Jones, 'The gentry of east Glamorgan: Welsh cultural dimensions, 1540–1640', *Morgannwg*, XXXVII (1993), 19.

28 *Stradling Correspondence*, XCIV, pp. 113–14.

29 Lawrence Stone, *The Crisis of the Aristocracy, 1558–1641* (Oxford, 1965), pp. 589–93.

30 *De Republica Anglorum*, pp. 74–5.

31 *History of the Gwydir Family*, pp. 31–2.

32 Heal and Holmes, *Gentry*, pp. 50–3.

33 HMC, *Salisbury MSS.*, X, pp. 98–9.

34 *Exchequer Proceedings (Equity) Concerning Wales Henry VIII–Elizabeth*, ed. Emyr Gwynne Jones (Cardiff, 1939), p. 48 (re.59/7).

35 W. Ll. Williams, 'A Welsh insurrection', *Y Cymmrodor*, XVI (1903), 1–93; Ralph A. Griffiths, *Sir Rhys ap Thomas and his Family: A Study in the Wars of the Roses and Early Tudor Politics* (Cardiff, 1993), pp. 91–8.

36 *Calendar of the Records of the Borough of Haverfordwest, 1539–1660*, ed. B. G. Charles (Cardiff, 1967), p. 34.

37 Penry Williams, *Council in the Marches of Wales*, pp. 181–204.

38 Ralph A. Griffiths, *Sir Rhys ap Thomas*, pp. 91–8.

39 *History of the Gwydir Family*, xvii–xxxviii.

40 Rice Merrick, *Morganiae Archaiographia: A Book of the Antiquities of Glamorganshire*, ed. Brian Ll. James (Barry, 1983), pp. 147–64.

41 *Calendar of Salusbury Correspondence, c.1553–1700*, ed. W. J. Smith (Cardiff, 1954), XXXIII, p. 33; *Gwaith Siôn Tudur*, ed. Enid Roberts (Cardiff, 1978), I, pp. 52–5, II, pp.45–7; Enid Roberts, 'Ymryson y Salsbrïaid, 1593', *TDHS*, XVII 1968, 8–46.

42 PRO Court of Requests 82/46 Elizabeth. Cited in M. Robbins, 'The agricultural, domestic, social and cultural interests of the gentry in south-east Glamorgan, 1540–1640' (unpublished University of Wales Ph.D. dissertation, 1974), I, p. 82.

43 HMC *Salisbury MSS.*, VIII, p. 423.

44 *Salusbury Correspondence*, no. 23, p. 30.

45 NLW MSS 9055E.721, 728.

46 J. Gwynfor Jones, 'Bishop William Morgan's dispute with John Wynn of Gwydir, 1603–04', *Journal of the Historical Society of the Church in Wales*, XXII (1972), 76.

47 D. R. Thomas, *The Life and Work of Bishop Davies and William Salesbury* (Oswestry, 1902), p. 21.

48 Richard Davies, *A Funerall Sermon*, Dii.

49 PRO SP 12/162/29.

50 Richard Davies, *A Funerall Sermon*, Dii.

51 NLW Peniarth MS 327,165. See E. D. Jones, 'Robert Vaughan of Hengwrt', *JMHRS*, I (1949) (i), p. 23.

[52] *Stradling Correspondence*, no. 11, p. 15.
[53] NLW Add.MS 464E.189.
[54] *Clenennau Letters and Papers*, no. 400, p. 114.
[55] *Statutes of Wales*, p. 154.
[56] *Calendar of Herbert Correspondence*, p. 88.
[57] NLW Llanstephan MS 36,49.
[58] A. H. Dodd, 'North Wales in the Essex revolt of 1601', *EHR*, LIX (1944), 368–9.
[59] HMC, *Salisbury MSS.*, X, p. 98; David Mathew, *The Celtic Peoples and Renaissance Europe* (London, 1933), p. 422.
[60] Kelso, *Doctrine of the English Gentleman*, pp. 70–3; Lawrence Stone and J. C. Fawtier Stone, *An Open Elite?*, pp. 45–7.
[61] *Stradling Correspondence*, CCXVII, p. 277.
[62] Stone, *Crisis of the Aristocracy*, chap. 2, pp. 21–64; A. J. Fletcher, 'Honour, reputation and local office-holding in Elizabethan and Stuart England', in *Order and Disorder in Early Modern England* (Cambridge, 1985), p. 92–3.
[63] R. R. Davies, *The Age of Conquest, 1063–1415* (Oxford, 1993), pp. 115–18.
[64] Ibid.
[65] *Stradling Correspondence*, CLXIV, p.202.
[66] *Statutes of Wales*, pp. 122–3.
[67] J. Hayward, *An Answer to the First Part of a Certaine Conference Concerning Succession* (1603), Sig. B4.; *The Book named the Governor*, p. 6. For further discussion of this theme see G. J. Schochet, *Patriarchalism in Political Thought* (Oxford, 1975).
[68] *Clenennau Letters and Papers*, no. 274, p. 79.
[69] Cheke, *The Hurt of Sedicion* [11, 12].
[70] *Clenennau Letters and Papers*, no. 297, p. 86; NLW MS 9051E.170.
[71] A. O. Evans, *A Memorandum on the Legality of the Welsh Bible* (Cardiff, 1925), pp. 84, 98, 122–3.
[72] *Rhagymadroddion*, pp. 79–80.
[73] *Clenennau Letters and Papers*, no. 233, p. 69.
[74] *Stradling Correspondence*, LVIII, p. 66.
[75] NLW MS 9053E.385.
[76] Ca. MS 4.58,85.
[77] William Vaughan, *The Golden-grove*, III, cap. 16.
[78] H. A. Lloyd, *Gentry of South-West Wales*, p. 105.
[79] *Pembrokeshire County History*, III, pp.81–2, 132–3.
[80] William Harrison, *The Description of England*, ed. Georges Edelen (New York, 1968), p. 175.
[81] P. S. Edwards, 'The parliamentary representation of Wales and Monmouthshire, 1542–1558' (unpublished University of Cambridge Ph.D. dissertation, 1970), pp. 83–4.
[82] *Clenennau Letters and Papers*, no. 398, p. 113.
[83] Neale, *House of Commons*, pp. 94–5, 99–128.
[84] *A Calendar of the Register of the Council in the Marches of Wales 1569–91*, ed. R. Flenley (London, 1916), pp. 94–5; H. G. Owen, 'Family politics in Elizabethan Merionethshire', *BBCS*, XVIII (1959), 185–91.
[85] *APC*, XV, p. 375; XXI, p. 37.
[86] D. Ll. Thomas, 'Further notes on the Council in the Marches', *Y Cymmrodor*, XIII (1899), 130.
[87] Bowen, St 26 Hen.VIII, c. 4, pp. 51–2.
[88] Ca. MS 4,474 ff., 40–2.
[89] Emyr Gwynne Jones (ed.), 'History of the Bulkeley family (NLW MS 9080E)', loc. cit.
[90] HMC, *Salisbury MSS.*, XI, p. 81.

91 Ibid., XII, p. 341.
92 *Penbrokshire*, III, pp. 114–15.
93 *CSPD* (1547–80), CXXIV, no. 12, p. 590.
94 Thomas Churchyard, *The Worthines of Wales* (London, 1776 edn.), pp. 91–3.
95 *Calendar Council in the Marches*, pp. 198, 212.
96 L. & P., VIII, no. 925, p. 363. Cited in D. Cyril Jones, 'The Bulkeleys of Baron Hill 1440–1621' (unpublished University of Wales MA dissertation, 1958), pp. 332–3.
97 Glanmor Williams, *Religion, Language and Nationality in Wales* (Cardiff, 1979), pp. 154–66. See also Francis Jones, 'The old families of Wales', in D. Moore (ed.), *Eighteenth-Century Wales* (Swansea, 1976), pp. 27–46.
98 A. O. Evans, *A Memorandum on the Legality of the Welsh Bible*, pp. 107–8.
99 J. Gwynfor Jones, *Concepts of Order and Gentility in Wales, 1540–1640* (Llandysul, 1992), pp. 197–247.
100 J. Griffiths (ed.), *The Two Books of Homilies, Appointed to be read in Church*, pp. 105–14.
101 W. Ogwen Williams, *Tudor Gwynedd* (Caernarfon, 1958), pp. 17–22.
102 D. Ll. Thomas, 'Further notes', 130–3.
103 *Calendar Council in the Marches*, pp. 98–9.
104 Ibid.
105 *Stradling Correspondence*, CXXXVIII, p. 165.
106 G. R. Elton, *England under the Tudors* (London, 1957 edn.), pp. 165–75, 398–404.
107 D. Ll. Thomas, 'Further notes', p. 130.
108 R. R. Davies, *Age of Conquest*, pp. 56–81.
109 T. Jones Pierce, 'Landlords in Wales', in Thirsk, *Agrarian History of England and Wales*, IV, pp. 357–81; Penry Williams, *Council in the Marches of Wales*, pp. 229–48.
110 William Harrison, *Description of England*, p. 413.
111 *Journals of the House of Commons*, I, *1547–1628* (London, 1803) p. 158; S. T. Bindoff, 'The Stuarts and their style', *EHR*, LX (1945), 203–4; *Clenennau Letters and Papers*, no. 204, p. 61; A. H. Dodd, 'Wales's parliamentary apprenticeship (1536–1625)', *TCS* (1942), 24–6; E. N. Williams, 'Sir William Maurice of Clenennau', *TCHS*, XXI, (1963), 93–4;
112 George Owen Harry, *The Genealogy of the High and Mighty Monarch, James . . . King of great Brittayne . . .* (London, 1604), pp. 39–40.
113 For bardic attitudes towards gentry with or without office see J. Gwynfor Jones, *Concepts of Order*, pp. 149–92.
114 Heal and Holmes, *Gentry*, pp. 48–135; Stone, *Crisis of the Aristocracy*, pp. 273–4.

Notes to Chapter 4: The Defence of the Realm

1 *Herbert Correspondence: The Sixteenth and Seventeenth-Century Letters of the Herberts of Chirbury, Powis Castle and Dolguog*, ed. W. J. Smith (Cardiff, 1978), no. 130, pp. 87–8.
2 James Howell, *Epistolae Ho-elianae (The Familiar Letters of James Howell)*, ed. J. Jacobs (London, 1892), I, p. 26.
3 Glanmor Williams, 'Prophecy, poetry and politics in medieval and Tudor Wales', in *Religion, Language and Nationality in Wales* (Cardiff, 1979), pp. 71–86; idem, *Henry Tudor and Wales* (Cardiff, 1985), passim; Ceri W. Lewis, 'The decline of professional poetry', in R. Geraint Gruffydd (ed.), *A Guide to Welsh Literature*, III, *c. 1530–1700* (Cardiff, 1997), pp. 33–5; A. D. Carr, *Owen of Wales: The End of the House of Gwynedd* (Cardiff, 1991), pp. 86–98.
4 Glyn Roberts, 'Wales and England: antipathy and sympathy, 1284–1485', in

A. H. Dodd and J. Gwynn Williams (eds.), *Aspects of Welsh History* (Cardiff, 1969), pp. 300–5 et seq.; ibid., 'Wyrion Eden: the Anglesey descendants of Ednyfed Fychan in the fourteenth century', pp. 179–214.

⁵ Gwyn A. Williams, *When was Wales? A History of the Welsh* (London, 1985), pp. 68–72.

⁶ Glyn Roberts, 'Wales and England', pp. 299–18. See also T. Gwynn Jones, 'Cultural bases: a study of the Tudor period in Wales', *Y Cymmrodor*, XXXI (1921), 161–92.

⁷ *Penbrokshire*, III, p. 55.

⁸ Richard Deacon, *John Dee* (London, 1968), pp. 99–100; P. J. French, *John Dee: The World of an Elizabethan Magus* (London, 1972), pp. 196–207; Gwyn A. Williams, *Welsh Wizard and British Empire: Dr John Dee and a Welsh Identity* (Cardiff, 1980); idem, *Madoc: The Legend of the Welsh Discovery of America* (Oxford, 1987).

⁹ Glanmor Williams, 'Some Protestant views of early British church history', *Welsh Reformation Essays* (Cardiff, 1967), pp. 207–19; idem, *Reformation Views of Church History* (London, 1970); R. Flower, 'William Salesbury, Richard Davies and Archbishop Parker', *NLWJ*, II i (1941), 7–14; A. O. Evans, *A Memorandum on the Legality of the Welsh Bible* (Cardiff, 1925), pp. 83–124.

¹⁰ *DNB*, XXXV, p. 302. See also T. Stephens, *An Essay on the Discovery of America by Madoc ap Owen Gwynedd in the Twelfth Century*, ed. L. I. Reynolds (London, 1893); Richard Deacon, *Madog and the Discovery of America* (London, 1966); David Williams, 'John Evans's strange journey', *TCS* (1948), 105–14.

¹¹ BL Cotton MS Augustus I, i, 1v.

¹² Gwyn A. Williams, *Madoc*, pp. 35–67.

¹³ Glanmor Williams, *Religion, Language and Nationality*, pp. 85–6.

¹⁴ *Calendar, Council in the Marches*, pp. 49–50; Emyr Gwynne Jones, 'Anglesey and invasion, 1539–1603', *TAAS* (1947), 26–37.

¹⁵ *The Stradling Correspondence*, ed. J. M. Traherne, (London, 1840), CLXVI, pp. 204–5; A. C. Miller, 'Sir William Morgan of Pencoed: "a man much to be accounted of"', *WHR*, IX (1978), 14–16; *APC*, XI, p. 280.

¹⁶ Glanmor Williams, *Renewal and Reformation: Wales c.1415–1642* (Oxford, 1993), pp. 358–73; Penry Williams, *The Council in the Marches of Wales under Elizabeth I* (Cardiff, 1958), pp. 111–17.

¹⁷ R. B. Wernham, *Before the Armada: The Growth of English Foreign Policy, 1485–1588* (London, 1966), pp. 355–405; idem, *After the Armada: Elizabethan England and the Struggle for Western Europe, 1588–1595* (Oxford, 1984), pp. 1–22.

¹⁸ NLW MS 9055E, 710.

¹⁹ Penry Williams, *Council in the Marches*, pp. 285–7; NLW MS 9055E.710.

²⁰ *Calendar of Star Chamber Proceedings concerning Wales*, ed. Ifan ab Owen Edwards (Cardiff, 1929), pp. 42, 128.

²¹ Wernham, *Before the Armada*, pp. 355–405.

²² NLW Mostyn MS 161,566.

²³ *Clenennau Letters and Papers*, nos. 21, 30, pp. 6–7, 9.

²⁴ *CSPD* (1611–18), LXVIII, no. 75, p. 123.

²⁵ *CSPD* (1627–8), LXXXVIII, no. 23, p. 487.

²⁶ *Penbrokshire*, III, p. 110.

²⁷ BL Royal MS 18B vii.

²⁸ R. Geraint Gruffydd, 'Gwasg ddirgel yr ogof yn Rhiwledyn', *Journal of the Welsh Bibliographical Society*, IX (1958), 5; idem, *Argraffwyr Cyntaf Cymru: Gwasgau Dirgel y Catholigion adeg Elisabeth* (Cardiff, 1972); W. R. Williams, *The Parliamentary History of the Principality of Wales, 1541–1895* (Brecknock, 1895), p. 65.

²⁹ HMC, *Salisbury MSS.*, VII, pp. 485–6.

³⁰ Ibid., XI, p. 460.

31 Ibid., XIII (Addenda), p. 478.
32 Ibid., XVII, p. 374.
33 Ibid., p. 216.
34 Ibid., IV, p. 8.
35 *APC*, XXV, p. 515 (App.).
36 Ibid., XXXII, pp. 493–4.
37 Ibid.
38 *Gwaith Siôn Tudur*, I, no. LVII, p. 235. See also L. & P., XX (Sept. 1585–May 1586), 668.
39 D. H. E. Roberts and R. A. Charles, 'Raff ap Robert ac Edwart ap Raff', *BBCS*, XXIV ii (1971), 298–300.
40 Ibid., 298; NLW Brogyntyn MS 6, 106.
41 W. Hughes, *The Life and Times of Bishop William Morgan* (London, 1891), pp. 123–4; *Rhagymadroddion a Chyflwyniadau Lladin*, p. 64.
42 *Hen Gerddi Gwleidyddol, 1588–1660*, ed. J. H. Davies (Cymdeithas Llên Cymru; Cardiff 1901), I, pp. 7–11.
43 *CSPD*, XIV (1603–10), XV, no. 95, p. 236. See A. J. Loomie, *The Spanish Elizabethans, the English Exiles and the Court of Philip II* (London, 1963), pp. 83–9.
44 *Canu Rhydd Cynnar*, ed. T. H. Parry-Williams (Cardiff, 1932), p. 372.
45 Ibid., p. 377. For further discussion of the cult of monarchy in Elizabeth I's reign see Roy Strong, *Gloriana: the Portraits of Queen Elizabeth I* (London, 1987).
46 *Canu Rhydd Cynnar*, p. 380.
47 Maurice Kyffin, *The Blessednes of Brytaine or a Celebration of the Queenes Holyday* [1587] (London, 1885 repr.), B1; W. J. Gruffydd, *Llenyddiaeth Cymru: Rhyddiaith o 1540 hyd 1660* (Wrexham, 1926), p. 87; *Gwaith Siôn Tudur*, II, p. 358; L. Hotson, *Mr W. H.* (London, 1964), pp. 74, 79–80.
48 D. H. E. Roberts and R. A. Charles, 'Raff ap Robert ac Edwart ap Raff', 299.
49 Maurice Kyffin, *Continuation of the Blessednes of Brytaine* (London, 1588), B3.
50 D. H. E. Roberts and R. A. Charles, 'Raff ap Robert ac Edwart ap Raff', 299.
51 *Gwaith Siôn Tudur*, I, p. 381.
52 *Cerddi Rhydd Cynnar*, ed. D. Lloyd Jenkins (Llandysul, 1931), p. 119.
53 Thomas Smith, *De Republica Anglorum*, ed. Mary Dewar (Cambridge, 1982), p. 88.
54 Roy Strong, *The Cult of Elizabeth: Elizabethan Portraiture and Pageantry* (London, 1977), pp. 11–12.
55 NLW MS 1559,241. See W. Ambrose Bebb, *Cyfnod y Tuduriaid* (Wrexham, 1939), p. 216.
56 NLW MS 9052E.205.
57 PRO SP 16/88/23.
58 *Gwaith Siôn Tudur*, I, LVII, p. 235; John Wynn, *History of the Gwydir Family and Memoirs*, ed. J. Gwynfor Jones (Llandysul, 1990), p. 64.
59 *Penbrokshire*, III, p. 112.
60 George Owen, *The Description of Pembrokeshire*, ed. Dillwyn Miles (Llandysul, 1994), p. 218.
61 *Penbrokshire*, III, p. 14.
62 HMC, *Salisbury MSS.*, XIV, p. 88; *APC*, XXX, p. 65.
63 Rice Merrick, *Morganiae Archaiographia*, ed. Brian Ll. James, pp. 67–8.
64 John Penry, *Three Treatises concerning Wales*, ed. David Williams (Cardiff, 1960), pp. 26–7, 34–5, 159–63.
65 Ibid., p. 43.
66 Ibid., pp. 40, 43.
67 Ibid., p. 27.
68 Ibid., pp. 27, 32, 34.
69 Ibid., pp. 52–8.

[70] Ibid., p. 60.

[71] Ibid., p. 61.

[72] Ibid., pp. 49, 61, 161.

[73] Ibid., pp. 162–3.

[74] Glanmor Williams, 'Sir John Stradling of St Donat's (1563–1637)', in Stewart Williams (ed.), *Glamorgan Historian*, IX (Cowbridge, 1966), 24.

[75] NLW MS 5666.

[76] William Vaughan, *The Golden-fleece* (1626), II, pp. 91–4.

[77] Ibid., III, p. 5.

[78] G. Tibbott, 'Welshmen with Prince Charles in Spain, 1623', *NLWJ*, I (1939), 91–4.

[79] A. H. Dodd, 'Wales's parliamentary apprenticeship (1536–1625)', *TCS* (1942), 64–5.

[80] NLW 9058E.1973.

[81] Rhys Prichard, *Y Seren Foreu neu Ganwyll y Cymry*, ed. Rice Rees (Wrexham, 1867), p. 260.

[82] *Epistolae Ho-elianae*, I, p. 213.

[83] Ibid., p. 154.

[84] *Clenennau Letters and Papers*, no. 162, p. 47. See also no. 115, p. 34.

[85] *Cerddi Rhydd Cynnar*, p. 121.

[86] P. L. Hughes and J. F. Larkin (ed.), *Tudor Royal Proclamations*, III, 1588–1603 (Yale, 1969), pp. 86–93 (esp. p. 89).

[87] Ibid., pp. 86–7.

[88] NLW MS 464E.241.

[89] J. Gwynfor Jones, 'The Welsh poets and their patrons', *WHR*, IX (1979), 250–3; *The Parliamentary Diary of Robert Bowyer, 1606–1607*, ed. D. H. Willson (London, 1931), pp. 206–7; *Clenennau Letters and Papers*, no. 474, pp. 134–5.

[90] *Clenennau Letters and Papers*, loc. cit.

[91] *Rhagymadroddion a Chyflwyniadau Lladin*, p. 44.

[92] Ibid., p. 87.

[93] John Stradling, 'Divine poems in seven several classes' (class 3, stanza 183), in *Epigrammatum libri quatuor* (1607), p. 40.

Notes to Chapter 5: The Protestant Church

[1] Glanmor Williams, *Renewal and Reformation: Wales c.1415–1642* (Oxford, 1993), pp. 316–23. The authoritative work on the Reformation era in Wales to 1603 is Glanmor Williams, *Wales and the Reformation* (Cardiff, 1997). For a discussion of the Protestant Church under Elizabeth I see chaps. 9, 11 and 12, pp. 280–337.

[2] Ibid., p. 306; David Williams, 'The miracle of St Donat's', *The Welsh Review*, VII(i) (1947), 33–8; T. G. Law, 'The miraculous cross of St Donat's, 1559–61', *EHR*, I (1886), 513–17.

[3] *Rhagymadroddion a Chyflwyniadau Lladin*, p. 94; R. Geraint Gruffydd, 'Y cyfieithu a'r cyfieithwyr', in R. Geraint Gruffydd (ed.), *Y Gair ar Waith: Ysgrifau ar yr Etifeddiaeth Feiblaidd yng Nghymru* (Cardiff, 1988), pp. 30, 33; Glanmor Williams, 'Bishop William Morgan and the first Welsh Bible', in *The Welsh and their Religion* (Cardiff, 1991), pp. 207–9.

[4] Glanmor Williams, *Welsh Reformation Essays* (Cardiff, 1967), p. 27.

[5] A. H. Dodd, 'Wales's parliamentary apprenticeship (1536–1625)', *TCS* (1942), 19.

[6] *DWB*, s.n.

[7] *Rhagymadroddion*, pp. 122–5.

8 J. Gwynfor Jones, 'Bishop William Morgan's dispute with John Wynn of Gwydir in 1603–04', *Journal of the Historical Society of the Church in Wales*, XXII (1972), 67–8.

9 *CSPD* (1611–18), LXI, no. 10, p. 2; J. Gwynfor Jones, 'Richard Parry, Bishop of St. Asaph: some aspects of his career', *BBCS*, XXVI (1975), 175–90, R. Geraint Gruffydd, 'Bishop Francis Godwin's injunctions for the diocese of Llandaff, 1603', *Journal of the Historical Society of the Church in Wales*, IV, 1954, 14–22.

10 Christopher Hill, *Economic Problems of the Church from Archbishop Whitgift to the Long Parliament* (Oxford, 1956), pp. 199–244; K. Fincham and P. Lake, 'The ecclesiastical policies of James I and Charles I', in K. Fincham (ed.), *The Early Stuart Church, 1603–1642* (London, 1993), pp. 23–50.

11 Glanmor Williams, 'The church', in Joan Thirsk (ed.), *The Agrarian History of England and Wales: IV, 1500–1640* (Cambridge, 1967), pp. 394–5.

12 Ibid.

13 D. R. Thomas, *The Life and Work of Bishop Davies and William Salesbury* (Oswestry, 1902), p. 44.

14 For background see Glanmor Williams, *Renewal and Reformation*, pp. 305–31; N. L. Jones, *Faith by Statute: Parliament and the Settlement of Religion, 1559* (London, 1982); Claire Cross, *Church and People 1450–1660: The Triumph of the Laity in the English Church* (London, 1987), pp. 124–52; F. Heal, *Of Prelates and Princes: A Study of the Economic and Social Position of the Tudor Episcopacy* (Cambridge, 1980).

15 R. O'Day, *The English Clergy: The Emergence and Consolidation of a Profession, 1558–1642* (Leicester, 1979), pp. 21–3, 234–6.

16 PRO SP 14/61/10; *CSPD* (1611–18), p. 2. See also J. Gwynfor Jones, 'Richard Parry, bishop of St Asaph', 178–9.

17 NLW MS 9061E.1440.

18 J. Gwynfor Jones, 'Thomas Davies and William Hughes: two Reformation bishops of St Asaph', *BBCS*, XXIX (i) (1981), 325–35; idem, 'The Reformation bishops of St Asaph', *Journal of Welsh Ecclesiastical History*, VII (1990), 17–40; *Pembrokeshire County History*, III, pp. 113–15; W. P. M. Kennedy (ed.), *Elizabethan Episcopal Administration*, III (Alcuin Club Collections, XXVII; 1924), pp. 139–52. See also R. Houlbrooke, 'The Protestant episcopate 1542–1603: the pastoral contribution', in F. Heal and R. O'Day, *Church and Society in England, Henry VIII to James I* (Basingstoke, 1977), pp. 78–98; J. Berlatsky, 'The Elizabethan episcopate: patterns of life and expenditure', in R. O'Day and F. Heal (ed.), *Princes and Paupers in the English Church, 1500–1800* (Leicester, 1981), pp. 111–22; Christopher Hill, *Economic Problems*.

19 S. Doran, *Elizabeth I and Religion, 1558–1603* (London, 1994), pp. 14–22; John Guy, 'The Tudor age', in K. O. Morgan (ed.), *The Sphere Illustrated History of Britain, 1485–1789* (London, 1985), pp. 48–51; Robert Ashton, *Reformation and Revolution* (London, 1984), pp. 141–69; A. G. Dickens, *The English Reformation* (London, 1964); D. Baker (ed.), *Reform and Reformation: England and the Continent c.1500–c.1750* (Oxford, 1979).

20 Ashton, *Reformation and Revolution*, pp. 141–69.

21 *Glamorgan County History*, IV, pp. 220–4; M. Gray, 'The cloister and the hearth: Anthony Kitchin and Hugh Jones: two Reformation bishops of Llandaff', *Journal of Welsh Religious History*, III (1995), 15–25.

22 D. R. Thomas, *Bishop Davies and William Salesbury*, p. 37.

23 Browne Willis, *A Survey of the Cathedral Church of St Asaph* (London, 1720), p. 251.

24 J. Gwynfor Jones, 'Thomas Davies and William Hughes', pp. 320–5.

25 *CSPD* (1547–80), XLIV, no. 27, p. 301; David Mathew, 'Some Elizabethan documents', *BBCS*, VI(i) (1931), 77.

[26] *Rhagymadroddion,* pp. 3–4.

[27] J. Gwynfor Jones, *Wales and the Tudor State, 1534–1603* (Cardiff, 1989), p. 236.

[28] Ibid., p. 237. See also Glanmor Williams, 'The achievement of William Salesbury', in *Welsh Reformation Essays* (Cardiff, 1967), pp. 194–5; *Rhagymadroddion,* pp. 4, 9.

[29] William Salesbury, *A Dictionary in Englyshe and Welshe* (London, 1547), preface [no pagination].

[30] Glanmor Williams, 'William Salesbury's *Baterie of the Popes Botereulx*', BBCS, XIII (1949), 146–50.

[31] William Salesbury, *Kynniver Llith a Ban,* ed. J. Fisher (Cardiff, 1931), preface, n.p.

[32] *Rhagymadroddion a Chyflwyniadau Lladin,* pp. 18–21.

[33] W. Hughes, *Life and Times of Bishop William Morgan* (London, 1891), pp. 121–2.

[34] *Rhagymadroddion,* p. 89.

[35] *CSPD* (1581–90), CXCI, no. 17, p. 339.

[36] *Rhagymadroddion,* p. 101.

[37] Ibid.

[38] *Exchequer Proceedings (Equity) concerning Wales,* ed. Emyr Gwynne Jones (Cardiff, 1939), p. 293.

[39] *A Funerall Sermon preached . . . by the reverend Father in God, Richard . . . Bishoppe of Saint Dauys at the Buriall of the Right Honourable Walter Earle of Essex and Ewe* (1577), Dii.

[40] A. O. Evans, *A Memorandum on the Legality of the Welsh Bible* (Cardiff, 1925), pp. 86–124.

[41] Ibid., p. 101.

[42] W. Hughes, *Life and Times of William Morgan,* p. 122.

[43] Ibid., pp. 126–7.

[44] J. Gwynfor Jones, 'Bishop Morgan's dispute', p. 74.

[45] Ibid.

[46] *Stradling Correspondence,* ed. J. M. Traherne, CCLVII, p. 331.

[47] Ibid., p. 332.

[48] R. Geraint Gruffydd, *The Translating of the Bible into the Welsh Tongue* (London, 1988), p. 64.

[49] For further discussion of Morgan's achievement see Glanmor Williams, 'Bishop William Morgan and the first Welsh Bible', in *The Welsh and their Religion* (Cardiff, 1991), pp. 173–229.

[50] R. Geraint Gruffydd, *Translating of the Bible,* p. 51.

[51] *Rhagymadroddion,* pp. 106–7.

[52] Ibid., pp. 109–10.

[53] John Penry, *Three Treatises,* p. 28.

[54] Ibid., p. 5.

[55] Ibid., p. 13.

[56] Ibid., p. 28.

[57] Ibid., pp. 59–60.

[58] Ibid., p. 60.

[59] J. Gwynfor Jones, 'John Penry: government, order and the "perishing souls" of Wales', *TCS* (1993), 66–74; R. Houlbrooke, 'The Protestant episcopate 1547–1603: the Protestant contribution', in F. Heal and R. O'Day (eds.), *Church and Society,* pp. 78–98.

[60] John Penry, *Three Treatises,* pp. 60–6, 84–7, 131–4.

[61] Ibid., p. 67.

[62] Ibid., p. 60.

[63] Ibid., p. 117.

[64] Ibid., p. 107.
[65] NLW MS 9061E.1445.
[66] *Rhagymadroddion*, pp. 89–102, 118–21, 126–35.
[67] Ibid., p. 100.
[68] Ibid., pp. 130–1.
[69] *Rhagymadroddion a Chyflwyniadau Lladin*, p. 103.
[70] Ibid., p. 103.
[71] *Rhagymadroddion*, p. 124. See R. Geraint Gruffydd, 'Dr Michael Roberts o Fôn a Beibl bach 1630', *TAAS* (1989), 25–41.
[72] PRO SP. 14 76/3.
[73] Emyr Gwynne Jones, *Cymru a'r Hen Ffydd* (Cardiff, 1951), pp. 61–2, 70–3; F. H. Pugh, 'Glamorgan recusants 1572–1611', *South Wales and Monmouth Record Society*, III (1954), 49–67; idem, 'Monmouthshire recusants in the reigns of Elizabeth and James I', ibid., IV (1957), 59–110; Glanmor Williams, 'Poets and pilgrims in fifteenth- and sixteenth-century Wales', *TCS* (1991), 69–98.
[74] BL, Lansdowne Coll. III, fo. 10; Edward Owen (ed.), *A Catalogue of the Manuscripts Relating to Wales in the British Museum*, Pt. I, p. 72.
[75] B. Reay, 'Popular religion', in B. Reay (ed.), *Popular Culture in Seventeenth-Century England* (London, 1985), pp. 91–119; Keith Thomas, *Religion and the Decline of Magic: Studies in Popular Beliefs in Sixteenth- and Seventeenth-Century England* (London, 1971); Patrick Collinson, 'Popular and unpopular religion', in *The Religion of Protestants: The Church in English Society 1559–1625* (Oxford, 1982), pp. 189–241.
[76] L. & P., XIII (Pt.i) (1538), no. 694, p. 264; W. G. Evans, 'Derfel Gadarn – a celebrated victim of the Reformation', *JMHRS*, XI(ii) (1991), 137–51.
[77] *CSPD* (1611–18), LXVII, no. 1, p. 84; LXVIII, no. 75, p. 123; (1627–28), LXXXVIII, no. 23, p. 48.
[78] *CSPD*, XI, no. 37, p. 172.
[79] Claire Cross, 'Churchmen and the royal supremacy', in Heal and O'Day, *Church and Society*, pp. 15–34. For a full study see P. Lake, *Anglicans and Puritans? Conformist Thought from Whitgift to Hooker* (London, 1988).
[80] *Rhagymadroddion*, p. 127.
[81] Rhys Prichard, *Y Seren Foreu, neu Ganwyll y Cymry*, ed. Rice Rees, pp. 17–21, 115–20.
[82] Ibid., p. 105.
[83] Ibid., p. 115.
[84] For an example of Penry's abrasive style see *Three Treatises*, p. 124.
[85] Glanmor Williams, 'Religion and Welsh literature in the age of the Reformation', in *The Welsh and their Religion*, pp. 138–72.
[86] W. J. Gruffydd, *Llenyddiaeth Cymru: Rhyddiaith o 1540 hyd 1660* (Wrexham, 1926), p. 106. See Glanmor Williams, 'Edward James a Llyfr yr Homilïau', in *Grym Tafodau Tân: Ysgrifau Hanesyddol ar Grefydd a Diwylliant* (Llandysul, 1984), pp. 180–98.
[87] J. Gwynfor Jones, 'Maurice Kyffin a Huw Lewys: dau amddiffynnydd y ffydd Brotestannaidd yng Nghymru yn 1595', in J. E. Caerwyn Williams (ed.), *Ysgrifau Beirniadol*, XXI (Denbigh, 1995), pp. 51–72.
[88] *Rhagymadroddion*, pp. 106–7.
[89] F. Heal, 'The idea of hospitality in early modern England', *Past & Present*, CII (1964), 66; G. Wheler, *The Protestant Monastery: or, Christian Oeconomicks* (London, 1698), p. 173.
[90] *The Works of William Laud*, V, ed. J. Bliss (Oxford, 1853), p. 329. For further background see Thomas Richards, *A History of the Puritan Movement in Wales, 1639–53* (London, 1920), pp. 1–30; G. F. Nuttall, 'Walter Cradock (1606?–1659): the man and his message', in *The Puritan Spirit: Essays and Addresses* (London,

1967), pp. 118–29; *The Two Books of Homilies appointed to be read in Churches*, ed. J. Griffiths (Oxford, 1859), X, pp. 105–17.

[91] Patrick Collinson, *The Elizabethan Puritan Movement* (London, 1967), p. 291 et seq.

[92] See E. C. E. Bourne, *The Anglicanism of William Laud* (London, 1947); N. Tyacke, *Anti-Calvinists: The Rise of English Arminianism c. 1590–1640* (Oxford, 1987); idem, 'Puritanism, Arminianism and Counter Reformation', in Conrad Russell (ed.), *The Origins of the English Civil War* (London, 1973), pp. 119–43; Collinson, *Elizabethan Puritan Movement*, p. 291 et seq.; *Works of William Laud*, V(ii), p. 345.

[93] Brian Ll. James, 'The evolution of a radical: The life and career of William Erbery (1604–54), *The Journal of Welsh Ecclesiastical History*, III (1986), 31–48.

[94] Thomas Richards, *History of the Puritan Movement*, pp. 23–30; Geraint H. Jenkins, *Protestant Dissenters in Wales, 1639–89* (Cardiff, 1991), pp. 9–14; idem, *Foundations*, pp. 43–6.

[95] Geraint H. Jenkins, *Foundations*, p. 28.

[96] R. Geraint Gruffydd, *'In that Gentile Country . . .': The Beginnings of Puritan Nonconformity in Wales* (Bridgend, 1975), pp. 14–18, 28–9; R. Tudur Jones, *Hanes Annibynwyr Cymru* (Swansea, 1966), pp. 41–4.

[97] Glanmor Williams, 'Landlords in Wales: the church', in Thirsk (ed.), *Agrarian History*, pp. 389–95.

[98] A. Tindal Hart, *The Country Clergy in Elizabethan and Stuart Times, 1558–1660* (London, 1958), pp. 59–85. For further discussion of the Church in the early seventeenth century see the studies in Kenneth Fincham (ed.), *The Early Stuart Church, 1603–1642* (London, 1993); R. Geraint Gruffydd, 'Bishop Francis Godwin's injunctions for the diocese of Llandaff', *Journal Hist. Soc. Church in Wales*, I, (1954), 14–22.

[99] *Rhagymadroddion*, p. 120.

[100] Lewis Bayly, *The Practice of Piety* (1640 edn.), preface, A5; A. H. Dodd, 'Bishop Lewes Bayly c.1575–1631', *TCHS*, XXVIII (1967), 13–36; NLW Brogyntyn MS 11,56; E. D. Jones, 'The Brogyntyn Welsh Manuscripts', *NLWJ*, VII(3) (1952), 165–8. See also M. Ellis, 'Cyflwyniad Rowland Vaughan, Caergai, i'w gyfieithiad o *Eikon Basilike*', *NLWJ*, I(3) (1940), 141–4.

Notes to Chapter 6: Family and Household

[1] Many weighty studies have appeared recently on the structure and perceptions of the family. Among the most important are the following: Lawrence Stone, *The Family, Sex and Marriage in England, 1500–1800* (New York, 1977); J. P. Jenkins, *The Making of a Ruling Class: Glamorgan Gentry 1640–1790* (Cambridge, 1983), pp. 193–238; F. Heal, *Hospitality in Early Modern England* (Oxford, 1990); R. Houlbrooke, *The English Family, 1450–1700* (London, 1984): K. Wrightson, *English Society, 1580–1680* (London, 1982).

[2] Lawrence Stone and J. C. Fawtier Stone, *An Open Elite? England 1540–1880* (Oxford, 1986), pp. 3–14.

[3] Thomas Pennant, *Tours in Wales*, ed. John Rhys (Caernarfon, 1883), I, p. 14.

[4] NLW Penrice and Margam Muniments, L.33. Cited in D. M. Cole, 'The Mansells of Oxwich and Margam, 1487–1631' (unpublished University of Birmingham MA dissertation, 1966), p. 55.

[5] *Penbrokshire*, III, p. 98; Francis Jones, 'Welsh pedigrees', in *Burke's Genealogical and Heraldic History of the Landed Gentry*, ed. L. G. Pine (London, 1952), lxix–lxxvi; T. M. Charles-Edwards, *Early Irish and Welsh Kinship* (Cambridge, 1993), pp. 169–74, 364–9, 431–59.

[6] *The Stradling Correspondence*, ed. J. M. Traherne (London, 1840), p. 289.

[7] Humphrey Llwyd, *Commentarioli Descriptionis Britannicae Fragmentum* (Cologne, 1572), tr. by Thomas Twyne as *The Breuiarye of Britayne* (London, 1573), fo. 60.

[8] Francis Jones, 'An approach to Welsh genealogy', *TCS* (1948), 348–86.

[9] John Wynn, *History of the Gwydir Family and Memoirs*, ed. J. Gwynfor Jones (Llandysul, 1990), p. 35.

[10] *Basilikon Doron*, tr. Robert Holland, [B2-C3]; J. Gwynfor Jones, 'Robert Holland a *Basilikon Doron* y brenin Iago', in J. E. Caerwyn Williams (ed.), *Ysgrifau Beirniadol* (Denbigh, 1997), pp. 161–88.

[11] *Funerall Sermon* (1577), Dii.

[12] NLW MS 9057E.923.

[13] NLW MS 9056E.878.

[14] John Penry, *Three Treatises concerning Wales*, ed. David Williams (Cardiff, 1960), pp. 28, 111.

[15] James Howell, *Epistolae Ho-elianae (The Familiar Letters of James Howell)*, ed. J. Jacobs (London, 1892), I, Bk I, Sec. I, no. II, p. 19.

[16] *The Autobiography of Edward, Lord Herbert of Cherbury*, ed. S. Lee (London, 1886), p. 10.

[17] *History of the Gwydir Family*, p. 49; M. Griffiths, ' "Very wealthy by merchandise"? Urban fortunes', in J. Gwynfor Jones (ed.), *Class Community and Culture in Tudor Wales* (Cardiff, 1989), pp. 197–235.

[18] Emyr Gwynne Jones, 'County politics and electioneering, 1558–1625', *TCHS*, I (1939), 40–6.

[19] *History of the Gwydir Family*, p. 59.

[20] Ibid., p. 60.

[21] Ibid., p. 63.

[22] Ibid., pp. 68, 72.

[23] Juan Luis Vives, 'Office and Duetie of a Husband' (1550), cited in Kenneth Charlton, *Education in Renaissance England* (London, 1965), p. 201.

[24] NLW MS 9052E.284.

[25] NLW MS 9056E.813.

[26] A. Everitt, *Change in the Provinces: The Seventeenth Century* (Leicester, 1969), pp. 5–15. For further discussion of the household see F. Heal and C. Holmes, *The Gentry in England and Wales 1500–1700* (London, 1994), pp. 282–9.

[27] P. L. Hughes and J. F. Larkin (eds.), *Tudor Royal Proclamations*, I, *1485–1553* (Yale, 1964), pp. 327, 451–3; II, *1553–87* (Yale, 1969), pp. 86, 541–3; III, *1588–1603* (Yale, 1969), pp. 169–72, 174–9; idem, *Stuart Royal Proclamations*, I (Oxford, 1973), no. 11, pp. 21–2.

[28] G. J. Williams and E. J. Jones (eds.), *Gramadegau'r Penceirddiaid* (Cardiff, 1934), p. 132.

[29] *Stradling Correspondence*, CCXLVIII, pp. 317–18.

[30] *Rhyddiaith Gymraeg: Detholion o Lawysgrifau a Llyfrau Printiedig*, II, *1547–1618*, Thomas Jones (Cardiff, 1988), pp. 132–9; F. Heal, 'The ideal of hospitality in early modern England', *Past and Present*, CII (1964), 80–9.

[31] J. Gwynfor Jones, 'Social and economic dimensions', in J. Gwynfor Jones, *Concepts of Order and Gentility in Wales 1540–1640* (Llandysul, 1992), pp. 197–247.

[32] *The Two Books of Homilies Appointed to be read in Churches*, ed. J. Griffiths (Oxford, 1859), pp. 105–6.

[33] Gerald of Wales, *The Journey Through Wales/The Description of Wales*, ed. Lewis Thorpe (London, 1978), pp. 251–2.

[34] Ibid., p. 261.

[35] T. Roberts and Ifor Williams (eds.), *The Poetical Work of Dafydd Nanmor* (Cardiff, 1923), X, p. 27; Saunders Lewis, 'Dafydd Nanmor', *Y Llenor*, IV (1925), 146.

[36] Ruth Kelso, *The Doctrine of the English Gentleman in the Sixteenth Century* (Boston, MA, 1954), pp. 21–30.

[37] Llwyd, *Breuiarye of Britayne*, fo. 60.

[38] W. G. Hoskins, 'The rebuilding of rural England, 1540–1640', *Past & Present*, IV (Nov. 1953), 44–59; E. Mercer, 'The houses of the gentry', *Past & Present*, V (May 1954), 11–32.

[39] S. R. Jones and J. T. Smith, 'The houses of Breconshire: V', *Brycheiniog*, XIII (1968–9), 13–16. See also E. Wiliam, '"Let use be preferred to uniformity": domestic architecture'. *Class, Community and Culture in Tudor Wales*, ed. J. Gwynfor Jones (Cardiff, 1989), pp. 159–96.

[40] H. J. Habakkuk, 'Daniel Finch, 2nd earl of Nottingham: his house and estate', in J. H. Plumb (ed.), *Studies in Social History: A Tribute to G. M. Trevelyan* (London, 1955), pp. 174–5.

[41] Ibid., p. 178.

[42] *Rhagymadroddion a Chyflwyniadau Lladin*, pp. 74–5.

[43] Ibid., p. 71.

[44] *Gwaith Guto'r Glyn*, ed. J. Ll. Williams and Ifor Williams (Cardiff, 1939), XLVII, p. 127.

[45] Saunders Lewis, 'Dafydd Nanmor', in R. Geraint Gruffydd (ed.), *Meistri'r Canrifoedd: Ysgrifau ar Hanes Llenyddiaeth Gymraeg gan Saunders Lewis* (Cardiff, 1973), X, pp. 80–92.

[46] Emyr Gwynne Jones (ed.), 'History of the Bulkeley family (NLW MS 9080E)', *TAAS* (1948), 21–2.

[47] Ibid.

[48] NLW MS 9059E.1188.

[49] John Leland, *Itinerary in Wales*, ed. L. Toulmin Smith (London, 1908), pp. 84 (Penrhyn), 85 (Gwydir), 108 (Tretŵr), 115 (Carew).

[50] *Penbrokshire*, III, p. 57.

[51] *Rhagymadroddion*, pp. 32–3.

[52] Francis Bacon, *Essays* (London, 1966 ed.), XLV, p. 180.

[53] Peter Smith, *Houses; Ancient Monuments Commission in Glamorgan: IV. Domestic Architecture from the Reformation to the Industrial Revolution*. Pt I, 'The greater houses', p. 354; Anc. Mon. Comm., *Caernarvonshire:East*, pp. 58–64; R. Turner, *Plas Mawr, Conwy* (Cardiff, Cadw (Welsh Historic Monuments), 1997).

[54] UCNW Plas Coch MSS 159, 185; Emyr Gwynne Jones, 'Some notes on the principal county families of Anglesey in the sixteenth and early seventeenth centuries', *TAAS* (1939), 66–7.

[55] *Penbrokshire*, I, p. 156.

[56] NLW MS 9052E.290.

[57] NLW MS 9055E.699.

[58] Stone, *Family, Sex and Marriage*, pp. 69–89, 113–36; M. Slater, 'The weightiest business: marriage in an upper-gentry family in seventeenth-century England', *Past & Present*, 72 (1976), 25–54; Heal and Holmes, *Gentry*, pp. 60–77.

[59] *Herbert Correspondence: The Sixteenth and Seventeenth-Century Letters of the Herberts of Chirbury, Powis Castle and Dolguog*, ed. W. J. Smith (Cardiff, 1978), p. 21.

[60] NLW MS 9059E.1188. See also J. Gwynfor Jones, *The Wynn Family of Gwydir: Origins, Growth and Development c.1490–1674* (Aberystwyth, 1995), p. 115 et seq.

[61] *Herbert Correspondence*, p. 6.

[62] H. Smith, *A preparation to mariage* ... (London, 1591).

[63] *Cerddi'r Ficer: Detholiad o Gerddi Rhys Prichard*, ed. Nesta Lloyd (Cyhoeddiadau Barddas, 1994), p. 102.

[64] Bayly, *Practice of Piety*, pp. 289–94; J. Gwynn Williams, 'Agweddau ar y gymdeithas Gymreig yn yr ail ganrif ar bymtheg', *Efrydiau Athronyddol*, XXXI (1968), 42–7.

[65] *Clenennau Letters and Papers*, no. 398, p. 113.

[66] John Davies, *Cambrobrytannicae Cymraecaeve Linguae Institutiones et Rudimenta* (1592), preface, 3a.

[67] *Stradling Correspondence*, CLXXXVII, p. 238.

[68] Lord Mostyn and T. A. Glenn, *History of the Mostyn Family of Mostyn* (London, 1925), p. 116.

[69] *Clenennau Letters and Papers*, no. 75, p. 22.

[70] *Glamorgan County History*, IV, pp. 105–6.

[71] *Stradling Correspondence*, CXXXVIII, p. 165.

[72] John Stradling, *Beati Pacifici: A Divine Poem written to the King* (1623), stanza 243.

[73] NLW MS 9052E.266; 9059E.1188.

[74] Gerald of Wales, p. 251; *History of the Gwydir Family*, p. 16.

[75] See Enid Roberts, 'Cywydd cymod Hwmffre ap Hywel ap Siencyn a'i geraint', *JMHRS*, IV (1964), 302–17.

[76] David Mathew, 'Some Elizabethan documents', *BBCS*, VI (1931), 74, 76–7.

[77] St 26 Hen.VIII c. 4, *The Statutes of Wales*, p. 51; *Stradling Correspondence*, CLXXXVII, p. 238.

[78] PRO E.36/191, fo. 24. I wish to thank my research student Mr Michael Jones for this reference. See also L. & P,. VII, no. 1456, p. 545. See also Peter R. Roberts, 'A petition concerning Sir Richard Herbert', *BBCS*, XX(i) (1964), 47–9.

[79] NLW MS 9054E.532.

[80] NLW MS 9059E.1172.

[81] Penry Williams, *The Council in the Marches of Wales under Elizabeth I* (Cardiff, 1958), pp. 290–3.

[82] J. E. Neale, *The Elizabethan House of Commons* (London, 1955), pp. 120–8.

[83] NLW MS 464E.235.

[84] *Calendar of the Caernarvonshire Quarter Sessions Records*: I. *1541–1558*, ed. W. Ogwen Williams (Caernarfon, 1956), lxxx, p. 133 (37, 39, 40).

[85] *Glamorgan County History*, IV, pp. 175–91; Gareth E. Jones, 'Local government and administration in sixteenth-century Glamorgan', *Morgannwg*, IX (1965), 11–37; H. G. Owen, 'Family politics in Elizabethan Merionethshire', *BBCS*, XVIII (1959), 185–91.

[86] *Clenennau Letters and Papers*, no. 270, p. 78.

[87] E. N. Williams, 'Sir William Maurice of Clenennau', *TCHS*, XXIV (1963), 78–97.

[88] *Calendar of Salusbury Correspondence c.1553–1700*, ed. W. J. Smith (Cardiff, 1954), no. 156, p. 79.

[89] *Stradling Correspondence*, CLXI, p. 198.

[90] Ibid., LXVIII, p. 66.

[91] NLW MS 9059E.1188.

[92] *Clenennau Letters and Papers*, no. 401, pp. 114–15.

[93] Thomas Parry (ed.), *The Oxford Book of Welsh Verse* (Oxford, 1962), no. 120, pp. 244–8.

[94] *Clenennau Letters and Papers*, no. 11, p. 3. See also no. 144, p. 42.

[95] NLW MS 9052E.206.

[96] Stone, *Family, Sex and Marriage*, pp. 6–7. See also J. J. Hurwick, 'Lineage and kin in the sixteenth-century aristocracy: some comparative evidence on England and Germany', in A. L. Beier, David Cannadine and J. M. Rosenheim (eds.), *The First Modern Society: Essays in English History in Honour of Lawrence Stone* (Cambridge, 1989), pp. 33–61; David Cressy, 'Kinship and kin interaction in early modern England', *Past & Present*, 113 (Nov. 1986), 38–69.

[97] J. Wilson, 'Icons of unity', *History Today*, XLIII (1993), 14–20.

[98] Thomas Churchyard, *The Worthines of Wales*, p. 106.

[99] Colin A. Gresham, *Eifionydd: A Study in Landownership from the Medieval Period to the Present Day* (Cardiff, 1973), pp. 114–15.

[100] A. H. Dodd, *Studies in Stuart Wales* (Cardiff, 1952), pp. 3–12; John Penry, *Three Treatises*, p. 111.

[101] Penry, *Three Treatises*, p. 60.

[102] Cited in W. J. Gruffydd, *Llenyddiaeth Cymru*, p. 113.

[103] Merfyn Morgan (ed.), *Gweithiau Oliver Thomas ac Evan Roberts: Dau Biwritan Cymreig* (Cardiff, 1981), [21] et seq.; R. O'Day, *The English Clergy: The Emergence and Consolidation of a Profession, 1558–1642* (Leicester, 1979); J. T. Cliffe, *The Puritan Gentry: The Great Puritan Families of Early Stuart England* (London, 1984).

[104] *Rhagymadroddion*, p. 124.

[105] Bodleian Library, Oxford, Ashmolean MS 174, p. 483. Cited in Gwyn R. Thomas, 'Sir Thomas Myddelton II, 1586–1666' (unpublished University of Wales MA dissertation, 1967), p. 28.

[106] T. T. Lewis (ed.), *Letters of the Lady Brilliana Harley* (Camden Society, 1854).

[107] Rowland Vaughan, *Yr Ymarfer o Dduwioldeb*, ed. John Ballinger (Cardiff, 1930), xiii–xv.

[108] Henry Lewis (ed.), *Hen Gyflwyniadau* (Cardiff, 1948), pp. 31–6.

[109] *Glamorgan County History*, IV, pp. 245–9.

[110] Morgan, *Oliver Thomas ac Evan Roberts*, p. 108.

[111] A. J. Fletcher, *Reform in the Provinces: The Government of Stuart England* (London, 1986), pp. 78–83.

[112] A. H. Dodd, 'The pattern of politics in Stuart Wales', *TCS* (1948), 23. See J. Gwynn Williams, 'Rhai agweddau ar y gymdeithas Gymreig yn yr ail ganrif ar bymtheg', 42–50.

Notes to Conclusion

[1] Gruffydd Robert, *Gramadeg Cymraeg gan Gruffydd Robert*, ed. G. J. Williams (Cardiff, 1939), preface [5–6].

[2] *Clenennau Letters and Papers*, no. 474, pp. 134–5.

[3] *James Howell, Epistolae Ho-elianae (The Familiar Letters of James Howell)*, ed. J. Jacobs (London, 1892), I, p. 88.

[4] Edward Owen (ed.), *A Catalogue of the Manuscripts Relating to Wales in the British Museum*, Pt.1 (London, 1900), p. 72 (citing BL Lansdowne MS 111, fo. 10).

[5] *Funerall Sermon*, Ei.

[6] Ralph A. Griffiths, *Sir Rhys ap Thomas and his Family: A Study in the Wars of the Roses and Early Tudor Politics* (Cardiff, 1993), pp. 88–111.

[7] See William Rees, *The Union of England and Wales* (Cardiff, 1948), pp. 13–14.

[8] *Clenennau Letters and Papers*, no.106, p. 31.

[9] *Calendar of Star Chamber Proceedings concerning Wales*, ed. Ifan ab Owen Edwards (Cardiff, 1929), p. 90.

[10] NLW Add.MS 465E.324.

[11] *Clenennau Letters and Papers*, no. 48, p. 15.

[12] John Wynn, *History of the Gwydir Family and Memoirs*, ed. J. Gwynfor Jones (Llandysul, 1990), p. 35.

[13] Lawrence Stone, *The Crisis of the Aristocracy, 1558–1641* (Oxford, 1965), pp. 12–20.

[14] Glanmor Williams, *Renewal and Reformation: Wales c.1415–1642* (Oxford, 1993), pp. 354–7.

[15] Peter R. Roberts, 'The union with England and the identity of "Anglican" Wales', *Transactions of the Royal Historical Society*, XXII (1972), 62–70.

[16] Glanmor Williams, 'Some Protestant views of early British church history', in *Welsh Reformation Essays* (Cardiff, 1967), pp. 207–19. For a full discussion of this theme see the same author's *Reformation Views of Church History* (London, 1970).

[17] *Rhagymadroddion*, pp. 5–16.

[18] Ibid., pp. 17–43; A. O. Evans, *A Memorandum on the Legality of the Welsh Bible* (Cardiff, 1925), pp. 83–124.

[19] *Rhagymadroddion*, pp. 89–96.

[20] Peter R. Roberts, 'The union with England and the identity of "Anglican" Wales', 70.

[21] William Vaughan, *The Arraignment of slander* (London, 1630), p. 323.

[22] John Davies, *Cambrobrytannicae Cymraecaeve Linguae Institutiones et Rudimenta* (London, 1592), preface [3]; *Rhagymadroddion a Chyflwyniadau Lladin*, p. 91; A. I. Pryce, *The Diocese of Bangor in the Sixteenth Century* (Bangor, 1923), pp. 11, 23.

[23] William Camden, *Remaines concerning Britaine* (London, 1614), p. 11.

[24] W. Ogwen Williams, 'The social order in Tudor Wales', *TCS* (1967 ii), 167–78; J. Gwynfor Jones, 'The gentry', in Trevor Herbert and Gareth E. Jones (eds.), *The Tudors* (Cardiff, 1988), pp. 10–30.

Bibliography

A. Primary Sources

(a) Manuscript

(i) British Library
Cotton MS Augustus 1, i, 1v
Harleian MSS 283 fo. 153; 6997 fo. 74
Royal MS 18B vii

(ii) South Glamorgan County Library
MSS 4.58, 85; 4.76, 13; 4.329, 11(old Hafod MS 12): 4.474

(iii) Gwynedd Archives Service
A Selection of Caernarfonshire Quarter Sessions Files (X/QS)

(iv) National Library of Wales
Additional MSS 464E–466E
Brogyntyn MS 6,106
Llanstephan MSS 36,49; 133,85, 144,31
MS 1559,241
MS 5666
MS 9051E–9061E
Mostyn MS 161,566
Peniarth MS 327,165
Tredegar MS 148

(v) Public Record Office
Court of Requests 82/46
E.134 8 James I (Mich. 3)
SP 12, 12/162/29, 252/42,16
St Cha. 8 James I, 14/61/10; 14/76/3; 16/88/23; 202/23; 207/32

(vi) University College of North Wales
Baron Hill MS 6720

(b) Printed

Acts of the Privy Council, ed. J. R. Dasent (London, 1890–).
A Funerall Sermon preached . . . by the reverend Father in God, Richard . . . Bishoppe of Saint Dauys at the Buriall of the Right Honourable Walter Earle of Essex and Ewe (London, 1577).
Bacon, Francis, *Essays* (London, 1966 edn.).
Basilikon Doron, tr. Robert Holland [1604] (Cardiff, 1931 repr.).
Bayly, Lewis, *The Practice of Piety* (London, 1640 edn.).
Bowen, Ivor (ed.), *The Statutes of Wales* (London, 1908).

Bowyer, Robert, *The Parliamentary Diary of Robert Bowyer, 1606–1607*, ed. D. H. Willson (London, 1931).
Calendar of Letters Relating to North Wales, ed. B. E. Howells (Cardiff, 1967).
Calendar of Salusbury Correspondence c.1553–1700, ed. W. J. Smith (Cardiff, 1954).
Calendar of Star Chamber Proceedings concerning Wales, ed. Ifan ab Owen Edwards (Cardiff, 1929).
Calendar of State Papers Domestic (London, 1856–).
Calendar of the Caernarvonshire Quarter Sessions Records, I. *1541–1558*, ed. W. Ogwen Williams (Caernarfon, 1956).
Calendar of the Records of the Borough of Haverfordwest 1539–1660, ed. B. G. Charles (Cardiff, 1967).
Calendar of the Register of the Council in the Marches of Wales, 1569–91, ed. Ralph Flenley (London, 1916).
Calendar of Wynn of Gwydir Papers, 1515–1690, ed. John Ballinger (Cardiff, 1926).
Camden, William, *Remaines concerning Britaine* (London, 1623).
Canu Rhydd Cynnar, ed. T. H. Parry-Williams (Cardiff, 1932).
Castiglione, Baldassare, *The Book of the Courtier*, ed. J. H. Whitfield (London, 1975).
Cerddi'r Ficer: Detholiad o Gerddi Rhys Prichard, ed. Nesta Lloyd (Cyhoeddiadau Barddas, 1994).
Cerddi Rhydd Cynnar, ed. D. Lloyd Jenkins (Llandysul, 1932).
Cheke, John, *The Hurt of Sedicion howe greueous it is to a Communewelth* [1549] (London, 1971 edn.).
Churchyard, Thomas, *The Worthines of Wales* (London, 1587: 1776 edn.).
Clenennau Letters and Papers in the Brogyntyn Collection, ed. T. Jones Pierce, Pt. I, (NLW, Aberystwyth, 1947).
Conran, Anthony, *The Penguin Book of Welsh Verse* (London, 1967).
Davies, Dr John, *Cambrobrytannicae Cymraecaeve Linguae Institutiones et Rudimenta* (London, 1592).
Davies, J. H. (ed.), *Gweithiau Morgan Llwyd o Wynedd* (Bangor and London, 1908).
Elizabethan Episcopal Administration, III, ed. W. P. M. Kennedy (Alcuin club Collections, XXVII; London, 1924).
Ellis, Henry (ed.), *Original Letters Illustrative of English History* (London, 2nd ser., 1827).
Elyot, Thomas, *The Book named the Governor*, ed. S. E. Lehmberg (London, 1962).
Evans. A. O., *A Memorandum on the Legality of the Welsh Bible* (Cardiff, 1925).
Exchequer Proceedings (Equity) concerning Wales Henry VIII–Elizabeth, ed. Emyr Gwynne Jones (Cardiff, 1939).
Gentleman's Magazine, The, LV (London, 1785).
Gerald of Wales, *The Journey Through Wales/The Description of Wales*, ed. Lewis Thorpe (Harmondsworth, 1978).
Gramadegau'r Penceirddiaid, ed. G. J. Williams and E. J. Jones (Cardiff, 1934).
Gwaith Guto'r Glyn, ed. J. Ll. Williams and Ifor Williams (Cardiff, 1939).
Gwaith Siôn Tudur, ed. Enid Roberts (Cardiff, 1978).
Harrison, William, *The Description of England* (London, 1599), ed. Georges Edelen (New York, 1968 edn.).
Harry, George Owen, *The Genealogy of the High and Mighty Monarch, James . . . King of great Brittayne . . .* (London, 1604).
Hayward, J., *An Answer to the First Part of a Certaine Conference Concerning Succession* (London, 1603).
Hen Gerddi Gwleidyddol, 1588–1660, ed. J. H. Davies (Cymdeithas Llên Cymru; Cardiff, 1901).
Herbert Correspondence: The Sixteenth and Seventeenth-Century Letters of the Herberts of Chirbury, Powis Castle and Dolguog . . ., ed. W. J. Smith (Cardiff, 1978).

Herbert, Edward Lord, *The Autobiography of Edward, Lord Herbert of Cherbury*, ed. S. Lee (London, 1886).

HMC, *Calendar of the Manuscripts of the Marquis of Salisbury (Hatfield House MSS)*, XVI (London, 1933).

Howell, Benjamin, *Law and Disorder in Tudor Monmouthshire* (Cardiff, 1995).

Howell, James, *Epistolae Ho-elianae (The Familiar Letters of James Howell)*, ed. J. Jacobs (London, 1892).

Hughes, P. L., and Larkin, J. F. (eds.), *Tudor Royal Proclamations:* I, 1485–1553 (Yale, 1964), II, 1553–87 (Yale, 1969), III, 1588–1603 (Yale, 1969).

Jones, Emyr Gwynne (ed.), 'History of the Bulkeley Family (NLW MS 9080E)', *TAAS* (1948).

Journals of the House of Commons, I, 1547–1628 (London, 1803).

Kyffin, Maurice, *The Blessednes of Brytaine or a Celebration of the Queenes Holyday* (London, 1587: 1885 edn.).

Kyffin, Maurice, *Continuation of the Blessednes of Brytaine* (London, 1588).

Lambarde, William, *Eirenarcha or the office of Justices of Peace* (London, 1581–2), ed. P. Glazebrook (London, 1972).

Larkin, J. F., and Hughes, P. L. (eds.), *Stuart Royal Proclamations*, I (Oxford, 1973).

Leland, John, *Itinerary in Wales*, ed. L. Toulmin Smith (London, 1908).

Letters and Papers, Foreign and Domestic, of the Reign of Henry VIII . . . , ed. J. S. Brewer, J. Gairdner and R. H. Brodie (London, 1862–1932).

Letters of the Lady Brilliana Harley, ed. T. T. Lewis (Camden Society, 1854).

Lewis, Henry (ed.), *Hen Gyflwyniadau* (Cardiff, 1948).

Lewis, Rice, *A Breviat of Glamorgan, 1596–1600*, ed. William Rees, *South Wales and Monmouth Record Society*, 3 (1954).

Llwyd, Humphrey, *Commentarioli Descriptionis Britannicae Fragmentum* (Cologne, 1572), tr. by Thomas Twyne as *The Breuiary of Britayne* (London, 1573).

Lyly, J., *Euphues. The Anatomy of Wit* (London, 1581).

Mathew, David, 'Some Elizabethan Documents', *BBCS*, VI (1931).

McCann, J. and Connolly, H., (eds.), 'Memorials of Father Augustine Baker and other documents relating to the English Benedictines', *Catholic Record Society Publications*, XXXIII (1933).

Merrick, Rice, *Morganiae Archaiographia: A Book of the Antiquities of Glamorgan-shire*, ed. Brian Ll. James (Barry, 1983).

Morgan, Merfyn (ed.), *Gweithiau Oliver Thomas ac Evan Roberts: Dau Biwritan Cymreig* (Cardiff, 1981).

Morrice, J. C. (ed.), *Barddoniaeth Wiliam Llŷn* (Bangor, 1908).

Nichols, J., *The Progresses and Public Processions of Queen Elizabeth . . .* I (London, 1788).

Notebook of John Penry, The, ed. A. Peel (Camden Society, 1944).

Owen, Edward (ed.), *Catalogue of Manuscripts relating to Wales in the British Museum*, 4 vols. (London, 1900–22).

Owen, George, *The Description of Penbrokshire*, ed. Henry Owen, 4 vols. (London, 1902–36).

Owen, George, *The Description of Pembrokeshire*, ed. Dillwyn Miles (Llandysul, 1994).

Pace, Richard, *De Fructu qui ex doctrina percipitur liber* (Basel, 1517).

Parry, Glyn (ed.), *A Guide to the Records of Great Sessions in Wales* (Aberystwyth, 1995).

Parry, Thomas (ed.), *The Oxford Book of Welsh Verse* (Oxford, 1962).

Peacham, Henry (the younger), *The compleat gentleman fashioning him absolute in the most necessary & commendable qualities concerning minde or bodie that may be required in a noble gentleman* (London, 1622).

Penry, John, *Three Treatises Concerning Wales*, ed. David Williams (Cardiff, 1960).

Powel, David, *Historie of Cambria, now called Wales* (Amsterdam, 1969 edn.).

Prichard, Rhys, *Y Seren Foreu, neu Ganwyll y Cymry*, ed. Rice Rees (Wrexham, 1867).

Read, Conyers (ed.), *William Lambarde on Local Government* (Ithaca, NY, 1962).

Report on the Manuscripts of Lord de L'Isle and Dudley preserved at Penshurst Place, III (London, 1936).

Robert, Gruffydd, *Gramadeg Cymraeg gan Gruffydd Robert*, ed. G. J. Williams (Cardiff, 1939).

Rhagymadroddion, 1547–1659, ed. Garfield H. Hughes (Cardiff, 1951).

Rhagymadroddion a Chyflwyniadau Lladin, 1551–1632, ed. Ceri Davies (Cardiff, 1980).

Rhyddiaith Gymraeg: Detholion o Lawysgrifau a Llyfrau Printiedig, II, *1547–1618*, ed. Thomas Jones (Cardiff, 1988).

Siddons, M. P., *The Development of Welsh Heraldry*, 3 vols (Aberystwyth, 1991 and 1993).

Smith, A. J., *John Donne: The Complete English Poems* (London, 1971).

Smith, H., *A preparation to mariage . . .* (London, 1591).

Smith, Thomas, *De Republica Anglorum*, ed. Mary Dewar (Cambridge, 1982).

Stradling Correspondence, The, ed. J. M. Traherne (London, 1840).

Stradling, John, *Beati Pacifici: A Divine Poem written to the King* (London, 1623).

Stradling, John, *The Storie of the Lower Borowes of Merthyrmawr*, ed. H. J. Randall and William Rees (Cardiff, 1932).

Summary Catalogue of the Manuscripts of South Glamorgan Libraries, Cardiff Central Library, compiled by G. C. G. Thomas and Daniel Huws (Aberystwyth, 1994).

William Lambarde and Local Government, ed. Conyers Reade (New York, 1962).

Works of William Laud, The, ed. W. Scott (I–II) and J. Bliss (III–VII) (Oxford, 1847–60).

Thomas, D. Aneirin (ed.), *The Welsh Elizabethan Catholic Martyrs: The Trial Documents of Saint Richard Gwyn and of the Venerable William Davies* (Cardiff, 1971).

Two Books of Homilies Appointed to be read in Churches, The, ed. John Griffiths (Oxford, 1859).

Vaughan, William, *The Golden-grove* (London, 1600).

Vaughan, William, *The Golden-fleece* (London, 1626).

Vaughan, William, *The arraignment of slander . . .* (London, 1630).

Wheler, G., *The Protestant Monastery: or, Christian Oeconomicks* (London, 1698).

Wynn, John, *History of the Gwydir Family and Memoirs*, ed. J. G. Jones (Llandysul, 1990).

Yr Ymarfer o Dduwioldeb, tr. Robert Vaughan, ed. John Ballinger (Cardiff 1930).

B. Secondary Works

Ashton, Robert, *Reformation and Revolution, 1558–1660* (London, 1984).

Baker, D. (ed.), *Reform and Reformation: England and the Continent c.1500–c.1750* (Oxford, 1979).

Barry, J., and Brooks, C. (eds.), *The Middling Sort of People: Culture, Society and Politics in England, 1550–1800* (London, 1994).

Bebb, W. Ambrose, *Cyfnod y Tuduriaid* (Wrexham and Cardiff, 1939).

Beier, A. L., *The Problem of the Poor in Tudor and Early Stuart England* (London, 1983).

Beier, A. L., *Masterless Men: The Vagrancy Problem in England, 1560–1640* (London, 1985).

Beier, A. L., Cannadine, David and Rosenheim, J. M. (eds.), *The First Modern Society: Essays in English History in Honour of Lawrence Stone* (Cambridge, 1989).

Bourne, E. C. E., *The Anglicanism of William Laud* (London, 1947).

Bowen, D. J., *Gruffudd Hiraethog a'i Oes* (Cardiff, 1958).

Carr, A. D., *Owen of Wales: The End of the House of Gwynedd* (Cardiff, 1991).

Carr, A. D., *Medieval Wales* (London, 1995).

Caspari, Fritz, *Humanism and the Social Order in Tudor England* (Chicago, 1954).

Charles-Edwards, T. M., *Early Irish and Welsh Kinship* (Cambridge, 1993).

Charlton, Kenneth, *Education in Renaissance England* (London, 1965).

Cliffe, J. T., *The Puritan Gentry: The Great Puritan Families of Early Stuart England* (London, 1984).

Collins, S. L., *From Divine Cosmos to Sovereign State* (Oxford, 1989).

Collinson, Patrick, *The Elizabethan Puritan Movement* (Cambridge, 1967).

Cooper, J. P., *Land, Men and Beliefs: Studies in Early-Modern History*, ed. G. E. Aylmer and J. S. Morrill (London, 1983).

Cross, Claire, *Church and People 1450–1660: The Triumph of the Laity in the English Church* (London, 1987).

Davies, Glenys, *Noddwyr Beirdd ym Meirion* (Dolgellau, 1974).

Davies, R. R., *Conquest, Coexistence and Change: Wales c.1063–1415* (Cardiff and Oxford, 1987, paperback edn., *The Age of Conquest, 1063–1415* Oxford, 1993).

Deacon, Richard, *Madog and the Discovery of America* (London, 1966).

Deacon, Richard, *John Dee* (London, 1968).

Dickens, A. G., *The English Reformation* (London, 1964).

Dictionary of National Biography, ed. L. Stephen and S. Lee (London, 1885–1900).

Dictionary of Welsh Biography to 1940, ed. J. E. Lloyd and R. T. Jenkins (London, 1959).

Dodd, A. H., *Studies in Stuart Wales* (Cardiff, 1952).

Doran, S., *Elizabeth I and Religion, 1559–1603* (London, 1994).

Edwards, J. Goronwy, *The Principality of Wales, 1267–1967: A Study in Constitutional History* (Caernarfon, 1969).

Ellis, S. G., *Tudor Ireland: Crown, Community and the Conflict of Cultures, 1470–1603* (London, 1985).

Ellis, S. G., and Barber, S. (eds.), *Conquest and Union: Fashioning a British State, 1485–1725* (London, 1995).

Elton, G. R., *England under the Tudors* (Cambridge, 1957 edn.).

Evans, Gwynfor, *Land of My Fathers* (Swansea, 1974).

Everitt, A., *Change in the Provinces: The Seventeenth Century* (Leicester, 1969).

Fincham, K. (ed.), *The Early Stuart Church: 1603–1642* (London, 1993).

Fletcher, A., *Reform in the Provinces: The Government of Stuart England* (London, 1986).

Fletcher, A., and Stevenson, J. (eds.), *Order and Disorder in Early Modern England* (Cambridge, 1985).

Fox, Levi (ed.), *English Historical Scholarship in the Sixteenth and Seventeenth Centuries* (Oxford, 1956).

French, P. J., *John Dee: The World of an Elizabethan Magus* (London, 1972).

Fussner, F. Smith, *The Historical Revolution, 1580–1640* (London, 1962).

Greenleaf, W. H., *Order, Empiricism and Politics: Two Traditions of English Political Thought, 1500–1700* (Oxford, 1964).

Gresham, Colin A., *Eifionydd: A Study in Landownership from the Medieval Period to the Present Day* (Cardiff, 1973).

Griffith, J. E. (ed.), *Pedigrees of Anglesey and Caernarvonshire Families* (Horncastle, 1914).

Griffith, William P., *Learning, Law and Religion: Higher Education and Welsh Society c.1540–1640* (Cardiff, 1996).

Griffiths, Ralph A. (ed.), *The Principality of Wales in the Later Middle Ages: The Structure and Personnel of Government*, I, *South Wales 1277–1536* (Cardiff, 1972).

Griffiths, Ralph A., *Sir Rhys ap Thomas and his Family: A Study in the Wars of the Roses and Early Tudor Politics* (Cardiff, 1993).

Gruffydd, R. Geraint, *Argraffwyr Cyntaf Cymru: Gwasgau Dirgel y Catholigion adeg Elisabeth* (Cardiff, 1972).

Gruffydd, R. Geraint (ed.), *Meistri'r Canrifoedd: Ysgrifau ar Hanes Llenyddiaeth Gymraeg gan Saunders Lewis* (Cardiff, 1973).

Gruffydd, R. Geraint, 'In that Gentile Country . . .': The Beginnings of Puritan Nonconformity in Wales* (Bridgend, 1975).

Gruffydd, R. Geraint, *The Translating of the Bible into the Welsh Tongue* (London, 1988).

Gruffydd, R. Geraint (ed.), *Y Gair ar Waith: Ysgrifau ar yr Etifeddiaeth Feiblaidd yng Nghymru* (Cardiff, 1988).

Gruffydd, R. Geraint, *A Guide to Welsh Literature*, III: *c.1530–1700*, 2nd edn., (Cardiff, 1997).

Gruffydd, W. J., *Llenyddiaeth Cymru: Rhyddiaith o 1540 hyd 1660* (Wrexham, 1926).

Hart, A. Tindal, *The Country Clergy in Elizabethan and Stuart Times, 1558–1660* (London, 1958).

Heal, F., *Of Prelates and Provinces: A Study of the Economic and Social Position of the Tudor Episcopacy* (Cambridge, 1980).

Heal, F., *Hospitality in Early Modern England* (Oxford, 1990).

Heal, F., and Holmes, C., *The Gentry in England and Wales, 1500–1700* (London, 1994).

Heal, F., and O'Day, R. (eds.), *Church and Society in England, Henry VIII to James I* (Basingstoke, 1977).

Herbert, Trevor, and Jones, Gareth E. (eds.), *Tudor Wales* (Cardiff, 1988).

Hill, Christopher, *Economic Problems of the Church from Archbishop Whitgift to the Long Parliament* (Oxford, 1956).

Hotson, L., *Mr W. H.* (London, 1964).

Houlbrooke, R., *The English Family, 1450–1700* (London, 1984).

Howells, B. E. (ed.), *Pembrokeshire County History*, III. *Early Modern Pembrokeshire* (Haverfordwest, 1987).

Hoyle, R. W. (ed.), *The Estates of the English Crown, 1588–1640* (Cambridge, 1992).

Hughes, W., *The Life and Times of Bishop William Morgan* (London, 1891).

Hurstfield, J., *The Elizabethan Nation* (London, 1964).

Hurstfield, J., and Smith, A. G., *Elizabethan England: State and Society* (London, 1972).

Huizinga, J., *The Waning of the Middle Ages* (London, 1955).

James, M., *Society, Politics and Culture: Studies in Early Modern England* (Cambridge, 1986).

Jarman, A. O. H., and Hughes, G. R. (eds.), *A Guide to Welsh Literature*, II (Swansea, 1979).

Jenkins, Geraint H., *Protestant Dissenters in Wales 1639–89* (Cardiff, 1991).

Jenkins, Geraint H. (ed.), *A Social History of the Welsh Language: The Welsh Language before the Industrial Revolution* (Cardiff, 1997).

Jenkins, J. P., *The Making of a Ruling Class: Glamorgan Gentry 1640–1790* (Cambridge, 1983).

Jenkins, J. P., *A History of Modern Wales, 1536–1990* (London, 1992).

Jones, Emyr Gwynne, *Cymru a'r Hen Ffydd* (Cardiff, 1951).

Jones, Gareth E., *The Gentry and the Elizabethan State* (Swansea, 1977).

Jones, J. Gwynfor, *Wales and the Tudor State, 1534–1603* (Cardiff, 1989).

Jones, J. Gwynfor (ed.), *Class, Community and Culture in Tudor Wales* (Cardiff, 1989).

Jones, J. Gwynfor, *Concepts of Order and Gentility in Wales 1540–1640* (Llandysul, 1992).

Jones, J. Gwynfor, *The Morgan Family of Tredegar: Origins, Growth and Advancement c.1340–1674* (Newport, 1995).

Jones, J. Gwynfor, *The Wynn Family of Gwydir: Origins, Growth and Development c.1490–1674* (Aberystwyth, 1995).

Jones, J. Gwynfor, *Law, Order and Government in Caernarfonshire, 1558–1640: Justices of the Peace and the Gentry* (Cardiff, 1996).

Jones, J. Gwynfor, *Beirdd yr Uchelwyr a'r Gymdeithas yng Nghymru c.1536–1640* (Denbigh, 1997).

Jones, N. L., *Faith by Statute: Parliament and the Settlement of Religion, 1559* (London, 1982).

Jones, R. Tudur, *Hanes Annibynwyr Cymru* (Swansea, 1966).

Jones, W. R. D., *The Tudor Commonwealth 1529–1559* (London, 1970).

Kelso, Ruth, *The Doctrine of the English Gentleman in the Sixteenth Century* (Boston, MA, 1954).

Lake, P., *Anglicans and Puritans? Conformist Thought from Whitgift to Hooker* (London, 1988).

Lewis, Saunders, *Tynged yr Iaith* (London, 1962).

Lewis, W. J., *Leadmining in Wales* (Cardiff, 1967).

Lloyd, H. A., *The Gentry of South West Wales, 1540–1640* (Cardiff, 1968).

Loomie, A. J., *The Spanish Elizabethans, the English Exiles and the Court of Philip II* (London, 1963).

Lovejoy, A. O., *The Great Chain of Being* (Boston, MA, 1936).

Manning, B., *The English People and the English Revolution* (London, 1976).

Mason, P., *The English Gentleman: The Rise and Fall of an Ideal* (London, 1982).

Mathew, David, *The Celtic Peoples and Renaissance Europe* (London, 1933).

Morgan, Gerald, *A Welsh House and its Family: The Vaughans of Trawsgoed: A Study of the Vaughan Family and Estate through Seven Centuries* (Llandysul, 1997).

Moore, D. (ed.), *Eighteenth-Century Wales* (Swansea, 1976).

Mostyn, Lord, and Glenn, T. A., *History of the Family of Mostyn of Mostyn* (London, 1925).

Neale, J., *The Elizabethan House of Commons* (London, 1955).

Nuttall, G. F., *The Puritan Spirit: Essays and Addresses* (London, 1967).

O'Day, R., *The English Clergy: The Emergence and Consolidation of a Profession, 1558–1642* (Leicester, 1979).

O'Day, R. and Heal, F. (eds.), *Princes and Paupers in the English Church, 1500–1800* (Leicester, 1981).

Owen, G. D., *Elizabethan Wales: The Social Scene* (Cardiff, 1962).

Owen, G. D., *Wales in the Reign of James I* (London, 1988).

Palmer, N., *A History of the Old Parish Church of Gresford* (Wrexham, 1905).

Plumb, J. H. (ed.), *Studies in Social History: A Tribute to G. M. Trevelyan* (London, 1955).

Powell, N. W., *Dyffryn Clwyd in the Time of Elizabeth I* (Ruthin, 1991).

Pryce, A. I., *The Diocese of Bangor in the Sixteenth Century* (Bangor, 1923).

Rabb, T. K., *The Struggle for Stability in Early Modern Europe* (Oxford, 1975).

Rees, William, *The Union of England and Wales* (Cardiff, 1948).

Rees, William, *Industry Before the Industrial Revolution*, 2 vols (Cardiff, 1968).

Richards, Thomas, *A History of the Puritan Movement in Wales, 1639–1654* (London, 1920).

Roberts, Glyn, *Aspects of Welsh History*, ed. A. H. Dodd and J. Gwynn Williams (Cardiff, 1969).

Róderick, A. J. (ed.), *Wales Through the Ages*, II (Llandybie, 1960).

Rowse, A. L., *The Elizabethan Renaissance: The Life of the Society* (London, 1971).

Royal Commission on Ancient Monuments in Wales and Monmouthshire (Inventories): Denbighshire (1914), Carmarthenshire (1917), Merioneth (1921), Pembrokeshire (1925), Anglesey (1937), Caernarfonshire (3 vols, 1956–64), Glamorgan (1976–).

Russell, Conrad, *The Origins of the English Civil War* (London, 1973).

Samaha, J., *Law and Order in Historical Perspective: The Case of Elizabethan Essex* (London, 1974).

Schochet, G. J., *Patriarchalism in Political Thought* (Oxford, 1975).

Sharpe, J. A., *Early Modern England: A Social History 1550–1760* (London, 1987).

Sharpe. R., *Criticism and Compliment: The Politics of Literature in the England of Charles I* (Cambridge, 1987).

Skeel, C. A. J., *The Council in the Marches of Wales: A Study in Local Government during the Sixteenth and Seventeenth Centuries* (London, 1903).

Smith, Peter, *Houses of the Welsh Countryside* (London, 1980 edn.).

Stephens, R., *Gwynedd, 1528–1547: Economy and Society in Tudor Wales* (Ann Arbor, MI, 1979).

Stephens, Thomas, *An Essay on the Discovery of America by Madoc ap Owen Gwynedd in the Twelfth Century*, ed. L. I. Reynolds (London, 1893).

Stevenson, B. (ed.), *The Home Book of Quotations* (New York, 1967 edn.).

Stone, Lawrence, *The Crisis of the Aristocracy, 1558–1641* (Oxford, 1965).

Stone, Lawrence, *The Family, Sex and Marriage in England 1500–1800* (New York, 1977).

Stone, Lawrence, and Fawtier Stone, J.C., *An Open Elite? England 1540–1880* (abridged version, Oxford, 1986).

Strong, Roy, *The Cult of Elizabeth: Elizabethan Portraiture and Pageantry* (London, 1977).

Strong, Roy, *Gloriana: The Portraits of Queen Elizabeth I* (London, 1987).

Thirsk, Joan (ed.), *Agrarian History of England and Wales:* IV. *1500–1640* (Cambridge, 1967).

Thomas, D. R., *The Life and Work of Bishop Davies and William Salesbury* (Oswestry, 1902).

Thomas, Keith, *Religion and the Decline of Magic: Studies in Popular Beliefs in Sixteenth- and Seventeenth-Century England* (London, 1971).

Tillyard, E. M. W., *The Elizabethan World Picture* (London, 1960).

Tomlinson, H. (ed.), *Before the English Civil War* (London, 1983).

Turner, R., *Plas Mawr, Conwy* (Cardiff, Cadw (Welsh Historic Monuments), 1997).

Tyacke, N., *Anti-Calvinists: The Rise of English Arminianism c.1590–1640* (Oxford, 1987).

Wagner, Anthony, *English Genealogy* (Oxford, 1960).

Wagner, Anthony, *Heralds of England: A History of the Office and College of Arms* (London, 1967).

Waters, W. H., *The Edwardian Settlement of North Wales in its Administrative and Legal Aspects, 1284–1343* (Cardiff, 1935).

Wernham, R. B., *Before the Armada: The Growth of English Foreign Policy, 1485–1588* (London, 1966).

Wernham, R. B., *After the Armada: Elizabethan England and the Struggle for Western Europe, 1588–1595* (Oxford, 1984).

Williams, G. J., *Traddodiad Llenyddol Morgannwg* (Cardiff, 1948).

Williams, Glanmor, *Reformation Views of Church History* (London, 1970).

Williams, Glanmor, *Welsh Reformation Essays* (Cardiff, 1967).

Williams, Glanmor (ed.), *Glamorgan County History,* IV. *Early Modern Glamorgan from the Act of Union to the Industrial Revolution* (Cardiff, 1974).

Williams, Glanmor, *Religion, Language and Nationality in Wales* (Cardiff, 1979).
Williams, Glanmor, *Grym Tafodau Tân: Ysgrifau Hanesyddol ar Grefydd a Diwylliant* (Llandysul, 1984).
Williams, Glanmor, *Recovery, Reorientation and Reformation: Wales c.1415–1642* (Oxford and Cardiff, 1987; *Renewal and Reformation: Wales c.1415–1642*, Oxford, 1993 edn.).
Williams, Glanmor, *Henry Tudor and Wales* (Cardiff, 1985).
Williams, Glanmor, and Jones, R. O. (eds.), *The Celts and the Renaissance: Tradition and Innovation* (Cardiff, 1990).
Williams, Glanmor, *The Welsh and their Religion* (Cardiff, 1991).
Williams, Glanmor, *Wales and the Act of Union* (Bangor, 1992).
Williams, Glanmor, *Wales and the Reformation* (Cardiff, 1997).
Williams, Gwyn A., *Welsh Wizard and British Empire: Dr John Dee and a Welsh Identity* (Cardiff, 1980).
Williams, Gwyn A., *When was Wales? A History of the Welsh* (London, 1985).
Williams, Gwyn A., *Madoc: The Legend of the Welsh Discovery of America* (Oxford, 1987).
Williams, Penry, *The Council in the Marches of Wales under Elizabeth I* (Cardiff, 1958).
Williams, Stewart (ed.), *Vale of History* (Cowbridge, 1960).
Williams, Stewart (ed.), *Glamorgan Historian*, V (Cowbridge, 1968).
Williams, W. Ogwen, *Tudor Gwynedd* (Caernarfon, 1958).
Williams, W. R., *The Parliamentary History of the Principality of Wales, 1541–1895* (Brecknock, 1895).
Williams, W. R., *The History of the Great Sessions in Wales, 1542–1899* (Brecknock, 1899).
Willis, Browne, *A Survey of the Cathedral Church of St Asaph* (London, 1720).
Wrightson, K., *English Society, 1580–1680* (London, 1982).

C. Articles and Chapters in Volumes

Barley, M. W., 'Rural housing in Wales', in Joan Thirsk (ed.), *Agrarian History of England and Wales:* IV. *1500–1640* (Cambridge, 1967).
Berlatsky, J., 'The Elizabethan episcopate: patterns of life and expenditure', in R. O'Day and F. Heal (eds.), *Princes and Paupers in the English Church*, 1500–1800 (Leicester, 1981).
Bindoff, S. T., 'The Stuarts and their style', *EHR*, LX (1945).
Carr, A. D., 'The Mostyns of Mostyn, 1540–1642', *FHSJ*, XXVIII (i) (1977–8); XXX (1981–2).
Carr, A. D., 'Gwilym ap Gruffydd and the rise of the Penrhyn estate', *WHR*, XV (1990).
Cooper, J. P., 'Ideas of gentility in early-modern England', in J. P. Cooper, *Land, Men and Beliefs: Studies in Early-Modern History*, ed. G. E. Aylmer and J. S. Morrill (London, 1983).
Cressy, David, 'Kinship and kin interaction in early modern England', *Past and Present*, CXIII (Nov. 1986).
Cross, Claire, 'Churchmen and the royal supremacy', in F. Heal and R. O'Day (eds.), *Church and Society in England: Henry VIII to James I* (London, 1977).
Davies. R. R., 'The twilight of Welsh law 1284–1536', *History*, LI, 172 (1966).
Dodd, A. H., 'Wales's parliamentary apprenticeship (1536–1625', *TCS* (1942).
Dodd, A. H., 'North Wales in the Essex revolt of 1601', *EHR*, LIX (1944).
Dodd, A. H., 'The pattern of Welsh politics in Stuart Wales', *TCS* (1948).
Dodd, A. H., 'The civil war in east Denbighshire', *TDHS*, III (1954).

Dodd, A. H., 'Wales under the early Stuarts', in A. J. Roderick (ed.), *Wales Through the Ages*, II (Llandybïe, 1960).

Dodd, A. H., 'Bishop Lewes Bayly c.1575–1631', *TCHS*, XXVIII (1967).

Ellis, M., 'Cyflwyniad Rowland Vaughan, Caergai, i'w gyfieithiad o *Eikon Basilike*', *NLWJ*, 1(3) (1940).

Emery, Frank, 'The farming regions of Wales', in Joan Thirsk (ed.), *Agrarian History of England and Wales: IV, 1500–1640* (Cambridge, 1967).

Evans, W. G., 'Derfel Gadarn – a celebrated victim of the Reformation', *JMHRS*, XI (ii) (1991).

Fincham, K., and Lake, P., 'The ecclesiastical policies of James I and Charles I', in K. Fincham (ed.), *The Early Stuart Church, 1603–1642* (London, 1993).

Fletcher, A. J., 'Honour, reputation and local office-holding in Elizabethan and Stuart England', in A. J. Fletcher and J. Stevenson (eds.), *Order and Disorder in Early Modern England* (Cambridge, 1985).

Flower, R., 'William Salesbury, Richard Davies and Archbishop Parker', *NLWJ*, II (1941).

Gray, M., 'Power, patronage and politics: office-holding and administration on the crown's estates in Wales', in R. W. Hoyle (ed.), *The Estates of the English Crown, 1588–1640* (Cambridge, 1992).

Gray, M., 'The cloister and the hearth: Anthony Kitchin and Hugh Jones, two Reformation bishops of Llandaff', *Journal of Welsh Religious History*, III (1995).

Griffiths, Ralph A., 'The rise of the Stradlings of St Donat's', *Morgannwg*, VII (1963).

Griffiths, Ralph A., 'The twelve knights of Glamorgan', in Stewart Williams (ed.), *Glamorgan Historian*, III (Cowbridge, 1966).

Gruenfelder, J. K., 'The Wynns of Gwydir and parliamentary elections 1604–40', *WHR*, IX (1978).

Gruffydd, R. Geraint, 'Gwasg ddirgel yr ogof yn Rhiwledyn', *Journal of the Welsh Bibliographical Society*, IX (1958).

Gruffydd, R. Geraint, 'Dr Michael Roberts o Fôn a Beibl bach 1630', *TAAS* (1989).

Gruffydd, R. Geraint, 'The Renaissance and Welsh literature', in Glanmor Williams and R. O. Jones (eds.), *The Celts and the Renaissance: Tradition and Innovation* (Cardiff, 1990).

Guy, John, 'The Tudor age', in K. O. Morgan (ed.), *The Sphere Illustrated History of Britain, 1485–1789* (London, 1985).

Gwyndaf, R., 'Sir Richard Clough of Denbigh c.1530–1570', *TDHS*, XIX (1970), XX (1971), XXII (1973).

Habakkuk, H. J., 'Daniel Finch, 2nd earl of Nottingham; his house and estate', in J. H. Plumb (ed.), *Studies in Social History* (London, 1955).

Ham, R. E., 'The four shire controversy', *WHR*, VIII (1977).

Heal, F., 'The ideal of hospitality in early Modern England', *Past & Present*, CII (1964).

Hoskins, W. G., 'The rebuilding of rural England', *Past & Present*, IV (1953).

Hoskins, W. G., 'Harvest fluctuations and English economic history, 1480–1619', *The Agricultural Historical Review*, XII (1964).

Hoskins, W. G., 'Harvest fluctuations and English economic history, 1620–1759', *The Agricultural History Review*, XVI (1968).

Houlbrooke, R., 'The Protestant episcopate 1547–1603: the Protestant contribution', in F. Heal and R. O'Day (eds.), *Church and Society in England: Henry VIII to James I* (London, 1977).

Howells, J. M., 'The Crosswood estate', *Ceredigion*, III (1956).

Hughes, Arwyn Ll., 'Rhai o noddwyr y beirdd yn sir Feirionnydd', *Llên Cymru*, X (1969).

Huizinga, J., 'The hierarchic conception of society', in *The Waning of the Middle Ages* (London, 1955).

James, Brian Ll., 'The evolution of a radical: the life and career of William Erbery (1604–54)', *The Journal of Welsh Ecclesiastical History*, III (1986).

Jones, Bobi, 'Beirdd yr uchelwyr a'r byd', in J. E. Caerwyn Williams (ed.), *Ysgrifau Beirniadol*, VIII (Denbigh, 1974).

Jones, E. D., 'Robert Vaughan of Hengwrt', *JMHRS*, I (1949).

Jones, E. D., 'The Brogyntyn Welsh manuscripts', *NLWJ*, VII (3) (1952).

Jones, E. D., 'The family of Nannau (Nanney) of Nannau', *JMHRS*, II (1953).

Jones, Emyr Gwynne, 'The Caernarvonshire freeholders and the Forest of Snowdon', in 'The Caernarvonshire squires, 1558–1625' (unpublished University of Wales MA dissertation, 1936).

Jones, Emyr Gwynne, 'County politics and electioneering, 1558–1625', *TCHS*, I (1939).

Jones, Emyr Gwynne, 'Anglesey and invasion, 1539–1603', *TAAS* (1947).

Jones, Emyr Gwynne, 'A Llandegai pew dispute', *TCHS*, IX (1948).

Jones, Francis, 'An approach to Welsh genealogy', *TCS* (1948).

Jones, Francis, 'The Vaughans of Golden Grove', *TCS* (1963).

Jones, Francis, 'The old families of Wales', in D. Moore (ed.), *Eighteenth-Century Wales* (Swansea, 1976).

Jones, Francis, 'Welsh pedigrees', in *Burke's Genealogical and Heraldic History of the Landed Gentry*, ed. L. G. Pine (London, 1952).

Jones, Francis, 'An approach to Welsh genealogy', *TCS* (1948).

Jones, Gareth E., 'Local government and administration in sixteenth-century Glamorgan', *Morgannwg*, IX (1965).

Jones, Gareth E., 'A case of corruption', in Stewart Williams (ed.), *Glamorgan Historian* (Cowbridge, 1968).

Jones, J. Gwynfor, 'Bishop William Morgan's dispute with John Wynn of Gwydir in 1603–04', *Journal of the Historical Society of the Church in Wales*, XXII (1972).

Jones, J. Gwynfor, 'Richard Parry, Bishop of St. Asaph: some aspects of his career', *BBCS*, XXVI (1975).

Jones, J. Gwynfor, 'The Welsh poets and their patrons c.1550–1640', *WHR*, IX (1979).

Jones, J. Gwynfor, 'Thomas Davies and William Hughes: two Reformation bishops of St Asaph', *BBCS*, XXIX(i) (1981).

Jones, J. Gwynfor, 'Governance, order and stability in Caernarfonshire c.1540–1640', *TCHS*, XLIV (1983).

Jones, J. Gwynfor, 'Concepts of continuity and change in Anglesey after the Acts of Union 1536–1603', *TAAS* (1990).

Jones, J. Gwynfor, 'The Reformation bishops of St Asaph', *Journal of Welsh Ecclesiastical History*, VII (1990).

Jones, J. Gwynfor, 'Sir John Wynn, junior, of Gwydir and Llanfrothen and the "Grand Tour" (1613–14)', *JMHRS*, XI (1993).

Jones, J. Gwynfor, 'John Penry: government, order and the "perishing souls" of Wales', *TCS* (1993).

Jones, J. Gwynfor, 'The gentry of east Glamorgan: Welsh cultural dimensions, 1540–1640', *Morgannwg*, XXXVII (1993).

Jones, J. Gwynfor, 'Maurice Kyffin a Huw Lewys: dau amddiffynnydd y ffydd Brotestannaidd yng Nghymru yn 1595', in J. E. Caerwyn Williams (ed.), *Ysgrifau Beirniadol*, XXI (Denbigh, 1995).

Jones, J. Gwynfor, 'Robert Holland a *Basilikon Doron* y brenin Iago', in J. E. Caerwyn Williams (ed.), *Ysgrifau Beirniadol* (Denbigh, 1997).

Jones, J. Gwynfor, 'The Welsh language and local government', in Geraint H. Jenkins (ed.), *A Social History of the Welsh Language: The Welsh Language before the Industrial Revolution* (Cardiff, 1997).

Jones, S. R., and Smith, J. T., 'The houses of Breconshire: V', *Brycheiniog*, XIII (1968–9).

Jones, T. Gwynn, 'Cultural bases: a study of the Tudor period in Wales', *Y Cymmrodor*, XXXI (1921).

Law, T. G., 'The miraculous cross of St Donat's, 1559–61', *EHR*, I (1886).

Lewis, Ceri W., 'The literary history of Glamorgan from 1550 to 1770', in Glanmor Williams (ed.), *Glamorgan County History*, IV (Cardiff, 1974).

Lewis, Ceri W,. 'Syr Edward Stradling, 1519–1609', in J. E. Caerwyn Williams (ed.), *Ysgrifau Beirniadol*, XIX (Denbigh, 1994).

Lewis, Ceri W., 'The decline of professional poetry' in R. Geraint Gruffydd (ed.), *A Guide to Welsh Literature c. 1530–1700*, III (Cardiff, 1997).

Lewis, Saunders, 'The essence of Welsh literature', in A. R. Jones and G. Thomas (eds.), *Presenting Saunders Lewis* (Cardiff, 1973).

Lewis, Saunders, 'Dafydd Nanmor', in R. Geraint Gruffydd (ed.), *Meistri'r Canrifoedd: Ysgrifau ar Hanes Llenyddiaeth Gymraeg gan Saunders Lewis* (Cardiff, 1973).

Marston, J. G., 'Gentry honour and royalism in early Stuart England', *Journal of British Studies*, XIII (1973–4).

Miller, A. C., 'Sir William Morgan of Pencoed: "a man much to be accounted of"', *WHR*, IX (1978).

Nuttall, G. F., 'Walter Cradock (1606?–1659): the man and his message', in *The Puritan Spirit: Essays and Addresses* (London, 1967).

Owen, H. G., 'Family politics in Elizabethan Merionethshire', *BBCS*, XVIII (1959).

Owen, Leonard, 'The population of Wales in the sixteenth and seventeenth centuries', *TCS* (1959).

Parry, B. R., 'Huw Nanney Hen (c.1546–1623), squire of Nannau', *JMHRS*, V (1972).

Pierce, T. Jones, 'Landlords in Wales' in J. Thirsk (ed.), *Agrarian History of England and Wales*, IV, *1500–1640* (Cambridge, 1967).

Powell, N. W., 'Crime and the community in Denbighshire during the 1590s', in J. Gwynfor Jones (ed.), *Class, Community and Culture in Tudor Wales* (Cardiff, 1989).

Redwood, P., 'The Games family versus the borough of Brecon 1589–1606', *Brycheiniog*, XXV (1992–3).

Roberts, D. H. E., and Charles, R. A., 'Raff ap Robert ac Edwart ap Raff', *BBCS*, XXIV (1971).

Roberts, Enid, 'Cywydd cymod i Hwmffre ap Hywel ap Siencyn a'i geraint', *JMHRS*, IV (1964).

Roberts, Enid, 'Ymryson y Salsbrïaid, 1593', *TDHS*, XVII (1968).

Roberts, Glyn, 'Wales and England, antipathy and sympathy, 1284–1485', and 'Wyrion Eden: the Anglesey descendants of Ednyfed Fychan in the fourteenth century', in A. H. Dodd and J. Gwynn Williams (eds.), *Aspects of Welsh History* (Cardiff, 1969).

Roberts, Peter R., 'A petition concerning Sir Richard Herbert', *BBCS*, XX (1964).

Roberts, Peter R., 'The union with England and the identity of "Anglican" Wales', *Transactions of the Royal Historical Society*, XXII (1972).

Roberts, Peter R., 'The "Act of Union" in Welsh History', *TCS* (1972–3).

Roberts, Peter R., 'A breviat of the effectes devised for Wales, c.1540–41', *Camden Miscellany*, XXVI (1975).

Roberts, Peter R., 'The "Henry VIII clause": delegated legislation and the Tudor principality of Wales', in T. G. Watkin (ed.), *Legal Record and Historical Reality* (London, 1989).

Roberts, Peter R., 'Tudor legislation and "the British tongue"', in Geraint H. Jenkins (ed.), *A Social History of the Welsh Language: The Welsh Language before the Industrial Revolution* (Cardiff, 1997).

Slater, M., 'The weightiest business: marriage in an upper-gentry family in seventeenth-century England', *Past & Present*, LXXII (1976).

Sharpe, K., 'Crown, parliament and localities: government and communities in early Stuart England', *EHR*, CI (1986), 321–50.

Smith, J. Beverley, 'Crown and community in the principality of north Wales in the reign of Henry Tudor', *WHR*, III (1966).

Styles, Philip, 'Politics and historical research in the early seventeenth century', in Levi Fox (ed.), *English Historical Scholarship in the Sixteenth and Seventeenth Centuries* (Oxford, 1956).

Thomas, D. Ll., 'Further notes on the Council in the Marches', *Y Cymmrodor*, XIII (1899).

Thirsk, Joan, 'The fashioning of the Tudor-Stuart gentry', *Bulletin of the John Rylands Library*, LXXII (1990).

Tibbott, G., 'Welshmen with prince Charles in Spain, 1623', *NLWJ*, I (1939).

Tyacke, N., 'Puritanism, Arminianism and Counter Reformation', in Conrad Russell (ed.), *The Origins of the English Civil War* (London, 1973).

Wiliam, E., ' "Let use be preferred to uniformitie": domestic architecture', in J. Gwynfor Jones (ed.), *Class, Community and Culture in Tudor Wales* (Cardiff, 1989).

Williams, David, 'The miracle of St Donat's', *The Welsh Review*, VII (i) (1947).

Williams, David, 'John Evans's strange journey', *TCS* (1948).

Williams, E. N., 'Sir William Maurice of Clenennau', *TCHS*, XXIV (1963).

Williams, Glanmor, 'William Salesbury's *Baterie of the Popes Botereulx*', *BBCS*, XIII (1949).

Williams, Glanmor, 'The Stradlings of St Donat's', in Stewart Williams (ed.), *Vale of History* (Cowbridge, 1960).

Williams, Glanmor, 'Rice Mansell of Oxwich and Margam (1487–1559)', *Morgannwg*, VI (1962).

Williams, Glanmor, 'The achievement of William Salesbury', in *Welsh Reformation Essays* (Cardiff, 1967).

Williams, Glanmor, 'Some Protestant views of early British church history', in *Welsh Reformation Essays* (Cardiff, 1967).

Williams, Glanmor, 'Landlords in Wales: the church', in Joan Thirsk (ed.), *Agrarian History of England and Wales:* IV. *1500–1640* (Cambridge, 1967).

Williams, Glanmor, 'Glamorgan Society, 1536–1642', in Glanmor Williams (ed.), *Glamorgan County History*, IV, *Early Modern Glamorgan from the Act of Union to the Industrial Revolution* (Cardiff, 1974).

Williams, Glanmor, 'Prophecy, poetry and politics in medieval and Tudor Wales', in *Religion, Language and Nationality in Wales* (Cardiff, 1979).

Williams, Glanmor, 'Edward James a Llyfr yr Homilïau', in *Grym Tafodau Tân: Ysgrifau Hanesyddol ar Grefydd a Diwylliant* (Llandysul, 1984).

Williams, Glanmor, 'Bishop William Morgan and the first Welsh Bible', in *The Welsh and their Religion* (Cardiff, 1991).

Williams, Glanmor, 'Religion and Welsh literature in the age of the Reformation', in *The Welsh and their Religion* (Cardiff, 1991).

Williams, G. J., 'The early historians of Glamorgan', in Stewart Williams (ed.), *Glamorgan Historian*, III (Cowbridge, 1966).

Williams, J. Gwynn, 'Rhai agweddau ar y gymdeithas Gymreig yn yr ail ganrif ar bymtheg', *Efrydiau Athronyddol*, XXX (1968).

Williams, Penry, 'Controversy in Elizabethan Glamorgan: the rebuilding of Cardiff bridge', *Morgannwg*, II (1958).

Williams, Penry, 'The attack on the Council in the Marches, 1603–42', *TCS* (1961, i).

Williams, Penry, 'The activity of the Council in the Marches under the early Stuarts', *WHR*, I (1961).

Williams, Penry, 'The political and administrative history of Glamorgan, 1536–1642', in Glanmor Williams (ed.), *Glamorgan County History*, IV (Cardiff, 1974).

Williams, W. Ogwen, 'The county records', *TCHS*, X (1949).

Williams, W. Ogwen, 'The survival of the Welsh language after the Act of Union of England and Wales: the first phase, 1536–1642', *WHR*, II (1964).

Williams, W. Ogwen, 'The social order in Tudor Wales', *TCS* (1967, ii).

Williams, W. Ll., 'A Welsh insurrection', *Y Cymmrodor*, XVI (1903).

Wilson, J., 'Icons of unity', *History Today*, XLIII (1993).

D. Unpublished Dissertations

Abraham, P. L., 'Contrasting cultures? Cultural propagation of the concept of order in early Stuart England c.1603–1648' (University of Wales MA, 1995).

Cole, D. M., 'The Mansells of Oxwich and Margam, 1487–1631' (University of Birmingham MA, 1966).

Edwards, P. S., 'The parliamentary representation of Wales and Monmouthshire, 1542–1558' (University of Cambridge Ph.D., 1970).

Hughes, Arwyn Ll., 'Noddwyr y Beirdd yn Sir Feirionnydd: casgliad o'r cerddi i deuluoedd Corsygedol, Dolau-gwyn, Llwyn, Nannau, Y Rug, Rhiwedog, Rhiw-goch, Rhiwlas ac Ynysmaengwyn' (University of Wales MA, 1969).

Jones, D. Cyril, 'The Bulkeleys of Baron Hill, 1440–1621' (University of Wales MA, 1958).

Jones, Emyr Gwynne, 'The Caernarvonshire squires, 1558–1625' (University of Wales MA, 1936).

Parry, T. E., 'Llythyrau Robert Vaughan, Hengwrt (1592–1667), gyda Rhagymadrodd a Nodiadau' (University of Wales MA, 1960).

Robbins, M., 'The agricultural, domestic, social and cultural interests of the gentry in south-east Glamorgan, 1540–1640' (University of Wales Ph.D., 1974).

Thomas, Gwyn R., 'Sir Thomas Myddelton II, 1586–1666' (University of Wales MA, 1967).

Index

A True Reporte (1587), 138
Aberbrân (Brecs.), 37
Aberbrân Fawr (Brecs.), 214
Abercerrig (Denb.), 138
Abergavenny, 35, 45, 53, 59, 208
Abergele (Denb.), 20, 138
Aber-mad (Cards.), 74
Abermarlais (Carms.), 23
Aberystwyth, 14
ach, 63–4
Acts of Parliament
  Act of Precedence (1559), 212
  Act of Supremacy (1559), 173, 175
  Act for the Translation of the
    Scriptures into Welsh (1563), *see*
    under Bible, Welsh
  Act of Uniformity (1559), 173
  Acts of Union (1536–43), *see under*
    Settlement, Tudor
Admonition to the Parliament, An
  (1572), 189
advenae, 7
Aeneas (of Troy), xxi, 134
Aequity of an Humble Supplication, The
  (1587), 29, 154, 186
America(s), 137, 139
Anglesey, 21, 22, 38, 47, 51, 62, 77,
  80, 88, 91, 123, 124, 125, 140,
  144, 193, 217, 225, 245
Antwerp, 25, 27, 152
Anwyl, Catherine (Parc, Mer.), 230
Anwyl, Robert (Parc, Mer.), 230
Apocrypha, The, 150
Apollo, 157
Apologia Ecclesiae Anglicanae (1562)
  (trans. into Welsh as *Deffyniad
  Ffydd Eglwys Loegr*), 174, 179
Aragon, 158
arbitration, 39
arddel, 35
arglwyddiaeth, 117, 126, 204, 239
Aristotle/Aristotelian, xiii, xiv, 60, 103
Arllechwedd Isaf, 89
Armada, Spanish, 62, 146, 147, 149,
  150, 153, 154, 155, 156, 161
Arminianism, 198

Arney, Rees (Llantarnam), 124
Arthur, prince of Wales, 70
Arthurian legend, xxi, 136
Ascham, Roger, xv, 96
Atlantis, 138
Aubrey, William, 46

Babylon, 151
Babington, Gervase, bp. of Llandaf
  (1591–5), 104, 114
Babington Plot (1586), 92, 149, 151
Bachymbyd (Denb.), 21, 92
Bachegraig (Denb.), 25
Bacon, Sir Francis, 216
Bagenal, Sir Henry, 160
Bancroft, Richard, bp. of London, 186
Bangor, 201
Barker, Richard, 2nd justice of North
  Wales, 118
Barlow, George, 121
Baron Hill, 62, 215
Barthol, 34, 152
Basaleg (Mon.), 21
Basilikon Doron (1598), 65, 69, 206
Basset, Arthur, 221
Basset family (Beaupré), 76
Baterie of the Popes Botereulx (1550),
  178
Bayly, Lewis, bp. of Bangor (1616–31),
  171, 190, 193, 201, 220, 230
Beaumaris, 9, 13, 18, 19, 38, 41, 62,
  77, 208
Beaupré (Glam.), 6
Bebb, W. Ambrose, xviii
Bedwellte (Mon.), 145
Berth-ddu, Y (Llanrwst), 143
Bewdley, 98
Bible, Welsh
  (1588), 147, 150, 167, 178, 181,
    182
  (1620), 191, 196
  (1630), 168, 191, 192, 196, 229
Bishops' Wars (1639), 144
Blackhall (Mont.), 166
Blessednes of Brytaine, The (1587), 149
Blundeville, Thomas, 96

Blunt, George, 98
Bodfel (Caerns.), 22
Bodidris (Denb.), 41
Bodowen (Anglesey), 91
Bodowyr (Anglesey), 66, 225
Bodwrda, Wiliam, 73
bonedd/bonheddig, xi, 11, 63, 71–2, 203, 204, 223
bonheddig cynhwynawl, 84, 204
Book named the Governor, The (1531), xv, 37, 61, 118
Book of Common Prayer, The (1552/1559), 173, 219
Book of Homilies, The (1547), 119, 196, 197
Book of Matins (1548), 219
Book of Sports, The (1633), 199
Books of Orders, The (1630–1), 80
Bosworth (1485), battle of, 204
Brampton Bryan, 230
Brecknock, 15; *see also* Brecon
Brecknock, archdeaconry of, 179
Brecknockshire (Breconshire), 46, 214
Brecon, 208
Brecon Priory, 25
Bret, Barbara, 8
Breuiary of Britayne, The (1573), 44
brëyr(iaid), 116, 203, 213
Bridges, Dr John, dn. of Sarum, 186
Brigstock, 217
Bristol, 24, 200
Britannicae Historiae Libri Sex (1585), 88
Briton Ferry (Glam.), 27
Broadmead, 200
Bromley, Sir Thomas, 207
Brutus of Troy, 132, 134, 185
Bryncunallt (Denb.), 18
Builth, 98
Bulkeley family (Anglesey), 9, 18, 19, 91, 123, 206
Bulkeley, Sir Richard (I), 38, 49, 126
Bulkeley, Sir Richard (II), 77
Bulkeley, Sir Richard (III), 41, 47, 57, 62, 120, 123, 124, 125, 151, 215
Burrington and Chew Norton, 200
Bushell, Thomas, 14

Cadiz, 159
Cadoxton-iuxta-Neath (Glam.), 191
Cadwaladr, King of Britain, 132
Caer Gai (Mer.), 230
Caernarfon, 144, 151, 208, 225
Caernarfonshire, 22, 38, 42, 48, 76, 77, 84, 89, 100, 119, 144, 180, 225, 226
Caerphilly Castle, 27
Calvin(ism), 173, 174
Cambridge, 207
    St John's College, 47
Cambrobrytannicae Cymraecaeve Linguae Institutiones . . . (1592), 25, 163, 214, 245
Camden, William, 8, 138, 245
Cân am y waredigaeth a gadd y Brytaniaid o law y Spaeniaid . . . (1588), 147
Canterbury, archiepiscopate of, 171
Caradog of Llancarfan, 138
Cardiff, 81, 199
Cardiff Castle, 25, 27
Cardigan, 208
Cardiganshire, 23, 51, 74, 82, 123
Cardiganshire leadmines, 14
Carew (Pemb.), 25, 26, 27, 125, 208
Carmarthen, 208
Carmarthen boroughs, 167
Carmarthenshire, 23, 244
Carne family (Glam.), 9, 120
Carne, Sir Edward, 27, 46
Cartwright, Thomas, 189
Car-wr y Cymru (1631), 194
Castellmarch (Caerns.), 46, 121
Castiglione, Baldassare, xiii, xiv, xv, 61
Castile, 158
Câteau-Cambrésis, Peace of, 173
Catherine de Valois, 8
Cecil family, 41
Cecil, Sir Robert, 125, 145, 171
Cecil, Sir William, Lord Burghley, 18, 71
Cefnamwlch (Caerns.), 18, 112, 123, 224
Cefnmabli (Glam.), 20
cenedl, 83
Charles I, 58, 111, 164, 231, 238
Charles, prince of Wales, 157, 158, 159, 201
Cheke, John, 102, 119
Cheshire, 62, 123
Chester, 24, 208
Chester, county palatine of, 4
Chirbury, xx
Chirk, 14, 165, 166
Chirk Castle, 25, 168
Chirk, lordship of, 5, 23
Church, Elizabethan, xviii, 57, 64, 164, 167–79, 243
Churchstoke, parish of, 180

Churchyard, Thomas, 125, 227
Cicero(nian), xiv, xv
Cinmel (Denb.), 20
Civil Wars, xviii, 7, 10, 14, 28, 29, 43, 53, 57, 59, 144, 168, 174, 202, 205, 210, 231
Clenennau (Caerns.), 21, 40, 214, 220, 221, 226, 230
Clochran (Ireland), 138
Clough, Sir Richard, 25, 27
Clwyd, Vale of, 26
cnapan, 152
Cochwillan (Caerns.), 46
Coed Alun (Caerns.), 76
Cogan Pill (Glam.), 51
Colet, John, xv
College of Arms, 64
Columbus, Christopher, 138
Commentarioli Descriptionis Britannicae Fragmentum (1572) (trans. into English as *Breuiary of Britayne, The*), 44
Complete Gentleman, The (1622), 63
Compton, William, 1st earl of Northampton, 221
Continuation of The Blessednes of Brytaine, The (1588), 149
Conway (III), John (Botryddan), 211
Conwy (Caerns.), 26, 191, 208, 216
Cope, Sir Anthony, 186
Corbett, Walter, 117
Cornwall, 134
Corsygedol (Mer.), 5, 26
Cotrel, Y (Glam.), 152
Cotton, John, 200
Council in the Marches, xxv, 32, 35, 36–7, 39, 48, 50, 66, 67, 68, 79, 80, 82, 84, 108, 109, 111, 114, 117, 120, 123, 124, 125, 126, 129, 144, 155, 161, 164, 186, 188
courts of law
Admiralty, 35, 46, 47
Chancery, 32, 35, 45, 46, 119, 210
Common Pleas, 32
county, 11, 51, 71, 145
Exchequer, 32, 35, 45, 70, 210
Great Sessions, xxv, 12, 20, 32, 34, 36, 50, 80, 113, 119
High Commission, 198
Quarter Sessions, 11, 38, 42, 51, 84, 89, 108, 112, 126 211
Requests, 32, 46
Star Chamber, 21, 32, 33, 35, 45, 67, 75, 107, 124, 141, 198

Westminster, king's courts at, 32
Coverdale, Miles, 180
Cradock, Sir Mathew, 13
Cradock, Walter, 197, 199, 200
Cranmer, Thomas, archbp. of Canterbury, 127
Craven, Elizabeth, 218
Creuddyn (Caerns.), 23, 84, 144
Cromwell, Thomas, xxiii, xxv, 14, 15, 49, 104, 126, 193
Crowther, Brian, 71
custos rotulorum, 33, 92
cymortha, 35, 91, 92, 241
Cynfal Fawr (Mer.), 25

Dafydd Nanmor, 28, 215
Danvers, Henry Baron, 2
Davies, Dr John (Siôn Dafydd Rhys), 25, 53, 56, 120, 214, 215, 245
Davies, Richard, bp. of St Asaph (1559–61) and St David's (1561–81), 57, 71, 110, 111, 119, 127, 170, 175, 176, 180, 181, 193, 216, 220, 240, 244
Davies, Thomas, bp. of St Asaph (1561–73), 176
Dee, Dr John, 137, 138, 139, 149
Deffynniad Ffydd Eglwys Loegr (1595), 179, 180; *see also Apologia Ecclesiae Anglicanae*
Denbigh, 21
Denbighshire, 13, 41, 123, 166, 224
Dent, Arthur, 228
deputy-lieutenants, 32, 38, 48, 69, 74, 75, 80, 101, 119, 141, 221, 241–2
De Republica Anglorum (1586), 19
Derfel Gadarn, 193
Description of England, The (1577), 7, 131
Description of Penbrokshire (1603), 84, 217
Devereux family (Lamphey, Pemb.), 2
Devereux, Robert, 2nd earl of Essex, 41, 69, 70, 71, 80, 109, 125, 141, 160
Devereux, Walter, 1st earl of Essex, 110, 240
Devereux, Walter, Lord Ferrers, 98, 109
'Dialogue of the Government of Wales' (1594), xxi, 19, 61, 101, 144, 152
Dictionary in Englyshe and Welshe, A (1547), 177
Dinefwr (Carms.), xxiii, 24, 108

Discourse on a North-west Passage
    (1576), 137
Dodd, A. H., xvi, 40–91
Dolgellau (Mer.), 27, 41, 82, 91
Dolwyddelan Castle (Caerns.), 6
Donne, John, 65
Dosbarth Byrr ar y rhan gyntaf i
    ramadeg Cymraeg (1567), 233
Downlee (Dunn Lee), Edward, 168
Drake, Sir Francis, 148
drudaniaeth, 28–9, 54
Drych Cristianogawl, Y (*c*.1585), 57
Dudley, Robert, earl of Leicester, 20,
    41, 69
Dunkirk, 159
Dwnn, Lewys, 64, 205

economic resources, 12–14, 24–31, 53–4
education, 44–9
Edward I, xxiv, 4
Edward IV, 2
Edward VI, xxv, 162, 165, 173, 178
Edwards family, Plas Newydd and
    Chirk (Denb.), 165, 166
Edwards, John (sen.), 166
Edwards John (III), 166
Edwards, Sir J. Goronwy, xxiv
Edwart ap Raff, 54, 113, 146, 149, 150
Egluryn Phraethineb (1595), 57
Eifionydd, 4, 21, 41, 88, 243
Eikon Basilike (1649), 201
Eiriannws (Caerns.), 89
Elizabeth I, 92, 129, 148–9, 165, 166,
    174, 184, 187, 246
Elizabeth, da. of James I, 89
Ellen, da. of John Lewis, Chwaen Wen,
    88
Elton, G. R., xx, 128
Elyot, Sir Thomas, xiii, xv, 37, 61, 73,
    86, 96, 118, 129, 225
Enfranchisement, Charters of
    (1505–8), xxii
Erasmus, Desiderius, 3
Erbery, William, 197, 199
Essex Revolt (1601), 146
Evans, Dr Gwynfor, xviii
Ewenni (Glam.), 9, 27, 120
Exhortation unto the Governors of Wales,
    An (1588), 155, 187, 188

familial connections, 203–10, 222–6
Fan, Y (Glam.), 20, 27, 51, 76, 145
Farnese, Alexander, duke of Parma,
    150, 152

Fetiplace, George, 50
Field, John, 189
Filmer, Sir Robert, 65, 118
Fitzhamo, Robert, earl of Gloucester,
    23
Flanders, 27, 146, 159
Fleming, William, 183
Flintshire, 28
Fonmon Castle (Glam.), 105
Forest of Snowdon, 20, 41
Forset, Edward, 65
Forty-two Articles (1553), 173
Fountain Gate (Cards.), 73
France, 13, 25, 38, 133, 134, 140, 143,
    147, 159, 161, 237
Frankfurt, 152
Frederick, king of Bohemia, 89, 157
Frondeg, Y (Anglesey), 91, 124
Funerall Sermon (1577), 71, 176, 240

gafael(-ion), 12
Gage, Agnes, Lady, 25
galanas, 12
galanterie, 61
Gamage, William, 51
Games family (Brecs.), 75
Games, John 75
Ganllwyd (Mer.), 14
gavelkind, 4, 6
Gellilyfdy (Flints.), 72, 231
genedigaeth-fraint, 118
General and Rare Memorials Pertayning
    to the Perfit Arte of Navigation
    (1577), 138
Geneva, 201
Geoffrey of Monmouth, 57, 132, 134,
    136, 137
Gerald of Wales, 63, 213, 222
Gerard, Sir William, 36, 50
Gilbert, Sir Humphrey, xv, 137, 138
Glamorgan, 13, 20, 23, 26, 27, 36, 39,
    41, 75, 81, 88, 91, 98, 101, 120,
    124, 216, 225
Glamorgan, Vale of, 13, 16, 20, 24, 165
Gloddaith (Caerns.), 23, 84, 144, 216
Gloucester, 145
Glyn Cywarch (Mer.), 45, 53
Glyndŵr Revolt, xxv, 6, 14, 58, 116,
    134, 135, 136
Glynn, Sir William (Glynllifon,
    Caerns.), 208, 240
Glynn, Thomas, 226
Godwin, Francis, bp. of Llandaf
    (1601–17), 169

Gogerddan (Cards.), 6, 18, 74
Golden-fleece, The (1626), 29, 157
Golden Grove (Carms.), 6, 23
Gower (Glam.), 13
Graduelys (*c.*1570),85
Grand Tour, 44, 65, 237
gravitas, xv, 11
grazia, xv
'Great Chain of Being', 85
Gregory XIII, pope, 174
Gresford (Denb.), 24
Gresham, Sir Thomas, 25
Greyfriars (Cardiff), 27
Griffith (Cefnamwlch), 18, 42
Griffith (Penrhyn), 20, 234
Griffith, Dr William (Caernarfon), 144
Griffith, John (Cefnamwlch), 76, 112, 123
Griffith, Sir Rhys (Penrhyn), 66
Griffith, Sir William (Penrhyn), 22
Gruffudd ap Cynan, 23
Gruffudd ap Llywelyn, xxiv
Gruffudd Hiraethog, 45, 73, 205
Gruffydd, Edward (Penrhyn), 126
Gruffydd, Morus (Plas Newydd), 21
Gruffydd, William (Porth-aml, Anglesey), 225
Guise faction, 142, 143
Gunpowder Plot, 148, 159
Gunter family (Usk), 25
Guto'r Glyn, xxii, 215
Gutun Owain, xxii, 138
gwaedogaeth, 222
gwehelyth, 12
gwely(au), 3, 5, 87
Gwent, 9
Gwenynog (Anglesey), 47
Gwerclas (Mer.), 25
Gwernyfed (Brecs.), 46
Gwilym ap Gruffudd (Penrhyn), 6
Gwydir (Caerns.), 6, 8, 26, 38, 44, 47, 77, 218
Gwydir Uchaf (Caerns.), 27
Gwyn (White), Richard, 46
Gwyn, Robert, 9, 57
Gwynedd, 10, 13, 23, 138
Gwynedd, princes of, 136
Gwynn, Dr John (Gwydir), 208
Gwynn, Hugh (Berth-ddu, Denb.), 143
Gwynn, Hugh (Pemb.), 108

Habsburgs, 153, 160, 184
Hakluyt, Richard, 138, 139

Hanbury, Richard, 14
Hanmer family (Hanmer, Flints.), 207
Harlech Castle, 242
Harley, Lady Brilliana, 230
Haroldston (Pemb.), 38, 74, 168, 240
Harrison, William, 77, 96, 122, 131
Harry, George Owen, 72, 132
Haverfordwest, 74, 108, 144
Hayward, Sir John, 65, 118
Henblas (Beaumaris), 91, 214, 215
Hengwrt (Mer.), 72
Henllan (Denb.), 27, 89
Henllys (Pemb.), 8, 18, 46
Henrietta Maria, Queen, 159
Henry IV, penal laws of, xxi, xxii, 49
Henry V, 8
Henry VIII, xx, xxi, xxii, 34, 68, 129, 143, 144, 223, 246
Henry, prince of Wales, 62, 69, 70, 133, 206, 215
Hensol (Glam.), 51
Herbert, Edward (Montgomery and Blackhall), 166
Herbert family (Raglan), 5, 20, 166
Herbert family (Montgomery), 5, 91, 159, 165, 209, 216
Herbert family (Swansea), 76, 216
Herbert, Henry, 2nd earl of Pembroke, 27, 35, 41, 48, 67, 69, 73, 80, 81, 89, 101, 102, 114, 119, 120, 125, 140, 143, 145, 155, 187, 188, 224, 225, 228
Herbert House (Cardiff), 27
Herbert, Lord (Chirbury), xx, 133, 207
Herbert, Sir Edward (Montgomery), 91, 240
Herbert, Sir Richard (Montgomery), 49, 91, 223
Herbert, Sir William, 1st earl of Pembroke, 8, 51
Herbert, Sir William (Raglan), 136
Herbert, Sir William (St Julian's), 1, 2, 168
Herbert, William (Cogan Pill), 51
Herefordshire, 230
Heylin, Rowland, 168
Historia Regum Britanniae (*c.*1136), 134
Historie of Cambria, The (1584), 138
History of the Gwydir Family, 8, 97, 99, 106, 109
Hoby, Sir Philip, 217
Hoby, Sir Thomas, xv
Holinshed, Ralph, 138

Holland, Piers (Cinmel), 20
Holland, Robert, 69, 191, 206
Holte, Sir Thomas, 35
Holywell (Flints.), 144
Homily of Obedience, The (1547), 61, 97, 212
Hooker, Richard, 186
House of Commons, 40, 122, 168
Howard of Effingham, William, Lord, 148
Howell, James, 102, 133, 158, 159, 207, 237
Hughes, Hugh, 217
Hughes, Humphrey, 25
Hughes, William, bp. of St Asaph (1573–1600), 167, 172
Huguenots, 159
Humphrey, Lawrence, xv
Hurault, Jacques, 96
Hurt of Sedicion howe greueous it is to a Communewelthe, The (1549), 102, 110
Huw Llwyd, 25
Huw Machno, 25, 184
Hywel ap Dafydd (Penyfed, Caerns.), 97

iaith, yr, xix
Iâl, 146, 151
Ieuan Llwyd Sieffrai, 160
Il Cortegiano, xiii, xiv, 61
Indies, 38
Inns of Court, 44, 45, 237
Ireland, 13, 58, 80, 134, 138, 140, 151, 160, 174, 208
Isle of Ré, 159
Israelites, 156
Italy, 13, 233, 237
Itinerary in Wales (1536–9), 4

James VI (Scotland) and James I (England), xxiv, 40, 65, 119, 131, 132, 133, 157, 162, 185, 206, 236
James, Edward, 191, 196, 197
James, Howell (Llandeilo Crosenni), 89
Jane, da. of John Wyn ap Huw, Bodfel, 22
Jeffreys, John (Acton), 51
Jenkins, David (Hensol), 51
Jesuits, 146, 148, 166, 174
Jewel, John, bp. of Salisbury, 174
John ap Maredudd (Eifionydd, Caerns.), 8

John Wyn ap Huw (Bodfel, Caerns.), 22
John Wyn ap Maredudd (Gwydir, Caerns.), 27, 38
Johnes, Henry, 120
Jones, Edward (Plas Cadwgan, Denb.), 151
Jones family (Abermarlais, Carms.), 23
Jones family (Usk), 25
Jones, Francis, 64
Jones, John (Gellilyfdy, Flints.), 72, 205, 231
Jones, Sir William (Castellmarch, Caerns.), 46, 121
Jones, Thomas (Fountain Gate, Cards.), 73
Jones, Thomas (Llanfair Cilgedin, Mon.), 147, 148, 149
Joseph of Arimathea, 57
justice of the peace, office of, 14, 33, 34, 78–9
Katherine, da. of Tudur ap Robert Fychan (Berain, Denb.), 22, 25
Kemeys, Edward, 20
Kemeys family (Cefnmabli, Glam.), 51
Ket, Robert, 102
Kilvey (Glam.), 13
Kitchin, Anthony, bp. of Llandaf (1545–63), 175
Kyffin, Edward, 184, 185, 197, 198
Kyffin family (Oswestry), 5
Kyffin, Maurice, 149, 179, 185, 186, 190, 197, 244
Kyffin, Morus (Maenan, Caerns.), 66, 67
Kynniver llith a ban (1551), 178

Lambarde, William, 33, 38, 62, 69, 213
Lampeter Velfrey (Pemb.), 122
Lancaster family, 135, 136
Lancastrians, 116
language, English, 8, 45, 49–53, 177
language, Welsh, 7, 8, 21, 45, 53, 177
La Rochelle, 159
Laud, William, 198, 199, 200
Laws of Ecclesiastical Polity, The (1593–1600), 174, 186
Ledbury, 98
Lee, Rowland, 14, 15, 20, 29, 35, 49, 62, 98, 223, 246
Leland, John, xxiii, 4, 215
Lewis ab Owain, Y Frondeg (Anglesey), 123
Lewis, Ellis, 230

Lewis family (Y Fan), 20, 27, 51, 76, 199
Lewis, Dr David, 35, 36, 46, 59, 78, 98, 108, 124, 126, 128, 129, 223, 241
Lewis, Rice, xx
Lewis, Saunders, xviii, 215
Lewkenor, Sir Richard, 125, 145
Lewys Glyn Cothi, xxii
Lewys, Huw, 93, 180, 190, 197
Leyshon, Thomas, 25
Linacre, Thomas, xv
Llanafan (Cards.), 23
Llanarmon (Llŷn), 191
Llanbeulan (Anglesey), 245
Llandaf, dioc. of, 169, 191, 201
Llandeilo Crosenni (Mon.), 89
Llanddeiniolen (Caerns.), 93, 180
Llan-ddew (Cards.), 74
Llanddewi Velfry (Pemb.), 122
Llanddowror (Carms.), 191
Llanddwywe (Mer.), 26
Llandenny (Mon.), 70
Llandygái (Caerns.), 65
Llanfaches (Mon.), 200
Llanfair Cilgedin (Mon.), 147
Llanfair-is-gaer (Caerns.), 21
Llanfedw (Glam.), xx, 21
Llanfrothen (Mer.), 8, 53, 230
Llangybi (Caerns.), 191
Llangyndeyrn (Carms.), 11, 29, 120, 157, 244
Llanidloes (Mont.), 46
Llanofer (Mon.), 147
Llanrhaeadr (Denb.), 21
Llanrhymni (Glam.), 21
Llanrwst (Denb.), 21, 77, 143, 168, 224
Llansilin (Denb.), 89
Llantarnam (Mon.), 25, 70, 124, 145, 165, 166, 193
Llantrithyd (Glam.), 20
Llantwit Major (Glam.), 222
Llanymddyfri (Carms.), 158, 194, 197, 219
Llanymynech (Mont.), 168
Lleweni (Denb.), 9, 18, 21, 41, 70, 89, 92, 150, 151, 208
Lloyd, David (Aber-mad, Cards.), 74
Lloyd, Edward (Llwyn-y-maen), 89
Lloyd family (Rhiwedog, Mer.), 18
Lloyd, John (Rhiwedog), 230
Lloyd, Lady Margaret, 230
Lloyd, Morgan (Llan-ddew, Cards.), 74, 82

Lloyd, Sir John (Bodidris, Denb.), 41
Lloyd, Sir Marmaduke, 51
Lloyd, William, 218
Llwybr hyffordd yn cyfarwyddo yr anghyfarwydd i'r nefoedd (1630), 190, 228; see also Plain Man's Pathway to Heaven, The
Llwydarth (Glam.), 73
Llwyd, Humphrey, 44, 46, 205, 213
Llwydiarth (Mont.), 5
Llwyd, Robert, 190, 191, 194, 197, 228, 229
Llwyd, Syr Ieuan (Iâl), 146, 151
Llwyn family (Dolgellau, Mer.), 41, 82, 91, 123
Llwyngwern (Mer.), 230
Llwyn-y-maen, 89
Llyfr Plygain, Y (1607), 196
Llŷn, 41, 42, 46, 73, 112, 148, 150, 224
Llywelyn ap Gruffudd, xxiv, 4
London, 24, 28, 43, 45, 53, 168, 206, 207, 208, 211, 221
Low Countries, 13, 25, 113, 133
Ludlow, 32, 40, 47, 50, 80, 82, 84, 98, 101, 107, 125, 143, 155, 161, 187, 208, 209, 221, 224
Luther, Martin, 3
Lyly, John, 85

mab darogan, y ('son of prophecy'), xx, xxi
Machen (Mon.), 4
Madog ab Owain Gwynedd, 137, 138, 139
Madrid, 179
Maecenas, 89
Maelor, 9
Maenan (Caerns.), 66
Maesyfelin (Cards.), 51
Mandan Indians, 138
Mansel, Anthony, 20, 109
Mansel family (Oxwich and Margam), 9, 18, 19, 25, 31, 41, 70, 73, 76
Mansel, Sir Edward, 27, 204, 222, 240
Mansel, Sir Rice, 9, 20, 26, 27, 240
Mansel, Sir Thomas, 44, 211
Mansfeld expedition, 159
Maredudd ab Ieuan ap Robert (Gwydir), 6
Maredudd ap Rhys, 139
Margam, 9, 18, 19, 25, 26, 31, 76, 208
Margam abbey, 9
Mary I, 143, 165

Mary Stuart (Queen of Scots), 142, 148, 155, 161, 166, 168
Massachusetts Bay, 200
Massacre of St Bartholomew's Day (1572), 140
Mathew family (Llandaf), 18, 41
Mathew family (Radyr), 13–14, 18, 41
Mathew, Sir George (Radyr), 8
Mathew, William (Radyr), 81, 101
Maurice, Sir William (Clenennau), 21, 40, 76, 87, 88, 100, 104, 112, 118, 120, 123, 132, 220, 221, 225, 226, 236
Mechain Iscoed (Powys), 73
Menai Straits, 62
Meredith, Rowland (Bodowyr, Anglesey), 66
Merioneth, 8, 21, 25, 27, 45, 51, 75, 77, 91, 95, 123, 225
Merlin, 134, 136
Merrick, Rice, xx, 27, 72, 108, 152
Meyricke, Sir Gelly, 68, 69, 125
Middleton, Hugh, 14
Middleton, Marmaduke, 110, 172, 176
Middleton, Sir Thomas (Chirk Castle and London), 14, 168, 229
Milan, 233
Milford Haven, 38, 144, 145, 151
Missouri, Upper, 138
Monmouth, 25
Monmouthshire, 16, 21, 25, 27, 89, 140, 151, 162, 168
Montague family (Brigstock), 217
Montefeltro family, xiv
Montefeltro, Frederick di, xiv
Montgomery, 5, 49, 91
Montgomeryshire, 41, 91, 123, 168, 180
More, Sir Thomas, x
Morgan, Edward (Llantarnam), 70
Morgan family (Llantarnam), 165
Morgan family (Tredegar), 6, 9, 18, 19, 20, 25, 145
Morgan, Henry (Llanrhymni), 21
Morgan, Rowland (Machen), 4
Morgan, Rowland (Tredegar), 21
Morgan, Sir Thomas (St George's, Glam. and Pen-carn, Mon.), 151
Morgan, Sir William (Pen-coed), 98, 140
Morgan, William, bp. of Llandaf (1595–1601) and St Asaph (1601–4), 77, 110, 147, 167, 168, 169, 178, 181, 182, 183, 184, 197

Morgan, William (Llantarnam), 166
Morison, Sir Richard, 119
Mostyn family (Flints.), 6, 13, 19, 23, 204, 206, 208, 216, 226, 234
Mostyn, William, 23
Mostyn, Sir Roger, 8, 28, 84, 207, 227, 240
Mostyn, Sir Thomas (d.1618), 51, 144, 227
Mostyn, Sir Thomas (d.1641), 20
Mostyn, Thomas (d.1558), 28
Mostyn, William, 216

Nanconwy, 6, 77, 243
Nannau family (Mer.), 6, 91
Nannau, Gruffudd, 75
Nannau Hen, Huw, 14, 27, 75, 95
Netherlands, 142, 147, 149, 237
Newfoundland, 29
New Testament, 173
Newton (Brecs.), 75
Newtown Hall (Mont.), 5
Nijmegen, 146
nobiliatores, 10
Northamptonshire, 217
Northern Earls, Rising of the (1569), 140, 161
Northop (Flints.), 150

Offa's Dyke, 42, 53, 213, 237, 244
Old Beaupré (Glam.), 216
Oll Synnwyr Pen Kembero Ygyd (1547), 177
optimates, 10
Oswestry, 89
Oswestry, lordship of, 5
Owain Gwynedd, 183
Owen ap John, 225
Owen ap Richard ap Rhys (Eiriannws), 89
Owen family (Bodowen and Y Frondeg), 91
Owen family (Llwyn, Mer.), 41
Owen family (Plas-du), 165
Owen, George, xx, xxi, 8, 18, 19, 24, 33, 34, 36, 46, 49, 55, 59, 61, 62, 67, 68, 69, 72, 78, 79, 84, 100, 101, 108, 125, 137, 140, 144, 151, 204, 216, 217, 245
Owen, Hugh (Gwenynog), 47, 193
Owen, Hugh (Plas-du), 148, 150, 159
Owen, John Lewis, Llwyn (Mer.), 82
Owen, Sir John (Clenennau), 230
Owen, William (Henllys), 46

Oxford, University of, 44, 45, 53, 183, 206
Oxwich, 9, 18, 26, 27, 208
Pura Wallia, xxiv, 4

Pace, Richard, 63
Palatinate, 157
Palmieri, Matteo, xiv
Parker, Matthew, archbp. of Canterbury, 176
parliamentary elections and feuds, 40–2, 91–3, 122–4
Parry, Richard, bp. of St Asaph, 145, 169, 171, 191, 192, 193
Parry, William, 150
Parson, Robert, 65
partible inheritance, 12
paterfamilias, xvii, xviii, 28, 97, 195, 206, 208, 220, 225, 230, 232
Patriarcha (c.1640), 118
Patrizi, Francesco, xiv
Peacham, Henry, xiii, xv, 63, 72, 96
Peckham, Sir George, 138
Pembrokeshire, 16, 18, 19, 24, 25, 27, 38, 56, 69, 100, 101, 108, 122, 125, 144, 145, 152, 191, 193, 204
penaduriaeth, 117
Penamnen (Caerns.), 6
Pen-carn (Mon.), 151
pencenedl, xvii, 28
Pen-llin (Glam.), 165
Pengwern (Chirk), 23
Penllwyn-sarth (serth) (Mon.), 21
Penrhyn (Caerns.), 6, 20, 126, 144, 208, 214
Penrhyn Creuddyn (Caerns.), 165, 166
Penrice (Glam.), 9
Penry, John, 29, 46, 153, 154, 155, 156, 157, 167, 168, 186, 187, 188, 189, 194, 197, 199, 206, 228
Pentyrch (Glam.), 14
Penyberth (Caerns.), 9
perchentyaeth, 28, 29, 211
Perl mewn Adfyd (1595), 180; *see also Spiritual and Most Precious Pearl, A*
Perri, Henri, 57
Perrot, Sir James, 40, 42, 69, 144, 151, 157, 168, 193
Perrot, Sir John, 26, 38, 74, 110, 121, 125, 151, 168, 240
Petrarch, xiv
Philip II, 142, 148, 150, 155, 161
Philipps family (Picton Castle), 18
Philipps, Sir John (Picton Castle), 69

Phillips, Fabian, 110
Picton Castle (Pemb.), 18, 25, 27, 69
Pilleth (Rads.), 232
Pius V, pope, 142
Plain Man's Pathway to Heaven, The (1610) (trans into Welsh as *Llwybr hyffordd yn cyfarwyddo yr anghyfarwydd i'r nefoedd*), 228
Plantagenets, 116
Plas Cadwgan (Denb.), 151
Plas Clough (Denb.), 25, 27
Plas Coch (Anglesey), 217
Plas-du (Llŷn), 148, 150, 159, 165, 193
Plas Iolyn (Denb.), 69
Plas Isaf (Llanrwst), 21
Plas Mawr (Conwy), 26, 208, 216
Plasnewydd (Chirk), 165, 166, 193
Plas Newydd (Porth-aml), 21
Plas-y-ward, 26, 46
plasty, xvii, 14, 23, 24, 28, 30, 66, 67, 87, 115, 132, 210, 211, 215, 217, 237
Plato, xiv, 103
Political Discourse or dialogue between a knight of the Commons-house of parliament . . . (1625), 157
Pontano, Gioviano, xiv
Ponticus, 88
Poor Law, 33, 79–80
Porth-aml (Anglesey), 225
Porth-aml (Brecs.), 214
Powel, Dr David, xx, xxi, 88, 89, 138
Powell, Anthony (Llwydarth), 73
Powell, Robert, 197
Powys Castle, 25, 165, 193, 216
Practice of Piety, The (1611) (trans. into Welsh as *Ymarfer o Dduwioldeb, Yr*), 190, 194, 201, 220, 230
Prendergast (Pemb.), 69
Price, Cadwaladr (Rhiwlas), 82, 145
Price, Charles (Pilleth), 232
Price, Dr Ellis, 69, 193
Price family (Mynachdy, Rads.), 41
Price family (Rhiwlas, Mer.), 9
Price, Leyshon, 27
Price, Richard (Brecon), 35, 59, 176, 180, 223, 241
Price, Richard (Gogerddan), 74, 82, 240
Price, Sir John, 9, 25, 49, 162, 176
Prichard, Humphrey, 163, 245
Prichard, Rhys, 158, 194, 195, 197, 219

primogeniture, 15
*Principal Navigations, Voyages, Traffiques
    and Discoveries of the English
    Nation* (1589), 139
priodawr, 10, 83, 84, 85, 114
priodoldeb, 10
Privy Council, 38, 39, 43, 48, 68, 80,
    81, 98, 108, 109, 144, 145, 160,
    187, 188, 212, 245
Pryce family (Newtown Hall), 5
Prydderch, Richard, 51
Prys, Edmwnd, archd. of Merioneth,
    54, 75, 96, 226
Pryse family (Gogerddan), 6, 18, 234
Puckering, John, Lord Keeper, 71
Pugh family (Penrhyn Creuddyn), 16
Pugh, Robert (Penrhyn Creuddyn), 166
Puleston family (Maelor), 9
Pum Llyfr Cerddwriaeth (c. 1570), xiv
Puritanism, 153–6, 184–202

Quakers, 199
Quintilian, xiv

Radnor, 232
Radnorshire, 41, 69, 71, 123
Radyr (Glam.), 8, 18, 81
Raglan (Mon.), 5, 20, 25, 136, 165,
    193, 208
Regnans in Excelsis, bull (1570), 142, 174
Remaines concerning Britaine (1623), 8
Renaissance, xiii–xiv, xix, 11, 24, 56–8,
    236
Rhann o Psalmae Dafydd Brophwyd
    (1603), 184, 198
Rhiryd, lord of Clochran, 138
Rhiwedog (Mer.), 18, 230
Rhiwlas (Mer.), 82, 145
Rhiwledyn (Caerns.), 144
Rhiw'r perrai (Glam.), xx
Rhys ap Gruffudd, Sir, xxiii, 24, 107,
    108, 241
Rhys ap Thomas, Sir, 26
Richard ap Hywel, 23, 204
Robert, Gruffydd, 233
Roberts, Dr Michael, 191
Roberts, Peter R., xxiii, xxv
Robeston West (Pemb.), 191
Robinson, Nicholas, bp. of Bangor
    (1566–85), 36
Roland ap Maredudd ap Rhys, 225
Roman Catholicism, 37–8, 70, 92, 139,
    142–8, 150–5, 165–7, 172–3,
    193–4

Rome, 146, 201
Roses, Wars of the, xxii
Rowland, Henry, 208
Rowlands, David, 190, 191
Royal Injunctions (1559), 173
Rug (Mer.), 14, 123

St Asaph, dioc. of, 171, 172, 176, 182
St David's, dioc. of, 172, 176, 201
St Donat's (Glam.), 9, 18, 25, 76, 109,
    163, 165, 166, 208, 215, 216, 221
St George's (Glam.), 151
St Grwst Church (Llanrwst), 26
St John, Oliver, 1st lord (Bletsoe and
    Fonmon), 31, 39, 105
St Julian's (Newport), 168
St Winifred's Well (Holywell), 144
Salcot, John (alias Capon), 104
Salesbury, Thomas (London), 185
Salesbury, William, 45, 57, 176, 177,
    178, 244
Salmau Cân (1621), 196
Salusbury family (Lleweni), 9, 18, 89,
    209
Salusbury family (Rug), 41, 91
Salusbury, Henry (Henllan), 73, 89
Salusbury, Henry (Llanrhaeadr), 21
Salusbury, Humphrey, 225
Salusbury, John (Bachymbyd), 21
Salusbury, Owen (Holt), 109
Salusbury, Owen (Rug), 111
Salusbury, Robert (Plas Isaf,
    Llanrwst), 21
Salusbury (II), Sir John, 41, 70, 85, 92,
    93, 109, 224
Salusbury, Sir Thomas, 28, 225
Salusbury, Thomas (Denbigh), 21
Salusbury, Thomas (recusant), 92, 150,
    151
sarhad, 12
Saxton, Christopher, 8
Scotland, 58, 143
Settlement, Edwardian (1284), xxii,
    xxiv, 58, 135, 204
Settlement, Tudor (1536–43), xi, xii.
    xvi, xix, xx, xxii, xxiii, xxiv, xxv,
    3–5, 7, 10, 11–12, 14, 15, 30, 31,
    34, 35, 36, 40, 49, 54–5, 58, 59,
    104, 111–13, 122, 128, 136, 152,
    182
Seven Shires, baron and justice of the,
    46
Shakespeare, William, 86
sheriffs, 32, 34, 78, 92

Ship Money, 43, 46
Shrewsbury, 129, 208
Shropshire, 180
Siddons, M. P., 64
Sidney, Sir Henry, 35, 36, 41, 88, 101, 112
Sidney, Sir Robert, Lord, Viscount Lisle, 89
Simwnt Fychan, 73, 205
Siôn Cain, 73
Siôn Phylip, 54, 95
Siôn Tudur, 54, 73, 85, 146, 150, 223
Smith, Henry, 218
Smith, Sir Thomas, 19, 34, 96, 99, 106, 150, 213
social structure, 15–24, 83–8
Society of the Mineral and Battery Works, 14
Somerset, 145, 200
Somerset, Charles, 1st earl of Worcester, 91
Somerset, Edward, 4th earl of Worcester, 125
Somerset, Elizabeth, wife of the 3rd Lord Powys, 218
Somerset family (Raglan), earls of Worcester, 165
Somerset, Henry, 2nd earl of Worcester, 98
Somerset, William, 3rd earl of Worcester, 204
Spain, 13, 25, 38, 98, 101, 119, 133, 134, 137, 138, 139, 140, 142, 146, 147, 149, 151, 152, 155, 157, 158, 159, 161, 163, 184
Spanish Infanta, 157
Spiritual and Most Precious Pearl, A (1550) (trans. into Welsh as Perl Mewn Adfyd), 180, 190
sprezzatura, xv
Stackpole (Pemb.), 25, 27
Stanley, Henry, 4th earl of Derby, 109
Starkey, Thomas, 119
Stedman family (Strata Florida), 23
Stone, Lawrence, 203, 227
Stradling family (St Donat's), 9, 18, 23, 73, 76, 209, 221
Stradling, Sir Edward, 25, 31, 39, 44, 51, 53, 56, 73, 79, 81, 88, 101, 104, 105, 109, 112, 114, 117, 120, 129, 183, 205, 211, 214, 215, 220, 221
Stradling, Sir John, 44, 157, 163
Stradling, Sir Thomas, 44, 165, 166

Strata Florida, 23
Styles, Philip, 72
Summons for Sleepers, A (1589), 211
Supplication unto the High Court of Parliament, A (1588), 155
Swansea, 13, 20, 204
'Sydanen' ('Sidanen'), 148

Tegeingl, 23
Terra Florida, 138
Thelwall, Simon, 26, 46
Thelwall, Sir Eubule (Plas-y-ward), 92
Thirty-Nine Articles (1563/71), 173
Thirty Years War, 133
Thomas, Oliver, 194, 230
Thomas, Sir William (Coed Alun), 76, 100
Thomas, William (Coed Alun), 151
Tintern, 14
Townshend, Sir Henry, 107, 114
Trawsgoed (Cards.), 23
Trecastell (Anglesey), 23
Tredegar (Mon.), 9, 18, 19, 20, 21, 145, 208
Trefalun (Denb.), 9, 18, 24, 41, 44, 46, 82, 168
Trefor family (Trefalun), 5, 9, 18, 24
Trefor, John, 24
Trefor, John (III), 44
Trefor, Sir Richard, 41, 82, 168, 224
Trefor, Sir Thomas, 46
Trefor, William, 46
Trefriw, 57
treftadaeth, 116
Tregarnedd (Anglesey), 23
Tremeirchion (Flints.), 25, 27
Trent, Council of (1545–65), 174
Tretŵr (Brecs.), 5, 20
Trew Law of Free Monarchies (1598), 65
Tri Chof Ynys Brydain, 72
Tudor, Henry, xx, xxi, xxii, 10, 70, 132, 134, 136, 204
Tudor, Jasper, 136
Tudur Aled, xxii
Turberville family (Pen-llin), 165
Turberville, James, 222
Twyne, Thomas, 44
tŷ cyfrifol, xvii, 23
Tyrone Rebellion (1598–1603), 141

uchelwriaeth, xvi, xviii, xix, 13, 18, 23, 30, 39, 55, 60, 82, 87, 94, 103, 115, 117, 136, 209, 212, 214, 225, 235, 236, 240

Ulster, 159
Urbino, xiv

Valladolid, 161
Valois, 160
Vaughan family (Clyro), 41
Vaughan family (Corsygedol), 5, 20
Vaughan family (Golden Grove), 6, 9,
  23, 234
Vaughan family (Llwydiarth), 5
Vaughan family (Trawsgoed), 9, 23
Vaughan family (Tretŵr), 5, 20
Vaughan, Gruffudd (Corsygedol), 26
Vaughan, Richard, bp. of Bangor
  (1595–7), 208
Vaughan, Robert (Hengwrt), 72, 73,
  111, 112
Vaughan, Rowland (Caer Gai), 190,
  201, 229
Vaughan, Thomas (Radnorshire), 8
Vaughan, William (Llangyndeyrn), 11,
  29, 93, 120, 121, 157, 244
Vesputius, Americus, 138
Villiers, George, duke of Buckingham,
  159
Virginia Company, 137
vita activa, xv, 2
vita contemplativa, 2
Vives, Juan Luis, 208

Wales, Marches of, xx, xxi, xxii, xxiv, 4,
  5, 6, 8, 9, 11, 30, 31, 35, 49, 92,
  99, 104, 116, 124, 128, 241
Wales, Principality of, xx, xxi, xxii,
  xxiv, xxv, 4, 6, 8, 11, 31, 49, 99,
  116, 241
Walsingham, Sir Francis, 36, 78, 138
Welshpool, 216, 218
Werdmüller, Otto, 180
Wheler, George, 198
Whitgift, John, archbp. of Canterbury,
  144, 167, 182
Wilcox, Thomas, 189
Wiliam ap Raff, 143
Wiliam Cynwal, 47, 73
Wiliam Llŷn, 73, 233
Wiliems, 'Sir' Thomas (Trefriw), 57,
  205, 233
Williams, David (Ystradfellte and
  Gwernyfed), 46

Williams family (Monmouth), 25
Williams, John, Lord Keeper, 46, 218
Williams, Sir Glanmor, 167
Williams, W. Ogwen, xxiii
Wiltshire, 120
'Winning of the Lordship of
  Glamorgan, The' (c. 1561–6), 23,
  109
Wolsey, Thomas, 216
Wrexham, 46, 151
Wright, Leonard, 211
Wroth, William, 197, 200
Wynn, Cadwaladr (Glyn Cywarch), 45,
  53
Wynn Ellis (Gwydir), 46
Wynn family (Gwydir), 19, 20, 21, 26,
  27, 42, 106, 123, 143, 206, 208,
  227
Wynn, Lady Grace (Gwydir), 218
Wynn, Lady Sydney (Gwydir), 218
Wynn, Morus (Gwydir), 208
Wynn, Owen, 3rd baronet (Gwydir),
  224
Wynn, Robert (Gwydir), 47, 216, 217
Wynn, Robert (Gwydir and Conwy),
  26, 208
Wynn, Sir John, 1st baronet (Gwydir),
  2, 4, 5, 8, 20, 23, 29, 46, 47, 50,
  51, 53, 70, 76, 77, 97, 99, 104,
  106, 109, 110, 120, 168, 182,
  206, 208, 209–10, 215, 218, 222,
  223, 224, 226, 227, 243
Wynn, Sir John Wynn, jun. (Gwydir),
  44, 210
Wynn, Sir Richard, 2nd baronet
  (Gwydir), 26, 158, 218, 222
Wynn, William (Glyn Cywarch), 45, 53
Wynn, William (Gwydir), 206

Ymarfer o Dduwioldeb, Yr (1630), 190;
  see also *Practice of Piety, The*
Yny lhyvyr hwnn (1546), 176
York(ist), 135, 136
Ystradfellte, 46

Zouche, Edward, 11th baron, 81, 98,
  114, 125, 161, 224, 242
Zwingli, 174